Builder's Guide to Room Additions

By Jack P. Jones

Craftsman Book Company

6058 Corte del Cedro / P.O. Box 6500 / Carlsbad / CA 92018

Acknowledgments

The author and publisher thank the following companies and organizations for furnishing materials used in the preparation of various portions of this book.

Asphalt Roofing Manufacturers Association — Rockville, Maryland
Brick Institute of America — Reston, Virginia
Kohler Co. — Kohler, Wisconsin
NuTone — Cincinnati, Ohio

This book is dedicated to those who build additional space for better living

Looking for other construction reference manuals?

Craftsman has the books to fill your needs. Call **toll-free** 1-800-829-8123,
order online http://www.craftsman-book.com or write to:
Craftsman Book Company, P.O. Box 6500, Carlsbad, CA 92018
for a **FREE CATALOG** of books, videos, audios and estimating software.

Library of Congress Cataloging-in-Publication Data

Jones, Jack Payne, 1928-
    Builder's guide to room additions / by Jack P. Jones.
        p.   cm.
    Includes index.
    ISBN 1-57218-031-5
    1. Dwellings--Remodeling. 2. Buildings--Additions--Design and
construction.   I. Title.
TH4816.2.J65   1996
690'.83--dc20   96-9549
                                                          CIP

© 1996 Craftsman Book Company

Cover photos by Peter Rintye, Hi Country Photography, Crestline, CA

Scott Markovich
Empire Construction, Crestline, CA

Russ Stehmeier
Stehmeier Construction, Running Springs, CA

Table of Contents

Starting Out

Construction of room additions and conversions is a $100-billion-plus per year business in this country. If you're already in the home-building business, you have the background and skill needed to succeed in this type of business.

This book will show you how to get jobs, plan the work, and then complete the project so you make a decent profit. We'll cover the problems you're likely to run into when converting basements, attics and garages or adding rooms to existing houses.

Both room conversions and room additions add living space. In that way they're both similar. But there is one major advantage to doing room conversions — you can work on conversions without worry about delays due to bad weather. That's the advantage. The disadvantage to conversions is that you have to work with the homeowner's family close at hand (and maybe even "helping" in the project).

Selling to and Satisfying the Homeowner

Homeowners add space and convert rooms because they need more living space. Additions and conversions solve an immediate problem. And they also provide a long-term advantage: better resale value. Make *value enhancement* a selling point when bidding any room addition or conversion job. Reroofing with asphalt shingles doesn't do much to enhance the value of a home. Everyone expects a house to have some suitable roof cover. But adding a porch, a bathroom, or a bedroom will increase the value of nearly any home. A wise owner understands that adding or converting space increases resale value.

I've found that homeowners who are adding a room or converting an attic or basement are good prospects for other work. Many will want the rest of their house brought up to the same standard as the new or newly-converted space. Be prepared to take on these profitable jobs. The extras can mean the difference between a decent profit and a bonus profit.

But here's a tip that can prevent disappointments. No matter how well you know your business, let the homeowner call the shots. Supply what the homeowner wants, not what you feel the home needs. Any design that doesn't take into consideration the desires of the homeowner isn't a good design, no matter what *you* think about it. A builder who has his own ideas about fixture colors, or floor and wall tile, is well-advised to keep those opinions confidential unless the homeowner asks for advice.

Of course, you have to point out things that can't work. For example, building codes and structural requirements limit what any builder can do economically. Of course, anything is possible on an unlimited budget. But you won't have many clients like that. If what the owner wants can't be done on a reasonable budget, be ready to explain that. The homeowner expects you to point out flaws in ideas he or she throws your way. After all, you're the professional.

Each job you take will have its challenges. And the greater the challenge, the better your chance for profit. The trick is to identify problems and solve them before they dissolve your profit and erode your reputation.

Labor is a budget-buster on most jobs. Here's a rule of thumb to follow when estimating labor costs: Assume that it will take twice as long to do most remodeling tasks as it does to do the same work in new construction. The manhour charts in this book are based on remodeling work and should improve the accuracy of your manhour estimates.

Designing an Addition

Before beginning serious design work, *always* find out what the code requires. For example, codes and zoning ordinances govern setbacks from property lines and streets. Most codes won't let you extend the front of a dwelling any nearer to the street. On narrow sites, the only direction you can expand may be to the rear. Be sure you know what the restrictions are. If you build an addition where an addition isn't allowed, don't expect to get paid for it.

When designing a room addition, approach the project about the same way you would if you were planning to build a house. But keep in mind that you're faced with limited options. Your choices of design, placement, materials, and access will be restricted. The design of any addition or conversion should blend into the design of the original home. Don't let your addition look like an afterthought. You're weaving a blanket, not making a patchwork quilt.

Still, there's plenty of room for innovation and creativity, as you'll see in later chapters. Common sense and a good eye for exterior appearance are your best guides. If you don't have the latter, use the former, and consult an architect.

Before the planning goes too far, think about conflicts and restrictions. For example, if there's a septic tank in the yard, mark the exact location before design goes too far. If the add-on will be on a concrete slab, think about drainage. Don't assume anything about the existing site. Do some investigation. For example, consider removal and replacement of topsoil. And what about power lines? I know of one builder who didn't give enough thought to an overhead power line. As it turned out, the power lines had the right to be right where they were. His wall framing had no rights at all. He had to remove the framing and relocate the addition elsewhere, at his expense.

As I said, your selection of materials and design options is almost unlimited. But I recommend against being a pioneer. You're working for homeowners who have their own tastes and prejudices. Your objective is to develop designs that are both acceptable to the owner and a good value. And no one solution fits all. Tailor your recommendations to the site, the owner and the best combination of skills and materials available. For example, a log house might be a good choice for a wooded hillside cabin. But I wouldn't recommend it for downtown Dallas.

Sizing an Addition

Avoid making a major addition to a small home in a neighborhood of small homes. For example, don't recommend investing $100,000 in a major addition to a home in a neighborhood of homes selling for $150,000. Nothing you can do will make one home on a street worth twice as much as any other home on the same street. That would be foolish. Instead, recommend adding a fourth bedroom and a third bathroom

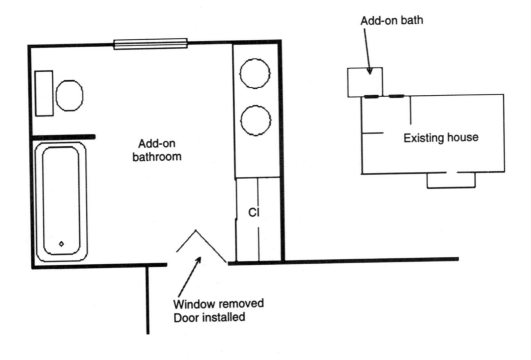

Figure 1-1
Bathroom addition to a small home

in a neighborhood of mostly four-bedroom, three-bath homes. That's always money well invested, especially if property values are increasing.

Consider carefully what's best for your client. Don't recommend a 10 x 12 addition if there's space for a 12 x 14 or larger room. How much more would it cost to go for the larger size? Suppose you can build the 10 x 12 addition for $50 a square foot. For an additional $2,400, you can build the larger room. You owe it to your client to discuss the option of going for the additional space. If your client is thinking about a 12 x 14 bedroom addition, explain the advantages of a 12 x 16 addition that includes an additional bathroom. Most homeowners understand that a 12 x 14 room doesn't cost much more than a 10 x 12 room. They'll also appreciate the closet space you can build into that extra 48 square feet of floor area.

When a homeowner is thinking about adding space, particularly a bedroom, suggest adding a bathroom as part of the project. That's nearly always a

good choice if space is available on the lot. An extra bathroom increases resale value and costs much less when added during other construction.

A bathroom may, of course, be the purpose of an addition. Suppose you're adding a bathroom to a master bedroom that's 12 x 12 (hardly a size that can be robbed of space for a bathroom). The adjoining rooms can't be spared for conversion to a bath. The owner doesn't want to close off any of the existing windows. The only solution may be to expand outward. Build a bathroom adjoining the master bedroom. Figure 1-1 shows an example.

Where feasible, put the bathroom where there are existing water and drain lines. That saves money, of course. But the cost of running those lines a few feet farther isn't very much.

And always try to keep room additions modular. Modular construction reduces wasted materials and cuts installation time. Check out the ideas in Chapter 8 before you finalize any design.

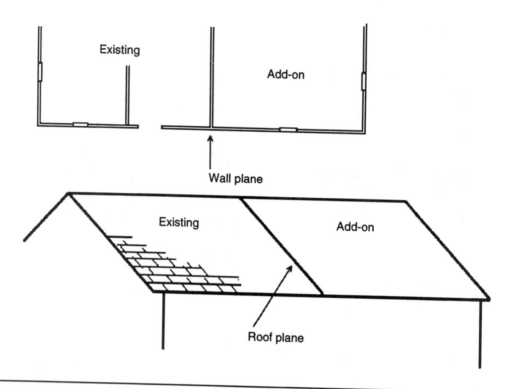

Figure 1-2
Joining planes

Adding to an Existing Structure

Every room addition requires joining two parts — the existing with the new. The completed structure should leave no obvious sign of the distinct parts. I'm sure you've seen add-ons that looked as if two different buildings were hauled in and shoved together. Blend your add-ons into the existing structure by using similar finish materials. Occasionally you may want the room interior to have a different look than the rest of the house. But the exterior finish should always match the existing building.

It's nearly impossible to match brick or stucco exteriors. The color and style of brick, block or stucco was probably discontinued years ago. Even if the same materials are still made, the existing finish has probably faded as it aged. The best you can do is get the closest match possible and then paint the entire house. That's not going to be a popular suggestion with most homeowners.

Older homes usually have molding and trim styles that are no longer made. You'll have a hard time find-

ing a mill to duplicate fancy trim such as spindles and scroll work. You might have to compromise on trim that's similar but doesn't match exactly. Another solution is to look for an older home in a neglected neighborhood. Find a home with trim of the style you need. Then try to negotiate with the owner — if the trim is salvageable.

Neighborhoods where preservationists are repairing and restoring old homes usually have a source for the trim you need. One good supplier of old-style trim is Vintage Wood Works, Highway 34 South, Box R, Quinlan, TX 75474. Phone 903-356-2158.

Matching old asphalt shingles is seldom worth the trouble. You'll probably want to replace the entire roof cover if the addition requires extending the roof line. Otherwise, your project will have that add-on look no matter what you do.

The ridge and slope of a roof, the roof's eaves and rake, the wall's plane and corners form the lines of a house. Each of these is part of the *building line.* Adding on at a building line is called *line* or *plane joining.* That's what was done in Figure 1-2.

At first glance, plane joining seems to be the best way to blend a new addition into an existing house. But it isn't. Any time you join at a building line, the joint will be obvious. The addition is going to look like an add-on. Matching exterior finish materials is nearly impossible if the joint is at a building line.

Any flaw at the building line will emphasize the joint between the two parts of the home. Say the roof ridge isn't level, the roof surface is wavy, or the wall is tilted. Any of these will work against you, making anything you do look bad.

Don't try to join one smooth surface to another smooth surface. Go for a break or offset. Step the roof line up or down where the addition intersects the roof line. Offset the foundation forward or back. Figure 1-3 shows several ways to make a break for a room addition.

A wall break can also smooth the transition between different exterior materials, such as where brick or stone joins wood siding. A home looks much better from the curb when you create a real break at the point of intersection.

Measuring Major Components

Avoid surprises when you build an addition. Be sure you know all the key measurements of the existing house. Establish finish floor lines, ceiling heights, rafter height, placement of doors and windows. Record all the measurements that might affect the room addition.

Figure 1-4 shows how to measure the key dimensions. Note that the roof overhang at the eaves is one of those key points. The overhang on the addition and the existing home should be the same.

From experience, I've learned it's best to find the finish floor height at several points. One of these points should be at the wall opening to the room addition. If the floor isn't level at this point, you'll have to adjust the floor height in the addition accordingly. It's no use creating a dead level floor in the addition if the floor in the adjoining room isn't exactly level. The owner will think you're the one who made the mistake. If you know that the existing floor isn't level, make adjustments so the two floor levels match.

Demolition

Demolition is a major part of most room addition jobs. You'll have at least some removal work on almost every room addition or conversion job. Unfortunately demolition is probably the hardest part of most jobs to estimate. Until you open up that wall or break out that foundation, it's hard to know what you'll find. But don't give up. Demolition estimates don't have to be pure guesswork. There's a lot you can do to anticipate costs. For example, you should be able to forecast problems of limited access on nearly every job:

◆ How close are the adjoining properties and buildings?

◆ How much space is there to handle and load debris?

◆ Will you have to work from a narrow or almost nonexistent yard?

◆ Is there enough space to back a truck in to catch the shingles as you remove them?

Answer these questions before beginning your demolition estimate.

How do you estimate the manhours required to remove a door or a partition wall? And if it's a load-bearing wall you're removing, don't forget to include the labor and materials required for temporary bracing. Good judgment and cost records from previous jobs will always be your best guide. Information in construction cost reference guides may help. (Several estimating books are described at the back of this book.)

Here's a rule of thumb to use if you don't trust your judgment, have no cost records and don't believe in published estimating data. Simply figure demolition manhours will be the same as installation manhours. For example, assume it takes about 1.5 manhours to lay a square (100 square feet) of three-tab square butt shingles on a roof. If you have no better numbers, assume the same amount of time (1.5 manhours) to remove a square of asphalt shingles. In most cases, this estimate will be generous — you'll need a little less time than estimated. But it's wise to be at least a little conservative when estimating any demolition. If you find something like lead paint or asbestos shingles, you'll need it.

A Breaking the wall and roof line

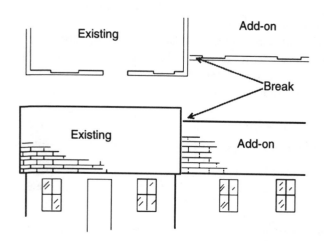

B Another way to break the lines

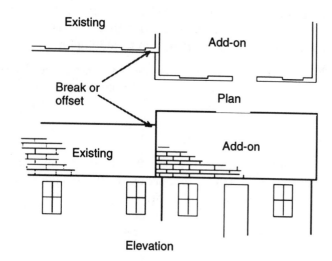

C Breaking with a satellite addition

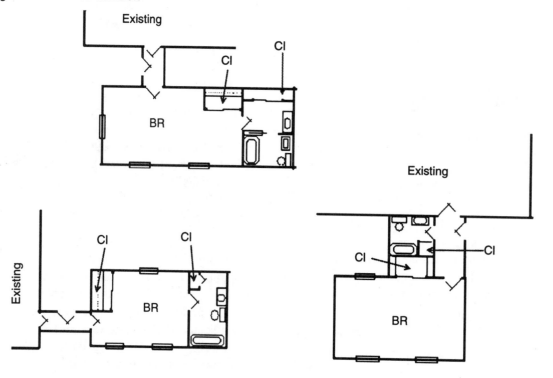

Figure 1-3
Creating breaks in an addition

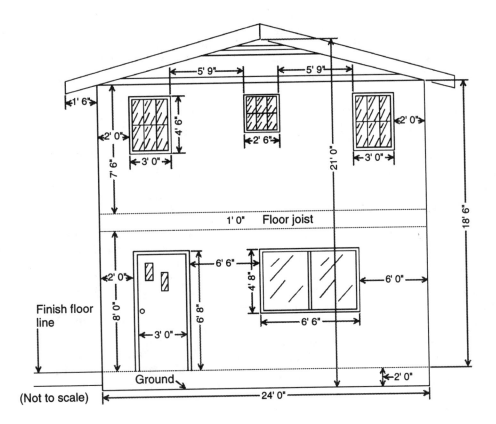

Figure 1-4
Key measuring points

Conserving Used Materials

During your negotiations with the homeowner, you may be asked to salvage and reuse existing materials whenever possible. For example, I've had owners ask me to reuse the sheathing and rafters I'm demolishing. I recommend avoiding salvage of framing. It takes too long, adding more to your labor cost than the price of new sheathing and rafters. That cuts into your profit. Instead, quote the job using all new materials. That ensures a professional job — and a profit. If the owner insists on salvage of materials, fine! Set them aside and let the owner deal with the problem. Don't try to install them yourself.

A word of caution on demolition. Sweep up all the nails and staples you take out during demolition work. Loose nails and staples are a safety hazard. Too often I've had employees, owners or children hurt by nails or staples removed during demolition. Leave the job site broom-clean at the end of each day to reduce the chance of injury to the homeowner and neighborhood kids. I try to keep nails and staples in my apron as I take materials apart. Provide a covered tin or box where nails and staples can be collected until they're ready for the trash bin. The homeowner will appreciate your thoughtfulness and your professionalism.

The Importance of Paperwork

I know home improvement contractors who work on a handshake without the benefit of written specifications or contract. I don't recommend doing business that way — even though I've been guilty of the practice more than once. When you've built a reputation in the community, clients tend to trust your word and honor your invoices. Just listen to what's needed, do the work, and present your bill. I've done work that way for repeat customers and have had very few problems — yet!

No matter how flattering it is to be trusted to work on a handshake, I recommend drawing up a "little memorandum of our agreement." It's not that you don't trust the homeowner. It's just that verbal communication is no more permanent than human memory and is always subject to interpretation. The homeowner knew exactly what he wanted and explained it to you precisely. And you listened carefully and knew exactly what he meant. It's just that he left out one little part. But that's OK because you already had that in mind (or at least thought you did). So you never found out that he didn't know that you didn't know what he knew.

Great!

That's your loss if you didn't put it in writing. My advice: Put it on paper. A written agreement protects both you and your client. It helps avoid disappointments that could become a major loss. The process of putting a verbal agreement down on paper will usually expose most potential misunderstandings. I think of it as cheap insurance.

The Contract

Figure 1-5 is a sample proposal and contract form you might want to use. This form includes the notice required by federal law that describes the customer's right to cancel. Figure 1-6 is the customer's cancellation notice.

Figure 1-7 is a job specifications form. It becomes part of the contract. This is where you specify the work to be done and materials to be installed.

Here are two contract drafting tips that could save you many times the cost of this book in the next year alone.

Tip One: The most important part of any contract is where you list what's excluded. Most construction disputes begin with the owner saying, "Hey! I thought you were going to include . . ." Don't leave room for that argument. Right under where you list what's included, list what's not included.

For example, if you're reroofing a home and only shingles are included in your bid, consider writing the following words into the agreement:

No flashing, sheathing, decking, masonry patching or replacing of rafters or vents is included in this proposal.

That should avoid most misunderstandings. It also puts the owner on notice that additional work may be needed, depending on what you discover when work begins. Of course, you're happy to bid on this extra work. But it will be at extra charge. Nothing but shingles is included in the contract.

Tip Two: Describe in the contract the materials you'll install, not the job you'll do. For example, if you're reroofing a home, the contract might say:

Furnish and install 1,600 square feet of three-tab, 240-pound, Class 3 composition shingles.

The worst thing you could say in the contract is "Reroof the home at 321 Main Street." What does that include? Who knows? Probably lots of flashing, sheathing, decking, masonry patching, rafters and vents.

I hope you get the point. You're a construction contractor, not an insurance company. If you discover that the deck is rotten, flashing has turned to dust and the sheathing won't even hold its own weight, *that's not your loss.* You're bidding the shingles. Everything else is extra.

The Plans

Your plans for an addition should be so clear and specific that anyone with construction experience could build what's required. Whether the plans are a roll with dozens of sheets prepared by an architect or a single sheet of 8½ x 11 paper, the measurements have to be clear.

Detailed plans will show a foundation plan, a basement plan if there's a basement, and front, rear and side elevations. A more complex job will include section and detail drawings.

A foundation plan shows the length and width of a structure, as well as its shape. It includes information on materials used for footings, pillars and foundation walls. An 8-inch-thick concrete footing 18 inches wide may be expressed as 8/18. A standard 8 x 8 x 16-inch concrete block foundation may be written as 8 x 8 x 16 CB. Figure 1-8 shows a foundation plan that's typical for a room addition.

A floor plan shows the work as it would be seen from directly above. The floor plan will show the location and size of wall openings, the door swing (right or left hand opening), room sizes, and wall thicknesses. It can also show the placement of light fixtures, wall

Proposal and Contract

Date _____ 19 _____

To _____

Dear Sir/Madam:

We propose to furnish all materials and perform all labor necessary to complete the following:

_____

_____

_____

Job location: _____

All of the above work to be completed according to the floor plan, job specifications, and terms and conditions on the back of this form, for the sum of:

Dollars ($ _____)

Payments to be made as the work progresses as follows:_____

_____

_____

the entire amount of the contract to be paid within _____ days after substantial completion and acceptance by the owner. The price quoted is for immediate acceptance only. Delay in acceptance will require a verification of prevailing labor and material costs. This offer becomes a contract upon acceptance by contractor but shall be null and void if not executed within 5 days from the date above.

By _____

"YOU, THE BUYER, MAY CANCEL THIS TRANSACTION AT ANY TIME PRIOR TO MIDNIGHT OF THE THIRD BUSINESS DAY AFTER THE DATE OF THIS TRANSACTION. SEE THE ATTACHED NOTICE OF CANCELLATION FORM FOR AN EXPLANATION OF THIS RIGHT."

You are hereby authorized to furnish all materials and labor required to complete the work according to the plans, job specifications, and terms and conditions on the back of this proposal, for which we agree to pay the amounts itemized above.

Owner _____

Owner _____

Accepted by Contractor _____   Date _____

Figure 1-5
Example proposal and contract

1. The Contractor agrees to commence work within (10) days after the last to occur of the following, (1) receipt of written notice from the Lien Holder, if any, to the effect that all documents required to be recorded prior to the commencement of construction have been properly recorded; (2) the materials required are available and on hand, and (3) a building permit has been issued. Contractor agrees to prosecute work thereafter to completion, and to complete the work within a reasonable time, subject to such delays as are permissible under this contract. If no first Lien Holder exists, all references to Lien Holder are to be disregarded.

2. Contractor shall pay all valid bills and charge for material and labor arising out of the construction of the structure and will hold Owner of the property free and harmless against all liens and claims of lien for labor and material filed against the property.

3. No payment under this contract shall be construed as an acceptance of any work done up to the time of such payment, except as to such items as are plainly evident to anyone not experienced in construction work, but the entire work is to be subject to the inspection and approval of the inspector for the Public Authority at the time when it shall be claimed by the Contractor that the work has been completed. At the completion of the work, acceptance by the Public Authority shall entitle Contractor to receive all progress payments according to the schedule set forth.

4. The plan and job specification are intended to supplement each other, so that any works exhibited in either and not mentioned in the other are to be executed the same as if they were mentioned and set forth in both. In the event that any conflict exists between any estimate of costs of construction and the terms of this Contract, this Contract shall be controlling. The Contractor may substitute materials that are equal in quality to those specified if the Contractor deems it advisable to do so. All dimensions and designations on the plan or job specification are subject to adjustment as required by job conditions.

5. Owner agrees to pay Contractor its normal selling price for all additions, alterations or deviations. No additional work shall be done without the prior written authorization of Owner. Any such authorization shall be on a change-order form, approved by both parties, which shall become a part of this Contract. Where such additional work is added to this Contract, it is agreed that all terms and conditions of this Contract shall apply equally to such additional work. Any change in specifications or construction necessary to conform to existing or future building codes, zoning laws, or regulations of inspecting Public Authorities shall be considered additional work to be paid for by Owner as additional work.

6. The Contractor shall not be responsible for any damage occasioned by the Owner or Owner's agent, Acts of God, earthquake, or other causes beyond the control of Contractor, unless otherwise provided or unless he is obligated to provide insurance against such hazards, Contractor shall not be liable for damages or defects resulting from work done by subcontractors. In the event Owner authorizes access through adjacent properties for Contractor's use during construction. Owner is required to obtain permission from the owner(s) of the adjacent properties for such. Owner agrees to be responsible and to hold Contractor harmless and accept any risks resulting from access through adjacent properties.

7. The time during which the Contractor is delayed in this work by (a) the acts of Owner or his agents or employees or those claiming under agreement with or grant from Owner, including any notice to the Lien Holder to withhold progress payments, or by (b) any acts or delays occasioned by the Lien Holder, or by (c) the Acts of God which Contractor could not have reasonably foreseen and provided against, or by (d) stormy or inclement weather which necessarily delays the work, or by (e) any strikes, boycotts or like obstructive actions by employees or labor organizations and which are beyond the control of Contractor and which he cannot reasonably overcome, or by (f) extra work requested by the Owner, or by (g) failure of Owner to promptly pay for any extra work as authorized, shall be added to the time for completion by a fair and reasonable allowance. Should work be stopped for more than 30 days by any or all of (a) through (g) above, the Contractor may terminate this Contract and collect for all work completed plus a reasonable profit.

8. Contractor shall at his own expense carry all workers' compensation insurance and public liability insurance necessary for the full protection of Contractor and Owner during the progress of the work. Certificates of insurance shall be filed with Owner and Lien Holder if Owner and Lien Holder require. Owner agrees to procure at his own expense, prior to the commencement of any work, fire insurance with Course of Construction. All Physical Loss and Vandalism and Malicious Mischief clauses attached in a sum equal to the total cost of the improvements. Such insurance shall be written to protect the Owner and Contractor, and Lien Holder, as their interests may appear. Should Owner fail so to do, Contractor may procure such insurance, as agent for Owner, but is not required to do so, and Owner agrees in demand to reimburse Contractor in cash for the cost thereof.

9. Where materials are to be matched, Contractor shall make every reasonable effort to do so using standard materials, but does not guarantee a perfect match.

10. Owner agrees to sign and file for record within five days after substantial completion and acceptance of work a notice of completion. Contractor agrees upon receipt of final payment to release the property from any and all claims that may have accrued by reason of the construction.

11. Any controversy or claim arising out of or relating to this contract shall be settled by arbitration in accordance with the Rules of the American Arbitration Association, and judgment upon the award rendered by the Arbitrator(s) may be entered in any Court having jurisdiction.

12. Should either party bring suit in court to enforce the terms of this agreement, any judgment awarded shall include court costs and reasonable attorney's fees to the successful party plus interest at the legal rate.

13. Unless otherwise specified, the contract price is based upon Owner's representation that there are no conditions preventing Contractor from proceeding with usual construction procedures and that all existing electrical and plumbing facilities are capable of carrying the extra load caused by the work to be performed by Contractor. Any electrical meter charges required by Public Authorities or utility companies are not included in the price of this Contract. unless included in the job specifications. If existing conditions are not as represented, thereby necessitating additional plumbing, electrical, or other work, these shall be paid for by Owner as additional work.

14. The Owner is solely responsible for providing Contractor prior to the commencing of construction with any water, electricity and refuse removal service at the job site as may be required by Contractor to effect the improvement covered by this contract. Owner shall provide a toilet during the course of construction when required by law.

15. The Contractor shall not be responsible for damage to existing walks, curbs, driveways, cesspools, septic tanks, sewer lines, water or gas lines, arches, shrubs, lawn, trees, clotheslines, telephone and electric lines, etc., by the Contractor, subcontractor, or supplier incurred in the performance of work or in the delivery of materials for the job. Owner hereby warrants and represents that he shall be solely responsible for the condition of the building with respect to moisture, drainage, slippage and sinking or any other condition that may exist over which the Contractor has no control and subsequently results in damage to the building.

16. The Owner is solely responsible for the location of all lot lines and shall if requested, identify all corner posts of his lot for the Contractor. If any doubt exists as to the location of lot lines, the Owner shall at his own cost, order and pay for a survey. If the Owner wrongly identifies the location of the lot lines of the property, any changes required by the Contractor shall be at Owner's expense. This cost shall be paid by Owner to Contractor in cash prior to continuation of work.

17. Contractor has the right to subcontract any part, or all, of the work agreed to be performed.

18. Owner agrees to install and connect at Owner's expense, such utilities and make such improvements in addition to work covered by this Contract as may be required by Lien Holder or Public Authority prior to completion of work of Contractor. Correction of existing building code violations, damaged pipes, inadequate wiring, deteriorated structural parts, and the relocation or alteration of concealed obstructions will be an addition to this agreement and will be billed to Owner at Contractor's usual selling price.

19. Contractor shall not be responsible for any damages occasioned by plumbing leaks unless water service is connected to the plumbing facilities prior to the time of rough inspection.

20. Title to equipment and materials purchased shall pass to the Owner upon delivery to the job. The risk of loss of the said materials and equipment shall be borne by the Owner.

21. Owner hereby grants to Contractor the right to display signs and advertise at the job site.

22. Contractor shall have the right to stop work and keep the job idle if payments are not made to him when due. If any payments are not made to Contractor when due, Owner shall pay to Contractor an additional charge of 10% of the amount of such payment. If the work shall be stopped by the Owner for a period of sixty days, then the Contractor may, at Contractor's option, upon five days written notice, demand and receive payment for all work executed and materials ordered or supplied and any other loss sustained, including a profit of 10% of the contract price. In the event of work stoppage for any reason, Owner shall provide for protection of, and be responsible for any damage, warpage, racking, or loss of material on the premises.

23. Within ten days after execution of this Contract, Contractor shall have the right to cancel this Contract should it be determined that there is any uncertainty that all payments due under this Contract will be made when due or that any error has been made in computing the cost of completing the work.

24. This agreement constitutes the entire Contract and the parties are not bound by oral expression or representation by any party or agent of either party.

25. The price quoted for completion of the structure is subject to change to the extent of any difference in the cost of labor and material as of the date and the actual cost to Contractor at the time materials are purchased and work is done.

26. The Contractor is not responsible for labor or materials furnished by Owner or anyone working under the direction of the Owner and any loss or additional work that results therefrom shall be the responsibility of the Owner. Removal or use of equipment or materials not furnished by Contractor is at Owner's risk, and Contractor will not be responsible for the condition and operation of these items, or service for them.

27. No action arising from or related to the contract, or the performance thereof, shall be commenced by either party against the other more than two years after the completion or cessation of work under this contract. This limitation applies to all actions of any character, whether at law or in equity, and whether sounding in contract, tort, or otherwise. This limitation shall not be extended by any negligent misrepresentation or unintentional concealment, but shall be extended as provided by law for willful fraud, concealment, or misrepresentation.

28. All taxes and special assessments levied against the property shall be paid by the Owner.

29. Contractor agrees to complete the work in a substantial and workmanlike manner but is not responsible for failures or defects that result from work done by others prior, at the time of or subsequent to work done under this agreement.

30. Contractor makes no warranty, express or implied (including warranty of fitness for purpose and merchantability). Any warranty or limited warranty shall be as provided by the manufacturer of the products and materials used in construction.

31. Contractor agrees to perform this Contract in conformity with accepted industry practices and commercially accepted tolerances. Any claim for adjustment shall not be construed as reason to delay payment of the purchase price as shown on the payment schedule. The manufacturers' specifications are the final authority on questions about any factory produced item. Exposed interior surfaces, except factory finished items, will not be covered or finished unless otherwise specified herein. Any specially designed, custom built or special ordered item may not be changed or cancelled after five days from the acceptance of this Contract by Contractor.

Figure 1-5 (continued)

Example proposal and contract

Notice To Customer Required By Federal Law

You have entered into a transaction on _____ which may result in a lien, mortgage, or other security interest on your home. You have a legal right under federal law to cancel this transaction without any penalty or obligation if you desire to do so within three business days from the above date, or any later date on which all material disclosures required under the Truth in Lending Act have been given to you. If you so cancel the transaction, any lien, mortgage, or other security interest on your home arising from this transaction is automatically void. You are also entitled to receive a refund of any down payment or other consideration if you cancel. If you decide to cancel this transaction, you may do so by notifying:

_____
(Name of Creditor)

at_____
(Address of Creditor's Place of Business)

by mail or telegram sent not later than midnight of _____ . You may also use any other form of written notice identifying the transaction as long as it is delivered to the above address no later than the stipulated time. This notice may be used for the purpose of cancelling transaction by dating and signing below.

I hereby cancel this transaction.

_____   _____
(Date)   (Customer's Signature)

Effect of rescission. When a customer exercises his right to rescind, he is not liable for any finance or other charge, and any security interest becomes void upon such a rescission. Within 10 days after receipt of a notice of rescission, the creditor shall return to the customer any money or property given as earnest money, down payment, or otherwise, and shall take any action necessary or appropriate to reflect the termination of any security interest created under the transaction. If the creditor has delivered any property to the customer, the customer may retain possession of it. Upon the performance of the creditor's obligations under this section, the customer shall tender the property to the creditor, except that if return of the property in kind would be impracticable or inequitable, the customer shall tender its reasonable value. Tender shall be made at the location of the property or at the residence of the customer, at the option of the customer. If the creditor does not take possession of the property within 10 days after tender by the customer, ownership of the property vests in the customer without obligation on his part to pay for it.

Figure 1-6
Customer's cancellation notice

Job Specifications

Contractor's Name _____   Owners's Name _____
Address _____   Address _____
City _____ State _____ Zip_____   City _____ State _____ Zip_____
Phone _____   Job Address _____
Prepared by _____   Phone _____
                                            Date _____ Job No. _____

Contractor proposes to provide the building permit, labor, materials and equipment necessary to complete installation of the following:

Walls
Removal _____
Tub area _____
Finish _____
Other areas _____
Finish _____
Wainscot _____
Finish _____
Other _____
Replacement _____
Size _____
Color _____
Size _____
Color _____
Size _____
Color _____
                    Total cost $ _____

Const. Requirements   Descr.
Removal_____ $ _____
Replacement _____ $ _____
Addition_____ $ _____
Relocate _____ $ _____
Floor _____ $ _____
Wall_____ $ _____
Ceiling _____ $ _____
Doors/windows _____ $ _____
              Total cost $ _____

Plumbing Requirements   Descr.
Removal_____ $ _____
Supply _____ $ _____
Waste_____ $ _____
Vent_____ $ _____
Gas _____ $ _____
Steam_____ $ _____
              Total cost $ _____

Ceilings
Removal _____
Description _____
Finish _____
Other _____
Replacement _____
Size _____
Color _____
                    Total cost $ _____

Floor
Removal _____
Underlayment _____
Cove _____
Finish _____
Sill _____
Other _____
Replacement _____
Total area _____
Type _____
Color _____
              Total cost $ _____

Ventilation
Fan _____
Venting _____
Switch _____
Other _____
Type _____
Timer _____
Humidistat _____
Other _____
                    Total cost $ _____

Figure 1-7
Job specifications and cost estimate

Access.   Finish No. Descr.   Cost
Matched tile _____
Tub trim _____
Grab bars _____
Bar soap dish _____
Soap dishes _____
Towel bars _____
Tumbler holder _____
Paper holder _____
Tissue dispenser _____
Mirrors _____
Hooks _____
Decorative items _____
Folding stools _____
                    Total cost $ _____

Medicine Cabinet(s)
Quantity _____
Mount _____
Color _____
Lights _____
Manufacturer's no. _____
Style _____
Mirror size _____
Type _____
                    Total cost $ _____

Fixtures & Fittings Color Descr.   Cost
Tub _____ $ _____
Whirlpool _____ $ _____
Shower cabinet _____ $ _____
Shower cove _____ $ _____
Toilet & seat _____ $ _____
Lavatory _____ $ _____
Bidet _____ $ _____
Lavatory faucets _____ $ _____
Lavatory fittings _____ $ _____
Lavatory valve _____ $ _____
Bath valve _____ $ _____
Shower head _____ $ _____
Diverter _____ $ _____
Tub fittings & overflow _____ $ _____
                    Total cost $ _____

Vanity   No. 1   No. 2
Cabinet style _____
Cabinet color _____

Manufacturer _____
Knob and pull no. _____
Hinge no. _____
Back plate no. _____
Doors _____
Shelves _____
        Total cost $ _____ Total cost $ _____

Enclosures
Description _____
Color _____
Door size _____
Rod length _____
Replacement _____
Size _____
Glass type _____
                    Total cost $ _____

Storage
Type _____
Doors _____
Shelves _____
Finish _____
Size _____
Drawer _____
Number _____
Hardware _____
                    Total cost $ _____

Heating/Cooling
Heating _____
Size _____
Manufacturer _____
Type _____
Cooling _____
Size _____
Manufacturer _____
Type _____
Duct _____
Registers _____
Size _____
Size/Color _____
                    Total cost $ _____

Figure 1-7(continued)
Job specifications and cost estimate

Electrical & Lighting
Removal _____
Service entrance _____
Wire outlets _____
Electrical heater _____
Wire lighting _____
Switches _____
Lighting _____
Replacement _____
New service _____
Wire switches _____
Electrical cooling _____
Wire fan _____
Outlets _____
Heat lamps _____
                    Total cost $ _____

Tops ( ) as per drawing attached
Material _____
Style _____
Color _____
Number of cutouts _____
Edge treatment _____
Splash height _____
Splash type _____
                    Total cost $ _____

Lavatories
Quantity _____
Mount _____
Style _____
Manufacturer & no. _____
Color _____
Material _____
                    Total cost $ _____

Contractor will do the following demolition and dispose of items removed:

☐ Vanity   ☐ Top   ☐ Lavatory   ☐ Tub
☐ Toilet   ☐ Shower enclosure
☐ Radiator   ☐ Medicine cabinet

☐ Bath fittings   ☐ Deteriorated pipe
☐ Partition _____   ☐ Electric
☐ Doors   ☐ Windows
☐ Heating equipment   ☐ Cooling equipment
☐ Ducting
☐ Flooring   (_____ sq. ft.)
☐ Wall covering   (_____ sq. ft.)
☐ Ceiling cover   (_____ sq. ft.)
            Total cost $_____

Contractor will make the following repairs:

Item	Description	Cost

            Total cost $_____

Total costs above	$_____
Tax	$_____
Total	$_____

Owner will furnish labor and material as follows:

Item	Description

These are the total and complete specifications for this job. Only the items checked or for which a cost is indicated are included in this job.

Contractor _____

Owner _____

Date _____

Figure 1-7 (continued)
Job specifications and cost estimate

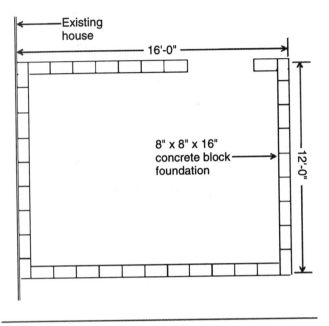

Figure 1-8
Addition foundation plan

switches and receptacles, and joist size and spacing. Figure 1-9 shows a floor plan for an addition. The front and side elevations of the addition could also be drawn as shown in Figure 1-10.

Elevation views show vertical dimensions. The dotted lines show what is below ground level. Exterior finishing materials and roof shingles may also be included on an elevation view.

Section and detail drawings are close-up views. They should eliminate any question about the critical sawing, fitting, and construction procedures. Figure 1-11 shows typical section and detail drawings. The main wall section shows a cross-section of the wall from footing to ridge.

Here's how I interpret the construction details in Figure 1-11:

There's a 2 x 10 header joist, a 2 x 10 floor joist, and cut-in blocks between the floor joists. Ceiling joists are 2 x 8s spaced 16 inches on center. They rest on the top plate and have 2 x 8 cut-ins. The rafters rest on a continuous 2 x 6 plate on top of the ceiling joists. In most plans, the rafters are sawed to fit directly on

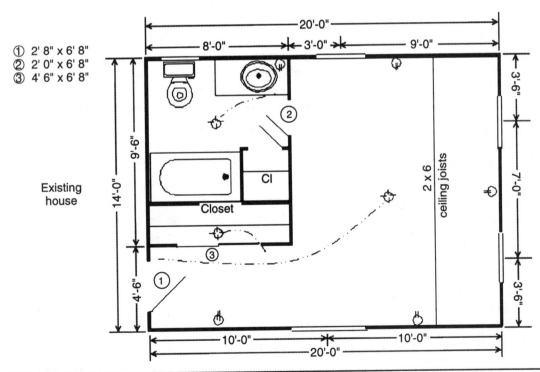

Figure 1-9
Floor plan of an addition

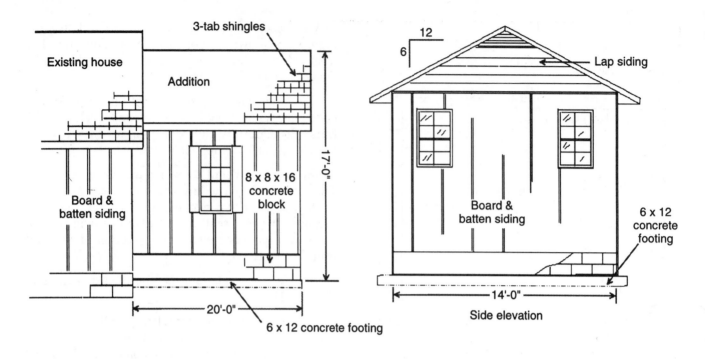

Figure 1-10
Elevations for the addition

top of the top plate. This plan allows for a horizontal soffit and a 2'6" overhang at the eaves. The rafter cut is 14'4⁹⁄₁₆". The roof pitch is 5/12. The distance from the bottom of the ceiling joist to the top of the ridge is 6'6½". Studs are placed 16 inches on center. The studs rest on a 2 x 4 sole plate and have a double 2 x 4 top plate. The top of the window is 6'9" above the finish floor. It shows the type of header that's commonly used for window and door openings in load-bearing walls. The basement ceiling height is 7'1⅝". The main floor ceiling height is 8'1".

The window panel drawing shows construction details for the panels under the front windows. The 2 x 10 sill is a joist header.

Figure 1-12 shows the type of detail drawing that's usually provided with stock house plans offered by a plan company. This sheet shows a series of detail drawings that could be used on many houses. Your local code may prohibit some of the details shown on stock house plans. Get the counsel of your building department on what the local code requires.

Figure 1-13 is a material description form. I use a form like this to list information about the quality,

size, type, style, and manufacturer of materials I plan to install. There isn't enough room on floor plans and elevations to describe everything you want to say about the materials you expect to install. Use this form to list all of that important information so you have an accurate, detailed, permanent record. Make it a part of the construction contract by referring to it in the contract. There's less room for controversy if a form like this is made part of the contract.

Use these or similar forms on each job and you'll eliminate most conflicts and misunderstandings. If you can't find a vendor who sells construction contract forms, copy the forms in this book and use them.

Who Pays for the Plans?

Floor plans are usually done at the expense of the owner. If you draw up the plans, be sure it's understood that you'll be paid for them. Include your fee in the bid. Don't hand over any plans until the contract is signed. Otherwise, the owner can shop around for a cheaper builder, using your plans.

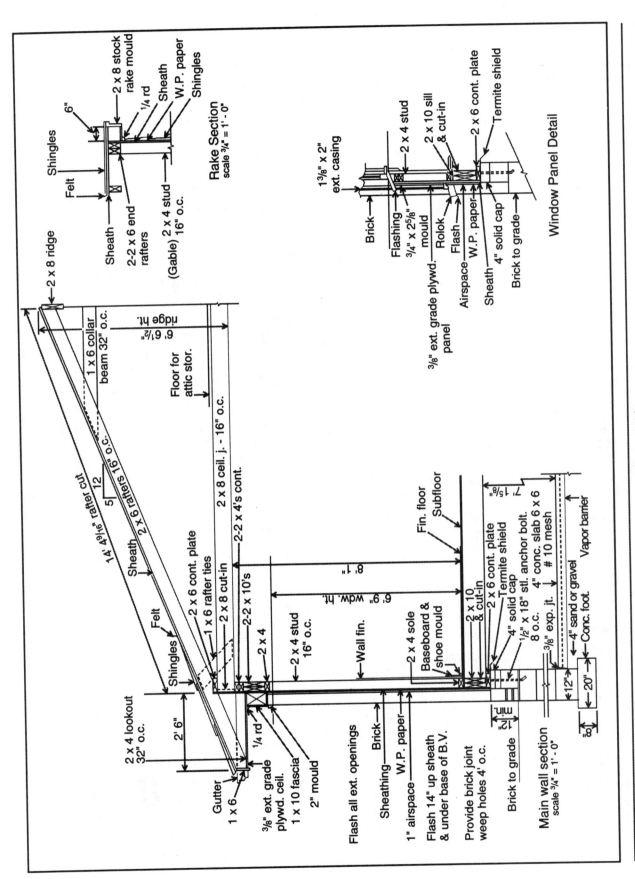

Figure 1-11
Section and details

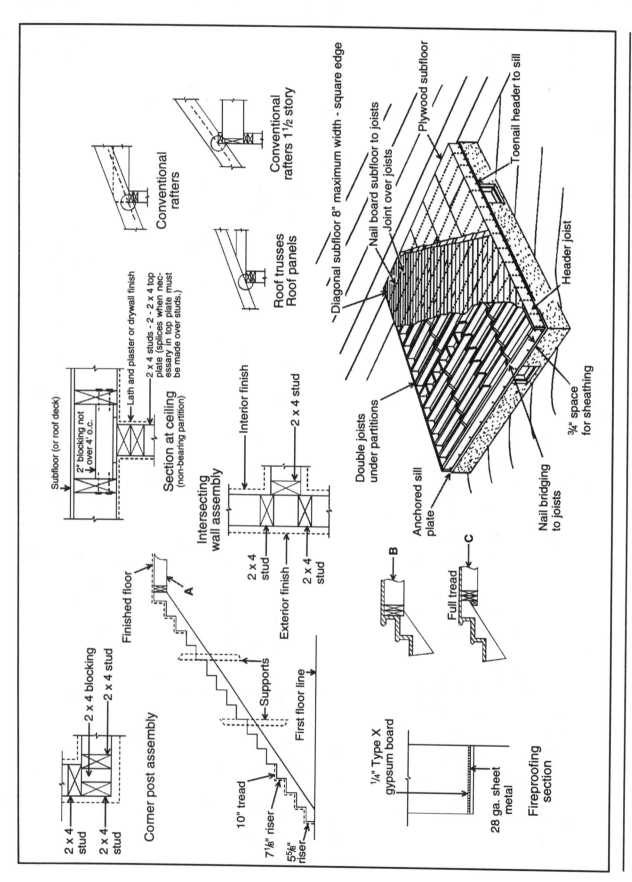

Figure 1-12
Standard construction details

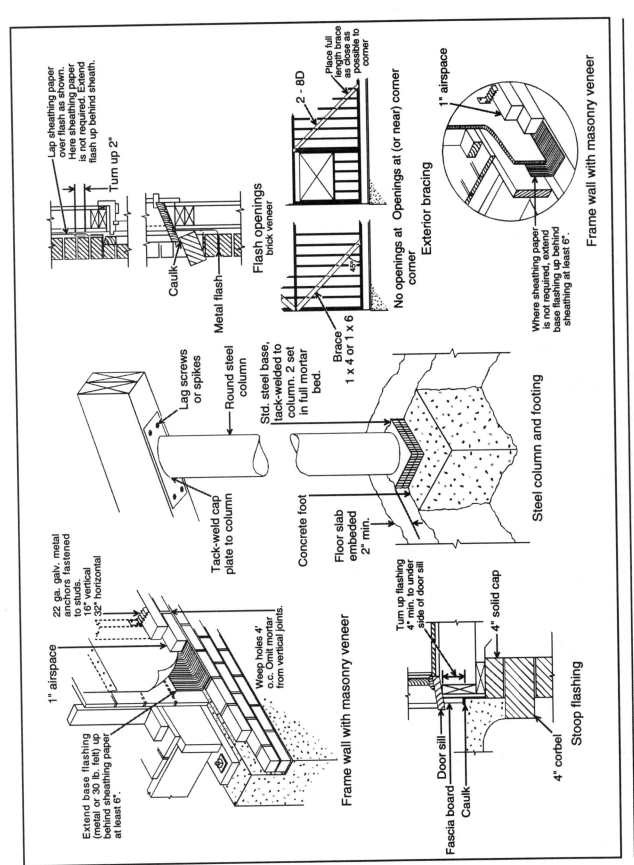

Figure 1-12 (continued)
Standard construction details

☐ Proposed Construction
☐ Under Construction

DESCRIPTION OF MATERIALS

No. _____
(To be inserted by FHA, VA or FmHA)

Property address _____ City _____ State _____

Mortgagor or Sponsor _____ _____
(Name)   (Address)

Contractor or Builder _____ _____
(Name)   (Address)

INSTRUCTIONS

1. For additional information on how this form is to be submitted, number of copies, etc., see the instructions applicable to the FHA Application for Mortgage Insurance, VA Request for Determination of Reasonable Value, or FmHA Property Information and Appraisal Report, as the case may be.

2. Describe all materials and equipment to be used, whether or not shown on the drawings, by marking an X in each appropriate check-box and entering the information called for in each space. If space is inadequate, enter "See misc." and describe under item 27 or on an attached sheet. THE USE OF PAINT CONTAINING MORE THAN THE PERCENTAGE OF LEAD BY WEIGHT PERMITTED BY LAW IS PROHIBITED.

3. Work not specifically described or shown will not be considered unless required, then the minimum acceptable will be assumed. Work exceeding minimum requirements cannot be considered unless specifically described.

4. Include no alternates, "or equal" phrases, or contradictory items. (Consideration of a request for acceptance of substitute materials or equipment is not thereby precluded.)

5. Include signatures required at the end of this form.

6. The construction shall be completed in compliance with the related drawings and specifications, as amended during processing. The specifications include this Description of Materials and the applicable Minimum Property Standards.

1. EXCAVATION
Bearing soil, type _____

2. FOUNDATIONS:
Footings: concrete mix _____; strength psi _____ Reinforcing _____
Foundation wall: material _____ Reinforcing _____
Interior foundation wall: material _____ Party foundation wall _____
Columns: material and sizes _____ Piers: material and reinforcing _____
Girders: material and sizes _____ Sills: material _____
Basement entrance areaway _____ Window areaways _____
Waterproofing _____ Footing drains _____
Termite protection _____
Basementless space: ground cover _____; insulation _____; foundation vents _____
Special foundations _____
Additional information: _____
_____

3. CHIMNEYS:
Material _____ Prefabricated *(make and size)* _____
Flue lining: material _____ Heater flue size _____ Fireplace flue size _____
Vents (material and size): gas or oil heater _____; water heater _____
Additional information: _____

4. FIREPLACES:
Type: ☐ solid fuel; ☐ gas burning; ☐ circulator *(make and size)* _____ Ash dump and clean-out _____
Fireplace: facing _____; lining _____; hearth _____; mantel _____
Additional information: _____

5. EXTERIOR WALLS:
Wood frame: wood grade, and species _____ ☐ Corner bracing. Building paper or felt _____
  Sheathing _____; thickness _____; width _____; ☐ solid; ☐ spaced _____" o.c.; ☐ diagonal _____
  Siding _____; grade _____; type _____; size _____; exposure _____; fastening _____
  Shingles _____; grade _____; type _____; size _____; exposure _____; fastening _____
  Stucco _____; thickness _____"; Lath _____; weight _____ lb.
  Masonry veneer _____ Sills _____ Lintels _____ Base flashing _____
Masonry: ☐ solid ☐ faced ☐ stuccoed: total wall thickness _____"; facing thickness _____"; facing material _____
  Backup material _____; thickness _____; bonding _____
  Door sills _____ Window sills _____ Lintels _____ Base flashing _____
  Interior surfaces: dampproofing, _____ coats of _____; furring _____
Additional information: _____
Exterior painting: material _____; number of coats _____
Gable wall construction: ☐ same as main walls; ☐ other construction _____

6. FLOOR FRAMING:
Joists: wood, grade, and species _____; other _____; bridging _____; anchors _____
Concrete slab: ☐ basement floor; ☐ first floor; ☐ ground supported; ☐ self-supporting; mix _____; thickness _____";
  reinforcing _____; insulation _____; membrane _____
Fill under slab: material _____; thickness _____"; Additional information: _____

7. SUBFLOORING: *(Describe underflooring for special floors under item 21)*
Material: grade and species _____; size _____; type _____
Laid: ☐ first floor; ☐ second floor; ☐ attic _____ sq. ft.; ☐ diagonal; ☐ right angles. Additional information: _____

8. FINISH FLOORING *(Wood only. Describe other finish flooring under item 21.)*

Location	Rooms	Grade	Species	Thickness	Width	Bldg. Paper	Finish
First floor							
Second floor							
Attic floor _____ sq. ft.							

Additional information: _____

Figure 1- 13
Description of materials form

9. PARTITION FRAMING:
Studs: wood grade, and species_____ size and spacing _____ Other _____
Additional information _____

10. CEILING FRAMING:
Joists: wood, grade, and species_____ Other _____ Bridging_____
Additional information: _____

11. ROOF FRAMING:
Rafters: wood, grade, and species _____ Roof trusses (see detail): grade and species _____
Additional information: _____

12. ROOFING:
Sheathing: wood, grade, and species _____ ☐ solid ☐ spaced _____" o.c.
Roofing _____; grade _____; size _____; type _____
Underlay_____; weight or thickness _____; size _____; fastening _____
Built-up roofing _____; number of plies _____; surfacing material _____
Flashing: material _____; gage or weight _____; ☐ gravel stops; ☐ snow guards
Additional information: _____

13. GUTTERS AND DOWNSPOUTS:
Gutters: material _____; gage or weight _____; size _____; shape _____
Downspouts: material_____; gage or weight _____; size _____; shape _____; number _____
Downspouts connected to: ☐ Storm sewer; ☐ sanitary sewer; ☐ dry-well.   ☐ Splash blocks: material and size _____
Additional information: _____

14. LATH AND PLASTER:
Lath ☐ walls, ☐ ceilings: material _____; weight or thickness _____ Plaster: coats _____; finish _____
Drywall ☐ walls, ☐ ceilings: material _____; thickness _____; finish _____;
Joint treatment _____

15. DECORATING: *(Paint, wallpaper, etc.)*

Rooms	Wall Finish Material and Application	Ceiling Finish Material and Application
Kitchen___		
Bath___		
Other___		

Additional information: _____

16. INTERIOR DOORS AND TRIM:
Doors: type _____; material _____; thickness_____
Door trim: type _____; material _____ Base: type _____; material _____; size _____
Finish: doors _____; trim _____
Other trim *(item, type and location)* _____
Additional information: _____

17. WINDOWS:
Windows: type _____; make _____; material _____; sash thickness _____
Glass: grade _____; ☐ sash weights; ☐ balances, type _____; head flashing_____
Trim: type _____; material _____ Paint _____; number coats_____
Weatherstripping: type _____; material _____ Storm sash, number _____
Screens: ☐ full; ☐ half; type _____; number _____; screen cloth material _____
Basement windows: type _____; material _____; screens, number _____; Storm sash, number _____
Special windows _____
Additional information: _____

18. ENTRANCES AND EXTERIOR DETAIL:
Main entrance door: material _____; width _____; thickness _____". Frame: material _____; thickness _____"
Other entrance doors: material _____; width _____; thickness _____". Frame: material _____; thickness _____"
Head flashing _____ Weatherstripping: type _____; saddles _____
Screen doors: thickness _____"; number _____; screen cloth material _____ Storm doors: thickness _____" number _____
Combination storm and screen doors: thickness _____"; number _____; screen cloth material _____
Shutters: ☐ hinged; ☐ fixed. Railings _____; Attic louvers_____
Exterior millwork: grade and species _____ Paint _____; number coats _____
Additional information: _____

19. CABINETS AND INTERIOR DETAIL:
Kitchen cabinets, wall units: material _____; linear feet of shelves _____; shelf width _____
  Base units: material _____; counter top _____; edging _____
  Back and end splash _____ Finish of cabinets _____ number coats _____
Medicine cabinets: make _____; model _____
Other cabinets and built-in furniture _____
Additional information: _____

20. STAIRS:

Stair	Treads		Risers		Strings		Handrail		Balusters	
	Material	Thickness	Material	Thickness	Material	Size	Material	Size	Material	Size
Basement ___										
Main ___										
Attic ___										

Disappearing: make and model number _____
Additional information: _____

Figure 1-13 (continued)
Description of materials form

21. SPECIAL FLOORS AND WAINSCOT: *(Describe Carpet as listed in Certified Products Directory)*

	Location	Material, Color, Border, Sizes, Gage, Etc.	Threshold Material	Wall Base Material	Underfloor Material
Floors	Kitchen _____				
	Bath _____				

	Location	Material, Color, Border, Cap, Sizes, Gage, Etc.	Height	Height Over Tub	Height in Showers (From Floor)
Wainscot	Bath _____				

Bathroom accessories: ☐ Recessed; material _____; number _____; ☐ Attached; material _____; number _____
Additional information: _____

22. PLUMBING:

Fixture	Number	Location	Make	Mfr's Fixture Identification No.	Size	Color
Sink _____						
Lavatory _____						
Water closet _____						
Bathtub _____						
Shower over tub _____						
Stall shower _____						
Laundry trays _____						

☐ Curtain rod ☐ Door ☐ Shower pan: material _____
Water supply: ☐ public; ☐ community system; ☐ individual (private) system★
Sewage disposal: ☐ public; ☐ community system; ☐ individual (private) system★
★Show and describe individual system in complete detail in separate drawings and specifications according to requirements.
House drain (inside): ☐ cast iron; ☐ tile; ☐ other _____ House sewer (outside): ☐ cast iron; ☐ tile; ☐ other _____
Water piping: ☐ galvanized steel; ☐ copper tubing; ☐ other_____ Sill cocks, number _____
Domestic water heater: type _____; make and model _____; heating capacity _____
_____ gph. 100° rise. Storage tank: material _____; capacity _____ gallons.
Gas service: ☐ utility company; ☐ liq. pet. gas; ☐ other _____ Gas piping: ☐ cooking; ☐ house heating.
Footing drains connected to: ☐ storm sewer; ☐ sanitary sewer; ☐ dry well. Sump pump; make and model _____
_____; capacity _____; discharges into _____

23. HEATING:
☐ Hot water. ☐ Steam. ☐ Vapor. ☐ One-pipe system. ☐ Two-pipe system.
☐ Radiators. ☐ Convectors. ☐ Baseboard radiation. Make and model _____
Radiant panel: ☐ floor; ☐ wall; ☐ ceiling. Panel coil: material _____
☐ Circulator. ☐ Return pump. Make and model _____; capacity _____ gpm.
Boiler: make and model _____ Output _____ Btuh.; net rating _____ Btuh.
Additional information: _____
Warm air: ☐ Gravity ☐ Forced. Type of system _____
Duct material: supply _____; return _____ Insulation _____, thickness _____ ☐ Outside air intake
Furnace: make and model _____ Input _____ Btuh.; output _____ Btuh.
Additional information: _____
☐ Space heater; ☐ floor furnace; ☐ wall heater. Input _____ Btuh.; output _____ Btuh.; number units _____
Make, model _____ Additional information: _____
Controls: make and types _____
Additional information: _____
Fuel: ☐ Coal; ☐ oil; ☐ gas; ☐ liq. pet. gas; ☐ electric; ☐ other _____; storage capacity _____
Additional information: _____
Firing equipment furnished separately: ☐ Gas burner, conversion type. ☐ Stoker: hopper feed ☐; bin feed ☐
Oil burner: ☐ pressure atomizing; ☐ vaporizing _____
Make and model _____ Control _____
Additional information: _____
Electric heating system: type _____ Input _____ watts; @ _____ volts; output _____ Btuh.
Additional information: _____
Ventilating equipment: attic fan, make and model _____; capacity _____ cfm.
kitchen exhaust fan, make and model _____
Other heating, ventilating, or cooling equipment _____

24. ELECTRIC WIRING:
Service: ☐ overhead; ☐ underground. Panel: ☐ fuse box; ☐ circuit-breaker; make _____ AMP's _____ No. circuits _____
Wiring: ☐ conduit; ☐ armored cable; ☐ nonmetallic cable; ☐ knob and tube; ☐ other _____
Special outlets: ☐ range; ☐ water heater; ☐ other _____
☐ Doorbell. ☐ Chimes. Push-button locations _____ Additional information: _____

25. LIGHTING FIXTURES:
Total number of fixtures _____ Total allowance for fixtures. typical installation, $ _____
Nontypical installation _____
Additional information: _____

Figure 1- 13 (continued)
Description of materials form

26

26. INSULATION:

Location	Thickness	Material, Type and Method of Installation	Vapor Barrier
Roof _____			
Ceiling _____			
Wall _____			
Floor _____			

27. MISCELLANEOUS: *(Describe any main dwelling materials, equipment, or construction items not shown elsewhere; or use to provide additional information where the space provided was inadequate. Always reference by item number to correspond to numbering used on this form.)* _____

_____
_____
_____
_____
_____
_____
_____
_____
_____

HARDWARE: *(make, material and finish.)* _____
_____
_____

SPECIAL EQUIPMENT: *(State material or make, model and quantity. Include only equipment and appliances which are acceptable by local law, custom and applicable FHA standards. Do not include items which, by established custom, are supplied by occupant and removed when he vacates premises or chattels prohibited by law from becoming realty.)* _____
_____
_____
_____
_____
_____
_____
_____

PORCHES:
_____
_____

TERRACES:
_____
_____

GARAGES:
_____
_____

WALKS AND DRIVEWAYS:
Driveway: width _____; base material _____; thickness _____"; surfacing material _____; thickness _____"
Front walk: width _____; material _____; thickness _____". Service walk: width _____: material _____; thickness _____"
Steps: material _____; treads _____"; risers _____". Cheek walls _____

OTHER ONSITE IMPROVEMENTS:
(Specify all exterior onsite improvements not described elsewhere, including items such as unusual grading, drainage structures, retaining walls, fence, railings, and accessory structures.)
_____
_____
_____

LANDSCAPING, PLANTING, AND FINISH GRADING:
Topsoil _____" thick: ☐ front yard; ☐ side yards; ☐ rear yard to _____ feet behind main building.
Lawns *(seeded, sodded or sprigged)*: ☐ front yard _____; ☐ side yards _____; ☐ rear yard _____
Planting: ☐ as specified and shown on drawings; ☐ as follows:

_____ Shade trees, deciduous, _____" caliper.	_____ Evergreen trees. _____' to _____', B&B.
_____ Low flowering trees, deciduous, _____' to _____'	_____ Evergreen shrubs. _____' to _____', B&B.
_____ High-growing shrubs, deciduous, _____' to _____'	_____ Vines, 2-year _____
_____ Medium-growing shrubs, deciduous, _____' to _____'	_____
_____ Low-growing shrubs, deciduous, _____' to _____'	_____

IDENTIFICATION. This exhibit shall be identified by the signature of the builder, or sponsor, and/or the proposed mortgagor if the latter is known at the time of application.

Date _____   Signature _____

Signature _____

Figure 1-13 (continued)
Description of materials form

2

Footings, Foundations and Slabs

The most important parts of any building are the parts that are hidden — those things you can't see. Your project begins with the footing, and that's where you can make or break the job.

There are, of course, no unimportant steps in building. You can't afford to be sloppy anywhere. But footings are unique because a mistake there can carry over into the rest of the job. If the footing isn't square or level, you'll have to make up for it somewhere down the line — and it's bound to be expensive. The idea is to get it right the first time. If you don't, then the sooner you fix it, the better.

Staking Out an Addition

Take these steps before you begin staking:

♦ Figure out where the lot boundaries are.

♦ Check that the addition satisfies the lot code requirements.

♦ Find out how deep the frost line is.

♦ Make sure there aren't any underground or overhead utility lines in the way.

♦ Avoid deep cuts, steep inclines, unnecessary steps, and excessive foundation wall height. In crawl-space construction, a minimum of 18 inches is required between the ground and the floor joists. A 24-inch space would require another course of concrete block — an unnecessary expense.

Staking out an addition always involves making square corners. To show you how to do this, I'll get a little technical for a moment. First, look at Figure 2-1. It shows how to use the 3-4-5 rule to make a square corner. It's called that because the triangle has sides that are 3, 4, and 5 feet long.

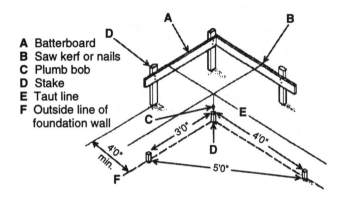

Figure 2-1
Using the 3-4-5 rule

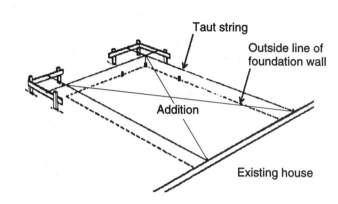

Figure 2-2
Squaring an addition

To find out if the corner is square, measure off 3 feet one way from the corner, and 4 feet the other way. Use a steel tape to get accurate measurements. If the corner is square, the measurement along the diagonal from the ends of the 3 and 4 foot sides will be exactly 5 feet. If it isn't, make the corner square by adjusting the side that's out of line until the diagonal is 5 feet long.

You can use longer lengths, as long as each one is a multiple of 3, 4, and 5 feet respectively. For example, you could use sides that are 6 and 8 feet. Then, if the diagonal is 10 feet, the corner is square.

You can check to make sure all the corners of a rectangle are square by measuring its two diagonals. If they're exactly the same length, the corners are square. When squaring an addition, attach a line to the existing house and make squaring adjustments at the batterboards. Figure 2-2 shows how to make sure an addition has square corners. Keep the string taut and securely fastened to the existing house as you make the diagonals equal.

Setting the Batterboards

As you can see in Figures 2-1 and 2-2, batterboards both establish key points at the site, and hold the layout string. Place the boards at least 4 feet from the outside line of your room addition, as shown in Figure 2-1.

To set batterboards, start by driving profile stakes into firm ground. Some builders brace them with diagonal boards, but this isn't usually necessary. Connect the tops of the stakes with horizontal boards, being careful to keep them at the same height. See Figure 2-3.

When you've set the continuous horizontal boards around the entire site, as shown in Figure 2-3 B, you can use a tape to mark the distances, such as footing depth and foundation wall height, at the same time. Figure 2-4 shows how a corner layout might look using a taut stringline. The continuous horizontal boards and the stringline serve the same purpose.

Figure 2-5 shows how you use a batterboard for squaring and excavation for shallow or deep footings. Cut kerfs (notches) on top of the boards to mark the exact points to attach the string. Then you can replace the string after you remove it for excavating, pouring footings, and material handling. When you replace the string, recheck the measurements and make sure the corners are still square. It's easy for batterboards to get bumped out of place.

When you're adding on to a house that sits on a sloping lot, be careful that you don't install drainage problems. The highest point on the ground should be your starting point because it controls the height of the foundation wall. See Figure 2-6. You'll want the foundation wall to be high enough so the finish grade slopes away from a house. Water pooling around the foundation will cause problems.

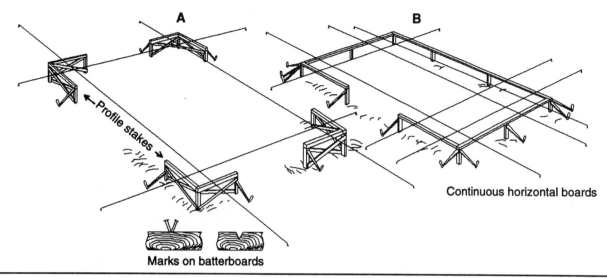

Figure 2-3
Layout using batterboards

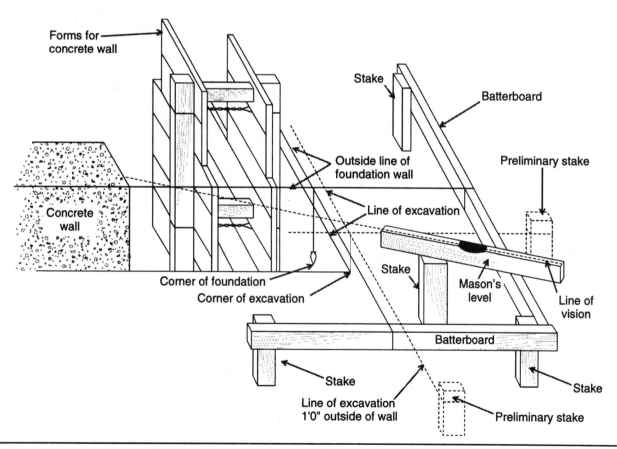

Figure 2-4
Construction lines

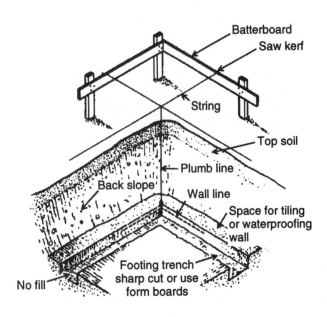

Figure 2-5
Proper location of a batterboard for squaring and excavation

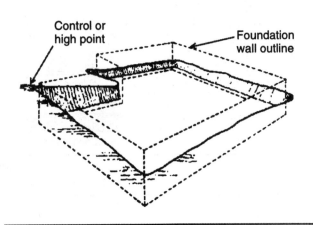

Figure 2-6
Establishing depth of excavation

Laying Out Satellite Additions

Satellite additions often form a T-shape. Fig. 2-7 shows how to place batterboards in satellite construction. Lay out a hallway or "connector" the same way as an addition, and square it the same way you square the addition. Normally, you can't change the dimensions adjacent to an existing wall because they're fixed points in the plan.

Dealing with Off-Square Corners

After you've taken pains to properly lay out an addition, squaring it to within an eighth of an inch of perfection, there's still something else to watch out for. If the building you're adding to isn't square, you might have to make some adjustments. You'll always want to do this in the least conspicuous place. Remember when we discussed adding on at planes and how difficult it can be to achieve a professional job? Well, in some cases it may be the only choice you have.

Look at Figure 2-8. The problem here is that there's no way you can square the addition without

creating an unsightly distortion in the common (plane) wall. What should you do? Just extend the common wall straight in line with the wall of the existing house, then work from that point. One approach is to build the common wall in line with the house and make corner B square. Wall C will be a few inches shorter than the common wall. Corners A and E will have to be off square, but this won't be obvious from the outside.

Planning the Footings

Unless you're building with pressure-treated wood, you'll probably want to use poured concrete footings for residential construction. Use wood stakes to set the height of the mix when poured. Work the surface smooth to make it easy to lay the foundation block or brick.

Always extend a footing below the frost line, and at least 6 inches below the finish grade. Check the code for your area for the specific depth for footings. For example, the footing depth for Anchorage, Alaska

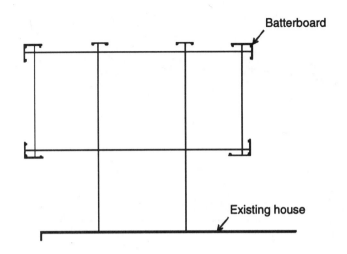

Figure 2-7
Locations of batterboards for squaring a T-shaped addition
(satellite) to an existing house

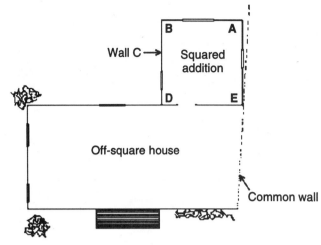

Figure 2-8
Off-square corners

is 42 inches. In Tampa, Florida it's only 6 inches. Always protect freshly-poured footings from freezing. Frozen concrete can't reach its maximum strength.

If you dig a footing trench too deep, you're not allowed to refill it with dirt. You have to use extra concrete. If the soil conditions won't let you use sharply-cut trenches for a footing, build a form for the footing. Reinforce a footing with steel rods any time it crosses a pipe trench.

Footing Sizes

Concrete footing sizes vary with soil type and the weight of a structure. You'll need to know the bearing value of the soil you're building on. The bearing value is the weight per square foot the soil will support, measured in tons per square foot. There are nine basic classes of soil type, each with the following bearing value:

Soil Type	Tons per SF
Sand, clean and dry	2.0
Sand, compact, not drained	4.5
Clay, deep beds, always dry	4.5
Clay, average, moist	3.5
Clay, soft	1.0

Soil Type	Tons per SF
Gravel, well-banded with coarse sand	4.5
Hard rock, thick layers, undisturbed	200.0
Soft rock, limestone strata	50.0
Soft rock, limestone, broken	15.0

Figure 2-9 shows the normal sizes for a conventionally-loaded wall on soil with an average bearing value of approximately 2,000 psf or more. Extend any excavation at least 6 inches into natural undisturbed soil to provide adequate bearing for the load of the structure. When you're building on fill, excavate through the fill to undisturbed soil.

If you're adding a second-story addition, you'll need to find out the size of the existing footing of the first story. If there's no basement, dig down outside an exterior wall to expose the footing. If there's a basement, you'll have to dig down the depth of the basement to reach the footing. Unless there's some evidence that the house has settled a lot, you're probably safe in adding that second floor. Use Figure 2-9 as a general guideline to find out if the footing is adequate. *But be sure to check your local building code for actual specifications.*

	Frame		Masonry or masonry veneer	
	Minimum thickness (inches)	Projection each side of wall (inches)	Minimum thickness (inches)	Footing projection each side of foundation wall (inches)
One story:				
No basement	6	2	6	3
Basement	6	3	6	4
Two story:				
No basement	6	3	6	4
Basement	6	4	8	5

Figure 2-9
Footing sizes

Stepped Footings

You'll need a stepped footing wherever the ground slopes more than 1 foot in 10. When planning a footing step, be sure the height of the vertical step isn't more than $3/4$ of the horizontal distance between steps. The horizontal distance between steps should be at least 2 feet. The vertical connection should be the same width as the footing, and at least 6 inches thick. Figure 2-10 shows these dimensions. Pour the vertical and horizontal runs at the same time so the two parts form a good bond.

Pier and Post Footings

In crawl-space construction, you'll probably use concrete block for building piers and foundation walls. Make pier footings at least 8 inches thick, and large enough to support the total load. In most areas, a 24 x 24-inch square footing is enough for a pier made of 8 x 8 x 16-inch concrete blocks spaced 8 feet on center. Figure 2-11 shows one method for using a pier footing.

Concrete Footing Mixes

For most footings, you'll use five-bag ready-mix. A five-bag mix has five bags of cement per cubic yard of concrete. After setting up for 28 days, the concrete should have a compressive strength of at least 2,000 psi. Generally, the more water you use with a mix, the weaker the concrete will be when it sets. Very hot weather dries concrete too quickly and stops the hardening process too soon. When it's hot, keep the fresh concrete moist for several days.

A good way to figure the concrete requirements for a footing is to multiply the total length of the footing in feet, times the width in feet, times the thickness in inches, and divide by 314. (This way you can avoid having to convert the thickness into the decimal portion of a foot.) For example, assume your room addition is 20 x 12 feet, with the 12-foot end joining the existing house. You'll need a footing for both the 20-foot runs, and one 12-foot run, which gives a total of 52 feet. If the footing is 18 inches wide (1.5 feet) and 6 inches thick, the computation is:

$$52' \text{ length x } 1.5' \text{ width} = 78 \text{ square feet}$$
$$78 \text{ SF x } 6'' \text{ thick} = 468$$
$$468 \div 314 = 1.49 \text{ cubic yards}$$

Round this off to 1.5 cubic yards. This doesn't include any pillars, but calculate those the same way and add them on to the total. If you calculate it by using a decimal of a foot for the thickness, you'll get a smaller answer, but this method allows for waste.

Treated Wood Foundations

The Permanent Wood Foundation (PWF) method uses pressure-treated lumber as a building foundation.

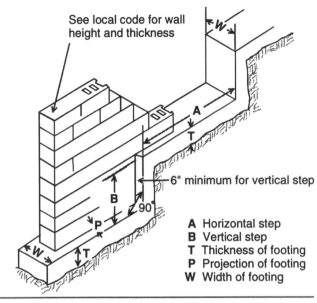

Figure 2-10
Stepped footings

A Horizontal step
B Vertical step
T Thickness of footing
P Projection of footing
W Width of footing

See local code for wall height and thickness

6" minimum for vertical step

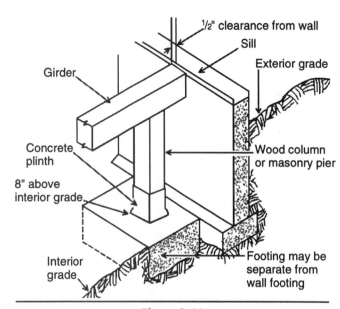

Figure 2-11
Pier footing in place

½" clearance from wall
Sill
Exterior grade
Girder
Concrete plinth
8" above interior grade
Wood column or masonry pier
Interior grade
Footing may be separate from wall footing

The lumber industry and the U.S. Forest Service developed this method with advice from the Federal Housing Administration and research data from the NAHB (National Association of Home Builders). The system combines proven construction techniques with good moisture-control practices. And there's another advantage: PWF lets you build during any weather since there's no concrete or masonry to worry about. For more information, contact:

American Forest & Paper Association
1250 Connecticut Avenue, NW, Second Floor
Washington, DC 20036

PWF is a structurally-engineered foundation using a gravel footing and a wood footing plate to transfer vertical loads to the soil. The studs and plywood sheathing resist lateral loads of the soil. The method uses 2 x 4s 16 inches on center where the backfill is shallow. If the fill is deep, use 2 x 6 studs 12 inches on center instead. Figure 2-12A shows how to construct a foundation wall for a crawl-space building. Figure 2-12B shows the wall supporting brick veneer. Figure 2-13 shows a center bearing support.

A PWF footing is a composite with a wood footing plate supported by a layer of gravel, coarse sand, or crushed stone (GSCS). The width of the footing plate depends on how much pressure the layer of grav-el, sand, or crushed stone can hold. The allowable bearing pressure on uncompacted GSCS is at least 3,000 psf.

In crawl-space construction, you need plywood panels only for the first 2 feet below a foundation top plate. There must be a minimum of 18 inches between the ground and the bottom of floor joists, as shown in Figure 2-12. Use lumber and plywood that's been treated as required by the American Wood Preservers Bureau Standard AWPB-FDN. Each piece of treated lumber or plywood bears the stamp of an approved inspection agency. Since the treatment involves impregnation with an inorganic arsenic pesticide, you need to take special precautions when you're using it. Wear a dust mask when you're sawing it, wash your hands immediately afterwards, and wash your clothing, separate from other laundry items, before rewearing it. Never burn it on an open fire or in a fireplace, or use it where it can come in contact with food. You can ask you dealer for a product information sheet that lists all of the precautions.

Hints for Crawl-Space Construction

I like the crawl-space method of building add-ons because it lets you get at wires, pipes, and drains. It's a practical way to build.

A PWF crawl-space wall

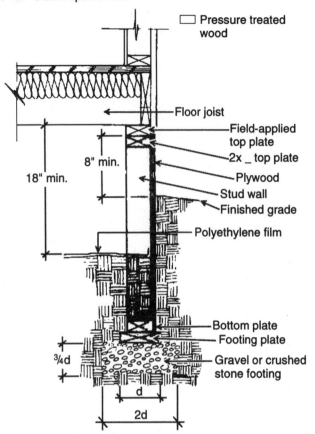

B PWF crawl-space wall with brick veneer on knee wall

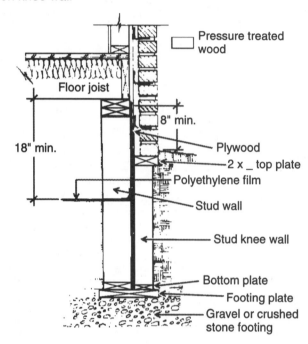

Figure 2-12
Permanent Wood Foundation (PWF) for a crawl-space building

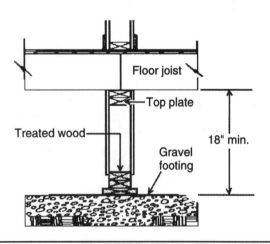

Figure 2-13
PWF crawl space center bearing support

Always ventilate the crawl space below an addition. You should also protect the crawl space from the ground moisture with a vapor barrier. Use a vapor barrier with a *perm value* of less than 1.0. (A perm is a measure of the permeability of a material. One perm means that no more than 1 gram of water vapor can travel through 1 square foot of the barrier per hour.) Plastic films, roll roofing, and asphalt-laminated paper all qualify. Check your local building code requirements.

A crawl space may open into a partial basement. If there's an openable basement window, you can omit wall vents. But you still need a vapor barrier over the soil.

In a crawl space that doesn't adjoin a basement, provide at least four foundation-wall vents near the corners of the building. The total net vent area should be $^1/_{160}$ of the ground area if you don't use a vapor barrier, and $^1/_{150}$ of the ground area if you do. For example, with no soil cover on a ground area of 600 square feet, you need a total net ventilating area of about 4 square feet. The best vents for crawl spaces have corrosion-resistant screens of No. 8 mesh.

In termite-prone areas, vents are extremely important. Moisture under the house attracts termites. Normally, I install a vent at each corner, plus additional vents spaced 8 to 10 feet on center between the corners.

Masonry and Concrete Foundations

By any standard, a masonry foundation is hard to beat. Concrete hollow block, brick, and stone make up the majority of masonry foundations. Over the years, I've mainly used 8 x 8 x 16-inch concrete block in foundation work and found the material highly satisfactory. The block are durable, relatively inexpensive, and they resist moisture and insects. They'll also support a second-story addition. See Figure 2-14 for a typical hollow block wall.

Allow at least 18 inches of clearance from the ground level to the bottom of floor joists, and 12 inches to the bottom of wood girders. A minimum of 2 feet is required between the ground and floor joists where mechanical equipment such as heating/cooling ducts run through a crawl space.

To ensure proper water drainage, make the outside finish grade lower than the ground level under the crawl space. If this isn't possible, put a drainage system under the structure to allow for water runoff. See Figure 2-15.

It's important that walls and piers supporting wood-frame construction extend at least 8 inches above the finish grade. Don't make the height of a foundation wall or pier more than four times its thickness unless it's reinforced in accordance with the local building code. The maximum height above grade of reinforced concrete, solid masonry, or filled cell blocks is ten times the smallest dimension of the block. Locate exterior piers and interior girder piers no more than 8 feet on center. Space the piers under exterior wall beams that run parallel to floor joists (at each end of a house), no more than 12 feet on center.

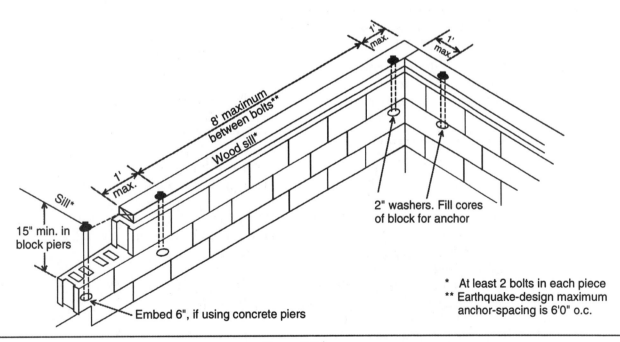

Figure 2-14
Hollow block wall with proper sill anchorage

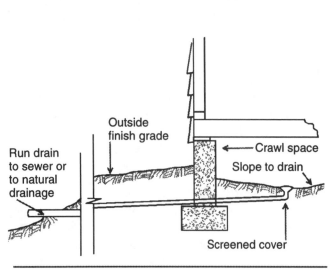

Figure 2-15
Crawl-space drainage

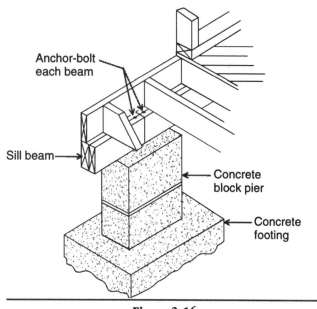

Figure 2-16
Free-standing exterior pier

You can reduce costs in brick veneer construction by using freestanding exterior piers instead of solid foundation walls. See Figure 2-16. In some areas, hollow block exterior piers supporting wood-frame walls must be filled with concrete or grout to prevent wind damage. If you don't use solid cap blocks for interior piers, you should fill the cells of the top course of hollow blocks with concrete or grout.

Look again at Figure 2-14. It shows how to anchor wood-frame floor and sills on hollow block walls. Use $1/2$ inch bolts (with a washer at each end), embedded at least 15 inches in block piers, and 6 inches in concrete piers.

Concrete Slab Construction

Building with poured cement slab floors is called slab-on-grade construction. Slabs make excellent floors if you grade, form, and finish them correctly. And for many jobs, you'll find it's cheaper to pour a slab — by up to a dollar a square foot of floor space, compared to a conventional foundation home. But if you're building in an isolated area, some distance from any ready-mix cement business, it can end up costing more because of the delivery cost.

Wet areas aren't good for slab construction. Even in dry areas, you must grade the site to keep surface and ground water from collecting under the slab. Make sure fill material is free of vegetation and trash. Also, clear out all the vegetation, topsoil, and foreign material before you begin constructing a slab.

Hints for On-Slab Construction

Many room additions you build will be on concrete slabs which are poured directly on the ground. This is a popular method, particularly in warmer climates. It's relatively easy to build this type of slab. Here are a few tips:

♦ Don't build a slab directly on sloping ground or a low-lying area. The greater the slope, the higher the costs for fill and retaining walls. A flat surface is ideal if it's not in a low-lying area where water drainage can be a problem.

♦ The drier the mix, the stronger the concrete will be when it sets up. Too much water may make the finishing easier, but it'll weaken the hardening process and may leave you with an unsatisfactory slab. Use only the amount of water it takes to make a mix pliable enough to make a smooth finish.

♦ Make sure heating and cooling ducts, sewer drain lines and water pipes installed under a slab are put in correctly *before* you pour. Discovering there's a problem after the slab is finished is going to make you very unhappy.

♦ Concrete slab-on-grade construction requires special precautions to keep moisture from damaging the flooring that covers it. The top of the slab should be at least 8 inches above the exterior finish grade. The bottom of wood sills or sleepers should be at least 8 inches above grade. Once you remove the top soil and run the utility lines, tamp 4 to 6 inches of gravel or crushed stone into place. You may need to do more, depending on the location of the slab in relation to the finish grade, the height of the ground water table, and the type of subsoil.

♦ In warm climates, your best protection against termites is to construct a monolithic slab by pouring the footing and slab at the same time. See Figure 2-17. Extend the vapor barrier under the footing. The bottom of the footing should be at least 1 foot below the natural grade line. You need solid, well-drained soil for this method.

♦ In areas with a deep frost line, build foundations or piers that extend below the frost line to solid bearing or unfilled soil. In room additions, the slab and foundation wall are usually separate. Figure 2-18 shows one method of building an independent slab and foundation. Figures 2-19 and 2-20 show two other methods.

♦ Reinforce concrete slabs with 6 x 6-inch No. 10 wire mesh, or use fiber-reinforced concrete. Check with your building code on this first. Slabs should be at least 4 inches thick.

♦ Steel trowel a slab for a smooth, dense surface. Flaws or even slightly uneven surfaces in a slab will really show under floor coverings like vinyl sheeting and tile.

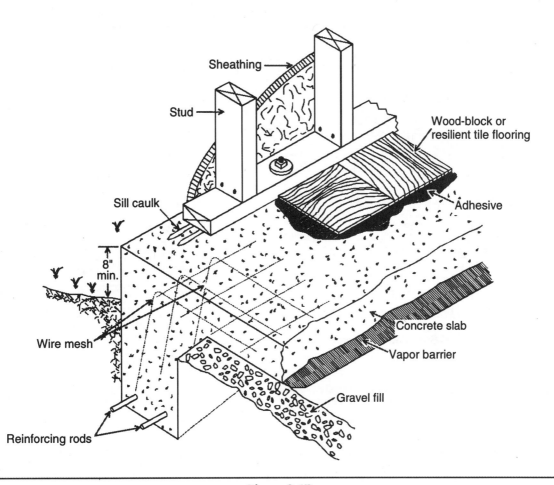

Figure 2-17
Monolithic slab

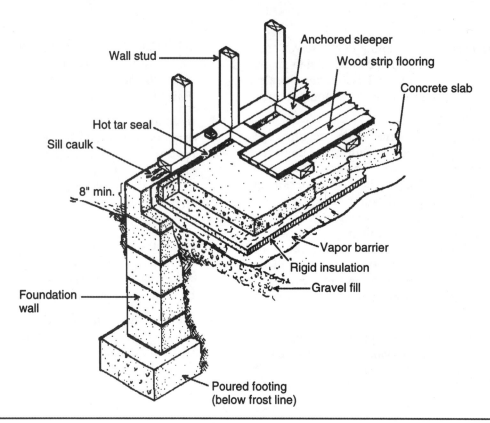

Figure 2-18
Independent concrete floor slab and wall

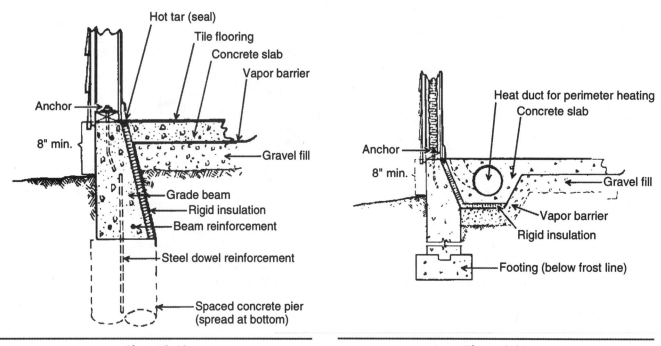

Figure 2-19
Reinforced grade beam for concrete slab

Figure 2-20
Full foundation wall for cold climates

Vapor Barriers

Always use a vapor barrier under a concrete slab. Check your building code for regulations on this. Usually the vapor barrier must have a vapor transmission rating of less than 0.5 perm, be strong enough to withstand ruptures, and resistant to moisture damage and rot. Always seal all seams in a vapor barrier with a waterproof mastic.

The following vapor barriers usually satisfy code requirements:

♦ Heavy plastic film, such as 6-mil or heavier polyethylene or similar plastic film laminated to a duplex-treated paper

♦ Three layers of 15-pound roofing felt mopped with hot asphalt

♦ Heavy asphalt-impregnated and vapor-resistant rigid sheet material with sealed joints

♦ 55-pound roll roofing or heavy asphalt-laminated duplex-treated paper

Slab Insulation

A slab with no insulation loses heat mainly around its perimeter. There's very little heat loss from the center. So use perimeter insulation to reduce heat loss. Figures 2-18, 2-19, and 2-20 show different methods of slab insulation. Use a high-quality closed-cell extruded polystyrene foam rigid insulation board which has high thermal resistance, long-lasting R-value, high compressive strength, and low moisture absorption. Place the board on top of a 6-mil polyethylene vapor barrier and pour the concrete slab directly over the insulation. AMOFOAM® SB is one trade name for this insulation board. It's available in 4 x 8 size and 1 inch, 1½ inches and 2 inches thick.

A glass fiber reinforced polyisocyanurate foam core rigid insulation board, such as THERMAX®, is also a good underslab insulation when used over 6-mil polyethylene. You can pour concrete right over the board. It comes in 4-foot widths in 8- and 9-foot lengths, ⅜ inch to 1 inch thick.

You can use mica aggregate (1 part cement to 6 parts aggregate) to increase the R-value of concrete to about 1.1 per inch of thickness. But don't use this where moisture might be a problem.

Estimating Manhours and Materials

To estimate the number of standard size (8 x 8 x 16) concrete blocks in a foundation wall, simply multiply the number of courses in the wall by the number of blocks in each course. To find the number of courses, multiply the height of the wall (in feet) times 1.5. Multiply the length of the wall times 0.75 to find the number of blocks in each course.

For a 4-foot high foundation wall that's 54 feet long, you'll need:

4 x 1.5 = 6 (the number of courses)
54 x 0.75 = 40.5 (the number of blocks per course)
6 x 40.5 = 243 blocks

This method counts corners twice, allowing approximately 2 percent per wall for waste. You'll also need a 70-pound bag of masonry cement and 3 cubic feet of sand for every 100 blocks you lay.

On a normal job, a mason should lay 30 concrete blocks (8 x 8 x 16-inch size) per hour. For lightweight blocks, add 10 percent. Figure standard brickwork at 6.5 hours for a mason, plus 5 hours for a laborer, per 100 square feet of wall space. Figure 2-21 gives a breakdown of labor required to place concrete block per 100 square feet of wall.

Here's a good rule of thumb for estimating the yards of concrete mix for a slab floor:

Multiply the length of the area in feet, times the width in feet, times the thickness in inches. Divide the result by 314. A slab 16 feet long, 12 feet wide and 4 inches thick would be:

16' (length) x 12' (width) x 4" (thickness) = 768

768 ÷ 314 = 2.45 cubic yards

The number of cubic yards of concrete mix required for the job is 2.45. Round this off to 2.5 cubic yards to allow for waste. A slab 22 feet long, 18 feet wide, and 5 inches thick would require 6.3 cubic yards.

If transit mix (delivered by truck ready to pour) isn't available, use Figure 2-22 as a guide to field-mix concrete.

Figure 2-23 gives a breakdown of labor and materials for slabs on grade.

Labor placing concrete block		
Work element	Unit (SF)	Man hours per unit
Concrete block, lightweight		
4" block	100 SF	10.50
6" block	100 SF	11.70
8" block	100 SF	12.80
10" block	100 SF	15.00
12" block	100 SF	17.90
Concrete block, hollow, standard weight		
4" block	100 SF	11.00
6" block	100 SF	12.00
8" block	100 SF	13.00
10" block	100 SF	15.00
12" block	100 SF	18.00

Time includes set-up, clean-up, joint striking one side only, cutting, pointing, steel alignment, and grout.
Suggested Crew: Small jobs, 1 mason, 1 helper

Figure 2-21
Labor placing concrete block

Maximum size of coarse aggregate	Approximate cement (bag) per CY	Approximate water per bag (gals.)	Approximate proportions (by volume) per bag of cement		
			Cement	Fine aggregate	Coarse aggregate
¾"	6.0	5	1	2½	2¾
1"	5.8	5	1	2½	3
1½"	5.5	5	1	2½	3½
2"*	5.2	5	1	2½	4

*Not for slabs or thin work

Figure 2-22
Field-mix concrete proportions

	Material per square foot		Labor	
Thickness	CF of concrete	SF per CY of concrete	Manhours per 100 LF forms and screeds	Manhours placing concrete per 100 SF
2"	0.167	167		
3"	0.25	108	Averages 22 linear feet per hour	Averages 2 hours
4"	0.333	81		
5"	0.417	65		
6"	0.50	54		

Placement includes finishing with topping. If topping is omitted, deduct 1.2 hours. Placement labor is based on ready-mix concrete direct from chute. Add ½ hour per cubic yard if concrete is pumped into place and 2 hours if concrete is wheeled up to 40 feet into place.

Figure 2-23
Labor and material for slabs on grade

Basement Conversion and Construction

The easiest way to expand living space in a house is to convert a properly-waterproofed basement. Many homeowners want to use the added space as a recreation room, office, hobby and craft space, or a study area. A basement also makes an ideal place for bedrooms. And you can add a bathroom without sewage pumping facilities if there are sewer lines running at or below the basement floor level. Because of the limited access, most basement conversions aren't suitable for living rooms.

Can the Basement Be Converted?

Homeowners think converting their basements should be simple because the floor, walls, and ceiling are already in place. All that's left is to put on the finish materials. Well, that's true in some cases. But not all. There are things you, the building expert, must consider before deciding that a basement can be converted.

Check the Ceiling Height

Before you take on a basement conversion, the first thing to consider is the ceiling height. Be sure to check your local code, however, because it may have different requirements than the ones shown here in Figure 3-1, Typical basement ceiling height requirements. A basement ceiling without habitable spaces can be as low as 6'8" (6'4" under girders). Basements with habitable spaces require a ceiling at least 7'6" high. If you put in a luminous or drop ceiling, that reduces the minimum ceiling height to 7'0". If there's a girder in the center of a basement that's lower than 6'4", you'll have to design the conversion with a partition under it.

In many basements, there are support columns under the girder. You can build a partition wall that encloses the columns. In large basements,

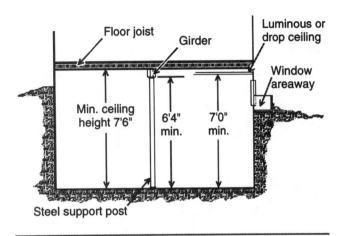

Figure 3-1
Typical basement ceiling height requirements

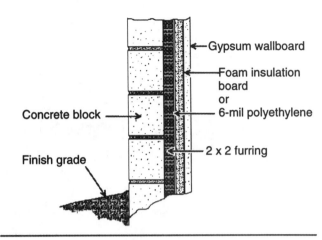

Figure 3-2
Preventing basement condensation

you may have to enclose additional columns that support a second girder. But you don't always have to disguise the columns. If your design doesn't easily incorporate a column in a wall, a bookcase, or a partial room divider, simply leave it alone if the girder it supports is over 6'4".

Is Dampness a Problem?

If the ceiling height is OK, the next factor to consider is whether the basement has any dampness problems. Remember, I started the chapter by mentioning the conversion of a "properly-waterproofed" basement. What if it's not properly waterproofed?

If there are only minor condensation problems, they can be minimized by regulating the basement ventilation. Advise the owners to keep the windows closed when the heater is going, and in the spring until warm weather has raised the temperature of the ground outside the walls. But the only real solution for condensation is a vapor barrier. Painting the walls doesn't do it, because the warm interior air will still hit the cool masonry wall. You need a barrier between the wall and the basement space to eliminate the problem.

The solution is to add a wall (Figure 3-2). Install furring strips (either 1 x 4s, 2 x 2s or 2 x 4s) and cover them with a vapor barrier. Six-mil polyethylene is a good choice. So is foam insulation board with a foil vapor barrier if you install it with the vapor barrier

facing the interior of the room. Then put up finish wall material like paneling or drywall, directly against the vapor barrier.

Suppose the basement is more than damp — it's *wet*. The problem is leakage, not condensation. Then you'll probably have to install a drain pipe. And if there's no sewer drain outlet or natural fall to take the water from the area, the job requires a sump pump. This is a good time to tell the homeowner the job isn't going to be quite as simple or cheap as he may have been hoping. There's information about drain pipes and sump pumps in the second part of the chapter on building a basement.

Finishing Basement Floors

You have to take special precautions to guard against moisture in concrete basement floors. If your examination of the basement shows no serious dampness, you can assume (or hope) that the basement was properly constructed, with gravel fill and a vapor barrier under the floor. But you don't want to base your entire conversion on assumptions or hopes.

I recommend finishing any concrete basement floor with a vapor barrier directly on top of the floor. Use 6-mil polyethylene and overlap the seams at least 6 inches. Seal the seams with a good quality silicone caulk Then install sleepers directly on the vapor barrier. I use pressure-treated 1 x 4s or 2 x 4s spaced 16 inches on center. See Figure 3-3.

Install a sheathing grade $\frac{1}{2}$-inch plywood or OSB panel subfloor directly on the sleepers. A layer of $\frac{5}{8}$-inch particleboard panels on top of the subfloor makes a strong base for carpeting or resilient flooring. Stagger the plywood panels so the joints don't line up, and so that their joints and ends don't match the joints and ends of the subfloor. Space according to the manufacturer's recommendations.

You'll find the procedures for installing floor covering, wall and ceiling finishes in later chapters on room additions and attic conversions.

Designing a Basement Conversion

Once you've decided that a conversion is feasible, it's time to think of design. If you have some experience remodeling or building, you already know that almost any reasonable design is possible within four walls. You can turn a drab, damp basement into a luxurious bedroom suite with an adjoining bathroom. Or you might develop a game room, study, and library. By cutting a doorway to the outside, you can turn a basement into an office with its own entrance.

But don't think basement conversions are all simple. There are times you have to work around obstacles and use your imagination to make the obstacle appear as a "part of the design." Often, there are small windows, so high on the basement wall that the top touches the bottom of the sill plate. Heating or air ducts suspended from the floor joists in a basement area can present a problem. We'll discuss how to get around these problems later in this chapter.

Basement stairways can sometimes present the biggest roadblock to a design. You might be able to move the stairs, but you can't move the landing unless you move the door leading from the first floor to the basement.

Figure 3-4 shows three ways to convert a basement with stairs located at an end wall by adding partitions, and in some cases a window and entrance door. Part A shows a recreation room with a half bath. Part B shows how the basement might be converted to an office, library, den, and half bath. And Part C adds two bedrooms, a bath and a storage room.

But suppose the stairs aren't at the end wall, but in the center of the basement. What then? Figure 3-5 shows one alternate design.

The basement stairway may be a problem in many conversions because it requires so much space. Where there's an outside entrance to the basement (or if you add one), consider replacing the stairway with a spiral staircase if it'll provide additional space in the conversion.

If the basements in Figures 3-4 and 3-5 are below the sewer lines running from the house, you'll have to put in a pump to lift the waste to the sewer line. Unless you're qualified in this area, you'll need to contact a plumbing company to give you a bid on the job.

Making a Basement Entrance

The ideal basement to convert is one that has its own entrance from the outside. A sloping lot is ideal for a basement with an outside entrance — especially if the lot slopes from rear of the building and is clear of any backfill.

Let's suppose the basement you're converting has no entrance door or windows. How can you provide them? Figure 3-6 shows two possibilities. You can build the stairs and entrance if you can meet the safety requirements. The basement stairway has to be at least 2'8" wide, with a tread of at least 11 inches, a maximum riser of $7\frac{1}{2}$ inches and a minimum riser of 4 inches.

Entrance doors are usually 3'0" wide. The landing at the bottom of the stairs must be at least as wide as

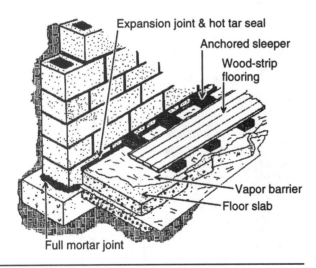

Figure 3-3
Installing sleepers on concrete floor

A Creating a rec room, laundry and half bath

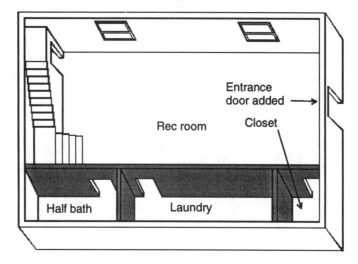

B Creating a library, office, den and half bath

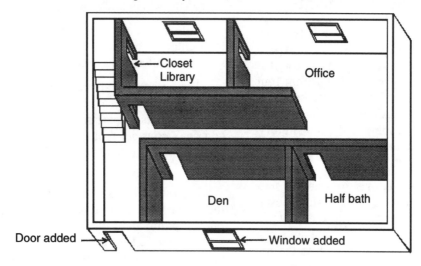

C Creating bedrooms, a bath and storage space

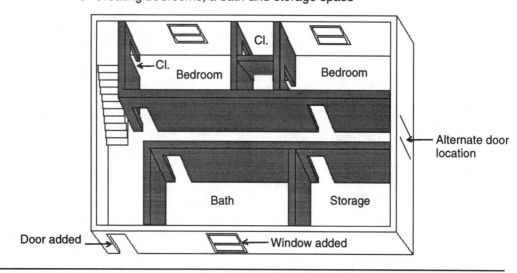

Figure 3-4
Three ways to convert an open basement

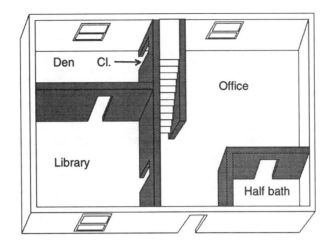

Figure 3-5
Conversion with stairs in center of basement

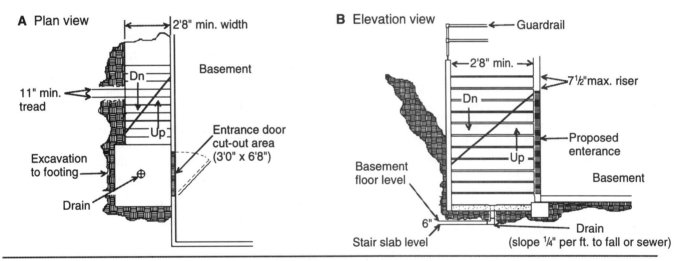

Figure 3-6
Excavation for an outside entrance door

the door. So you'll need 3 feet for the landing and space for the run of the stairs.

Assume the height from the top of the basement floor to finish grade is 7 feet. The top of the bottom landing should be at least 6 inches below the basement floor level. The finish grade and landing at the top of the stairs will take about 6 inches more, so the stair height is 8 feet from the top of the bottom landing to the top of the top landing. The 8-foot height will need

13 risers at $7\frac{3}{8}$ inches for a total run of about 11 feet. Figure 3-7 shows the stairs and entrance.

When you're sure your design meets the requirements, begin by excavating the dirt down to the footing, as shown in Figure 3-6. The next step is to make a form for the concrete basement steps. Cut the ground to a 30 to 35-degree angle. Undisturbed soil is best as a base for the steps. Chapter 7 covers step-by-step details in stairway construction. Skip ahead to that

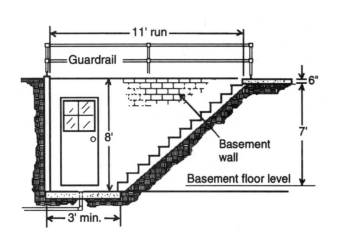

Figure 3-7
Entrance stairway run and height

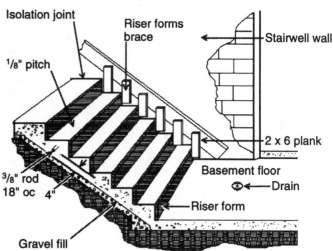

Figure 3-8
Forming concrete basement steps

chapter if you want to learn how to figure out the rise and tread of the steps and how to lay out stairs.

Now look at Figure 3-8. Use a 2 x 6 along each side of the steps and brace it to a side wall or with stakes driven into the ground. If the steps will butt against a side wall, mark the location of the riser and tread on the wall. Nail supports for the riser forms to the 2 x 6 at the marked locations. The riser form (board) should be the same width as the height of the riser. Install all riser forms and brace them so they'll hold when you pour the concrete.

Pour the steps directly on the ground unless there's a dampness problem. If the soil is damp, pour a 1-inch layer of dry sand, gravel, or crushed stone to help drain excess water. Place $^3/_8$-inch reinforcement rods parallel to the treads, 18 inches on center.

Don't use a wet mix. You want concrete that doesn't slump very much. Work the concrete against the face of the riser forms for a good finish. Give the treads a broom finish so they won't be slippery.

Pitch treads $^1/_8$ inch downward toward the front of the step so they'll drain properly. When concrete has set, remove the forms.

Build in a drain at the bottom of the steps, preferably in the center of the concrete landing. Install a strainer cover plate on the drain. Don't use perforated drain pipe. Use solid plastic pipe to drain the water

away. If there's no storm sewer, natural fall, or ditch, run the drain to a sump pump well.

Install an isolation joint where steps join a building. Use $^1/_2$-inch-thick asphaltum-impregnated felt. Simply cut the felt to fit the contour of the steps flush with the surface.

Build the walls of the stairwell the same way you build a basement wall. Waterproof the walls on the fill side. You don't want seepage through the stairwell walls to ruin the appearance of the finish.

Provide a handrail for the stairway, and a guardrail at the side and rear of the stairwell.

Cutting a Doorway

Use care here. Measure the exact dimensions for the door and framing materials. You don't want to cut the hole too large or too small. Figure 3-9 shows a doorway cut into a basement wall.

Before you make the cut on the exterior side of the basement wall, remove parging and sealing material from the wall in the door and stairwell area. Later, you'll seal the wall with a paint-compatible sealer, and paint the area.

Locate the position for the door, using a level to plumb the cut lines. Mark the top and bottom positions and snap a chalk line through the points. Make sure

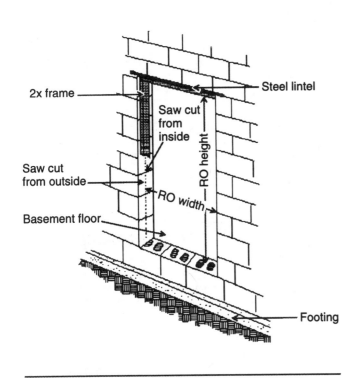

Figure 3-9
Cutting a doorway in a basement wall

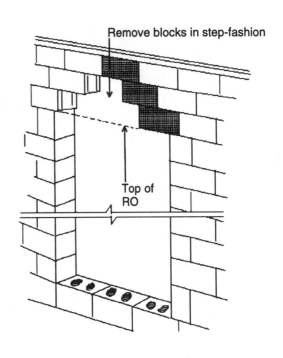

Note: The shaded blocks may also have to be removed

Figure 3-10
Removing blocks above an opening

the cutting lines are exact when you cut openings both inside and outside the walls. Drill through the wall at the top right corner of the opening and measure all cutting lines from that point.

When cutting through masonry, I use a power saw with a masonry blade. It makes a neat job and you have little patchwork to do. Of course, you have to make an inside and outside cut because the blade isn't large enough to cut through a concrete block wall. Be sure to always use protective goggles over your eyes, and a protective face mask. If you have an old power saw, use it for masonry cutting. The resulting dust and grit can be damaging.

If you'd rather use a cold chisel to cut out a door, go ahead. But don't try to cut completely through the wall as you go. Instead, etch a shallow cut and keep repeating the etching until the surface cracks. Repeat the action on the other side of the wall, cutting a line in the masonry until it cracks the length of your line. Then you can start removing the masonry pieces and dress the opening. Follow the same steps when cutting window openings.

Providing Header Supports for Door Openings

The opening you cut for a door won't extend from the top of a basement wall to the floor framing. Window openings can, however, depending on window size, finish grade level, and design.

To install a steel lintel above a door or window opening, begin by removing the blocks above the opening in step-fashion (Figure 3-10). Then install the lintel (Figure 3-11). But there's a catch. Of course the lintel is longer than the opening is wide.

On a really good day, the lintel's position will fall exactly at mortar joints. But in the remodeling world, good days are rare. If you are having one of those days though, and the lintel's position does fall exactly at the mortar joint, just rake out the joints each side of the opening, slide the lintel into position and fill the joints with mortar. On a normal day, you'll have to saw a notch in the masonry to put the lintel in (as on the left in Figure 3-11). Make the notch wide enough to allow a half-inch mortar joint at the top and bottom of the lintel. If you try to chisel out the notch, you may

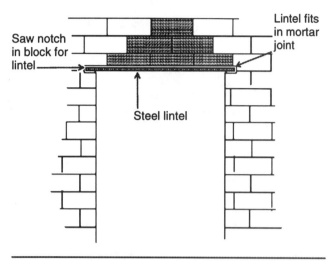

Figure 3-11
Installing steel lintel in rough opening

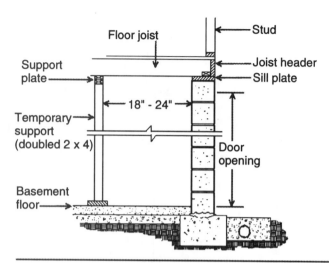

Figure 3-12
Using a temporary support when cutting an opening

loosen the block entirely. If that happens, remove the block, install the lintel in a mortar base, and relay the blocks over the lintel. In Figure 3-11, the blocks that have to be relaid are shaded.

When to Use Temporary Supports

If you'll look ahead to Figures 4-8, 4-9, and 4-10 in Chapter 4, you'll see the structural strength of the floor framing immediately on top of the foundation wall. There's a 2 x 6 or larger sill plate and, in some cases, a joist header on side walls. The end walls also have a 2 x 6 or larger sill plate and a joist stringer. (The end walls, except in hip roof construction, don't support roof weight.)

Whether or not you need to provide temporary supports for the floor when you take out a section of the basement wall for door and window openings depends on the size of the sill plate and whether it's continuous over the opening area.

If the framing also includes a joist header or stringer running continuous over the opening, you won't need temporary support for the floor if you're just cutting a 3- to 4-foot opening in a one-story structure. For a two-story house, you want to be on the safe side. Build a temporary support as shown in Figure 3-12.

Framing a Door Opening

Use 2-by pressure-treated wood to frame door openings in basement walls to guard against weather deterioration and termite attacks. Build the door frame by nailing the top member and threshold to both side pieces. Then install the frame in the masonry opening using anchor bolts with lead shields. Drill holes in the masonry so you can place the lead shields flush with the surface of the masonry. Line up the shields with their corresponding positions on the frame member, mark the location on the frame and drill holes for the bolts. Use a minimum of three bolts for each side. See Figure 3-13.

Make the 2-by door framing flush with the surface of the interior finish wall and inset from the exterior wall to leave room for molding (Figure 3-14). This technique works for doors and windows framed with 2-by material.

Providing Windows for Basement Conversions

A basement with habitable rooms below grade must have natural light. A basement without windows is like a cave. And the requirements for natural light

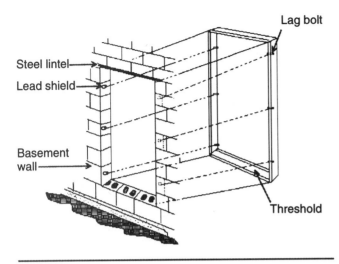

Figure 3-13
Framing a door opening

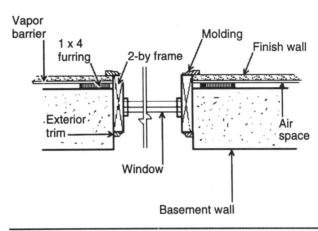

Figure 3-14
Framing and finishing a basement opening

and ventilation for a basement change when you convert it to habitable space. Finished basement spaces require natural light from a glazed area that's 8 percent of the floor area. They also need ventilation openings of at least 4 percent of the floor area. A window that opens can meet both natural light and ventilation requirements. Let's see how you calculate this:

A 12- x 12-foot bedroom has 144 square feet, so it needs natural light area that's 8 percent of 144, or 11.52 square feet. A 2- x 3-foot window provides 6 square feet. Two windows that size are 12 square feet, which meets the natural light requirement. They also more than meet the ventilation requirement.

The size of a basement window is also important for another reason. Every room used for sleeping, living, or dining must have at least two ways to get out of the room. At least one of the ways must be by a door or stairway that makes an unobstructed path to the outside at street or ground level. Each sleeping room (unless it has two doors providing separate means of escape or a door leading outside of the building directly) must have at least one outside window which can be opened from the inside without the use of tools. The sill height of the window can't be more than 44 inches above the floor. Its open area must be at least 5.7 square feet, and there must be a net clear opening at least 24 inches high and 20 inches wide. This is so people can get out if the door is blocked by the fire.

Basement Window Areaways

Basement windows that are below grade must have areaways. Figure 3-15 shows two methods of installing areaways at windows.

Framing a Window

The frame you build for a window opening depends on the kind of window you'll install. A double-hung window with brick molding can be installed in a 1 x 8 frame (for an 8-inch-thick wall). A 2-by frame works best for steel casement and similar windows. Install the frame just like you install the door frame we discussed earlier.

Slope the bottom member of the frame so moisture drains away from the window. Caulk the joint between the frame and the masonry. Then after you get the window in, caulk the joints between all masonry and wood joints with a quality, nondrying caulk.

How to Construct a Window Sill

Like the window opening, the sill depends on the type of window. A double-hung window comes with a sill designed to shed water, as shown in Figure 3-16. Other style windows might require a masonry sill with a slope to drain water away from the wall, as shown in

A Anchored to basement wall

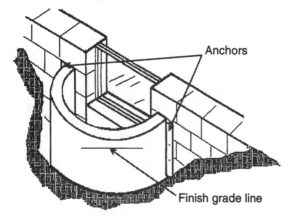

B Resting on masonry ledge

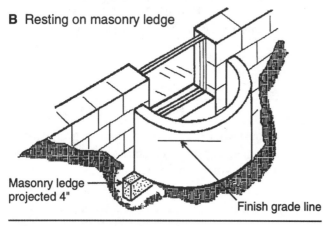

Figure 3-15
Window areaways

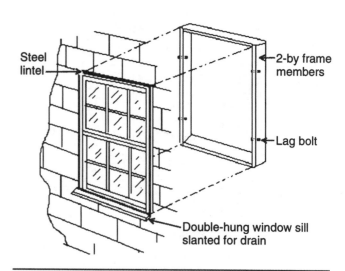

Figure 3-16
Frame and window installation

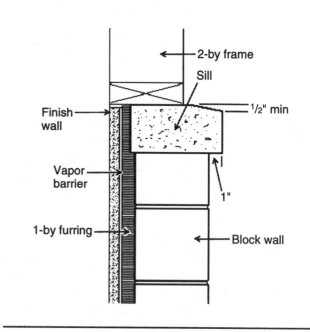

Figure 3-17
Formed masonry window sill

Figure 3-17. In a window like this, you have to consider the sill before cutting the opening in the basement wall. The opening height must allow for the thickness of the masonry sill plus the top and bottom framing.

Having cut the opening to allow for the thickness of the masonry sill (4 inches minimum) and the framing, measure the length of the rough opening from the lintel. (The rough opening should allow a snug fit for the window frame.) Mark the point on both sides of the opening to mark the top surface of the masonry sill.

Take care that the concrete you pour for the sill won't fill the cells of the block below the sill. Place metal screen or building paper 5 or 6 inches down inside the cells of the top layer of block. Secure form boards at the position you marked on both sides of the opening for the sill. Build the form to allow a 1-inch

projection beyond the outside wall to divert drainage from the wall. Use clamps to secure the form boards to the wall, as shown in Figure 3-18. Brace the form from below.

Fill the form with concrete mix that's not too wet. Use a trowel and slope the sill for a drop of a minimum of $1/2$ inch to the front edge.

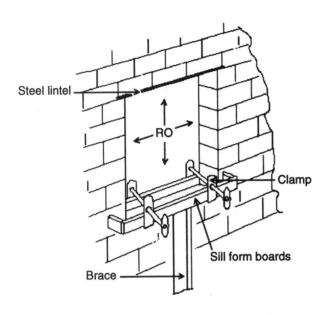

Figure 3-18
Installing sill form boards

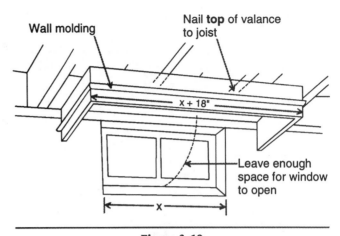

Figure 3-19
Three-sided valance around a basement window

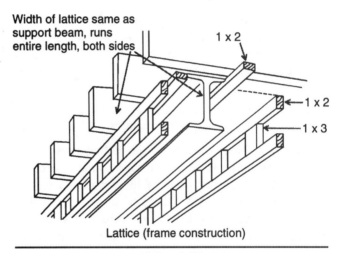

Figure 3-20
Boxing in a beam

Boxing Around Windows, Beams and Stairs

As a practical matter, most basement windows are located as high as possible in a basement wall, leaving little space for the finish ceiling and trim. To get around this problem, build a three-sided valance around each window, using ¼-inch plywood for the top, and 1 x 6-inch white pine for the three sides. Make the valance wide enough to allow the window to open, and long enough to accommodate the open draperies (usually about 9 inches on each side of the window). Attach the top of the completed valance to the bottom of the ceiling joists as shown in Figure 3-19. Then install wall molding at the desired level.

Boxing Around Iron Support Beams

Here's a general rule for basement conversions: If you can't move it, cover it. For example, a steel girder is a load-bearing beam that you can't move or remove. But you'll probably want to disguise it. One solution is to construct wooden lattices to attach to both sides of the beam. Use 1 x 2-inch wooden strips and 1 x 3-inch center supports spaced 16 inches on center to construct

each lattice. Nail lattices to 1 x 2-inch cleats installed on each side of the beam, as shown in Figure 3-20.

Enclose the support beam by nailing to each lattice a finish material that matches the room's finish walls. Attach the same material to the exposed face of the beam by driving nails into the base of the lattice frames. To finish the box, attach the corner moldings as shown in Figure 3-21.

Snap a chalk line on the finished box at the new ceiling height, and nail wall molding along the line to hold the ceiling finish.

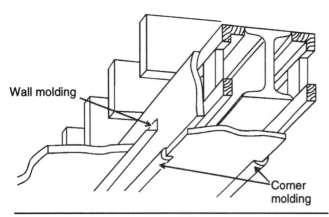

Figure 3-21
Finishing the beam enclosure

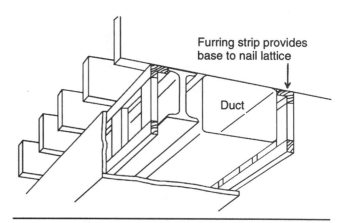

Figure 3-22
Enclosing a beam and duct

In basements with heating and cooling air ducts, the ducts often run parallel to the support beams. You can build latticework to enclose both support beam and ducts, as shown in Figure 3-22.

Boxing Around Basement Stairways

Nail 1 x 3-inch cleats into the ceiling joists. The distance from the old ceiling (if any) to the new ceiling will determine the width of the valance material. Using 1 x 4-inch or 1 x 6-inch white pine, nail the valance into the cleats. Cover the seam with standard molding. Install the wall molding at the height desired, as shown in Figure 3-23.

Estimating Basement Conversions

Excavating

Use the table in Figure 3-24 as a guideline for excavating. In most instances, you'll have to do the work by hand. Heavy equipment working close to a basement can cause damage to basement walls and grounds.

Estimate a trench at its actual size plus 1 foot outside for working room. For walls that will be waterproofed, figure 2 extra feet for working room.

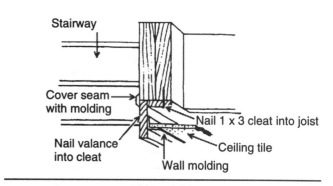

Figure 3-23
Finishing a stairwell

The amount of trench a laborer can excavate varies with the type of dirt, the height it must be lifted to, the extent of digging required, and the weather conditions.

Use a pick to loosen the dirt, and a round-pointed, long-handled shovel to lift it. It takes 150 to 200 shovels of dirt to excavate a cubic yard under normal conditions.

A deeper trench requires more dirt handling. The dirt must be rehandled once for depths of 6 to 10 feet. For every two or three diggers, you'll need one man for rehandling the dirt. The rehandler will probably stand on a stage or platform that can be moved as required.

If the dirt won't be used as fill, add manhours to spread the loose dirt over the site or haul it off.

	Trench depth in feet			
Soil type	3	5	8	10
Light	0.7	0.75	0.85	0.9
Medium	0.85	0.9	0.9	1.0
Heavy	1.1	1.10	1.25	1.3
Hard pan	1.3	1.4	1.6	1.7

Figure 3-24
Labor hours per cubic yard for hand excavation

Wall thickness (inches)	Manhours per LF
8	0.25
10	0.35
12	0.50

Time includes cutting line on both sides of the wall.

Figure 3-25
Skilled manhours required to cut door and window openings in concrete block basement walls

Door and Window Openings

Figure 3-25 shows the skilled manhours required to cut door and window openings in concrete block basement walls. The labor in this table includes the cutting line on both sides of the wall.

Figure 3-26 shows the skilled manhours required to install the door or window frame and unit in the prepared opening.

Estimate 3 skilled manhours to build forms and pour a masonry window sill.

Boxing-in Windows, Beams and Stairs

Basement boxing is time consuming and the work must be first class. Estimate lattice and boxing at 10 skilled manhours per 50 linear feet.

Designing and Building a Basement for an Addition

There are just two ways to build a basement: the right way and the wrong way. A properly-designed and constructed basement remains dry. If it's built any other way, it will either leak or have condensation problems — or both. A basement that's always damp isn't suitable for habitation, and if you're the one who converted it, it's not going to do your reputation a lot of good either.

Basement dampness comes from two sources: water seepage and condensation. When water comes through the floor or walls, the basement is leaking. Condensation is caused by the basement's interior air (usually dry and warm) hitting the cool masonry basement walls, causing water vapor to condense on the walls. Condensation happens any time the surface temperature of the wall is below the dew point temperature of the air. Appliances like washers, dryers and hot water heaters in the basement will raise the relative humidity and temperature.

Building Concrete Block Walls

Concrete blocks are often a good choice for building basement walls. Consider these factors when you design a concrete block basement wall:

Unit	Manhours per unit
Installing the frame	
Door (3' x 6'0")	2.5
Window (casement, 2 leaves, 3'10" x 4'2")	2.0
Installing the unit	
Door (solid core, exterior)	3.5
Window	2.0
Time includes installing door threshold and exterior trim.	

Figure 3-26
Skilled manhours required to install frame and unit in opening

♦ Pressure on the wall, which depends on the depth of the basement that's below grade and the soil type. Unusual soil conditions such as organic silts, organic clays, peat or sand may require a soil test, and an engineered design.

♦ Weight of the vertical load the wall must support

♦ Wall thickness required by the local code

♦ Length or height of the wall between lateral supports

♦ Maximum depths below grade. For residential basement walls 8, 10, and 12 inches thick, see Figure 3-27. It shows maximum depths below grade for both frame and block construction so you can compare them.

♦ Masonry foundation walls should extend at least 8 inches above the finish grade.

A basement wall is supported at its bottom by the footing and basement floor slab. The first-floor construction supports the top of the wall. Obviously, you can't backfill until after you've built the first floor to support the top of the wall.

A basement wall acts as a beam in the horizontal span to carry part of the earth load (pressure) from the side. The distribution of this pressure between the vertical and horizontal spans depends on:

♦ Wall height and length

♦ Wall stiffness in the vertical and horizontal spans

The total lateral load is divided equally between the horizontal and vertical spans if a wall's length

between supports isn't greater than its height. The lateral load is carried entirely in the vertical span when a wall's length between supports is 3½ to 4 times its height. The distribution of the lateral load falls somewhere between these limits for other ratios of wall length to height.

You can increase the stability of a basement wall by increasing its stiffness in the vertical or horizontal spans, or by reducing the length of one span (generally the horizontal span). You can make a wall stiffer in the vertical span by embedding vertical steel in the hollow

Nominal wall thickness	Maximum depth below grade	
	Frame wall	Concrete block wall
Hollow load-bearing		
8"	5'	5'
10"	6'	7'
12"	7'	7'
Solid load-bearing		
8"	5'	7'
10"	7'	7'
12"	7'	7'
Based on FHA "MPS" for average soil conditions.		

Figure 3-27
Maximum depths below grade for
concrete block and frame walls

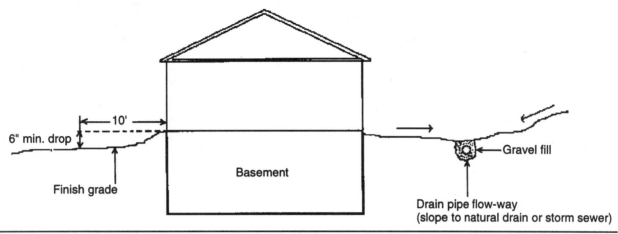

Figure 3-28
Finish grade slope

cores and the filling the cores with grout. To make it stiffer in the horizontal span, build a bond beam (a specially reinforced horizontal strip of a wall designed to act as a beam), or embed horizontal steel joint reinforcement in the mortar.

Lateral support in the horizontal span is provided by a wall's corners, by the intersecting partition walls, and by any pilasters (or similar supports) built into it. You can also use a pilaster to support a building's heavy center beams. A pilaster should project from a wall about 1/12 of the vertical span between supports. The pilaster's width should be about 1/10 of the horizontal span between supports. Make sure you follow the local building code.

Instead of using a center beam for lateral support, you can kill two birds by using the partition wall that divides the space into different areas.

Excavation

Building an addition with a basement can be a high-profit project. Use care in estimating the job. Remember, you have to handle a great deal of dirt, and dirt estimating is tough. This is a real easy place to lose your shirt. If you need more information on estimating excavation, you can read *Handbook of Construction Contracting, Volume 2*. There's an order form at the back of this book.

Don't forget that when you excavate an area around a basement, you have to excavate extra to allow working room for laying and sealing the exterior walls.

Finish Grade Slope

Slope the finish grade away from all sides of a basement. Ground water flowing toward a basement "stacks" against its walls and can overwork the drainage system. Slope the finish grade away from the house for at least 10 feet with a minimum 6-inch drop. Make water flow away from a yard by grading or putting in drain pipe. See Figure 3-28.

Use eave gutters and downspouts to divert run-off water from the roof to the slope or drain pipe. During a heavy rain, water running off the roof can cause water to stack against the basement walls.

Water has to have some way to escape. Trapped water creates hydrostatic pressure as the water table rises (Figure 3-29). Water trapped by the footings creates tremendous pressure under a basement floor. That's why a basement's waterproofing is so important.

When you design a basement, take great care with the drainage and waterproofing. You *don't* want to be known as the contractor who built the Jones' leaky basement — not if you want to stay in business, that is.

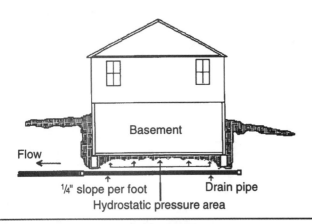

Figure 3-29
Elevation view of footing drain installed around house

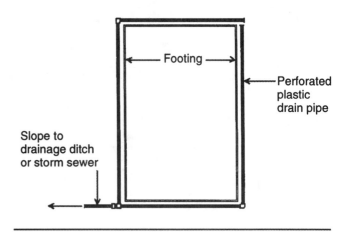

Figure 3-30
Plan view of footing drain installed around house

Basement Footings

Poured concrete makes a good basement footing. The soil under the footing should be firm and undisturbed, and the footing must go below the frost line. Make the footing twice as wide as the thickness of the wall it supports.

Install the footing and foundation drains so water can flow, by gravity or mechanical means, to a discharge area like a ditch or storm drainage system. See Figures 3-29 and 3-30. Perforated plastic drain pipe will do the job.

Install drain pipe as shown in Figures 3-31 and 3-32. Cover the pipe with 6 to 8 inches of coarse gravel or crushed rock. Be sure to pour at least a 2- to 4-inch layer of gravel or crushed stone under a drain pipe.

Suppose the lot is located in a low area, or there's no sewer drain outlet or natural fall to take the water from the area. Then you need a sump pump to take water from the drain pipe to a higher elevation, where it can flow to a storm drain or natural ground-fall away from the house. Figure 3-33 shows how it works.

Install the sump pump on a concrete base in a pump well or housing of concrete block. Lay the basement footing drain pipe so the water runs into the well. The pump should turn on automatically when the well fills to a set level. Follow the pump manufacturer's installation and operating instructions.

Make sure the sump well is large enough for someone to service the pump, and provide a strong steel or pressure-treated wood cover.

Pouring Concrete Slab Basement Floors

Before pouring the slab, make sure the ground is level and undisturbed. The slab should rest directly on the inner edge of the footing or on compacted gravel fill. Pour 4 to 6 inches of crushed stone fill on the ground, then grade and tamp it. Lay sheets of 6-mil polyethylene as a vapor barrier over the fill. Overlap edges 12 inches or more and seal with a good quality silicone caulk. Turn up the edges of the membrane to the top of the slab.

Find and mark the finish floor level at all corners. Then snap a chalk line to use as a guide when pouring and finishing the concrete. A $3\frac{3}{4}$-inch-thick finished slab makes a sound basement floor, although your code may specify a different thickness.

Pouring and Finishing the Concrete

You'll want the concrete in a good workable consistency with a slump of 4 to 5 inches. "Stiff" concrete with a low water-cement ratio may have a slump of only 3 inches, while a "wet" concrete may have a

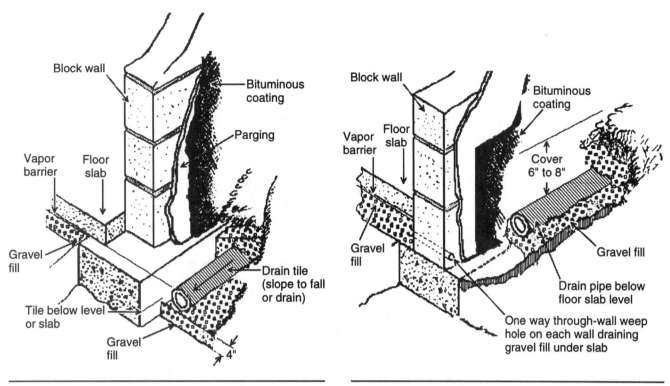

Figure 3-31
Installing drain tile beside footing

Figure 3-32
Installing drain pipe on top of footing

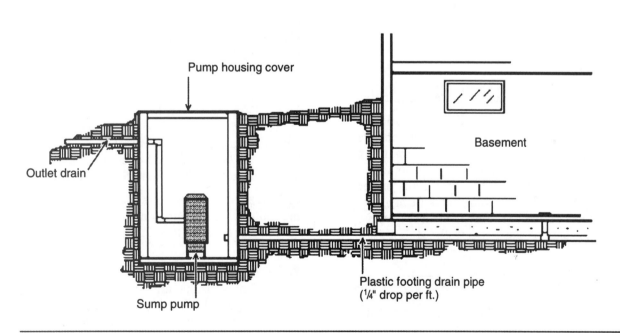

Figure 3-33
Installing a sump pump

slump as high as 6 inches. The slump is measured by placing concrete in a 12 inch high cone-like container with an 8-inch diameter top. After it's filled with concrete and struck flush, the container is lifted off of the concrete. The amount, in inches, by which the top surface slumps from the original shape is the slump. A five-bag, 3000 psi mix is fine for most basement floors. You don't need a stronger mix since the floor isn't subject to freeze-thaw cycles, or salt and alkali action.

When you have concrete butting concrete, you need expansion joints. Install them along the length of all walls with 1/2-inch-thick asphaltum-impregnated felt the depth of the slab. Make a control joint with a groover down the center of a floor where the partition or support columns will be located. A control joint is a shallow groove to control cracks in the surface of a floor.

Trowel finish the floor to a hard, smooth level finish. The only pitch should be around the drain. Unless you're experienced at pouring and finishing concrete floors (and have enough workers to finish the concrete before it sets up), subcontract the job. It takes a lot of experience and special tools to properly finish a concrete floor.

It's a good idea to put a sump pit in the floor to guard against possible flooding. Some codes require a sump pit. Even if yours doesn't, explain to the homeowner why the sump pit is important.

How to Construct Concrete Block Walls

A solid, well-constructed wall is essential to water-seal a basement. Lay the first course of concrete blocks in a full bed of mortar. Lay the remaining courses with a face-shell bedding of horizontal and vertical joints, 3/8 inch thick (full mortar joints on the top and ends of each block). Tool joints firmly after the mortar has stiffened (thumbprint hard) unless you're going to parge or plaster the wall.

Building the Bearing Course

To distribute the vertical loads evenly, build the bearing (top) course solidly, as follows:

1. Fill the cores of hollow blocks with mortar or concrete, as shown in Figure 3-34. But first install

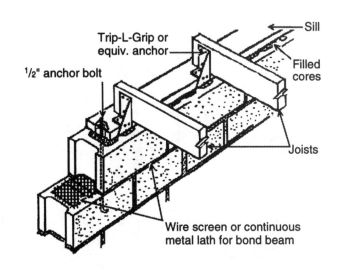

Figure 3-34
Top course and floor anchoring details

wire screen in the joint under the cores you're going to fill to keep the fill out of the cores below. To make the top course a reinforced bond beam, install a continuous strip of metal lath and allow the mortar or concrete to pass through the lath to fill the cores of the lower course. Or use a bond beam block with the transverse webs depressed at the top to permit a channel path for horizontal reinforcing bars within the wall. Place 1/2-inch-diameter anchor bolts that extend at least 15 inches into the filled cores. Space the anchor bolts not more than 6 feet on center. Put one bolt not more than 12 inches from each end of the sill plate.

2. Figure 3-35 shows how to use solid-top blocks for the course that supports the floor joists. The joists must have a minimum of 3 inches overlap (bearing) on the blocks. Embed one end of the twisted steel plate anchors into the horizontal mortar joint.

3. A third alternative uses a reinforced bond beam as the top unit, as explained above and in Figure 3-34. Use the beam to resist wind and seismic forces.

You'll need to pay special attention to concrete block basement walls that are 10 or 12 inches thick as required in Figure 3-27. Basement walls require the best running bond pattern for maximum stability and a pleasing interior finish. See Figure 3-36. An L-corner block (indented to 8-inch thickness) allows the block to be laid in a running bond. Check the criteria for

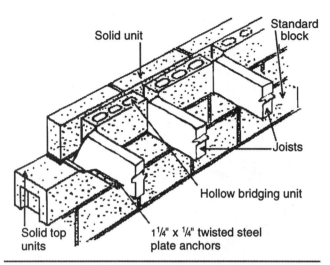

Figure 3-35
Solid top construction technique

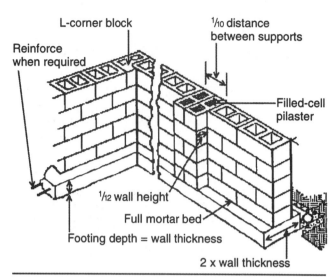

Figure 3-36
Construction details for 10 and 12 inch walls

pilasters, footing size and reinforcement. Use L-corner units, or fill in with bricks. If the soil is an unreliable Group III or Group IV (Figure 3-27), reinforce the footing.

Anchoring the Sill Plate and Joists

First, anchor the sill plates with ½-inch diameter bolts which extend at least 15 inches into the filled block cores (Figure 3-34). Then toenail the floor joist to the sill, or anchor it with a Trip-L-Grip, or similar anchor. Anchor the ends of the joists (butting and resting directly on the block wall) at 6-foot intervals, or at every fourth joist. See Figure 3-35.

Also anchor the joists that are parallel to the side walls at intervals of not more than 8 feet. Figure 3-37 shows how. Embed the split end of the anchors in the mortar joint, or bend the end down into a block core filled with mortar. The anchor should span at least three joists. Nail the anchors to the undersides of the joists. Cross-brace at each anchor and in between at intervals required by the local building code.

Anchoring Intersecting Walls

Use metal straps, spaced not more than 32 inches vertically (every fourth course), to anchor intersecting walls to basement walls. The metal straps in Figure 3-38

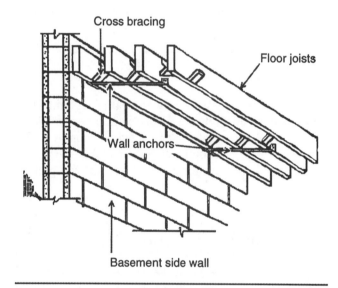

Figure 3-37
Wall anchors for joists parallel to a wall

are 30 inches long, ¼ inch thick, and 1¼ inches wide. Put metal lath or wire screen over the core of the block course below where the metal strap is anchored to support the mortar or concrete fill. Bend the ends of the straps, and anchor them with the fill. Rake out the mortar where two walls intersect, and caulk the intersection to form a control joint. The control joint lets the building move slightly without damage.

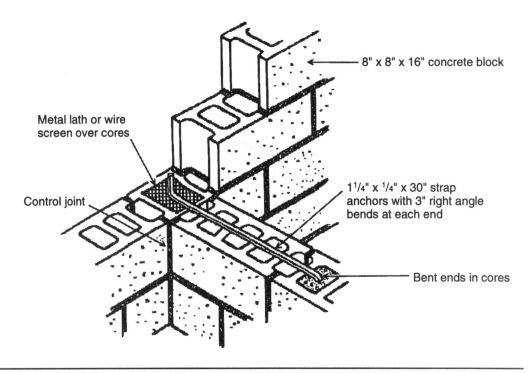

Figure 3-38
Anchoring an intersecting wall

You can use essentially the same techniques as those shown in Figure 3-38 to tie non-bearing partitions. If the partition won't be a lateral support for the basement wall, substitute strips of metal lath or galvanized hardware cloth for the steel straps if you prefer.

Waterproofing Basement Walls

To waterproof a basement in well-drained soils, you need to put a continuous, effective coating from a point above the finish grade to a point below the top of the footing. But before you do that, you should:

1. Clean the outside of the walls and parge them with a ¼-inch coat of portland cement-sand plaster.

2. Dampen the walls to get proper curing of the cement plaster.

3. Follow this with a brush coat of a bituminous (tar or asphalt) coating. Be sure to let the plaster coat cure and dry before applying the bituminous coat or you won't get the proper adhesion.

4. Apply a second coat to eliminate pin holes.

5. Finally, cover the walls with a heavy, troweled-on coat of cold, fiber-reinforced asphaltic mastic.

Figures 3-39 shows an end view of waterproofed walls in well-drained soil. But in wet and impermeable soils, there's more to do. Look at Figure 3-40. Install a through-wall weep hole or pipe on each wall to drain water from under the slab. Dowel the wall to the footing if the floor might not support the wall laterally (for example, where there's a bituminous joint between the floor and wall). Next, clean the exterior of the wall. Then waterproof with one of the following:

♦ Two ¼-inch thick coats of portland cement plaster, plus two brush coats of bituminous waterproofing

♦ One ¼-inch-thick coat of portland cement plaster, plus one heavy troweled-on coat of cold, fiber-reinforced asphaltic mastic

♦ A waterproof membrane extending from the edge of the footing to the finish grade. The membrane should be a 2-ply hot-mopped felt, 6-mil polyvinyl chloride, 55-pound roll roofing or similar material. Seal all laps and fix the membrane firmly to the wall.

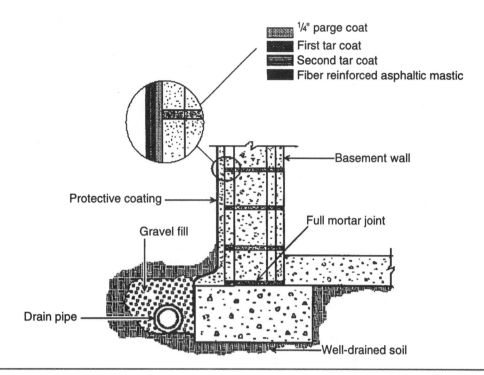

Figure 3-39
Minimum waterproofing requirements in well-drained soil

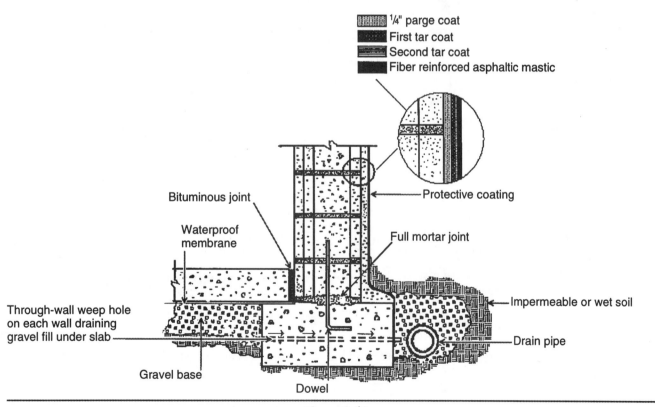

Figure 3-40
Extensive waterproofing requirements in wet soil

Installing a Drainage System

A properly-installed drainage system drains water away from, and not into, a basement. Lay perforated plastic drain pipe that's at least 4 inches in diameter on a bed of crushed stone around the perimeter of the basement wall, as shown in Figures 3-39 and 3-40. Place 6 to 8 inches of crushed stone above the drain pipe. As an added precaution, many builders place a minimum of 4 inches of crushed stone under the drain pipe. Slope the drain pipe to a positive fall or storm drain. Drain the area under a floor slab with one-way through-wall weep holes on each wall that has a drain pipe if you use a crushed stone base under the slab.

Estimating Block Walls

The best blocks you can use for basement wall construction are Hollow Load Bearing ASTM C90 and Solid Load Bearing ASTM C145. They meet the stan-dards of the American Society for Testing and Materials (ASTM). Use high- or moderate-strength mortars because they provide a strong bond to resist the pressure of the backfill. Figure 3-41 lists construction mortar mixes. Type S (moderate strength) mortar is especially good. Where transit mix (delivered by truck ready to pour) is not available, you can field mix cement for slabs or basement floors using the proportions shown in Figure 3-42.

To reduce the number of blocks you have to cut on the job, use full-length and half-length concrete blocks. Figure 3-43 shows the number of blocks and the amount of mortar you need for each 100 square feet of basement wall. The amounts in the table are for mortar joints that are $3/8$ inch thick, and use face-shell mortar bedding. They include a 10 percent waste allowance.

Figure 3-44 gives manhours for laying concrete block per 100 square feet of wall.

	Parts by volume of:			
Mortar type	Portland cement	Masonry cement	Hydrated lime	Sand, damp (loose volume)
M	1	1	—	Not less than $2\frac{1}{4}$ and not more than 3 times the sum of the volumes of the cements and lime
(high strength)	1	—	$\frac{1}{4}$	
S	$\frac{1}{2}$	1	—	
(moderate strength)	1	—	over $\frac{1}{4}$ to $\frac{1}{2}$	
N	—	1	—	
(low strength)	1	—	over $\frac{1}{2}$ to $1\frac{1}{2}$	

Figure 3-41
ASTM specs for unit masonry (ASTM C-270)

Maximum size of coarse aggregate (inches)	Approximate cement (bags) per CY	Approximate Water (gals) per bag	Approximate proportions (by volume) per bag of cement		
			Cement	Fine aggregate	Coarse aggregate
$3/4$	6.0	5	1	$2\frac{1}{2}$	$2\frac{3}{4}$
1	5.8	5	1	$2\frac{1}{2}$	3
$1\frac{1}{2}$	5.5	5	1	$2\frac{1}{2}$	$3\frac{1}{2}$
2*	5.2	5	1	$2\frac{1}{2}$	4
*Not for slabs or thin work					

Figure 3-42
Concrete proportions

Actual height of units (inches)	Units per 100 SF	CF mortar per 100 SF
7⅝ (modular)	113	8.5
3⅝ (modular)	225	13.5
8 (nonmodular)	103	8.0

Figure 3-43
Estimating wall materials

Work element	Unit (SF)	Manhours per unit
Concrete block, lightweight		
4" block	100	10.50
6" block	100	11.70
8" block	100	12.80
10" block	100	15.00
12" block	100	17.90
Concrete block, hollow, standard weight		
4" block	100	11.00
6" block	100	12.00
8" block	100	13.00
10" block	100	15.00
12" block	100	18.10

Time includes set-up, clean-up, joint striking one side only, cutting, pointing, steel alignment, and grout.
Suggested Crew: Small jobs, 1 mason, 1 helper

Figure 3-44
Labor placing concrete block

4

Floor Framing

Framing is often called rough carpentry work. But there's a limit to how rough you can make it. The more care you use in framing, the easier it'll be to do the finishing work. Exact measurements and accurately-fitted joints during framing make it easy to achieve a professional finish. If you make a mistake in framing, you'll just have to spend extra time to cover it up during the finishing process.

Framing Basics

Before you start sawing lumber and driving nails, there are some important basic things you should know — lumber sizes and strengths, what size nails to use, and minimum joist grades. No book of this type would be complete without this basic reference material.

Figure 4-1 shows typical lumber product classifications. It helps to know these classifications because they're part of a builder's vocabulary. Knowing them will help you understand what's going on when you buy lumber at the yard, look over house plans, or discuss construction with a fellow tradesman.

Many have entered the building trades believing that a 2 x 4 is a full 2 inches by 4 inches. This was probably the case back in the days before lumber was planed to a smooth surface. I've used rough-sawn (unplaned) lumber such as 4 x 10s, 2 x 4s, and 1 x 8s that did measure the full dimensions, but they were special orders from the mill. The 2 x 4 you buy at the lumberyard these days will actually be $1\frac{1}{2}$ inches by $3\frac{1}{2}$ inches. These are the dry measurements. The green size will be slightly larger, as shown in Figure 4-2.

There's a nail size for every task. While some carpenters prefer to use a 16d for almost all framing jobs, it's often best to use an 8d or 10d for toenailing 2-by stock. The lumber is less likely to split. Figure 4-3 shows the sizes of common wire nails. Figure 4-4 is the recommended schedule for nailing, framing, and sheathing wood-frame structures.

	Thickness (inches)	Width (inches)
Board lumber	1	2 or more
Light framing	2 to 4	2 to 4
Studs	2 to 4	2 to 6, 10 and shorter
Structural light framing	2 to 4	2 to 4
Structural joists and planks	2 to 4	5 and wider
Beams and stringers	5 and thicker	More than 2 greater than thickness
Posts and timbers	5 x 5 and larger	Not more than 2 greater than thickness
Decking	2 to 4	4 to 12 wide
Siding	Thickness expressed by dimension of butt edge size at thickest and widest points	
Moldings		

Lengths of lumber generally are 6' and longer in multiples of 2'.
Source: Western Wood Products Association

Figure 4-1
Typical lumber product classifications

Floor Joists

The distance a floor joist has to span determines its size. However, all wood species don't have the same structural strength — and using different grades within the same species also affects the allowable span. Figure 4-5 lists the minimum grades and joist sizes required for house depths from 20 to 32 feet in 1-foot intervals, based on 40 pounds per square foot (psf) uniform live load, framing with center girder, nominal 2-inch thick band (header) joists, and 2 x 4 sill and center bearing plates.

Close figuring and attention to detail in floor framing can save you money. For example, look at Figure 4-6. The wider the sill plate, the shorter the span. Where joists bear on a center girder, the clear span of each joist is half the house depth (measured between the outside surfaces of the exterior studs), minus the thickness of the band header joist, minus the length of joist bearing on the foundation wall sill plate, minus half the width of the bearing plate on the center support.

Assuming you use 2 x 4 sill plates and a 2 x 4 center bearing plate, the clear span is half the house depth minus 5¼ inches. The joist span is the unsupported area of the joist run. Using a 2 x 6 or 2 x 8 sill or bearing plate instead of a 2 x 4 reduces the clear span. That

may allow you to use a smaller size and/or a lesser grade of lumber at a lower cost.

Floor Framing Techniques

Figure 4-7 shows the components you'll use in framing a floor. The sill plate bears directly on the foundation wall, as shown in Figure 4-8, and should be of treated wood or foundation redwood or cedar. A sill sealer may be required between the foundation wall and the sill to control moisture penetration of the sill. Check with your local code concerning sill plate and sealer.

On exterior freestanding piers, you can install a sill beam as shown in Figure 4-9. Install a metal shield or barrier between the sill and the pier or foundation wall in termite areas. A sill sealer is not generally required when you install a termite shield.

There are two general types of wood-sill construction: platform and balloon framing. The platform method usually uses a *box sill*, a sill plate anchored (when required) to the foundation wall or piers. See Figure 4-10. The plate supports the joists and joist header which are anchored to the sill. A sill for

Thicknesses			Face widths		
Nominal (inches)	Minimum dressed		Nominal (inches)	Minimum dressed	
	Dry* (inches)	Green* (inches)		Dry* (inches)	Green* (inches)
Boards **					
1	3/4	26/32	2	1 1/2	1 9/16
			3	2 1/2	2 9/16
			4	3 1/2	3 9/16
			5	4 1/2	4 5/8
			6	5 1/2	5 5/8
			7	6 1/2	6 5/8
1 1/4	1	1 1/32	8	7 1/4	7 1/2
			9	8 1/4	8 1/2
			10	9 1/4	9 1/2
			11	10 1/4	10 1/2
1 1/2	1 1/4	1 9/32	12	11 1/4	11 1/2
			14	13 1/4	13 1/2
			16	15 1/4	15 1/2
Dimension					
2	1 1/2	1 9/16	2	1 1/2	1 9/16
			3	2 1/2	2 9/16
2 1/2	2	2 1/16	4	3 1/2	3 9/16
			5	4 1/2	4 5/8
3	2 1/2	2 9/16	6	5 1/2	5 5/8
			8	7 1/4	7 1/2
			10	9 1/4	9 1/2
3 1/2	3	3 1/16	12	11 1/4	11 1/2
			14	13 1/4	13 1/2
			16	15 1/4	15 1/2
Dimension					
4	3 1/2	3 9/16	2	1 1/2	1 9/16
			3	2 1/2	2 9/16
			4	3 1/2	3 9/16
			5	4 1/2	4 5/8
			6	5 1/2	5 5/8
			8	7 1/4	7 1/2
			10	9 1/4	9 1/2
4 1/2	4	4 1/16	12	11 1/4	11 1/2
			14		13 1/2
			16		15 1/2
Timbers					
5 & thicker	—	1/2 off	5 & wider	—	1/2 off

*These are minimum dressed sizes. Source: American Softwood Lumber Standard, PS 20-70.

**Boards less than the minimum thickness for 1" nominal but 5/8" or greater thickness dry (11/16" green) may be regarded as American Standard Lumber, but such boards shall be marked to show the size and condition of seasoning at the time of dressing. They shall also be distinguished from 1" boards on invoices and certificates.

Figure 4-2
Nominal size chart for softwood lumber

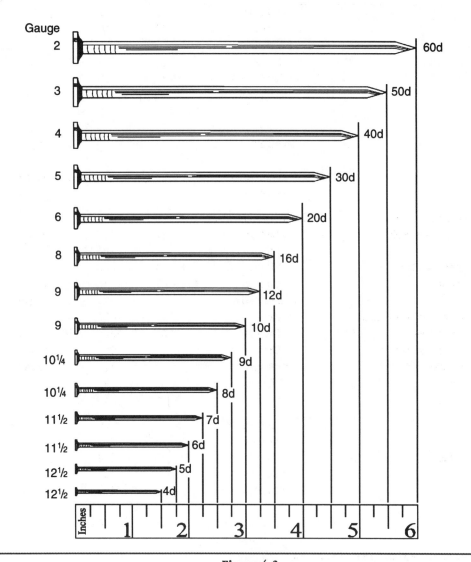

Figure 4-3
Sizes of common wire nails

balloon framing is shown in Figure 4-11. We'll discuss balloon framing in detail in Chapter 5.

To tie in new floor framing that's on the same level as the old, build the foundation wall (or free-standing piers) the same height as the existing foundation wall. Use same size lumber for the floor framing. Whether you're installing the floor joist of the addition parallel or perpendicular to the existing joists, you make the tie-in joint the same way. Nail a joist directly to the existing floor joists as a stringer if the new joists run parallel, or as a header if the new joists run perpendicular. See Figure 4-12.

Except for the tie-in joint, the foundation and floor framing is independent of the existing house and is a complete unit of its own as shown in Figure 4-7.

Girders

Southern yellow pine, cypress, redwood, and Douglas fir are good choices for girders and sills. I like to use lumber treated with a good preservative for sill and girder work. In the South, where I build, I need it because termites and rot can be a problem.

Joining	Nailing method	Number	Size	Placement
Header to joist	End-nail	3	16d	
Joist to sill or girder	Toenail	2	10d or	
		3	8d	
Header and stringer joist to sill	Toenail		10d	16" on center
Bridging to joist	Toenail ea. end	2	6d	
Ledger strip to beam, 2" thick	Face-nail	3	16d	At each joist
Subfloor, boards:				
1 x 6 and smaller	Face-nail	2	8d	To each joist
1 x 8	Face-nail	3	8d	To each joist
Subfloor, plywood:				
At edges	Face-nail		8d	6" on center
At intermediate joists	Face-nail		8d	8" on center
Subfloor (2 x 6, T&G) to joist or girder	Blind-nail (casing) & face-nail	2	16d	
Sole plate to stud, horizontal assembly	End-nail	2	16d	At each stud
Top plate to stud	End-nail	2	16d	
Stud to sole plate, upright assembly	Toenail	4	8d	
Sole plate to joist or blocking	Face-nail		16d	16" on center
Double studs	Face-nail, stagger		10d	16" on center
End stud of intersecting wall to ext. wall stud	Face-nail		16d	16" on center
Upper top plate to lower top plate	Face-nail		16d	16" on center
Upper top plate, laps and intersections	Face-nail	2	16d	
Continuous header, two pieces	Each edge		12d	12" on center
Ceiling joist to top wall plates	Toenail	3	8d	
Ceiling joist laps at partition	Face-nail	4	16d	
Rafter to top plate	Toenail	2	8d	
Rafter to ceiling joist	Face-nail	5	10d	
Rafter to valley or hip rafter	Toenail	3	10d	
Ridge board to raftger	End-nail	3	10d	
Rafter to ridge board	Toenail	3	10d	
Collar beam to rafter:				
2" member	Face-nail	2	12d	
1" member	Face-nail	3	8d	
1" diagonal let-in brace to each stud and plate (4 nails at top)		2	8d	
Built-up corner studs:				
Studs to blocking	Face-nail	2	10d	Each side
Intersecting stud to corner studs	Face-nail		16d	12" on center
Built-up girders and beams, 3 or more members	Face-nail		20d	32" on center, each side
Wall sheathing:				
1 x 8 or less, horizontal	Face-nail	2	8d	At each stud
1 x 6 or greater, diagonal	Face-nail	3	8d	At each stud
Wall sheathing, vertically applied plywood:				
$\frac{3}{8}$" and less thick	Face-nail		6d	6" edge
$\frac{1}{2}$" and over thick	Face nail		8d	12" intermediate
Wall sheathing, vertically applied fiberboard:				
$\frac{1}{2}$" thick	Face-nail		1 $\frac{1}{2}$" roofing nail	3" edge & 6" intermediate
$\frac{25}{32}$" thick	Face-nail		1 $\frac{3}{4}$" roofing nail	
Roof sheathing, boards, 4", 6" 8" wide	Face-nail	2	8d	At each rafter
Roof sheathing, plywood:				
$\frac{3}{8}$" and less thick	Face-nail		6d	6" edge and 12" intermediate
$\frac{1}{2}$" and over thick	Face-nail		8d	

Figure 4-4
Recommended schedule for nailing, framing, and sheathing of wood-frame structures

Species	Joist spacing	Joist size	House depth (measured between outside surfaces of exterior studs), in feet													Grading rule agency*
			20	21	22	23	24	25	26	27	28	29	30	31	32	
Balsam fir	16"	2 x 8	No.2	No.2	No.2	No.2	No.2[c]	No.1[c]								NeLMA NH&PMA
		2 x 10	No.3	No.3	No.3	No.3[a]	No.2	No.2	No.2	No.2	No.2	No.2	No.2[c]	No.1[a]		
	24"	2 x 8	No.2[c]	No.1[a]												
		2 x 10	No.2	No.2	No.2	No.2	No.2	No.2[c]	No.1	No.1[c]						
California redwood (open grain)	16"	2 x 8	No.3[c]	No.2	No.2	No.2[a]	No.1[b]									RIS
		2 x 10	No.3	No.3	No.3	No.3	No.3	No.3[c]	No.2	No.2	No.2	No.2[a]	No.1[a]			
		2 x 12						No.3	No.3	No.3	No.3	No.3	No.3[b]	No.2	No.2	
	24"	2 x 8	No.2	No.1[a]												
		2 x 10	No.3	No.3[c]	No.2	No.2	No.2	No.2	No.2[c]	No.1[c]						
		2 x 12		No.3	No.3	No.3	No.3	No.3[c]	No.2	No.2	No.2	No.2	No.2	No.2[a]	No.1[b]	
Douglas fir-larch	16"	2 x 8	No.3	No.3	No.3	No.2	No.2	No.2	No.2	No.2	No.1[b]					NLGA WCLIB WWPA
		2 x 10				No.3	No.3	No.3	No.3	No.3	No.3[a]	No.2	No.2	No.2	No.2	
		2 x 12									No.3	No.3	No.3	No.3	No.3	
	24"	2 x 8	No.2	No.2	No.2	No.2	No.2[c]	No.1[c]								
		2 x 10	No.3	No.3	No.3	No.3[a]	No.2	No.2	No.2	No.2	No.2	No.2	No.2[b]	No.1[a]	No.1[c DENSE]	
		2 x 12				No.3	No.3	No.3	No.3	No.3	No.3[b]		No.2	No.2	No.2	
Douglas fir-south	16"	2 x 8	No.3	No.3	No.3[c]	No.2	No.2	No.2[a]	No.1[c]							WWPA
		2 x 10				No.3	No.3	No.3	No.3	No.3	No.3	No.2	No.2	No.2	No.2[c]	
		2 x 12									No.3	No.3	No.3	No.3	No.3	
	24"	2 x 8	No.2	No.2	No.2[a]	No.1[c]										
		2 x 10	No.3	No.3	No.3	No.3[c]	No.2	No.2	No.2	No.2	No.2[b]	No.1[c]				
		2 x 12				No.3	No.3	No.3	No.3	No.3[a]	No.2	No.2	No.2	No.2	No.2	
Eastern hemlock-tamarack	16"	2 x 8	No.3	No.3[c]	No.2	No.2	No.2[b]	No.1[a]								NeLMA NLGA
		2 x 10			No.3	No.3	No.3	No.3	No.3[a]	No.2	No.2	No.2	No.2[a]	No.1	No.1[c]	
	24"	2 x 8	No.2	No.2[a]	No.1[a]											
		2 x 10	No.3	No.3	No.3[c]	No.2	No.2	No.2	No.2	No.2[c]	No.1[b]					
Eastern spruce	16"	2 x 8	No.2	No.2	No.2	No.2	No.2[a]	No.1	No.1[c]							NeLMA NH&PMA
		2 x 10	No.3	No.3	No.3	No.3	No.3[b]	No.2	No.2	No.2	No.2	No.2	No.2	No.2	No.1	
	24"	2 x 8	No.2[b]	No.1	No.1[a]											
		2 x 10	No.3[c]	No.2	No.2	No.2	No.2	No.2[a]	No.1	No.1	No.1[b]					
Englemann spruce-alpine fir or Englemann spruce-lodgepole pine	16"	2 x 8	No.2	No.2	No.2	No.2	No.2[c]	No.1[a]								WWPA
		2 x 10	No.3	No.3	No.3	No.3[a]	No.2	No.2	No.2	No.2	No.2	No.2	No.2[c]	No.1	No.1[c]	
		2 x 12				No.3	No.3	No.3	No.3	No.3			No.2	No.2	No.2	
	24"	2 x 8	No.2[c]	No.1[a]												
		2 x 10	No.2	No.2	No.2	No.2	No.2	No.2[c]	No.1	No.1[c]						
		2 x 12	No.3	No.3	No.3	No.3[c]		No.2	No.2	No.2	No.2	No.2	No.2[c]	No.1	No.1	
Hem fir	16"	2 x 8	No.3[a]	No.2	No.2	No.2	No.2	No.2	No.2[c]							NLGA WCLIB WWPA
		2 x 10		No.3	No.3	No.3	No.3	No.3[a]	No.2	No.2	No.2	No.2	No.2[c]	No.2	No.2	
		2 x 12					No.3	No.3	No.3	No.3	No.3	No.3	No.3[c]			
	24"	2 x 8	No.2	No.2[c]	No.1	No.1										
		2 x 10	No.3	No.3[c]	No.2	No.2	No.2	No.2	No.2	No.2[c]	No.1	No.1[a]				
		2 x 12	No.3	No.3	No.3	No.3	No.3	No.3[a]		No.2	No.2	No.2	No.2	No.2	No.2	
Idaho white pine or Western white pine	16"	2 x 8	No.2	No.2	No.2	No.2[a]	No.1	No.1[a]								WWPA
		2 x 10	No.3	No.3	No.3	No.3[a]	No.2	No.2	No.2	No.2	No.2	No.2	No.1	No.1	No.1[b]	
		2 x 12			No.3	No.3	No.3	No.3	No.3	No.3[c]		No.2	No.2	No.2		
	24"	2 x 8	No.1	No.1[b]												NLGA
		2 x 10	No.2	No.2	No.2	No.2	No.2[a]	No.1	No.1[b]							
		2 x 12	No.3	No.3	No.3	No.3[c]	No.2	No.2	No.2	No.2	No.2	No.2[a]	No.1	No.1	No.1[c]	

[a] Nominal 2 x 6 sill plate and 2 x 4 center bearing plate; or width of sill plate plus one-half width of center bearing equal to 7 1/4" or more.
[b] Nominal 2 x 6 sill plate and 2 x 6 center bearing plate; or width of sill plate plus one-half width of center bearing equal to 8 1/4" or more.
[c] Nominal 2 x 8 sill plate and 2 x 8 center bearing plate; or width of sill plate plus one-half width of center bearing equal to 10 7/8" or more.

Based on construction with center girder, nominal 2" thick band (header) joists, and except where footnoted, nominal 2 x 4 sill and 2 x 4 center bearing plates.

Figure 4-5
Minimum joist grades for different house depths 40 psf uniform live load

Species	Joist spacing	Joist size	House depth (measured between outside surfaces of exterior studs), in feet													Grading rule agency*
			20	21	22	23	24	25	26	27	28	29	30	31	32	
Lodgepole pine	16"		No.1[a] (centered across depths)													WWPA
		2 x 8	No.2	No.2	No.2	No.2	No.2	No.2[c]								
		2 x 10	No.3	No.3	No.3	No.3	No.3	No.2	No.2	No.2	No.2	No.2	No.2	No.2[a]	No.1[c]	
		2 x 12						No.3	No.3	No.3	No.3	No.3[a]		No.2	No.2	
	24"	2 x 8	No.2	No.1	No.1[a]											
		2 x 10	No.3[a]	No.2	No.2	No.2	No.2	No.2	No.2[c]	No.1	No.1[b]					
		2 x 12		No.3	No.3	No.3	No.3[a]		No.2	No.2	No.2	No.2	No.2	No.2[b]	No.1	
Northern pine	16"	2 x 8	No.3[c]	No.2	No.2	No.2	No.2	No.2[a]	No.1[c]							NeLMA NH&PMA
		2 x 10	No.3	No.3	No.3	No.3	No.3	No.3[c]	No.2	No.2	No.2	No.2	No.2	No.2[c]		
	24"	2 x 8	No.2	No.2[b]	No.1	No.1[c]										
		2 x 10	No.3	No.3[c]	No.2	No.2	No.2	No.2	No.2[a]	No.1	No.1	No.1[c]				
Ponderosa pine-sugar pine	16"	2 x 8	No.2	No.2	No.2	No.2	No.2[b]	No.1[c]								WWPA
		2 x 10	No.3	No.3	No.3	No.3	No.2	No.2	No.2	No.2	No.2	No.2	No.2[a]	No.1[a]		
		2 x 12					No.3	No.3	No.3	No.3	No.3[a]		No.2	No.2	No.2	
	24"	2 x 8	No.2[c]	No.1	No.1[c]											
		2 x 10	No.2	No.2	No.2	No.2	No.2	No.2[c]	No.1	No.1[a]						
		2 x 12	No.3	No.3	No.3	No.3[a]		No.2	No.2	No.2	No.2	No.2	No.2[b]	No.1	No.1	
Southern pine	16"	2 x 8	No.3	No.3	No.3[a]	No.2	No.2	No.2	No.2[c]	MG No.2[b]	No.1[b]					SPIB
		2 x 10			No.3	No.3	No.3	No.3	No.3	No.3	No.3[c]	No.2	No.2	No.2	No.2	
		2 x 12									No.3	No.3	No.3	No.3	No.3	
	24"	2 x 8	No.2	No.2	No.2[c]	No.2	No.2[c]	No.1[c]								
		2 x 10	No.3	No.3	No.3	No.3[b]	No.2	No.2	No.2	No.2	No.2	MG No.2	MG No.2[b]	No.1[a]	No.1[c] DENSE	
		2 x 12			No.3	No.3	No.3	No.3	No.3	No.3[c]	No.2	No.2	No.2	No.2	No.2	
Southern pine KD (15% mc)	16"	2 x 8	No.3	No.3	No.3	No.3[b]	No.2	No.2	No.2	No.2	No.1	No.1[b] DENSE				SPIB
		2 x 10			No.3	No.3	No.3	No.3	No.3	No.3	No.3[b]	No.2	No.2	No.2	No.2	
		2 x 12										No.3	No.3	No.3	No.3	
	24"	2 x 8	No.2	No.2	No.2	No.2	No.2[a]	No.1[c]								
		2 x 10	No.3	No.3	No.3	No.3	No.3[b]	No.2	No.2	No.2	No.2	No.2[c]	MG No.2	No.1	No.1[c]	
		2 x 12			No.3	No.3	No.3	No.3	No.3	No.3	No.3[a]	No.2	No.2			
Spruce-pine fir Coast Sitka spruce or Sitka spruce	16"	2 x 8	No.2	No.2	No.2	No.2	No.2	No.2[a]	No.1	No.1[a]						NLGA
		2 x 10	No.3	No.3	No.3	No.3	No.2	No.2	No.2	No.2	No.2	No.2	No.2	No.2[c]	No.1	
		2 x 12					No.3	No.3	No.3	No.3	No.3[a]		No.2	No.2		
	24"	2 x 8	No.2[b]	No.1	No.1[c]											WCLIB
		2 x 10	No.2	No.2	No.2	No.2	No.2	No.2[a]	No.1	No.1						
		2 x 12	No.3	No.3	No.3	No.3[a]		No.2	No.2	No.2	No.2	No.2	No.2[a]	No.1	No.1	
Western hemlock	16"	2 x 8	No.3	No.3[a]	No.2	No.2	No.2	No.2	No.2	No.1[b]						WWPA
		2 x 10			No.3	No.3	No.3	No.3	No.3	No.3	No.3[c]	No.2	No.2	No.2	No.2	
		2 x 12								No.3	No.3	No.3	No.3	No.3	No.3[a]	
	24"	2 x 8	No.2	No.2	No.2[a]	No.1	No.1[c]									
		2 x 10	No.3	No.3	No.3[b]	No.2	No.2	No.2	No.2	No.2	No.2[b]	No.1	No.1[b]			
		2 x 12			No.3	No.3	No.3	No.3	No.3[c]		No.2	No.2	No.2	No.2	No.2	
White woods (Western woods)	16"	2 x 8	No.2	No.2	No.2	No.2[a]	No.1[b]									WWPA
		2 x 10	No.3	No.3	No.3	No.3[a]	No.2	No.2	No.2	No.2	No.2	No.2[a]	No.1[a]			
		2 x 12					No.3	No.3	No.3	No.3	No.3	No.3[c]	No.2	No.2	No.2	
	24"	2 x 8	No.1	No.1[b]												
		2 x 10	No.2	No.2	No.2	No.2	No.2[a]	No.1	No.1[a]							
		2 x 12	No.3	No.3	No.3	No.3[c]	No.2	No.2	No.1	No.1[a]	No.2	No.2	No.2[a]	No.1	No.1[c]	

[a] Nominal 2 x 6 sill plate and 2 x 4 center bearing plate; or width of sill plate plus one-half width of center bearing equal to 7¼" or more.

[b] Nominal 2 x 6 sill plate and 2 x 6 center bearing plate; or width of sill plate plus one-half width of center bearing equal to 8¼" or more.

[c] Nominal 2 x 8 sill plate and 2 x 8 center bearing plate; or width of sill plate plus one-half width of center bearing equal to 10⅞" or more.

* NeLMA — Northeastern Lumber Manufacturers Association
NH&PMA — Northern Hardwood and Pine Manufacturers Association
RIS — Redwood Inspection Service
NLGA — National Lumber Grades Authority, a Canadian Agency
WCLIB — West Coast Lumber Inspection Bureau
WWPA — Western Wood Products Association
SPIB — Southern Pine Inspection Bureau

Figure 4-5 (continued)
Minimum joist grades for different house depths 40 psf uniform live load

A Clear span of joist

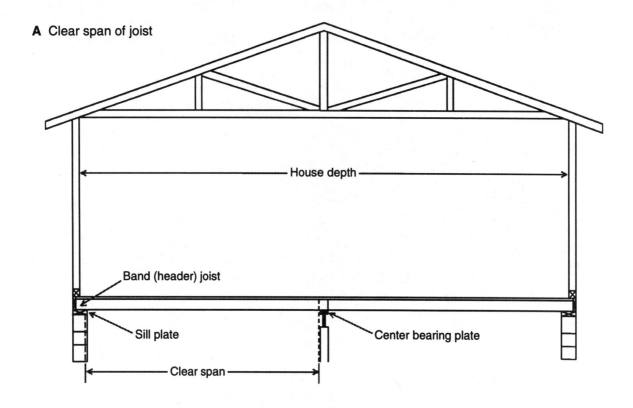

B Size of sill and center bearing plates

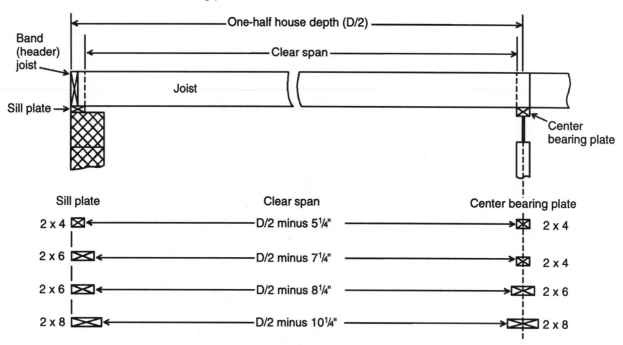

Sill plate	Clear span	Center bearing plate
2 x 4	D/2 minus 5¼"	2 x 4
2 x 6	D/2 minus 7¼"	2 x 4
2 x 6	D/2 minus 8¼"	2 x 6
2 x 8	D/2 minus 10¼"	2 x 8

Figure 4-6
Using wider bearing plates to reduce clear spans

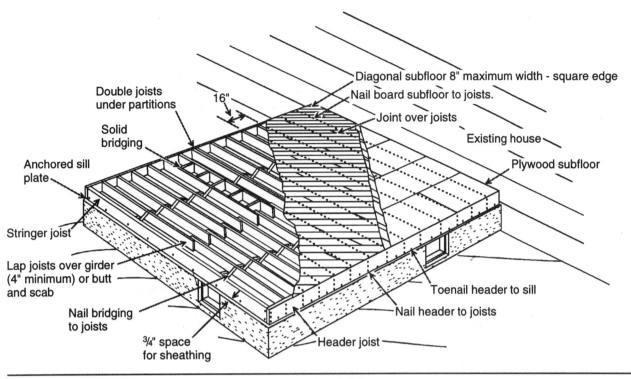

Double joists under partitions

Solid bridging

Anchored sill plate

Stringer joist

Lap joists over girder (4" minimum) or butt and scab

Nail bridging to joists

¾" space for sheathing

16"

Diagonal subfloor 8" maximum width - square edge

Nail board subfloor to joists.

Joint over joists

Existing house

Plywood subfloor

Toenail header to sill

Nail header to joists

Header joist

Figure 4-7
Typical floor framing

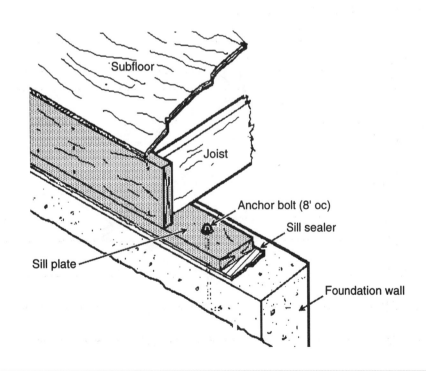

Subfloor

Joist

Anchor bolt (8' oc)

Sill sealer

Sill plate

Foundation wall

Figure 4-8
Sill plate anchored on foundation wall

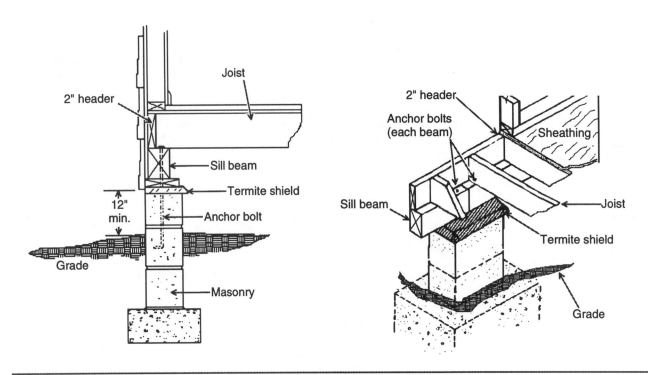

Figure 4-9
Sill beam anchored on freestanding pier

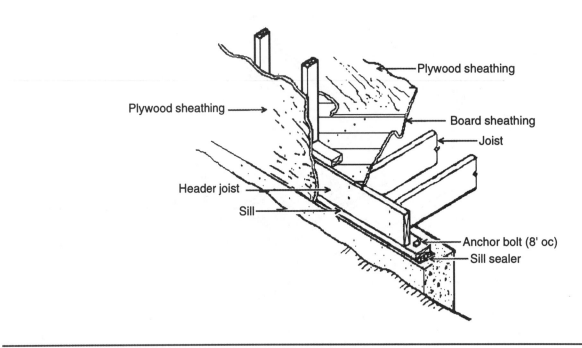

Figure 4-10
Platform framing with a box sill

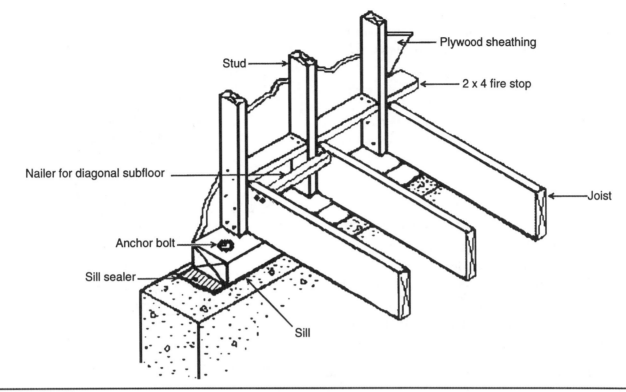

Figure 4-11
Balloon frame sill

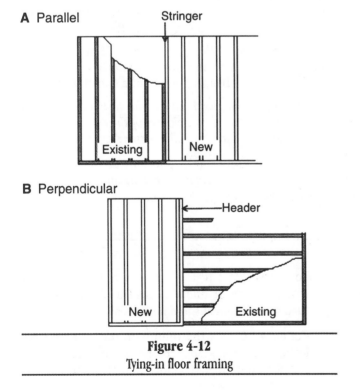

Figure 4-12
Tying-in floor framing

Girder spacing depends on the length and depth of the joists and the location of the bearing partitions on the floor above the joists. As a general rule, don't space girders more than 16 feet apart. For a span of 25 feet, one girder is enough if you put it midway between each of the other supports. Use two equally-spaced girders in a 35-foot span.

You have to consider how the length, width, and depth of a girder affect its strength when you decide on girder or beam size. It works like this:

Length — If a girder is supported at each end and has a load that's spread evenly along its entire length, it'll bend. A girder twice as long, with the same load per foot of length, will bend much more and may break. If the length is doubled, the safe load isn't cut in half, it's reduced to only a quarter of the original load. But if there's a single concentrated load at the center, doubling the length *will* cut the safe load in half. The greater the unsupported length of a girder, the stronger it must be. You can increase girder strength by using a stronger material or by using a larger beam.

Width — Doubling the width of a girder doubles its strength. One double-width girder can carry the same load as two single-width girders placed side by side.

Depth — Doubling the depth of a girder means it can carry 4 times as much weight. So, a beam 3 inches wide and 12 inches deep can carry 4 times the load of a beam 3 inches wide and 6 inches deep. If you need a stronger beam, it's cheaper to increase the depth than the width.

Girder-Joist Layout

Figure 4-7 shows a simple method of girder-joist installation which lets the joists bear directly on a girder. In this method, the top of the girder must be flush with the top of the sill plate.

Keep in mind that horizontal wood shrinkage is usually greater at the girder than at the foundation in this type of girder construction. Use joist hangers, stirrups, and supporting ledger strips to minimize the amount of horizontal wood subject to shrinkage (Figures 4-13 and 4-14). They make the amount of shrinkage at the inner beam and the outer walls nearly equal.

In this method, the joists must always bear on the ledger. Depending on the size of your joists and wood girders, there are several ways to support them on a ledger strip. One is to notch the joists, as shown in Figure 4-14 A. The connecting scab shown in Figure 4-14 B makes an unbroken horizontal tie and a nailing area for the subfloor. Figure 4-14 C shows a steel strap that ties the joists together. Use this method when the top of a beam is level with the top of the joists.

You can also tie the joists together with plywood or OSB (oriented strand board) subfloor panels as shown in Figure 4-14 D, eliminating the steel strap. This usually saves materials and labor. Simply arrange the panel layout so panels will overlap the opposing joists at the girder a minimum of 12 inches. This may require cutting panels for the first row but you'll get a solid tie.

No matter which method you use, leave a small space above the beam to allow for shrinking joists. Each of these methods provides about the same shrinkage at the outer walls and the center girder because the 2-inch ledger is the same thickness as the outer wall sill.

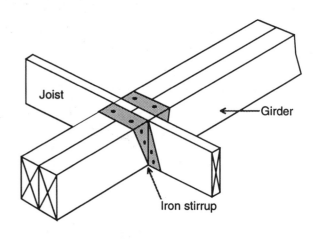

Figure 4-13
Using iron stirrups to hang joists

How to Figure Joist Lengths

Wood joists are made in 2-foot length increments. Joists 12 feet and longer normally have a plus tolerance of $\frac{1}{2}$ inch or more, allowing for squaring and sawing shorter lengths. A saw blade can eat up $\frac{1}{8}$ inch for each cut. If there wasn't a little extra allowance, two 6-foot joists cut from a 12-foot member would be a little short of standard length after the sawing.

Use this rule of thumb (shown in Figure 4-15) to calculate joist length in normal platform construction with lapped joists bearing on top of a center girder:

The length of the joist is one-half the room or house depth, minus the thickness of the band joist, plus the overlap of the joists at the center support.

Notice in Figure 4-15 that half of the lap length must be at least $1\frac{1}{2}$ inches. That means the total joist overlap must be at least 3 inches.

Glued Floor Systems

To add stiffness to a floor system, field-glue plywood subflooring or underlayment to the joists. This will also reduce squeaks and nail pops.

Figure 4-16 lists the minimum requirements for field-glued floor systems for house or room depths from 20 feet to 32 feet. The joist and plywood require-

A Notched joists

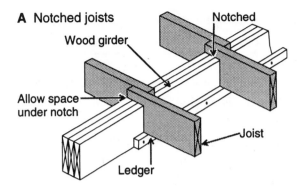

B Scab tie between joists

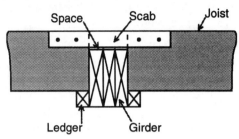

C Flush joists

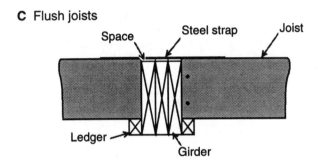

D Lay panel to overlap girder

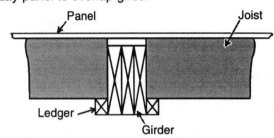

Figure 4-14
Using a ledger on center gider

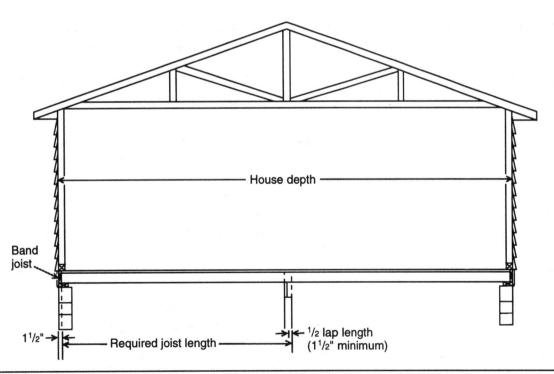

Figure 4-15
Required joist length

Species	Joist spacing	Joist size	Plywood under-layment thickness	House depth (measured between outside surfaces of exterior studs), in feet												
				20	21	22	23	24	25	26	27	28	29	30	31	32
Balsam fir	16"	2 x 8	1/2	—	—	—	—	—	No.1	No.1[c]	—	—	—	—	—	—
		2 x 10	1/2	—	—	—	—	—	—	—	—	—	—	—	No.1	No.1
California redwood (open grain)	16"	2 x 8	1/2	—	—	—	No.2	No.2	No.2[a]	No.1[b]	—	—	—	—	—	—
			19/32	—	—	—	—	—	—	—	No.1[c]	—	—	—	—	—
			23/32	—	—	—	—	—	—	—	No.1[a]	—	—	—	—	—
		2 x 10	1/2	—	—	—	—	—	—	—	—	—	—	No.2	No.2	No.1[a]
			19/32	—	—	—	—	—	—	—	—	—	—	—	—	No.2[b]
	24"	2 x 8	23/32	No.2	No.2	No.1	No.1[b]	—	—	—	—	—	—	—	—	—
		2 x 10	23/32	—	—	—	—	—	—	No.2[a]	No.1	No.1	No.1[b]	—	—	—
		2 x 12	23/32	—	—	—	—	—	—	—	—	—	—	—	No.2	No.2
Douglas fir-larch	16"	2 x 8	1/2	—	—	—	—	—	—	—	No.2	No.2[c]	No.1[c]	—	—	—
			19/32	—	—	—	—	—	—	—	—	—	No.1[a]	—	—	—
			23/32	—	—	—	—	—	—	—	—	—	—	No.1[c]	—	—
	24"	2 x 8	23/32	—	—	—	—	—	No.1	No.1[c]	—	—	—	—	—	—
		2 x 10	23/32	—	—	—	—	—	—	—	—	—	—	—	No.1	No.1

Figure 4-16
Joist grades for joists used with field-glued subflooring (40 psf live load)

ments agree with the maximum clear spans specified by most building codes.

Field-gluing can also reduce the joist size or grade. This cuts the cost of materials. If you look again at Figures 4-5 and 4-16 and compare the joist sizes for a particular house depth, both with and without a field-glue system, you'll get an idea of the savings.

Here's an example: For a 28-foot room depth without field-gluing, you'll use No. 1 Douglas fir-larch or southern pine 2 x 8s, 16 inches on center, with 2 x 6 sill and center bearing plates. For a 28-foot room depth with field-gluing, you can use No. 2 joists of the same size and species, with the same spacing, and with only 2 x 4 sill and center bearing plates.

Using a little glue on a job will save you money if it lets you use a lower, more readily available grade of lumber. Also, you space nails 12 inches on center in glued panels, compared to 6 inches and 10 inches for nonglued construction. To apply glue, use a caulking gun and run a bead along the top of the floor joist following the glue manufacturer's instructions.

Using Spliced Joists

Off-center spliced joints provide another way to cut costs. If you splice two unequal joist lengths together so the splice isn't in the center of the span, the joist span can be longer. You must, of course, alternate the splices for extra support, just as you would stagger subflooring. Use plywood or metal plates tied to both sides of the joists for a firm splice. See Figure 4-17. Splicing can increase joist stiffness by up to 40 percent.

It's hard to believe that a spliced joist is as strong as a solid one-piece joist. But research by the National Association of Home Builders Research Foundation, Inc. has shown that properly-designed 2 x 8 spliced joists, spaced at 24 inches on center, with glue-nailed 5/8-inch plywood sheathing, are structurally adequate for a 28-foot depth with a center bearing.

The NAHB actually built a demonstration house with a floor section of spliced joists in combination with a glue-nailed plywood subfloor. Full length 28-foot joists were preassembled from No. 2 hem-fir lumber by splicing two 2 x 8s together. One was 18 feet long and the other 10 feet. The splice was made with

Species	Joist spacing	Joist size	Plywood under-layment thickness	House depth (measured between outside surfaces of exterior studs), in feet												
				20	21	22	23	24	25	26	27	28	29	30	31	32
Douglas fir-south	16"	2 x 8	1/2	—	—	—	—	—	No.2	No.2	No.2[a]	No.1[c]	—	—	—	—
			19/32	—	—	—	—	—	—	—	—	No.2[c]	—	—	—	—
			23/32	—	—	—	—	—	—	—	—	No.2[b]	No.1[c]	—	—	—
	24"	2 x 10	1/2	—	—	—	—	—	—	—	—	—	—	—	—	No.2
		2 x 8	23/32	—	—	No.2	No.2[b]	No.1	No.1[a]	—	—	—	—	—	—	—
		2 x 10	23/32	—	—	—	—	—	—	—	—	No.2	No.2[b]	No.1	No.1	No.1[b]
Eastern hemlock Tamarack	16"	2 x 8	1/2	—	—	—	—	—	No.2	No.2	No.2[b]	No.1[a]	—	—	—	—
			19/32	—	—	—	—	—	—	No.2[a]	—	No.1[c]	—	—	—	—
			23/32	—	—	—	—	—	—	—	—	No.1[a]	—	—	—	—
		2 x 10	1/2	—	—	—	—	—	—	—	—	—	—	No.2	No.2	No.2[a]
			19/32	—	—	—	—	—	—	—	—	—	—	—	—	No.2
	24"	2 x 8	23/32	—	No.2	No.2[c]	No.1	No.1[a]	—	—	—	—	—	—	—	—
		2 x 10	23/32	—	—	—	—	—	—	—	—	No.2	No.1	No.1	No.1	No.1[c]
Eastern spruce	16"	2 x 8	1/2	—	—	—	—	—	—	No.1	No.1[b]	—	—	—	—	—
Englemann spruce Alpine fir	16"	2 x 8	1/2	—	—	—	—	—	No.1	No.1[c]	—	—	—	—	—	—
		2 x 10	1/2	—	—	—	—	—	—	—	—	—	—	—	—	No.1
Hem-fir	16"	2 x 8	1/2	—	—	—	—	—	—	No.1	No.1[a]	—	—	—	—	—
			19/32	—	—	—	—	—	—	—	—	No.1	—	—	—	—
	24"	2 x 10	23/32	—	—	—	—	—	—	—	—	—	No.1	No.1[c]	—	—
Lodgepole pine	16"	2 x 8	1/2	—	—	—	—	—	No.1	No.1[a]	—	—	—	—	—	—
		2 x 10	1/2	—	—	—	—	—	—	—	—	—	—	—	—	No.1
	24"	2 x 8	23/32	—	—	No.1	No.1[c]	—	—	—	—	—	—	—	—	—
		2 x 10	23/32	—	—	—	—	—	—	—	—	—	No.1	No.1[c]	—	—
Northern pine	16"	2 x 8	1/2	—	—	—	—	—	—	No.1	No.1	No.1[c]	—	—	—	—
			19/32	—	—	—	—	—	—	—	—	No.1[a]	—	—	—	—
			23/32	—	—	—	—	—	—	—	—	No.1	—	—	—	—
		2 x 10	1/2	—	—	—	—	—	—	—	—	—	—	—	—	No.2[b]
	24"	2 x 8	23/32	—	—	—	No.1	—	—	—	—	—	—	—	—	—
		2 x 10	23/32	—	—	—	—	—	—	—	—	—	No.1	No.1[c]	—	—
Ponderosa pine Sugar pine	16"	2 x 8	1/2	—	—	—	—	—	No.1	No.1[a]	—	—	—	—	—	—
		2 x 10	1/2	—	—	—	—	—	—	—	—	—	—	—	No.1	No.1
	24"	2 x 10	23/32	—	—	—	—	—	—	No.1	MG/No.2	MG	MG	—	—	—
Southern pine	16"	2 x 8	1/2	—	—	—	—	—	—	No.2[a]	MG/No.2	No.2	No.2	No.1[c]	—	—
			19/32	—	—	—	—	—	—	—	—	—	No.1[a]	No.1[c]	—	—
	24"	2 x 8	23/32	—	—	—	—	—	No.1	No.1[b]	—	—	—	—	—	—
		2 x 10	23/32	—	—	—	—	—	—	—	—	MG	MG	—	No.1	No.1
Southern pine KD (15% mc)	16"	2 x 8	1/2	—	—	—	—	—	—	No.2	No.2	No.2[a]	No.1[a]	—	—	—
			19/32	—	—	—	—	—	—	—	—	—	No.2[c]	No.1[c]	—	—
			23/32	—	—	—	—	—	—	—	—	—	—	No.1[b]	—	—
	24"	2 x 8	23/32	—	—	No.2	No.2[c]	No.1 MG	No.1[a] MG	—	—	—	—	—	—	—
		2 x 10	23/32	—	—	—	—	—	—	—	—	—	—	MG	No.2[c]	No.1
Western hemlock	16"	2 x 8	1/2	—	—	—	—	—	—	No.2	No.2[b]	No.1	No.1[c]	—	—	—
			19/32	—	—	—	—	—	—	—	—	—	No.1[a]	—	—	—
			23/32	—	—	—	—	—	—	—	—	—	No.1[c]	—	—	—
	24"	2 x 8	23/32	—	—	No.1	No.1[c]	—	—	—	—	—	—	—	—	—
		2 x 10	23/32	—	—	—	—	—	—	—	—	—	—	No.1	No.1[b]	—
White woods (Western woods)	16"	2 x 8	1/2	—	—	—	—	No.1	No.1[a]	—	—	—	—	—	—	—
		2 x 10	1/2	—	—	—	—	—	—	—	—	—	No.2	No.1	No.1	No.1[c]

[a] Nominal 2 x 6 sill plate and 2 x 4 center bearing plate; or width of sill plate plus one-half width of center bearing equal to 7¼" or more.

[b] Nominal 2 x 6 sill plate and 2 x 6 center bearing plate; or width of sill plate plus one-half width of center bearing equal to 8¼" or more.

[c] Nominal 2 x 8 sill plate and 2 x 8 center bearing plate; or width of sill plate plus one-half width of center bearing equal to 10⅞" or more.

Figure 4-16 (continued)
Joist grades for joists used with field-glued subflooring (40 psf live load)

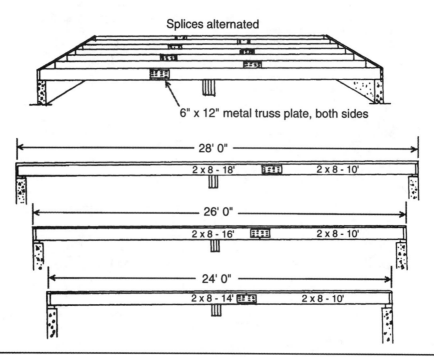

Figure 4-17
Off-center spliced joists span farther than simple joists of the same dimension

standard 6 x 12-inch truss plates on both sides. The joists were installed 24 inches on center, with the splices alternating on either side of the center support, as shown in Figure 4-17. Then T&G ⅝-inch-thick plywood sheathing was glue-nailed to the joists with the T&G joint glued. During full-scale loading tests, this floor system was stiffer and stronger than a conventional floor.

For houses or rooms up to 28 feet deep with center bearing, use a 2 x 8 off-center spliced-joist floor system. For other depths, make spliced joists from standard lengths of the same quality 2 x 8 lumber, as shown in Figure 4-17. The off-center splicing system offers all the benefits of the in-line joist system, plus an increased span capability. Figure 4-18 shows the layout of the in-line floor joist system over a center support for both preassembled and unassembled joists.

Figure 4-19 shows two types of joist trusses. The I-beam spans up to 25 feet spaced 24 inches on center with no center support for floor loads up to 60 psf. The open-web flat truss can span 30 feet spaced 24 inches on center with no center support. Conventional floor framing, however, is probably the most practical for work on the typical small addition.

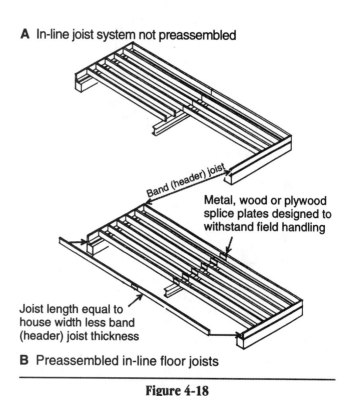

A In-line joist system not preassembled

Band (header) joist

Metal, wood or plywood splice plates designed to withstand field handling

Joist length equal to house width less band (header) joist thickness

B Preassembled in-line floor joists

Figure 4-18
In-line floor joist systems

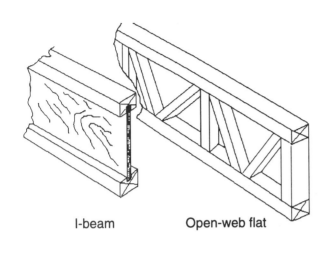

I-beam   Open-web flat

Figure 4-19
Two types of joist trusses

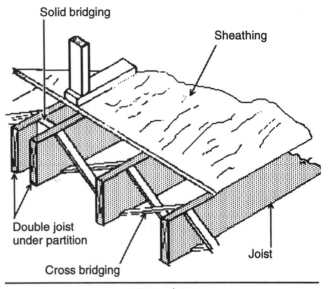

Solid bridging

Sheathing

Double joist
under partition

Cross bridging

Joist

Figure 4-20
Solid and cross bridging

Solid and Cross Bridging

Figure 4-20 shows solid and cross bridging. Unless required by code, many builders skip this part because they believe that bridging doesn't strengthen the floor and may, in fact, magnify the vibrations caused by someone walking on the floor. However, if the joist material is still green, you'll need bridging to keep the joists from twisting out of plane and causing rises or dips in the floor.

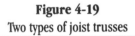

Subflooring

Subflooring provides a working platform and a base for the finish floor. Apply subflooring directly to floor joists. Plywood sheathing or OSB in 4 x 8-foot size is commonly used for this purpose. You could also use boards, but few builders apply board subfloors any more because they're expensive and time-consuming to install. If you did use boards, you'd choose square-edge or T&G boards that are 8 inches or less wide, and at least $3/4$ inch thick. Plywood

sheathing panels can be $3/8$ inch to $3/4$ inch thick, depending on joist spacing and type of finish floor. Figure 4-21 shows the minimum thickness of plywood needed for subflooring. OSB panels $7/16$ to $1 3/8$ inch thick are available for various joist spacings.

A good system for subflooring is to nail (or glue-nail) $1/2$-inch plywood or $7/16$-inch OSB to the floor joists. Then, after walls and ceilings are finished, you can install $5/8$-inch particleboard underlayment. Before putting the particleboard down, I like to apply 15-pound felt over a subfloor as a vapor barrier and cushion for the underlayment.

Using Sturd-I-Floor

There are also other subfloor systems available. For instance, using APA-rated Sturd-I-Floor panels can be a more cost-effective system than using double-layer floors. This flooring method is ideal where you're using a plank and beam frame system. The panels are strong enough to lay directly on top of the girders without using joists. Figure 4-22 A shows the system for joists spaced 32 inches on center. Figure 4-22

Panel identification index (1), (2), (3), and (4)	Plywood thickness (inches)	Maximum span (5) (inches)	Common nail size and type	Nail spacing (inches)	
				Panel edges	Intermediate
30/12	3/8	12(6)	8d	6	10
32/16	1/2	16(7)	8d(8)	6	10
36/16	3/4	16(7)	8d	6	10
42/20	5/8	20(7)	8d	6	10
48/24	3/4	24	8d	6	10
1 1/8" groups 1 & 2	1 1/8	48	10d(9)	6	6
1 1/4" groups 3 & 4	1 1/4	48	10d(9)	6	6

Notes:
(1) These values apply for Structural I and II, Standard sheathing and C-C exterior grades only.
(2) Identification index appears on all panels except 1 1/8" and 1 1/4" panels.
(3) In some non-residential buildings, special conditions may impose heavy concentrated loads and heavy traffic requiring subfloor constructions in excess of these minimums.
(4) Edges shall be tongue and grooved or supported with blocking for square edge wood flooring, unless separate underlayment layer (1/4" minimum thickness) is installed.
(5) Spans limited to values shown because of possible effect of concentrated loads. At indicated maximum spans, floor panels carrying identification index numbers will support uniform loads of more than 100 psf.
(6) May be 16" if 25/32" wood strip flooring is installed at right angles to joists.
(7) May be 24" if 25/32" wood strip flooring is installed at right angles to joists.
(8) 6d common nail permitted if plywood is 1/2".
(9) 8d deformed shank nails may be used.

Figure 4-21
Minimum thickness of plywood adequate for subflooring

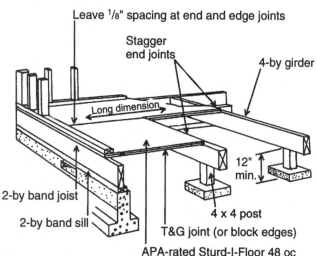

A Over supports 32" oc

Leave 1/8" spacing at end and edge joints
Stagger end joints (optional under carpet & pad)
APA-rated Sturd-I-Floor 48 oc
2 x 2 ledger or framing anchors
Joists 32" oc (2 x 10s typical)
Long dimension
2-by band joist
2-by band sill
Center girder (three 2 x 12s typical)
T&G joint (or block edges)

B Over supports 48" oc

Leave 1/8" spacing at end and edge joints
Stagger end joints
4-by girder
Long dimension
2-by band joist
2-by band sill
12" min.
4 x 4 post
T&G joint (or block edges)
APA-rated Sturd-I-Floor 48 oc

Figure 4-22
APA-rated Sturd-I-Floor 48 oc (2-4-1)

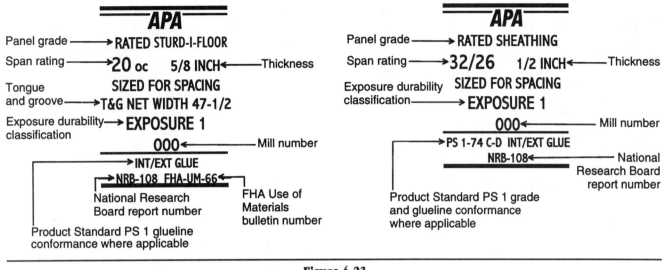

Figure 4-23
Typical APA registered trademarks

B shows how to install the panels over 4-by girders spaced 48 inches on center. Here, the girders can be either 2-by joists spiked together, 4-by lumber, lightweight steel beams, or wood-steel floor trusses. When you use doubled 2-by material, make sure the top edges are flush so the panel end joints will be smooth.

Using Plywood and OSB Subflooring

Most add-on experts use plywood and OSB wherever they can because of their strength, durability, availability, and time-saving features. In addition, the panels make for a professional job.

Plywood comes in many different grades. For sheathing subfloors, you can use any interior grade with a fully-waterproof adhesive (the same adhesive used in exterior plywood). Use waterproof interior grades of underlayment and subflooring where there's likely to be a lot of moisture, such as at plumbing fixtures. Use standard sheathing grades in other areas.

Some grades of plywood you can use for subflooring are Standard, Structural I and II, and C-C Exterior. Each plywood panel should be stamped with a mark such as those shown in Figure 4-23. The stamping tells you what spacing of rafters and floor joists you can use with different thicknesses of plywood. For example, a marking of 32/16 means that the maximum spacing for the panel is 32 inches for rafters and 16

inches for floor joists. Since each panel is stamped with an identification index, you always know its strength capability.

Always install plywood with the grain direction (of the outer plies) at right angles to the joists. Use 8d common or 7d ring or screw-shank nails to fasten 1/2-

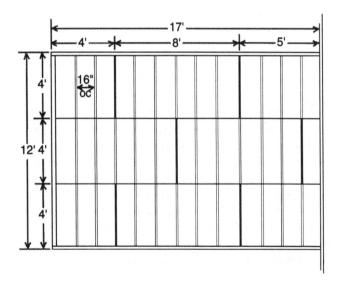

Figure 4-24
Subfloor panel layout, 12 x 17 room addition

Spacing	Edges (inches)	Ends (inches)
Underlayment or interior wall lining	1/32	1/32
Combination subfloor underlayment	1/16	1/16
Subflooring (under wet or humid conditions, spacing should be doubled)	1/8	1/16

Figure 4-25
Plywood location and spacing

Built-up girders		
Size of girder	BF per LF	Nails per 1000 BF
4 x 6	2	53
4 x 8	2.66	40
4 x 10	3.33	32
4 x 12	4	26
6 x 6	3	43
6 x 8	4	32
6 x 10	5	26
6 x 12	6	22
8 x 8	5.33	30
8 x 10	6.66	24
8 x 12	8	20

Figure 4-26
Built-up girders

to ³⁄₄-inch thick panels to the joists at each bearing. Space nails 6 inches apart along all edges and 10 inches apart along other members. Space nails 6 to 7 inches apart at all joists and blocking if the plywood will serve as both subfloor and underlayment.

Figure 4-24 shows how to lay out panel subflooring in a house 12 feet deep with in-line joists. Stagger the subflooring panels for extra strength, so you can use the half pieces efficiently. Use this same system when you work with larger dimensions.

Leave an expansion gap between the ends and edges of all adjoining plywood panels whether you're laying interior or exterior grades. Figure 4-25 shows spacing requirements. This spacing is based on field experience studies done by the American Plywood Association.

Estimating Materials

To figure your lumber needs in board feet, multiply the width times the thickness in inches times the length in feet, and divide by 12. A board foot is 1 square foot of wood 1 inch thick (based on nominal dimensions). A 2 x 8 that's 16 feet long has 21.33 board feet (2 x 8 x 16 ÷ 12 = 21.33), and 48 pieces have 1,024 board feet. Figure 4-26 shows the board feet per linear foot of lumber in a built-up girder, and the nails needed per 1,000 board feet.

Figure 4-27 shows the number of floor joists required for joist spacing from 12 to 60 inches and spans up to 40 feet. You can, of course, quickly find the number of joists required by dividing the length of

the addition, in feet, by the joist spacing center to center, in feet. Add one joist for the end and one joist for each double joist used under wall partitions.

Suppose you have a room addition that's 16 feet wide and 24 feet long, with joists installed 16 inches on center, and you're using 8-foot long 2 x 10s for the joists. So:

24' ÷ 1.3' (16" oc) = 18

Add 1 for the end joist to get a total of 19.

You'll need 19 joists for one side or bay. Since there's one bay on each side of the center girder, you'll need 38 joists in all. Now, a 4 x 8 plywood panel has 32 square feet. The 16 x 24 room addition has 384 square feet. Divide 384 by 32 and you see that you need 12 panels for the subfloor.

Figure 4-28 shows the nail requirements for various tasks. If you're installing 2 x 8 floor joists, you'll need 252 16d nails per 1,000 board feet of lumber. That's 5 pounds of nails. Use the chart as a handy reference when you're estimating a job.

Length of span	Joist spacing									
	12"	16"	20"	24"	30"	36"	42"	48"	54"	60"
6	7	6	5	4	3	3	3	3	2	2
7	8	6	5	5	4	4	3	3	3	2
8	9	7	6	5	4	4	3	3	3	3
9	10	8	6	6	5	4	4	3	3	3
10	11	9	7	6	5	4	4	4	3	3
11	12	9	8	7	5	5	4	4	3	3
12	13	10	8	7	6	5	4	4	4	3
13	14	11	9	8	6	5	5	4	4	4
14	15	12	9	8	7	6	5	5	4	4
15	16	12	10	9	7	6	5	5	4	4
16	17	13	11	9	7	6	6	5	5	4
17	18	14	11	10	8	7	6	5	5	4
18	19	15	12	10	8	7	6	6	5	4
19	20	15	12	11	9	7	6	6	5	5
20	21	16	13	11	9	8	7	6	5	5
21	22	17	14	12	9	8	7	6	6	5
22	23	18	14	12	10	8	7	7	6	5
23	24	18	15	13	10	9	8	7	6	6
24	25	19	15	13	11	9	8	7	6	6
25	26	20	16	14	11	9	8	7	7	6
26	27	21	17	14	11	10	8	8	7	6
27	28	21	17	15	12	10	9	8	7	6
28	29	22	18	15	12	10	9	8	7	7
29	30	23	18	16	13	11	9	8	7	7
30	31	24	19	16	13	11	10	9	8	7
31	32	24	20	17	13	11	10	9	8	7
32	33	25	20	17	14	12	10	9	8	7
33	34	26	21	18	14	12	10	9	8	8
34	35	27	21	18	15	12	11	10	9	8
35	36	27	22	19	15	13	11	10	9	8
36	37	28	23	19	15	13	11	10	9	8
37	38	29	23	20	16	13	12	10	9	8
38	39	30	24	20	16	14	12	11	9	9
39	40	30	24	21	17	14	12	11	10	9
40	41	31	25	21	17	14	12	11	10	9

One joist has been added to each of the above quantities to take care of the extra joist required at end of span. Add for doubling joists under all partitions.

Figure 4-27

Number of wood joists required for floors

Description of material	Unit of measure	Size and type of nail	Number of nails required	Pounds of nails required
Wood shingles	1,000 BF	3d common	2,560	4
Individual asphalt shingles	100 SF	7/8" roofing	848	4
Three in one asphalt shingles	100 SF	7/8" roofing	320	1
Wood lath	1,000 BF	3d fine	4,000	6
Wood lath	1,000 BF	2d fine	4,000	4
Bevel or lap siding, ½" x 4"	1,000 BF	6d coated	2,250	*15
Bevel or lap siding, ½" x 6"	1,000 BF	6d coated	1,500	*10
Byrkit lath, 1" x 6"	1,000 BF	6d common	2,400	15
Drop siding, 1" x 6"	1,000 BF	8d common	3,000	25
⅜" hardwood flooring	1,000 BF	4d finish	9,300	16
¹³⁄₁₆" hardwood flooring	1,000 BF	8d casing	9,300	64
Softwood flooring, 1" x 3"	1,000 BF	8d casing	3,350	23
Softwood flooring, 1" x 4"	1,000 BF	8d casing	2,500	17
Softwood flooring, 1" x 6"	1,000 BF	8d casing	2,600	18
Ceiling, ⅝" x 4"	1,000 BF	6d casing	2,250	10
Sheathing boards, 1" x 4"	1,000 BF	8d common	4,500	40
Sheathing boards, 1" x 6"	1,000 BF	8d common	3,000	25
Sheathing boards, 1" x 8"	1,000 BF	8d common	2,250	20
Sheathing boards, 1" x 10"	1,000 BF	8d common	1,800	15
Sheathing boards, 1" x 12"	1,000 BF	8d common	1,500	12½
Studding, 2" x 4"	1,000 BF	16d common	500	10
Joist, 2" x 6"	1,000 BF	16d common	332	7
Joist, 2" x 8"	1,000 BF	16d common	252	5
Joist, 2" x 10"	1,000 BF	16d common	200	4
Joist, 2" x 12"	1,000 BF	16d common	168	3½
Interior trim, ⅝" thick	1,000 BF	6d finish	2,250	7
Interior trim, ¾" thick	1,000 BF	8d finish	3,000	14
⅝" trim where nailed to jamb	1,000 BF	4d finish	2,250	3
1" x 2" furring or bridging	1,000 BF	6d common	2,400	15
1" x 1" grounds	1,000 BF	6d common	4,800	30

Note: Cement-coated nails sold as ⅔ pound equals 1 pound of common nails.

Figure 4-28
Standard nail requirements

Item	Manhours Skilled	Manhours Unskilled
Sill, bolted & grouted per 100 LF	3	2
Joists, per 1,000 BF	—	—
2 x 6	18	7
2 x 8	16	6
2 x 10	15	5
Built-up girders, per 1,000 BF	13	5
Joist bridging, 1 x 3 or 1 x 4 per 1,000 pieces	4	—
Floor sheathing, plywood or OSB per 1,000 SF	9	4
Subflooring, diagonal boards per 1,000 BF	12	5
Subflooring, right angle boards per 1,000 BF	10	5

Figure 4-29
Manhours for installing floors

Estimating Manhours

You can only estimate manhours for any building task on the basis of general guidelines. Your best method of estimating should be based on your own manhour records for your crews. If you don't have these records, use Figure 4-29 as a guideline.

Here's an example using these estimates. For a 16 x 24 addition that requires 19 floor joists (2 x 10 x 8 feet), the board footage is:

19 x 2 x 10 x 8 ÷ 12 = 254 BF

Using Figure 4-29, it takes 15 skilled manhours and 5 unskilled hours to install 1,000 board feet of 2 x 10 floor joists. So it would take 3.8 skilled (15 x .254)

and 1.3 unskilled manhours (5 x .254) to install 19 joists in the 16 x 24 addition.

What about the girder? In our example, we'll double a 2 x 10 to get a 4 x 10 girder. The length will be 23'6". Using Figure 4-26, a 4 x 10 has 3.33 board feet per linear foot. Our girder, then, will have 3.33 x 23.5 for a total of 78.25 board feet. Built-up girders require 13 skilled manhours and 5 unskilled hours per 1,000 BF. So it'll take 1 skilled manhour (13 x .078) and 0.39 unskilled hours (5 x .078) to build the girder.

Using Figure 4-29 as a guide, it'll take about 3.5 skilled manhours and 1.54 unskilled hours to nail down 12 sheets of plywood which total 384 square feet.

5

Wall Framing

The addition is generally an independent structure built onto the house without removing any of the exterior finish (brick, siding, etc.) of the existing house. The framing members are butted to or flushed with the exterior finish wall. Of course, the door opening is cut in the wall. In the event the exterior is removed, the framing members of the addition are nailed in the conventional manner to the framing members of the existing house for solid tie-in.

Builders around the country use several different framing techniques. Usually, when you start out in the business, you find out which method suits you best, and then stick with it. It's easier and cheaper to use a system that you're familiar with. However, when framing additions, it's generally better to use the same framing technique in the addition as in the existing structure to ensure the same horizontal wood shrinkage.

In this chapter we'll cover modern braced, western or platform, balloon, and plank and beam framing. Let's start with modern braced framing.

Modern Braced Framing (MBF)

MBF comes from an old technique called early brace framing which used posts and beams mortised and tenoned together. Diagonal braces were used to strengthen the structure. Many old barns built this way are still standing. Now, MBF uses side-wall and center studs cut to the same length. MBF gets its rigidity from diagonal braces let into the studs at the corners, or other locations depending on where the openings in the side or end walls are. You can also use plywood or structural strength panels instead of let-in bracing.

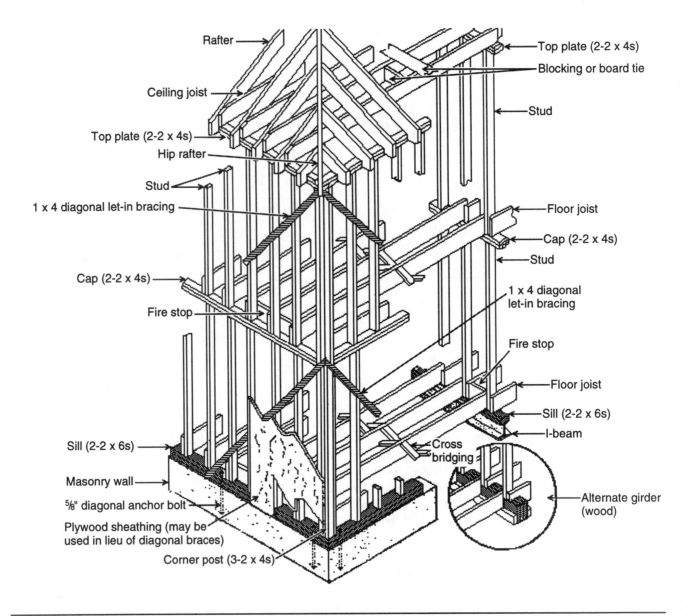

Rafter

Ceiling joist

Top plate (2-2 x 4s)

Hip rafter

Stud

1 x 4 diagonal let-in bracing

Cap (2-2 x 4s)

Fire stop

Sill (2-2 x 6s)

Masonry wall

⅝" diagonal anchor bolt

Plywood sheathing (may be used in lieu of diagonal braces)

Corner post (3-2 x 4s)

Top plate (2-2 x 4s)

Blocking or board tie

Stud

Floor joist

Cap (2-2 x 4s)

Stud

1 x 4 diagonal let-in bracing

Fire stop

Floor joist

Sill (2-2 x 6s)

I-beam

Cross bridging

Alternate girder (wood)

Figure 5-1
Modern braced framing

Figure 5-1 shows details of this method. Attach the side-wall studs to the sill or plate. Attach the partition studs to the girder or sill. To make sure the outside and inside walls shrink uniformly, use a steel girder as shown in the figure.

Lap and spike the joists to the side-wall studs The joists may run continuously between the two opposite side walls, or you can side-lap and spike them at the center partition, depending on the additions depth. These joists form a tie for the two side walls. They are bridged (where required) and supported by the full width of the sill and girder. Install fire stops at the ends of all joists.

To keep the structure from twisting, lay diagonal flooring in opposite directions on the upper and lower levels, or install plywood or OSB subflooring.

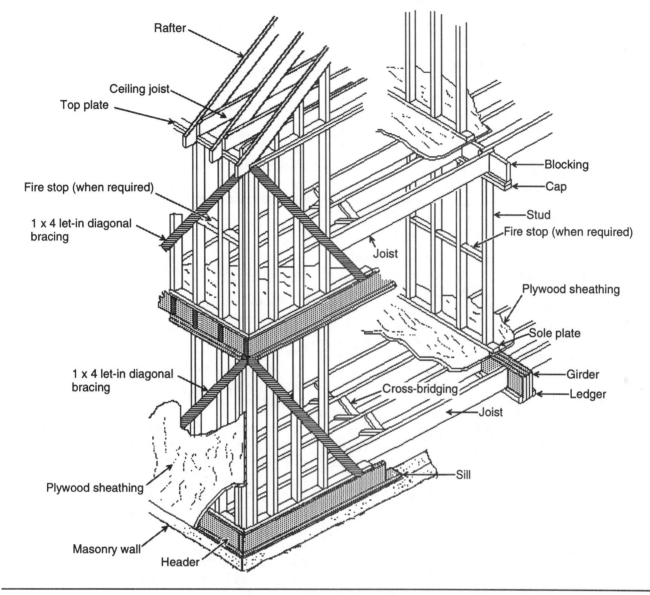

Figure 5-2
Western (platform) framing

Western (or Platform) Framing (WF)

Like most builders, I have my preferences when it comes to framing. Over the years I've used the western (platform) system more than any other. Whether you're building a one-story or a two-story house or addition, it lets you put wall framing together on a deck (floor) and raise it into place.

WF is probably the fastest and safest form of wood-frame construction. It's similar to MBF except the ends of the joists form a bearing surface for the side and center wall studs. This provides equal shrinkage at the side and end walls.

WF lets you use more short material for studs. The studding extends only one story and rests on a sill plate nailed on top of the subfloor. A plate on top of the studding for the first floor carries the second floor joists. No wood fire stops are required because the subfloor panels or boards extend to the outside edge of the building. Figure 5-2 shows this method. Generally you build the walls horizontally on the floor, and then raise them into place in a single operation.

This horizontal assembly or "tilt-up" saves a great deal of time. Some builders prefer to install the sole plate, nailing it in place on the subfloor, and then assemble the studs to the top plate on the deck. Then they lift the wall into place and toenail the studs to the sole plate. This takes more time but also makes a sound wall.

You build each story of the building as a separate unit. Lay the subfloor before you raise the side walls to provide a safe working platform. If you've ever tried framing a house without this platform, you can appreciate the efficiency and safety it provides.

In western framing, you use a continuous header at the first floor. Make this header the same width as the joists and rest its bottom edge on the sill. To form a box sill, make sure the outside face of the header is flush with the outside edge of the sill. If you're working with a second floor, instead of a continuous header, extend the joists flush to the outside of the plate and put blocking between the joists.

Frame outside WF wall members the same way as interior partitions. This makes the shrinkage uniform in both outside walls and partitions. If you're using steel beams, make sure the wood you use is the same cross-section size as the sills to give equal shrinkage.

Mark the sole plate and the top plate for stud placement, window, and door openings. Mark partition intersections at the same time. Lay the sole plate out where you're going to install it. Temporarily tack it in place at both ends. Lay the top plate on the floor alongside the sole plate. Using a square, measure and mark both the top plate and the sole plate for all studs, openings and intersections. When the studs and joists are on the same spacing, align the side wall studs directly over the floor joists.

Lay out precut studs, window and door headers, cripple studs, jamb studs (studs supporting headers), corner posts, intersection T's and window sills. Precut studs are delivered to the job site ready to be nailed in place without cutting. They're precut for a finished 8-foot high ceiling in a wall having a nominal 2 x 4 sole plate and a double 2 x 4 top plate.

Nail the top and sole plates to the studs using 16d nails. Install window and door framing and cut for let-in bracing, if required. Then erect, plumb and brace the entire wall frame. See Figure 5-3.

You normally preassemble the corner posts, T's, and headers so you can install them during horizontal assembly of the wall frame. To preassemble complete window units horizontally, nail the double stud (full stud and jamb stud), header, sill, and cripples together. Assemble door opening units on the deck in the same manner. You can also install the sheathing before raising the wall.

In high wind areas, anchor the stud wall to the foundation as shown in Figure 5-4. Structural sheathing, such as plywood or OSB extending down over the sill, also makes a good anchor.

Balloon Framing (BF)

Balloon framing is less common than modern braced framing and western framing in most parts of the country. Figure 5-5 shows the details of balloon framing. Notice that the second floor joists are carried by a ribbon let into the studs. BF uses long side-wall and end-wall studs. Fire stops are required between the studs.

There are some advantages to balloon framing. First, the outside studs go up quickly because they extend the full two stories, from the sill to the roof plate. At the second-story level, rest the joists on a 1 x 4 or 1 x 6 ribbon or ledger board and nail them against the studs. You can also build the load-bearing partitions this way. The preferred method, however, is shown in Figure 5-5. Rest the attic or ceiling joists on the double top plate. Another advantage is that BF reduces shrinkage by keeping the amount of horizontally-laid lumber at a minimum.

There's also a disadvantage. There's a strong "flue effect" in balloon framing. Be sure to use blocking, both at the sills and at half-story heights, to make the structure safer. Most codes require fire stops. Figure 5-6 shows 2 x 4 blocking between the studs. This provides strength as well as a good fire stop.

BF isn't as rigid as braced types of framing until after you apply the outside sheathing. After sheathing, a BF building is as strong and stiff as the other types. If you nail the sheathing board diagonally or install plywood vertically, you can omit the 1 x 4 diagonal braces. In many cases, plywood panels at each corner provide the necessary bracing.

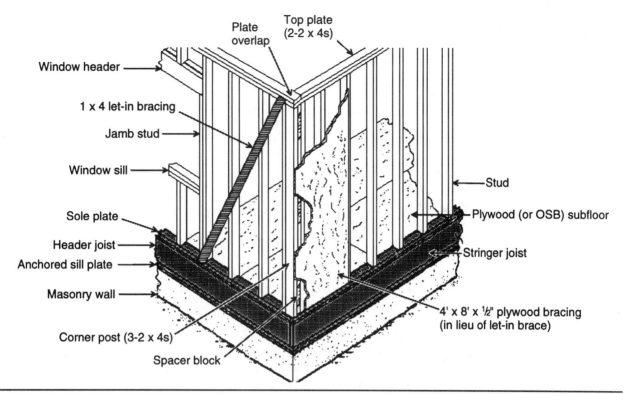

Figure 5-3
Wall framing detail — platform construction

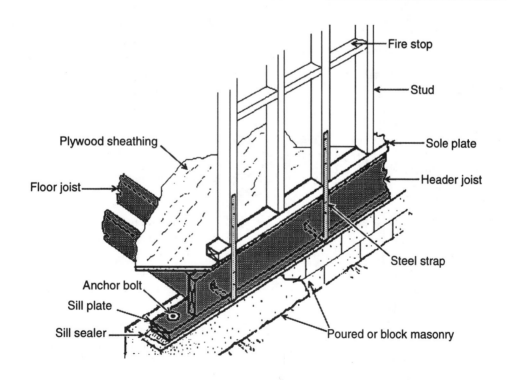

Figure 5-4
Wall-anchoring straps

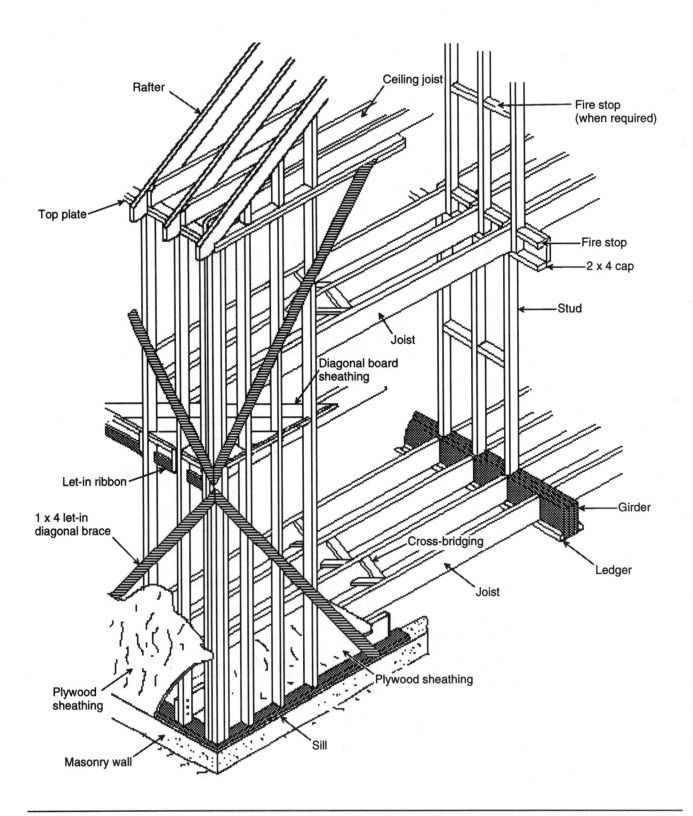

Figure 5-5
Balloon framing

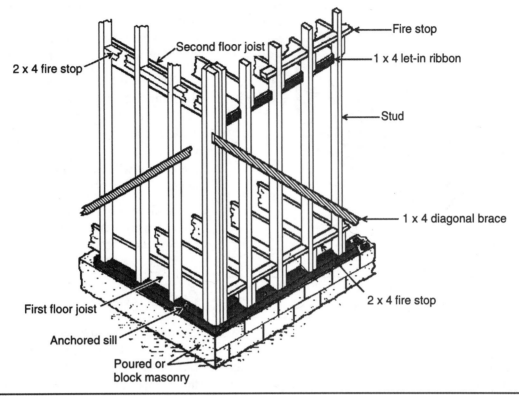

2 x 4 fire stop

Second floor joist

Fire stop

1 x 4 let-in ribbon

Stud

1 x 4 diagonal brace

2 x 4 fire stop

First floor joist

Anchored sill

Poured or block masonry

Figure 5-6
Wall framing — balloon construction

Plank and Beam Framing (P&B)

Plank and beam framing (also called post and beam framing) is a modern building style adaptable to some types of construction. It works well with one-story structures, large glass areas, modular setups, open-span planning, and natural finish materials. P&B can make good use of glue-laminated beams where large spans are required.

P&B framing concentrates the structural load on fewer, and larger, framing members than conventional construction. To some degree, it's similar to the old braced frame system. It has the advantage of reducing carpentry manhours. Using planks continuously over two or more spans, plus eliminating most interior and exterior finishes, can cut costs further. Use it for framing floors and roofs in combination with ordinary wood stud or masonry walls, or as the skeleton frame in curtain wall construction. Figure 5-7 shows P&B framing.

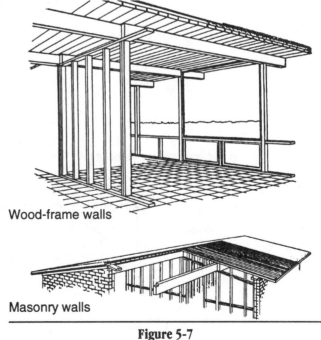

Wood-frame walls

Masonry walls

Figure 5-7
Plank and beam framing

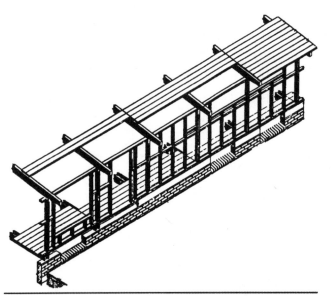

Figure 5-8
Modular plank and beam framing

foot spacing for beams and columns can use 16-foot planks running continuously over two spans. Figure 5-8 shows how this might look. Sheets of 4 x 8 drywall and plywood will also fit the walls without cutting.

The wide beam spacing and 2 x 6 or 2 x 8 T&G dual-function planking can eliminate conventional ceiling construction. This saves on ceiling joists, bridging, and finishing materials such as drywall. If you stain and seal the planks before installing them, the ceiling will be complete when you nail the planks in place.

While P&B uses a lot less material and labor, top quality workmanship is essential. All joints must fit exactly since there are fewer contacts between members.

Corner Posts

Figure 5-9 shows three ways to build corner posts. For MBF, BF and WF techniques, the standard post (A) is the one most used. It requires three studs and three 2 x 4 blocks that are 12 inches or longer. A block is placed at each end and at the mid-span. It is probably the most rigid of the three assemblies.

P&B lends itself to modular concepts. If you lay out your addition in 2-foot modules, there will be a minimum of cutting, fitting, and waste. The key is deciding what the spacing will be. For example, an 8-

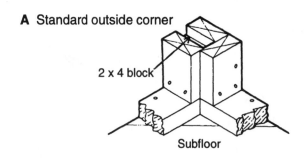

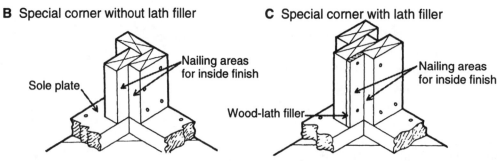

Figure 5-9
Examples of corner stud assembly

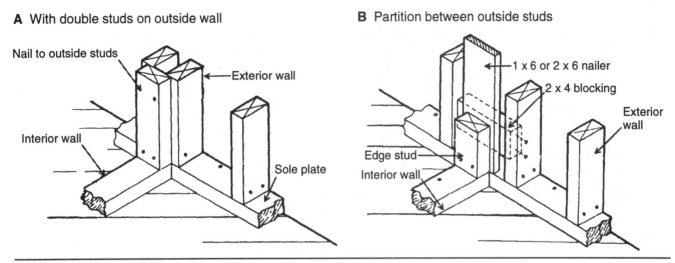

A With double studs on outside wall

Nail to outside studs

Exterior wall

Interior wall

Sole plate

B Partition between outside studs

1 x 6 or 2 x 6 nailer

2 x 4 blocking

Exterior wall

Edge stud

Interior wall

Figure 5-10
Intersection of interior wall with exterior wall

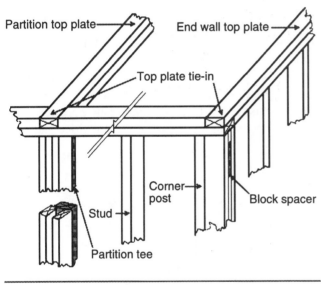

Partition top plate

End wall top plate

Top plate tie-in

Corner post

Block spacer

Stud

Partition tee

Figure 5-11
Top plate tie-in

Figure 5-10 shows two common ways to build the intersection interior and exterior walls. The method with double studs on the outside wall provides a nailing surface at the corners. The partition between outside studs uses short pieces of 2 x 4 blocking between the studs to support and provide backing for a 1 x 6 nailer. I don't like this method. It takes too much time. The first method goes together quickly and provides a strong wall tie-in.

Figure 5-11 shows how to tie in the top plates for solid-built walls and partitions. Lap the top plate over the joints of the first member at all corners and wall intersections. Use at least two 16d nails at the overlaps. Stagger 16d or 12d nails about 16 inches apart to firmly join the two plate members. Be sure to plumb and align the wall before nailing the second member. Use a taut string to align the outside walls, as shown in Figure 5-12. This is very important because the rafters won't fit and end walls won't be straight if the walls aren't aligned.

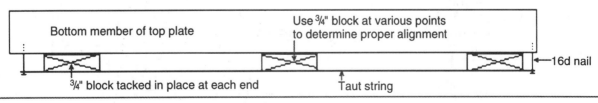

Bottom member of top plate

Use ¾" block at various points to determine proper alignment

16d nail

¾" block tacked in place at each end

Taut string

Figure 5-12
Wall alignment method

Figure 5-13
1 x 6 let-in diagonal bracing installed on interior side of wall

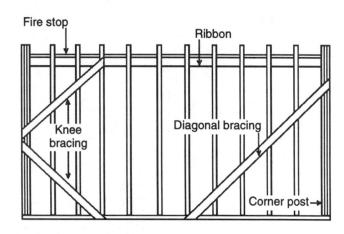

Figure 5-14
Bracing a wall section

Use temporary braces to set the walls plumb and aligned. Leave the braces in place until the roof is on and the sheathing is applied to the outside walls.

Build let-in diagonal braces at the corners of each wall of each story after you erect and plumb the walls. A 1 x 4 is big enough to brace a one-story structure. In two-story framing and high wind areas, 1 x 6s are better. Cut a notch in each stud at the point where the brace crosses it. Fit the brace flush with the surface of the studs. You can put it on the exterior or interior side (Figure 5-13) of the stud. Use knee braces as shown in Figure 5-14 if there's an opening near the corner that keeps you from using a corner diagonal brace. However, a brace can extend under a window opening as shown in Figure 5-15.

Constructing End and Interior Walls

Figure 5-16 shows the usual method for framing a wall and ceiling in platform construction for a 1½ or 2-story house with finished rooms above the first floor. Toenail the edge floor joist to the top wall plate with 8d nails spaced 16 inches on center. Install the sole plate, subfloor, and wall framing the same way as you would a first floor.

In balloon framing (Figure 5-17), the studs continue through the first and second floors. Nail the edge joist to each stud with three 10d or larger nails. Install

2 x 4 fire stops at the first and second-story levels between each stud.

Both loadbearing and nonbearing walls make up the interior partitions in a house with conventional joist and rafter construction. Walls running at right angles to the floor joists are usually loadbearing. Walls running parallel to the joists are usually nonbearing. You can use 2 x 3 studs in nonbearing partitions. The loadbearing walls hold up the second floor and roof,

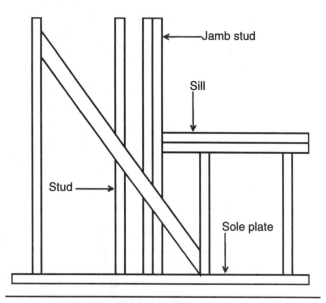

Figure 5-15
1 x 6 let-in diagonal brace extending past window opening

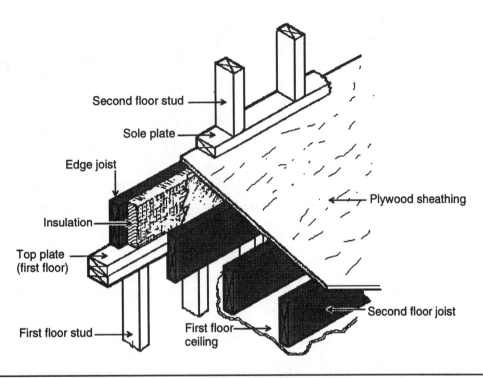

Figure 5-16
End-wall framing (platform construction)

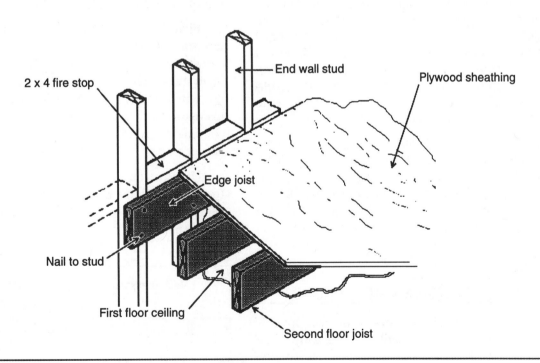

Figure 5-17
End-wall framing (balloon construction)

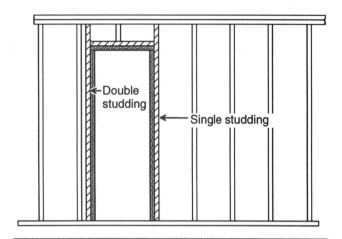

Figure 5-18
Double stud door opening for loadbearing wall

Figure 5-19
Two 2 x 10s and 2 x 4 base make a header strong enough to support two-story construction

and should be framed with 2 x 4s. I prefer to use 2 x 4 studs throughout a house, as do most of the builders I know. If you use 2 x 3 studs, you have to use 2 x 3 sole plates and top plates. That's too many different sizes of lumber to keep up with.

Interior walls must also have a sole plate. You can use a single or double top plate in an interior wall. But if you use a single top plate, the precut studs will be too short. You'll have to order a full 8-foot 2 x 4 and cut it to fit. This is a waste of time and materials. And with a single top plate, you can't use the upper member of the top plate to tie the intersecting walls together by overlapping. It's really a lot simpler and faster to use only double top plates on all walls.

You can use a single stud to frame a door opening in a nonbearing partition, and a double stud in a load-bearing wall. The problem with single stud framing is the opening won't have a solid feel or sound when the door is slammed shut. See Figure 5-18 for single and double studding.

How to Frame Doors and Windows

The member used over doors and windows is called a header. It's usually built up from 2-by members, spaced with ³⁄₈-inch lath or wood strips. You can also build one without the spacers, using a ³⁄₈-inch empty space.

The longer the span of an opening, the deeper its header must be to support the ceiling and roof loads bearing down on the side walls. To give a header added strength, sandwich ³⁄₈-inch-thick plywood or OSB between the members. Nail through both the 2-by pieces and the spacer when you nail the header members together.

Figure 5-19 shows my preferred method of framing headers, with doubled 2 x 10s resting on a 2 x 4 member, and the header supported at its ends by the jamb studs. Figure 5-15 shows the sill construction for the window in Figure 5-19. Figure 5-20 shows an alternate way to frame headers, with the jamb studs continuous from the sole plate to the bottom of the header.

Usually you use the same species for headers as for floor joists in a house. Use the following chart as a general guide when you're figuring materials for different spans.

Maximum span (feet)	Header size (inches)
3½	2 x 6
5	2 x 8
6½	2 x 10
8	2 x 12

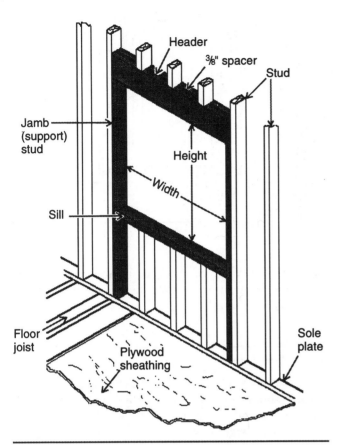

Figure 5-20
Window header and framing

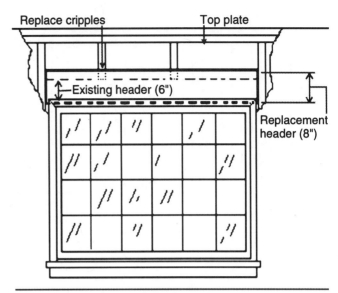

Figure 5-21
First floor header replacement

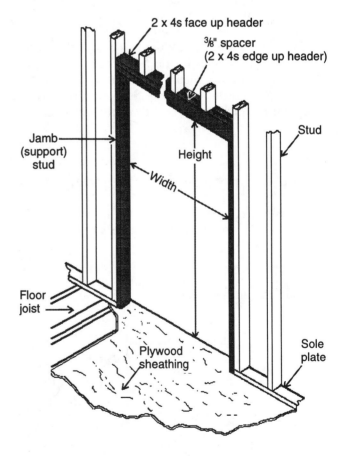

Figure 5-22
2 x 4 header for interior door

If the span of a first-floor header in the existing house exceeds the maximum allowable span, replace it with the size shown in the chart. To do this, remove a section of the interior or exterior finish wall above the opening. If the header was built in the conventional manner, it'll be supported by jamb studs and made of doubled 2 x 6 or wider members. Remove the members and replace the cripples to fit the replacement header as shown in Figure 5-21.

Frame headers for exterior doors the same as windows, using the same dimension lumber. You can frame interior door openings in nonbearing partitions using double 2 x 4s with the face flat, or vertical, as shown in Figure 5-22.

Doors are usually 6'8" high. Use this height plus an allowance for the thickness and clearance of the head jambs and the finish floor. Depending on the thickness of the finish floor, about 6'10" to 6'11" is usually enough.

Open one side

Opening either end

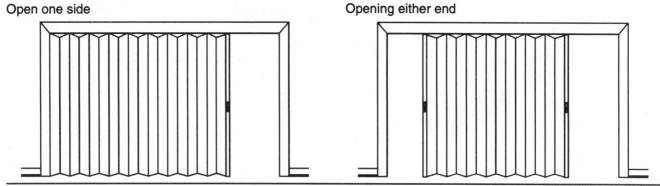

Figure 5-23
Making a partition with folding doors

Folding Partitions

Folding partitions or doors are made in vinyl and wood. Stabilized wood cores make the panels warp-free. Wood veneer and vinyl-film surfaces resist damage in normal service and prolonged hard use. An all-wood construction unit should stay properly aligned throughout its life. Follow the manufacture's instructions when installing. Figure 5-23 shows some types of folding partitions. Figure 5-24 shows a folding door in extended and stack position. Stack dimension is the space the door takes up when it's all the way open.

Window Types and How to Install Them

If you keep informed about the latest technology in windows, you'll always have suggestions to

increase the value of a house and the comfort of the homeowner at the same time. Let's look at some common window terms.

Double-Hung Windows

A double-hung window has separate upper and lower sliding sashes, traditionally both the same size. But a contemporary double-hung window may have an upper sash larger than the bottom sash. Some double-hung windows have a pivoting sash and optional snap-out wood window dividers, called muntins, which make it easier to wash the windows. Figure 5-25 shows a double-hung window. If you can raise or lower a window's sash, it's a vent window. You can't open a fixed window.

Manufacturers today sell wood-frame windows with aluminum-clad coating systems that withstand

Folding door in closed position

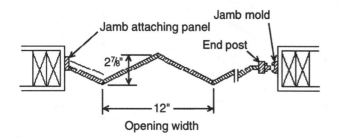

Folding door in stacked position

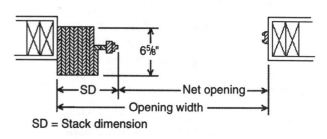

Figure 5-24
Stack position

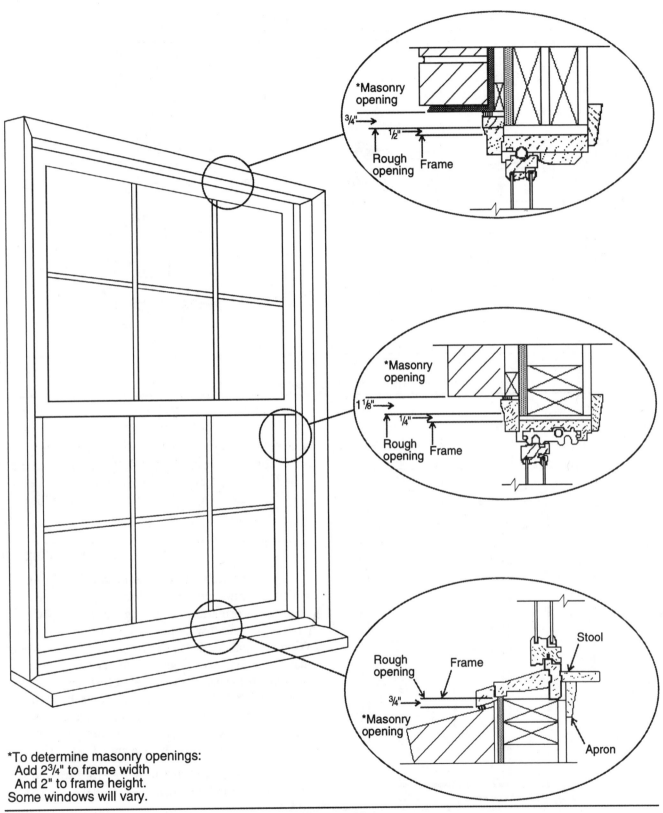

*Masonry opening

3/4"
Rough opening
1/2"
Frame

*Masonry opening

1 1/8"
Rough opening
1/4"
Frame

Stool
Rough opening
Frame
3/4"
*Masonry opening
Apron

*To determine masonry openings:
  Add 2 3/4" to frame width
  And 2" to frame height.
Some windows will vary.

Figure 5-25
Double-hung window

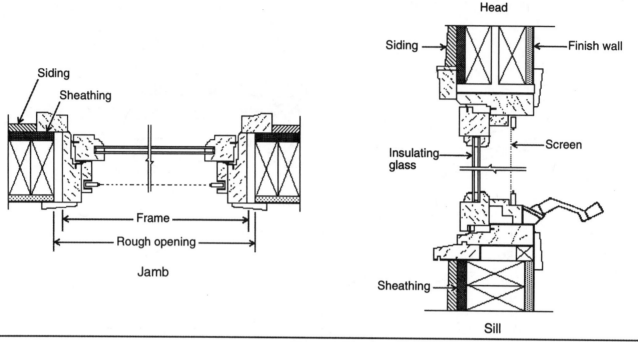

Figure 5-26
Installation details showing casement window in siding wall

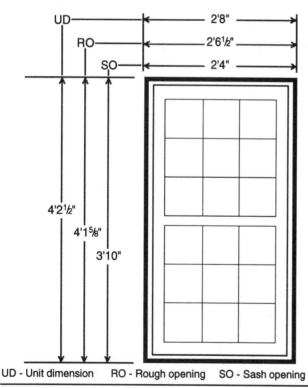

UD - Unit dimension   RO - Rough opening   SO - Sash opening

Figure 5-27
Rough opening determined by sash openings

acid rain, severe temperature changes, salt spray, and other forms of environmental attack. This coating, called cladding, comes in many colors. And double-glazed windows have valuable insulation qualities.

Rough Opening Size

Figure 5-26 shows window installation details in 2 x 4 frame, brick veneer construction, including rough opening information. The rough opening (RO) of a particular window depends on the way it's built. Windows that are the same size, but made by different manufacturers, may require different rough openings. Be sure to measure a window before you frame the opening it's going into. Most of us have had to reframe a RO because we believed what the supplier told us about the RO requirements. Play it safe. Measure and save yourself time and effort.

Figure 5-27 gives the RO sizes for different sizes of wood double-hung windows. For these windows, add $\frac{1}{2}$ inch to frame width and height for typical installation. For masonry openings, add $2\frac{3}{4}$ inches to frame width and 2 inches to frame height.

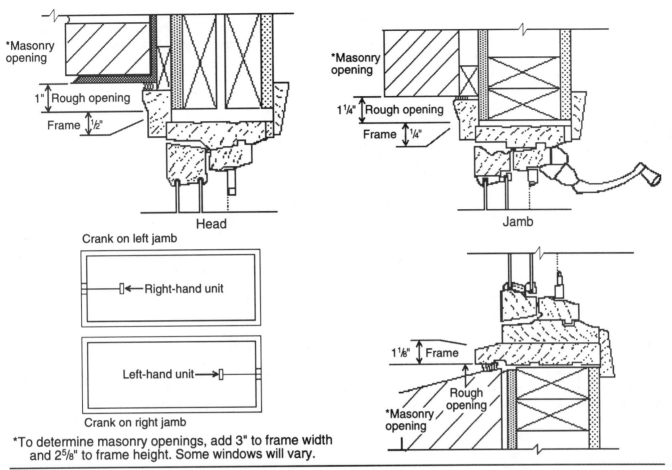

Head

Jamb

Crank on left jamb

Right-hand unit →

Left-hand unit →

Crank on right jamb

*To determine masonry openings, add 3" to frame width and 2⅝" to frame height. Some windows will vary.

Figure 5-28
Installation details showing awning window in brick veneer wall

For window combinations, use the single-unit formulas to combine frame widths and heights. Be sure to add enough space for mullion reinforcement, if necessary. A mullion is a framing member, such as a 2 x 4, installed between adjacent window or door units to separate them. You'll need mullion reinforcement for any window combination where four units meet at a common corner.

Casement and Awning Windows

Casement windows are mounted on the sides of a window frame with hinges that let them swing outward. Awning windows are casement windows that hinge at the top of a frame. Some casement and awning windows rotate almost 180 degrees. Then the outside of the window is as easy to clean as the inside.

Figure 5-28 shows installation details in a 2 x 4 frame, brick veneer construction.

Bay Windows

Many bay windows hang in the shape of a polygon and jut about 2 feet from the house. They can be designed as a projecting window with seats or full-height bays. They are created by pairing three or more windows. Casement bows are windows installed on a radius. Typically, they are made of four or more windows.

A bow or bay window can make interior space seem larger by bringing in more light and giving a broader view than regular picture windows.

Storm Windows

If you put them in correctly, storm windows, such as aluminum frame and screen storm windows that you install permanently, can cut down on a home's energy costs during both summer and winter. Another benefit is that a storm window protects the window behind it, so the homeowner has less painting and general maintenance to do. Storm windows provide a double thickness of glass with a dead air space that helps prevent condensation on the glass surface in cold weather.

Glazing Systems

Glazing is the glass in a window. A double-glazing system may start with two panels of glass, $^{13}/_{16}$ inch apart. The two panels form an air space that's nearly twice as wide as standard insulating glass. Of course, you can also get windows made with standard insulating glass.

You can get windows with tinted glazing which shield against the sun's warmest and brightest rays by reflecting them away from the interior of a home. This really combats solar heat gain, eye-straining glare, faded furnishings, and air-conditioning costs. Compared to uncoated double glass panels, bronze-tinted glass is 79 percent more energy efficient, and it keeps interiors cooler during hot summer days.

You can get low emissivity or "Low-E" glass for cool climates. By allowing the sun's warming rays to enter and reflect radiant heat back into a room, Low-E glass adds to a room's light and comfort. Windows with Low-E cut down on condensation, glare, faded fabrics, and especially, energy costs by much as 57 percent over uncoated double glass panels.

Built-In Shades and Blinds

Built-in shades and blinds are manufactured in double-glazed windows. The shades fit into a $^{13}/_{16}$-inch air space between the exterior glass and a removable double-glazing panel so they aren't subject to dust and damage. Slats tilt to any angle, from open to closed, for control of heat gain or loss, light, glare, and privacy.

Oyster white and dark brown blinds cut heat loss through glass by as much as 62 percent compared to single unshaded glass. They can reduce air-condition-ing costs up to 82 percent by cutting solar heat gain. Some colors hold in interior heat by reflecting it back into a room during winter, and directing outside heat away during summer.

Trusses

If you use roof trusses, you won't need loadbearing interior partitions. Then the interior wall locations will depend on the room size, not the need for support. Use the bottom chord of the trusses to anchor crossing partitions. When the partition walls are located between, and parallel to, trusses, use 2 x 4 blocks nailed between the lower chords to anchor the partition top plate. Trusses are commonly spaced 24 inches on center. You can space studs 16 inches or 24 inches on center.

Fastening Blocks

You need fastening blocks (lath nailers) at all horizontal and vertical fastening points for drywall, plaster-base lath or tile. In other words, all inside corners in the wall and ceiling must have a solid backing to nail finish materials to. Look back to Figure 5-8 for two methods of installing studs where walls intersect.

Figure 5-29 shows three ways to make horizontal lath nailers at a junction of wall and ceiling framing. In section A, double ceiling joist above a wall, space the joists so that each joist provides a nailing base. In section B, a parallel wall is located between two ceiling joists, and the spacing is wider. Here you need to nail a 1 x 6 board to the top plate and space the backing blocks 3 to 4 feet on center. Usually, you can find some 2-by scrap material to use as lath nailers. Fasten the nailers to the top plate with 16d nails.

In a partition wall running at right angles to the ceiling joists, let in 2 x 6 blocks between the joists as shown in Figure 5-29, section C. Nail the blocks to the top plate and toenail to the ceiling joists. Use 2-by scrap material if you have it.

Estimating Studs for Western and Modern Braced Framing

You'll need about the same board feet of stud material for western (platform), modern braced fram-

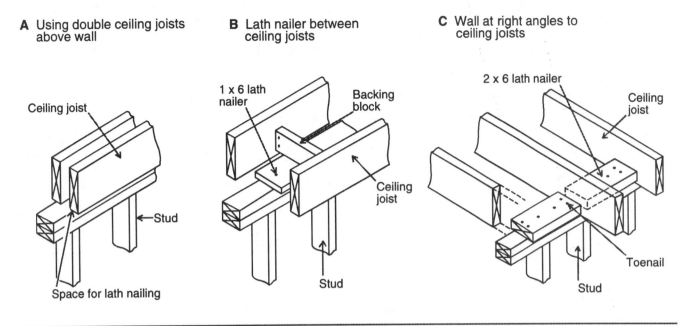

A Using double ceiling joists above wall

Ceiling joist

Stud

Space for lath nailing

B Lath nailer between ceiling joists

1 x 6 lath nailer

Backing block

Ceiling joist

Stud

C Wall at right angles to ceiling joists

2 x 6 lath nailer

Ceiling joist

Toenail

Stud

Figure 5-29
Horizontal lath nailers at junction of wall and ceiling framing

ing and balloon framing. The difference is in the length of the studs. First, measure the linear feet around the outside walls. Then measure the linear feet of partitions running parallel to the joists and the linear feet of partitions running at right angles. If there's a second floor, measure it the same way.

For walls with no openings, you find the number of studs you need by multiplying the length of a wall in feet by 0.75 and then adding one stud. This gives you the number of studs spaced 16 inches on center.

To make it easier, use Figure 5-30 to estimate partition studs. Figure 5-31 gives the board feet per square foot of area, and nails required per 1,000 board feet for all standard stud walls.

For walls with openings, estimate one stud for each linear foot of wall with studs spaced 16 inches on center. This allows for doubled studs at corners and window and door openings.

For the top and bottom plates, multiply the linear feet of all walls and partitions by 2. Multiply the linear feet of all walls by 3 if you use double top plates.

Estimating Studs for Balloon Framing

The exterior wall studs in balloon framing extend from the sill to the top plate of the second story. Figure the partition studs the same way you do for western framing. In balloon framing, you also have to figure full-length studs for double studding at openings. Use shorter lengths under and over openings, including from the top of the first floor window and door openings to the top plate of the second story. To allow for waste, add 10 percent to the stud total.

Balloon framing requires a ribbon. To estimate ribbon requirements, measure the linear feet of the outside walls supporting second-story floor joists. A wall running parallel to the floor joists doesn't need a ribbon. See Figure 5-17.

The stud requirements for MBF, as well as planks and beams for P&B construction, vary widely due to the many different spacings available. Consult the plans to determine material quantities for these framing methods.

Length of partition (feet)	Number of studs required	Length of partition (feet)	Number of studs required
		11	9
2	3	12	10
3	3	13	11
4	4	14	12
5	5	15	12
6	6	16	13
7	6	17	14
8	7	18	15
9	8	19	15
10	9	20	16

Figure 5-30
Partition studs required 16" on center

Exterior-wall studs			
Size of studs	Spacing on center	BF per sq. ft. of area	Nails per 1000 BF (lbs)
2 x 3	12"	.83	30
	16"	.78	
	20"	.74	
	24"	.71	
2 x 4	12"	1.09	22
	16"	1.05	
	20"	.98	
	24"	.94	
2 x 6	12"	1.66	15
	16"	1.51	
	20"	1.44	
	24"	1.38	

Includes an allowance for corner bracing.

Partition studs			
Size of studs	Spacing on center	BF per sq. ft. of area	Nails per 1000 BF (lbs)
2 x 3	12"	.91	25
	16"	.83	
	24"	.76	
2 x 4	12"	1.22	19
	16"	1.12	
	24"	1.02	
2 x 6	16"	1.48	16
	24"	1.22	

Includes an allowance for top and bottom plates, end studs, blocks, backing, framing around openings, and normal waste.

Figure 5-31
Board feet per square foot for wall studs

Estimating Manhours for Studding

It takes 21 skilled and 6 unskilled labor hours to install 1,000 board feet of exterior wall studding (including plates). Partition studding takes 20 skilled and 5 unskilled hours.

Let's see how this works. A 12 x 20 addition with an 8-foot high ceiling and 2 x 4 studs spaced 16 inches on center has 1.05 board feet per square foot of wall area. See Figure 5-31. The square footage of the 20-foot wall is 20 times 8, or 160 SF. For 160 SF of wall area you need 160 times 1.05, or 168 board feet of lumber.

The skilled hours needed will be:

$21 \times 168 \div 1000 = 3\frac{1}{2}$ hours

The unskilled hours needed will be:

$6 \times 168 \div 1000 = 1$ hour

To frame the 20-foot exterior wall will take $3\frac{1}{2}$ skilled and 1 unskilled hours.

A partition with an 8-foot ceiling height and 2 x 4 studs 16 inches on center has 1.12 board feet per square foot of wall area. A 12-foot partition has 96 square feet of wall area. This wall area uses 96 times 1.12, or 108 board feet of lumber, and requires 20 skilled and 5 unskilled hours per 1,000 square feet. The skilled hours to frame the partition are:

$20 \times 108 \div 1000 = 2.2$ hours

The unskilled hours needed are:

$5 \times 108 \div 1000 = 0.5$ hour

So the partition will require 2.2 skilled and 0.5 unskilled hours.

6

Ceiling and Roof Framing

Ceiling and roof framing is precision work. The key to quality is to hire an experienced framer who's familiar with this phase of building to do the work. If you can't find someone like that, learn how to do it yourself — the right way. This chapter will give you the instructions you need to do the job right.

Whether you're framing an entire house or an addition, the procedure is the same. If you install trusses, you're putting up the ceiling and roof framing in one operation. If you build the conventional way — called "stick" building — you install the ceiling and rafter frame separately after you've finished the wall framing. I prefer to "stick" build a ceiling and roof when framing small houses and room additions. In this chapter we'll first look at framing a ceiling. Then we'll go on to framing the roof.

The Ceiling Joists

Ceiling joists run from exterior wall to exterior wall, or from exterior wall to load-bearing interior walls, usually across the shortest dimension of the structure. Ceiling joists lock a structure together, resist the outward thrust of the rafters on pitched roofs, and provide a nailing surface for the finish ceiling.

You'll usually frame a ceiling with joists of 2-by lumber, often 2 x 6s for a one-story structure and 2 x 8s or larger for a two-story structure. The ceiling joist size, of course, depends on the span, the spacing and the kind of wood you use. Most builders space ceiling joists 16 inches on center. Spacing them 24 inches on center is acceptable if you use a wider joist. Just make sure you follow the building code in your area.

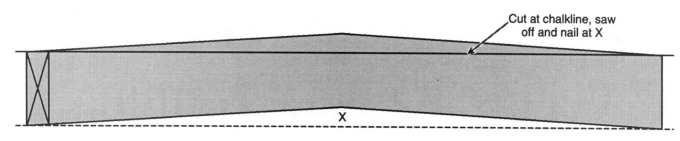

Figure 6-1
Eliminating excess crown

Crowning and Trimming the Joists

When installing floor or ceiling joists, always place the crown (the curved side) of a joist up. A moderate crown, such as $1/4$ inch in 8 feet, is acceptable, but it's best to remove anything more than $1/4$ inch. To remove the excess crown from a joist, first place the joist on your saw bench. Then snap a chalk line the full length of the joist and saw along the line. Finally, tack the waste to the bottom edge of the joist, to avoid possible problems caused by the underside of the joist being uneven. Figure 6-1 shows how to do it.

Before installing the joists, always cut the end of the joist to the angle of the rafter pitch. If you don't, the corner of the joist sitting on top of the exterior wall top plate or cap will stick out above the rafter. Then you'll have to cut it off with a saw or hatchet before you can put on the roof sheathing.

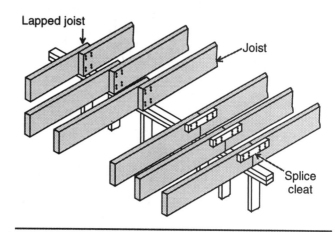

Figure 6-2
Lap or butt joist at load-bearing partition

Installing the Joists

Toenail the joists to the plate at the outer and inner walls with 8d nails. Where joists join at a load-bearing partition, they can either overlap or butt together. If they overlap, spike them together securely at the overlap and toenail to the plate. If they butt, use splice cleats to strengthen the joint. See Figure 6-2.

Nail ceiling joists to rafters at an exterior wall with 16d nails, as shown in Figure 6-3. (Notice that the joists have been trimmed to match the rafter angle.) In high wind areas, anchor joists and rafters to the wall framing with metal straps. If ceiling joists are perpendicular to a rafter run, use collar beams and cross ties on rafters to resist thrust.

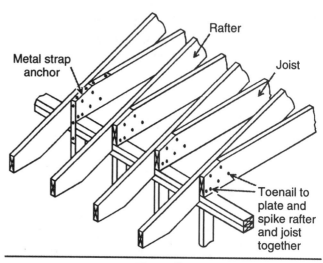

Figure 6-3
Nail ceiling joists to rafters at exterior wall

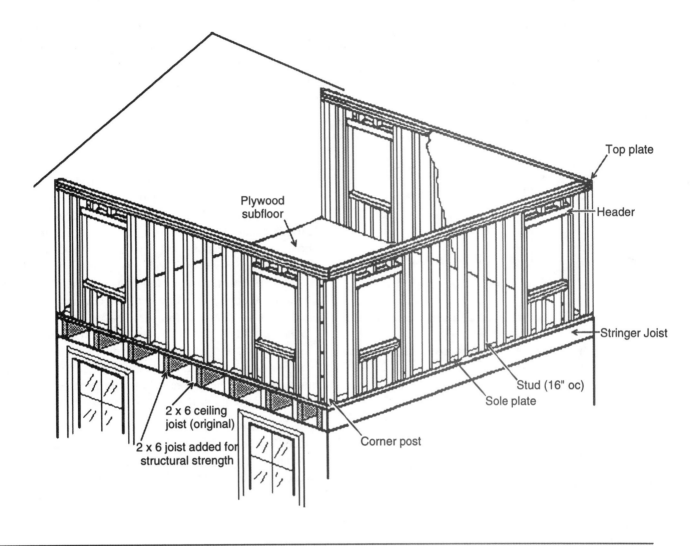

Figure 6-4
Adding a second story after removing roof

Ceiling Joists for a Second-Story Addition

Building a second-story addition takes careful planning. You have to remove the existing roofing, sheathing, and rafters, then protect the first floor ceiling and contents from the weather. That means there's always pressure to get the job done quickly. That's why some builders say that if there's one job where everything conspires to ruin you, it's adding a second-story addition. It's more than likely that one of your crew will accidentally drop a hammer or 2 x 4 through the first floor ceiling or break a window. Although I don't enjoy adding second-floor additions to occupied homes, I've never refused a job, because it's high-profit work.

The ceiling joists of the original first floor become the floor joists for the second-floor addition. Depending on the span of the joists, you can usually double the joists with 2 x 6s as shown in Figure 6-4 to support the load. Place the 2 x 6 adjacent to the existing joist and toenail with 8d nails to the top plate and face nail to the joist with 12d or 16d nails staggered 24 inches on center.

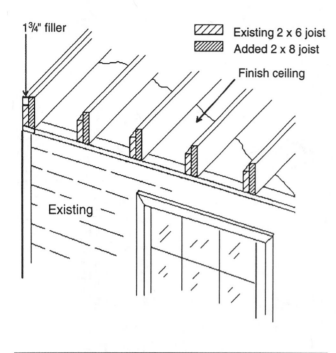

1¾" filler

▨ Existing 2 x 6 joist
▧ Added 2 x 8 joist

Finish ceiling

Existing

Figure 6-5
Reinforcing first-floor ceiling joists for a second-floor addition

If doubling the joists with same-size members won't carry the load, add a wider 2-by such as a 2 x 8 or 2 x 10 (depending on the span) as shown in Figure 6-5. This won't disturb the ceiling finish of the first floor. Figure 6-6 is a sample span table for Southern pine floor joists. But make sure to check the span tables in your local code to find the joist size that's right for your job. And be careful when doubling a joist that you don't damage any electrical lines or insulation.

Figure 6-7 shows minimum ceiling heights for an attic conversion, exposed-beam ceiling or vaulted ceiling. Unless you have the plans for the home you're adding to, physical measurement of the house is the only sure way to determine the height between all major components.

Installing a Flush Beam

Sometimes you'll want a continuous flush ceiling over a large span, such as in a large, open room addition. In this case, use a flush beam to replace a load-bearing partition. Use a nail-laminated beam with suf-

ficient load-carrying capacity to support the ends of the joists. Toenail the joists to the beam and support them with metal joist hangers, wood hangers, or a ledger. You can also use a flush beam to support both joists and rafters. All of these methods are shown in Figure 6-8.

Post and Beam Framing

A low-pitched or flat roof is often used on a post and beam framed house. It may have a conventional rafter-joist combination, or thick wood decking spanning between the beams. You can use a solid or spaced post and beam as support for the sole plate and roof beam. Figure 6-9 shows both a solid and a spaced post and beam. You fasten the solid post and beam together with metal angles nailed to the top plate, the sole plate, and the roof beam. Fasten the spaced beam and post together with ⅜-inch or thicker plywood cleats extending between, and nailed to, the spaced members. You can fasten a wall-header member between beams with joist hangers. These connections are necessary to keep the roof from blowing off during high winds.

If you use a continuous header between spaced posts, fasten the beams well and reinforce them at the corners with lag screws or metal straps as shown in Figure 6-10. Predrill pilot holes when you use lag screws so you don't split any members.

Planning the Roof

Now, let's look at the some of the basic parts of a roof. Rafters are the basic framing members for all pitched roofs. There are several types of rafters — common, jack, hip and valley, for example. Rafters support the sheathing and roof covering material.

The *run* of a rafter is measured horizontally from the outside of the wall plate to the point directly under the ridge board. This distance is one-half the span of the roof. See Figure 6-11.

The *rise* of a rafter is measured vertically from the top of the wall plate to where the measuring line (shown by the dotted line in Figure 6-11) meets the ridge board.

Size and spacing (inches)	Inches oc	Dense Sel Str KD and No. 1 Dense KD	Dense Sel Str, Sel Str KD, No. 1 Dense and No. 1 KD	Sel Str, No. 1 and No. 2 Dense KD	No. 2 Dense, No. 2 KD and No. 2	No. 3 Dense KD	No. 3 Dense	No. 3 KD	No. 3
2 x 5	12.0	10-3	10-0	9-10	9-8	**9-3**	**8-11**	**8-6**	**8-3**
	13.7	9-9	9-7	9-5	9-3	**8-7**	**8-4**	**8-0**	**7-9**
	16.0	9-3	9-1	8-11	8-9	**8-0**	**7-9**	**7-5**	**7-2**
	19.2	8-9	8-7	8-5	8-3	**7-3**	**7-1**	**6-9**	**6-6**
	24.0	8-1	8-0	7-10	7-8	**6-6**	**6-4**	**6-0**	**5-10**
2 x 6	12.0	12-6	12-3	12-0	11-10	**11-3**	**10-11**	**10-5**	**10-1**
	13.7	11-11	11-9	11-6	11-3	**10-6**	**10-3**	**9-9**	**9-5**
	16.0	11-4	11-2	10-11	10-9	**9-9**	**9-6**	**9-0**	**8-9**
	19.2	10-8	10-6	10-4	10-1	**8-11**	**8-8**	**8-3**	**8-0**
	24.0	9-11	9-9	9-7	9-4	**8-0**	**7-9**	**7-4**	**7-1**
2 x 8	12.0	16-6	16-2	15-10	15-7	**14-10**	**14-5**	**13-9**	**13-3**
	13.7	15-9	15-6	15-2	14-11	**13-11**	**13-6**	**12-10**	**12-5**
	16.0	15-0	14-8	14-5	14-2	**12-10**	**12-6**	**11-11**	**11-6**
	19.2	14-1	13-10	13-7	13-4	**11-9**	**11-5**	**10-10**	**10-6**
	24.0	13-1	12-10	12-7	12-4	**10-6**	**10-2**	**9-9**	**9-5**
2 x 10	12.0	21-0	20-8	20-3	19-10	**18-11**	**18-5**	**17-6**	**16-11**
	13.7	20-1	19-9	19-4	19-0	**17-9**	**17-2**	**16-5**	**15-10**
	16.0	19-1	18-9	18-5	18-0	**16-5**	**15-11**	**15-2**	**14-8**
	19.2	18-0	17-8	17-4	17-0	**15-0**	**14-6**	**13-10**	**13-5**
	24.0	16-8	16-5	16-1	15-9	**13-5**	**13-0**	**12-5**	**12-0**
2 x 12	12.0	25-7	25-1	24-8	24-2	**23-0**	**22-4**	**21-4**	**20-7**
	13.7	24-5	24-0	23-7	23-1	**21-7**	**20-11**	**19-11**	**19-3**
	16.0	23-3	22-10	22-5	21-11	**19-11**	**19-4**	**18-6**	**17-10**
	19.2	21-10	21-6	21-1	20-8	**18-3**	**17-8**	**16-10**	**16-3**
	24.0	20-3	19-11	19-7	19-2	**16-3**	**15-10**	**15-1**	**14-7**

Floor Joists — *30 psf live load. Sleeping rooms and attic floors. (Spans shown in light face type are based on a deflection limitaion of L/360. Spans shown in bold face type are limited by the recommended extreme fiber stress in bending value of the grade and includes a 10 psf dead load.)*

Figure 6-6
Southern pine floor joists — sample span table

A Attic conversion

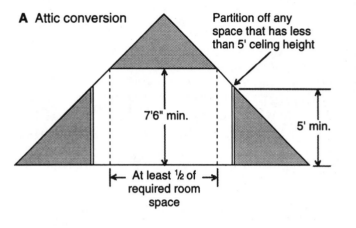

B Exposed-beam ceiling

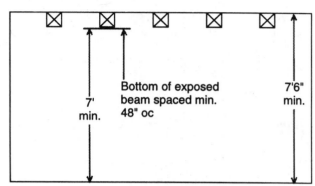

C Vaulted ceiling

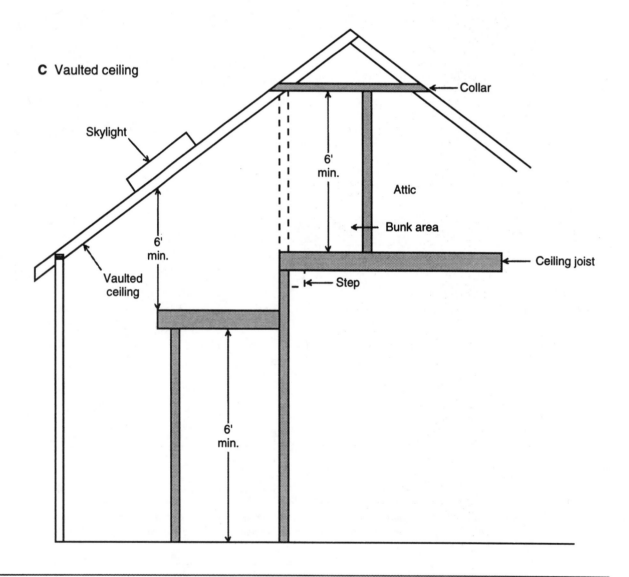

Figure 6-7
Required ceiling heights

A Metal joist hanger

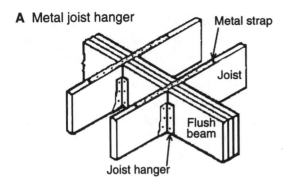

B Wood joist hanger

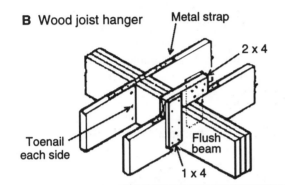

C Two 2 x 12s form the beam

Figure 6-8
Flush ceiling framing

A Solid roof beam

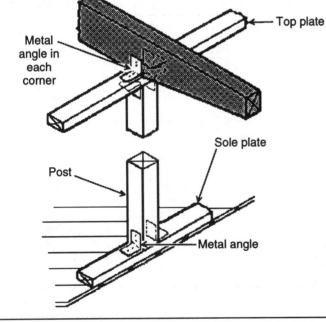

B Spaced roof beam

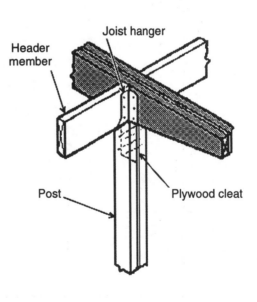

Figure 6-9
Post and beam framing

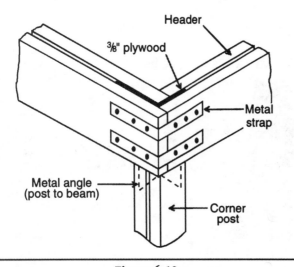

Figure 6-10
Post and beam corner connection with continuous header

The *roof overhang*, which is also called the *eaves* or *rafter tails*, is the lower end of a rafter that extends beyond the building line. You have to add its length to the calculated length of the rafter to find the actual length. If the plans and specs don't detail the finish for the overhang of a roof rafter, you must decide what design to use. If rafter ends will be enclosed by a cornice, you'll have to cut the ends accordingly.

Start with Roof Pitch

The pitch of a roof is usually expressed as the number or inches of vertical rise in 12 inches of run. The rise is given first. For example, 6 in 12 means that the roof rises 6 inches in each 12 inches of horizontal run, as shown in Figure 6-11.

Another way of describing the pitch of a roof is the slant, or slope, from the ridge board to the wall plate. Because this slope changes if the rise (height of ridge board) or span changes, it's expressed as the ratio of the rise to the span. For example, a "$\frac{1}{3}$ pitch" roof means the rise is $\frac{1}{3}$ of the span, and "$\frac{1}{4}$ pitch" means that the rise is $\frac{1}{4}$ of the span. See Figure 6-15. To figure out the pitch of a roof, use the ratio of rise/span. For example, in Figure 6-11, the rise is 4 feet and the span 16 feet. The ratio of these measurements is $\frac{4}{16}$ or $\frac{1}{4}$ pitch.

The overall *rafter length* usually includes the overhang, as shown in Figure 6-12.

The *roof span* is the distance between the outer faces of the wall plates that support the rafters. In a gable roof with a centered ridge, the span is twice the run of a rafter. Figures 6-12, 6-13, and 6-14 show run, rise, and span for different types of roofs.

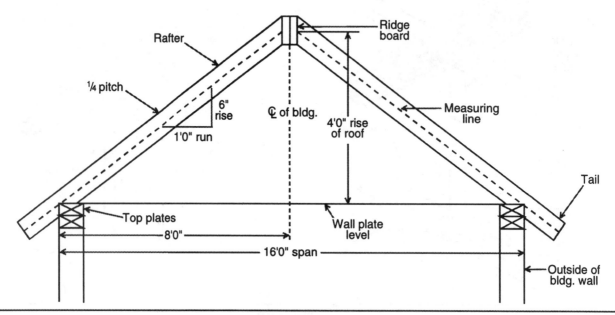

Figure 6-11
Roof definitions

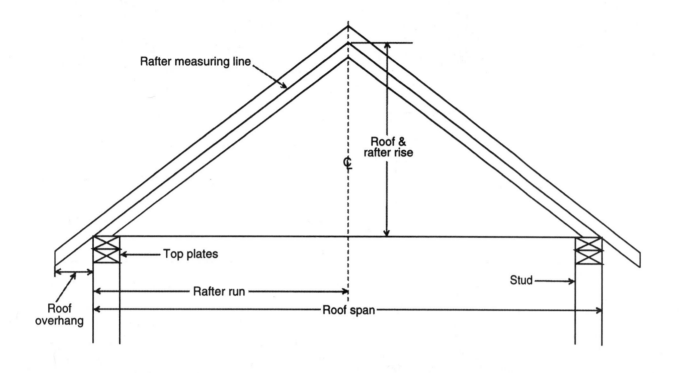

Figure 6-12
Rise and run of rafter — gable roof

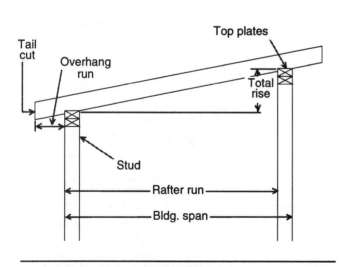

Figure 6-13
Shed roof details — rafter rise and run

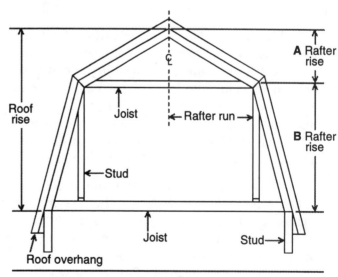

Figure 6-14
Rise and run of rafter — gambrel roof

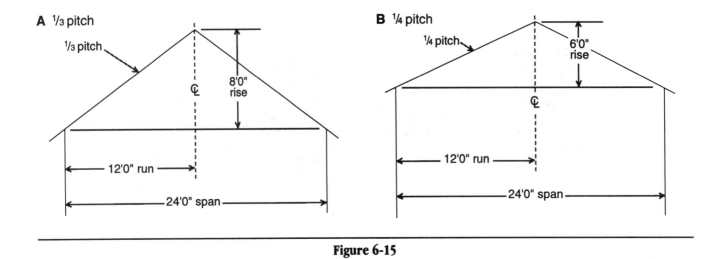

Figure 6-15
Roof pitch

Figure 6-16 shows the common roof pitches and a steel square (also called a carpenter's square or framing square). The square's body (the blade) is up and the figures on it represent inches of rise on a roof. The tongue of the square is horizontal, and the 12 on it represents 1 foot of run. For example, 6 inches on the body would be a 6 in 12 roof, or a ¼ pitch. A little later we'll learn how to use the square to lay out a rafter.

Roof Slopes for Add-on Rooms

The slope of the roof of the existing house will usually dictate the slope of the roof for your addition. A compatible roof line is essential if you don't want your room addition to look "tacked on." As a room addition contractor you're expected to know how to plan, frame, and tie-in the addition as one complete unit. Figure 6-17 shows one way to add an addition to a house with a smooth transition in the roof lines.

Climate, materials, buyer's preferences, and trends affect roof slopes and styles. For example, you can use asphalt strip shingles on roofs as low as 3 in 12. Generally, wood shingles perform well only on 5 in 12 or steeper slopes, but by doubling the underlay and decreasing the exposure distance of wood, you can use wood shingles on lesser slopes, even down to 3 in 12.

Flat Roofs

Flat roofs are often called shed or single-construction roofs. Figure 6-18 show two such roofs. A flat roof has one kind of member that provides both roof and ceiling support. In other words, the rafter and joist are the same piece. Flat roofs require larger-size mem-

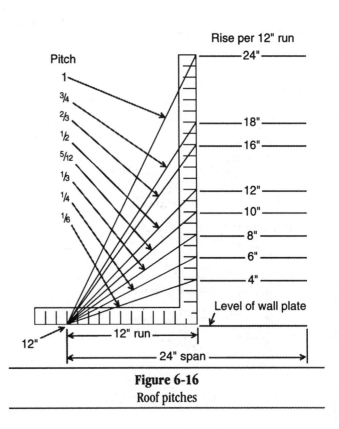

Figure 6-16
Roof pitches

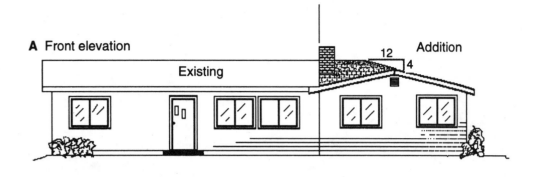

A Front elevation

Existing

12
4

Addition

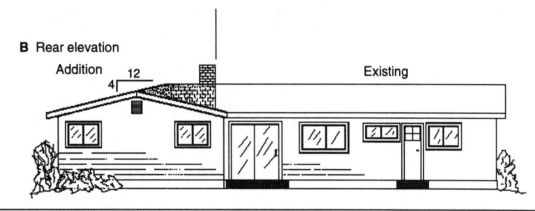

B Rear elevation

Addition

12
4

Existing

Figure 6-17
Plan addition roof lines carefully

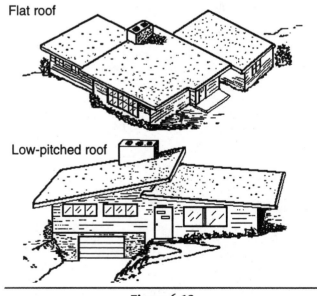

Flat roof

Low-pitched roof

Figure 6-18
Single-construction roofs

bers than roofs with a steeper pitch because they carry both roof and ceiling loads.

Install the roof decking directly on the joists and apply the finish ceiling to the underside. The joists for these flat roofs may be dead level, or have a slight pitch. I recommend tapering or notching the joists to fit lower on the top plate of the back wall so the roof has a slight slope for drainage. That keeps water from forming puddles on the roof.

Note in Figure 6-18 that ample overhang beyond the walls is part of the shed roof design. Figure 6-19 shows how to make an overhang on all sides of a flat roof. Nail lookout rafters to a double header and toe-nail them to the wall plate with 8d nails. The distance from the double header to the wall line is usually twice the overhang. Add a nailing header to the rafter ends to attach the soffit and fascia boards.

A Side and end overhang of less than 3'

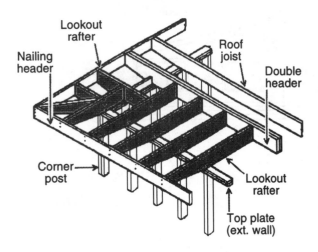

B Side and end overhang of more than 3'

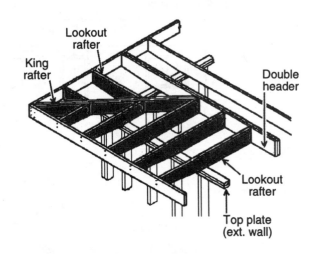

Figure 6-19
Construction details of low-pitched or flat roofs

Regardless of the type of soffit, be sure to provide ventilation between the insulation and roof decking between each rafter so moisture can escape. That reduces winter condensation problems.

Pitched Roofs

In pitched roofs, both ceiling joists and rafters are required. If you install roof trusses, the truss has a rafter and a ceiling joist.

Figure 6-20 A shows a simple gable roof. Both rafters and ceiling joists are required to form the attic space under the roof. Cut all rafters to the same length and pattern. Nail each 2 x 6 rafter at the top to a 1 x 8 or 2 x 8 ridge board. A 2-inch-thick ridge board adds extra support and provides a nailing area for each rafter end.

Figure 6-20 B is a variation of the gable roof. This is basically a one-story house since the majority of the rafters rest on the first floor top plate. Slopes for this type of roof must be from 9 in 12 to 12 in 12 to provide headroom in the second story. This Cape Cod style provides the maximum living space for the material used.

A hip roof is shown in Figure 6-20 C. Hip roofs eliminate the gable ends. Many do-it-yourself home-

A Gable roof

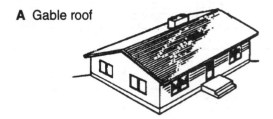

B Gable roof with dormers

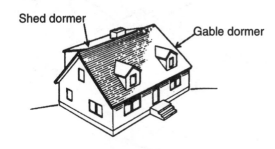

C Hip roof

Figure 6-20
Types of pitched roofs

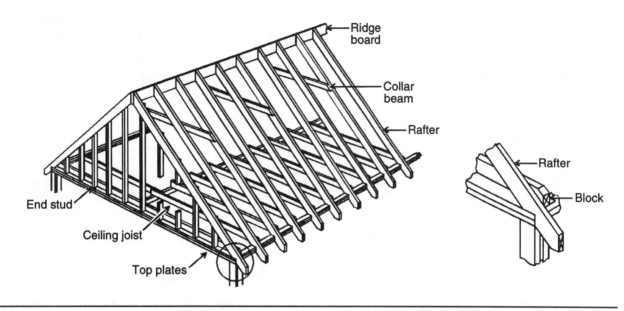

Figure 6-21
Overall view of gable roof framing

owners like this type of roof because they don't have to climb high ladders to paint and maintain the fascia. In hip roof construction, you secure the center rafters to the ridge board. Hip rafters support the shorter jack rafters. Carry the cornice lines around the perimeter of the house.

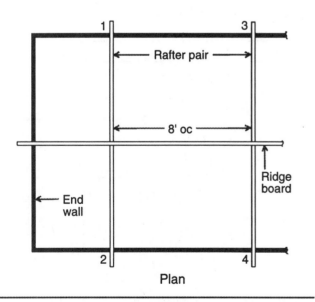

Figure 6-22
Begining rafter erection

Pitched-Roof Construction

In pitched-roof construction, nail the ceiling joists in place after the interior and exterior wall framing is done. Rafters are usually precut to length, with angles cut at the ridge and eave, and notches cut for the top plate. See Figure 6-21. No. 2 grade wood is normally adequate for rafters and most species of softwood framing lumber are acceptable for roof framing. But you need to stay within the limits of the span table for the species of wood you use. There are detailed instructions for figuring and cutting rafters later in this chapter.

Put up rafters in pairs or in pair groups as shown in Figure 6-22. Rafters 1 and 2 support each other, and 3 and 4 support each other. A crew of two can begin rafter installation by nailing rafters 1 and 3 to the horizontal ridge board, using the top of the ceiling joists as a platform. One framer can then raise the ridge board into position while the other tacks the ends of rafters 1 and 3 at the top plate. Then they tack rafters 2 and 4 at the plate with their peak ends resting against the ridge board. When the nailing is complete, the entire system is solidly supported. Then it's a simple matter to fill in the intermediate rafters in pairs to complete the rafter installation.

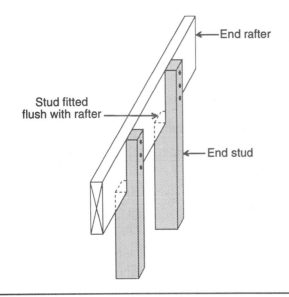

Figure 6-23
Fitting gable end studs to end rafter

Cut the studs for gable end walls to fit, and nail them to the end rafters and the top plate of the end wall as shown in Figure 6-23. With a gable overhang, you have a fly (or floating) rafter that goes out beyond the end rafter as shown in Figure 6-24. Nail this fly rafter to the lookout rafters and roof sheathing.

Another way to support a fly rafter is shown in Figure 6-25. Here, you extend the ridge board and the bottom member of the top plate of the side wall to fit flush with and support the outside edge of the fly rafter.

Some builders rely on the roof decking alone to support a fly rafter but I don't consider this good construction practice. There's too much chance of the roof beyond the gable sagging.

Hip Roof Construction

If the addition you're building will have a hip roof, leave off the first joist at the end wall to allow for the rafter run. In low-pitch hip roofs, you may also have to leave off the second joist. In this case, you can use a stub joist at the end wall as shown in Figure 6-26.

The middle of a hip roof is framed like a gable roof. But at the ends, you'll install hip rafters which extend from each outside corner of the wall to the ridge board at a 45-degree angle. Extend jack rafters

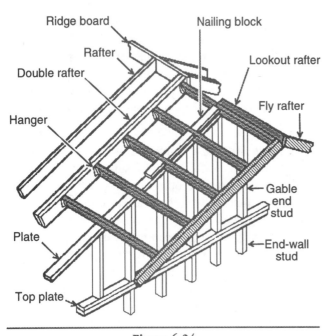

Figure 6-24
Gable overhang construction details

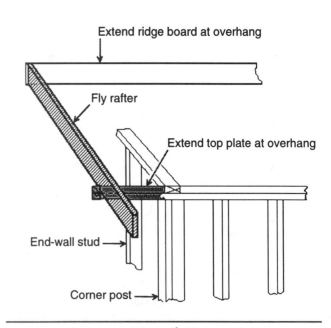

Figure 6-25
Alternate gable overhang construction

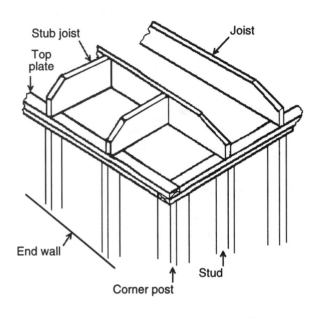

Figure 6-26
Hip roof framing

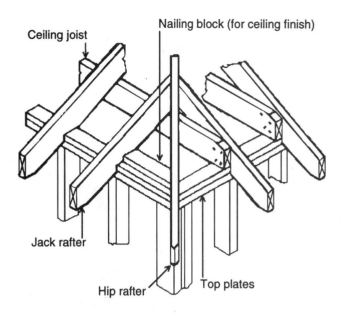

Figure 6-27
Construction details for a hip roof corner

from the top plates to the hip rafters as shown in Figure 6-27.

Use 2 x 4 collar beams between opposing rafters if the roof span is long or the slope is flat. Nail them to each rafter with four 16d nails. (Figure 6-21). For steep slopes and shorter spans, use 1 x 6s as collar beams. Nail them with 8d nails on every third pair of rafters. In 1½-story houses, use 2 x 4s as collars at each pair of rafters. The collars also serve as ceiling joists for the finished rooms.

Valleys and Dormers

A valley is the internal angle formed where two sloping roof surfaces meet. A valley rafter forms the bottom of a valley. When two equal-size roof sections come together, use double valley rafters that are 2 inches deeper than the common rafters. These extra inches will provide full contact with the jack rafters. Nail jack rafters to the ridge and toenail to the valley rafter with three 10d nails. Figure 6-28 shows valley framing.

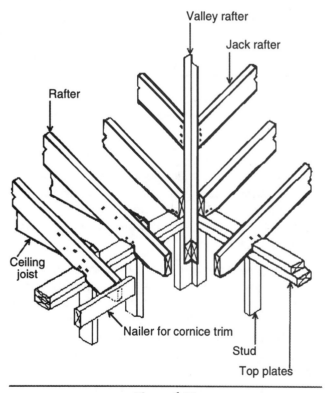

Figure 6-28
Construction details for a hip roof valley

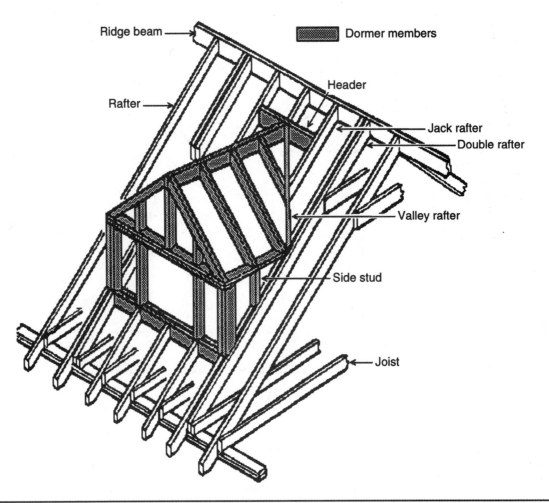

Ridge beam
Dormer members
Header
Rafter
Jack rafter
Double rafter
Valley rafter
Side stud
Joist

Figure 6-29
Dormer framing technique

Dormers can provide a lot of space when you convert an attic to living space. They can also help an addition to blend in with the style of the existing house. We'll cover attic conversion using dormers in detail in a later chapter.

For now, let's just take a look at framing for a dormer, since it's part of framing the roof (Figure 6-29). Double the rafters at each side of the dormer. The side studs and the short valley rafters rest on these members. Or you can carry the side studs past a doubled rafter to bear on a sole plate nailed to the floor framing and the subfloor. You can use this type of framing for the side walls of shed dormers. Look back to Figure 6-20, part B. Tie the valley rafter to the roof framing with a header.

Calculating Rafter Length

There's no place for guesswork in rafter construction. It takes exact measurements and precise cutting to make sure the rafters will fit properly. In the rest of this chapter, we'll go through each step for measuring, cutting, and fitting rafters for hip and gable roofs.

The bird's eye view of a plan with intersecting hip roofs shown in Figure 6-30 will give you a better understanding of how the pieces fit together.

Figure 6-31 shows how to find the intersection of the hip rafters with the ridge board at point B. Notice that distance AB is equal to BC. Line DB, the diagonal of the square ABCD, shows the run of the hip rafter.

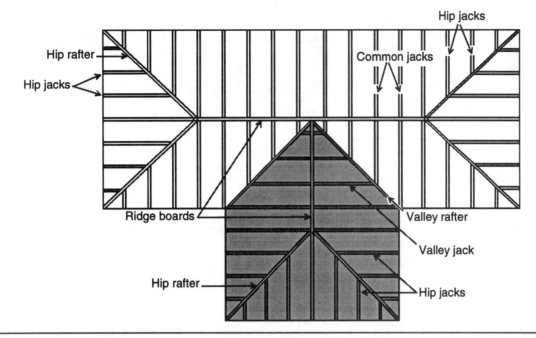

Figure 6-30
Plan view of intersecting hip roofs

In regular hip roof construction, the length of the ridge is the building length minus the building width. Let's see how this works. Say you're building a 40-foot-long addition with a regular hip roof. The room is 20 feet wide. What's the length of the ridge?

$$Ridge = length - width$$
$$= 40' - 20'$$
$$= 20'$$

Now there are several ways you can figure out the length of the rafters. One of the simplest is to use the rafter table on a framing square, like the one shown in Figure 6-32. If you know the rise, you can find the length of the rafter. Assume the pitch is 8 in 12, which is 8 inches of rise for each foot of run. Below the 8-inch mark on the body of the square is the "Length Common Rafters Per Foot Run." (In this case it's 14.42 inches.) The next line, "Length Hip or Valley Rafter Per Foot Run," reads 18.76 inches.

The run for the common rafter in line AB, Figure 6-31, is 10 feet. To find the common rafter length, multiply the per-foot run (14.42 inches) by 10 feet (the run).

$$14.42" \times 10' = 144.2" = 12.01'$$

The hip rafter (line BD, Figure 6-31) runs at a 45-degree angle to the sides of the building. It's longer than the common rafters because of the extra distance

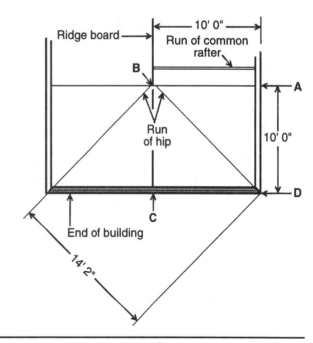

Figure 6-31
Finding the hip rafter length

Figure 6-32
Rafter table

from the corner of the building to the center of the span. From the framing square, take the second figure under the 8-inch mark, 18.76 inches, and multiply by 10 feet (the run of the common rafter).

$$18.76" \times 10' = 187.6" = 15.633' = 15'7\tfrac{5}{8}"$$

These lengths for the common and hip rafters are the *mathematical lengths*: the length from the outside edge of the wall plate to the center of the ridge board. You find the *actual length* by subtracting half the thickness of the ridge board that the rafter butts against, and adding the length of the overhang. That's the true length of the rafter along the measuring line.

You can use your square to find the approximate length of a common rafter without referring to the rafter table. The rise of the rafter (in feet) is represented on the tongue of the square. The run (in feet) is represented on the body. Measure the length of the diago-

nal between these two points. This measurement, expressed in feet, is the rough length of the rafter.

For example, assume that the total rise of a rafter is 9 feet and the run is 12 feet. Find 9 and 12 on the square, as shown in Figure 6-33, and measure the diagonal. This will be 15 feet. If there's a cornice overhang, add the overhang length. If the overhang will be 12 inches, you'll need 16-foot stock.

Calculating the Cuts on Rafters

There are several ways to find the cuts on rafters. Each of the three common methods (the graphic, the rafter table, and the step-off) works well. The graphic method is often preferred by draftsmen because they can make the layout with drafting instruments.

If you're a carpenter, you'll find the rafter table or step-off method convenient because you lay out the work with your framing square. Regardless of which method you use, you can check your work using the rafter tables printed on the framing square.

Lay out all rafters in the same relative position to avoid confusion. Crown each board by sighting along it to find the slight bow, or crown, near the middle of the board. The rafter will be stronger if the crowned edge is up. Hold the board with the crowned (top) edge toward you.

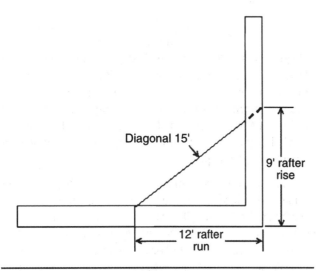

Figure 6-33
Finding rough length of rafter

Laying Out a Common Rafter Using the Step-Off Method

Hold the tongue (short leg) of the steel square in your left hand and the body (long leg) in your right

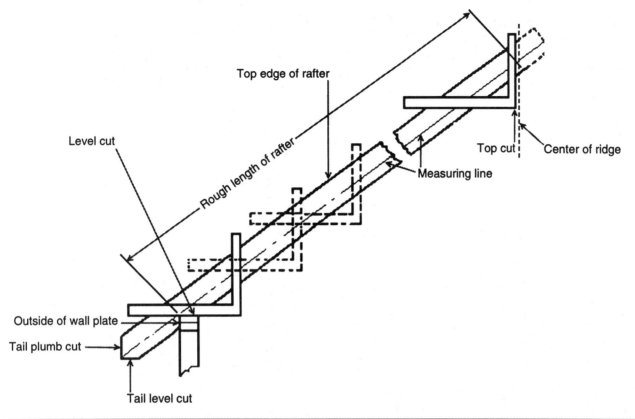

Figure 6-34
Common rafter lay-out — step-off method

hand. This way, the tongue will form the vertical, or top, cut of the rafter and the body will form the level, or seat cut, as shown in Figure 6-34.

Locating the Measuring Line on a Rafter

Make the first rafter, which you'll use as a pattern, out of straight stock of the correct rough length. Lay this piece flat across two sawhorses and place the square near the right-hand end, leaving enough stock on the right for the overhang. See Figure 6-35.

Place the 12-inch mark on the outside edge of the body (representing the run of the roof), and the appropriate inch mark on the outside edge of the tongue (representing the rise of the roof) at the top edge of the rafter. See points A and F of Figure 6-35. Draw the line AB on the rafter to mark the top of the wall plate. Then measure $3\frac{5}{8}$ inches along this line, from B to C, to find the outside top corner of the plate. Make sure it's far enough from the right end of the rafter to allow

for the tail (overhang). Then gauge the measuring line (CD) parallel to the edge of the rafter and mark it with a chalk line.

When using the step-off method to lay out a rafter, it helps to fasten a wooden fence or small metal clamps to the tongue and body of the square. The fence is merely a guide made with a straight 1 x 2 board at least 32 inches long and clamped to the square. Or you can use $\frac{1}{2}$ x 2-inch plywood. We'll use a fence in our examples. But many skilled carpenters don't bother with the fence. They carefully place the square at each step.

Let's do an example, based on a building 24 feet wide. The slope of the rafter will be 9 in 12. To find the exact length of the rafter, lay the square on the stock so the 12-inch mark on the outside of the body is at point C, as in Figure 6-36. Put the 9-inch mark on the outside edge of the tongue on the measuring line at E. It's important that these two marks are exactly on the measuring line for the next step.

131

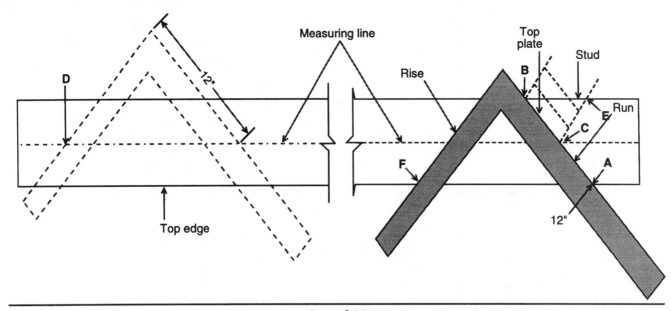

Figure 6-35
Locating rafter measuring line

Put the fence against the rafter stock, as shown at the far right of Figure 6-36. Keep the square from moving and adjust the fence so its edge lies against the top edge of the rafter. Tighten the fence on the square. Mark along the outside edges of the square's tongue and body. Find point E on the measuring line. Slide the square to the left until the 12-inch mark is over E (position 2 on Figure 6-36) and again mark along the tongue and body. Do this as many times as there are feet of run for the rafter (12 in this case). The successive positions of the square are shown by the numbers 1 through 12 on Figure 6-36.

When you get to the last position, draw a line along the tongue across the rafter to mark the centerline of the ridge board. Do each step in this process

carefully, and make all marks clearly. It just takes a small mistake to make your cut rafter useless.

Laying Out a Rafter for an Odd Span

Assume that the building span is an odd number, say 25 feet wide. The slope of the rafter is 9 in 12. The run of the rafter will be half the width of the building, or 12'6".

You lay out this rafter the same as the one just described, except that at the end you'll take an extra half step for the added 6 inches of the rafter. After marking the twelfth step, put the square on the top edge of the rafter as shown in Figure 6-37. Now move the square until the 6 on the outside of the body is

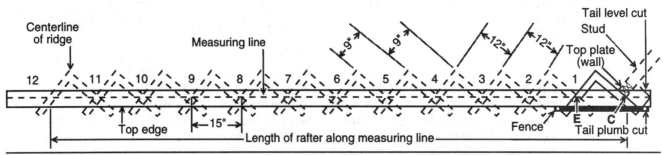

Figure 6-36
Laying out a common rafter (step-off method)

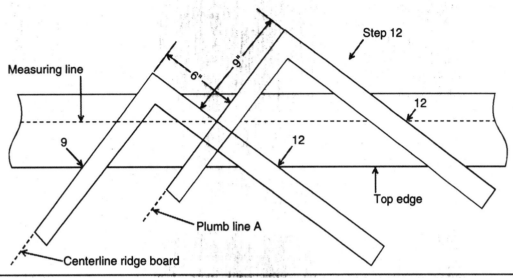

Figure 6-37
Additional half-step

right over line A from step 12. Draw a line along the outside edge of the tongue. This line shows the centerline of the ridge board.

Allowing for the Ridge Board

The last line marked on the rafter shows where to cut the rafter if all rafters will be butted against each other without a ridge board. Since most roofs have a ridge board, the rafter you just laid out will be too long by half the thickness of the ridge board.

To lay out the actual cutting line, as shown in Figure 6-38, measure half the thickness of the ridge board at a right angle to the last line (position 12 in Figure 6-36). Then slide the square back for this distance. Keep the fence tight against the rafter. Mark the plumb cut along the edge of the tongue. This line should be inside of, and parallel to, the original line marking the end of the rafter.

Cutting the Rafter

The *bottom cut*, or *seat cut*, of the rafter (often called the *birdsmouth*) is a combination of level and plumb cuts. The level cut (line BC, Figure 6-35) rests on the top face of the side wall plate. The plumb cut (CE) fits against the outside edge of the wall plate.

Lay out the plumb cut by squaring a line from line AB, Figure 6-35, through point C. This line CE represents the plumb cut.

How to Cut the Tail

If the rafter tail is like the one shown in Figure 6-34, make the plumb cut along the measuring line as shown. Find the level cut at the end of the tail by sliding the square toward the tail. Mark the rafter where the body crosses both the plumb and measuring line.

For a box cornice as shown in Figure 6-39, you have to cut the rafter tail differently. Lay out the level and plumb cuts as before. Then allow for the thickness of the sheathing, since it extends into the rafter notch up to the top of the plate. To do this, lay out line AB parallel to line CD. Make it the thickness of the sheathing away from CD. Then extend the line of the level cut at D to meet AB. The rafter will now fit over the plate and sheathing.

If a 12-inch piece will be used at E, continue the line of the level cut through B to F on the top edge of the rafter. Lay the body of the square along this line. Put the 12-inch mark of the outside edge directly over point B. Mark a line GH along the outer edge of the tongue across the rafter. The tip of the rafter is at the spot where this line meets the measuring line at H. Square the line HJ across the rafter from line GH to locate J.

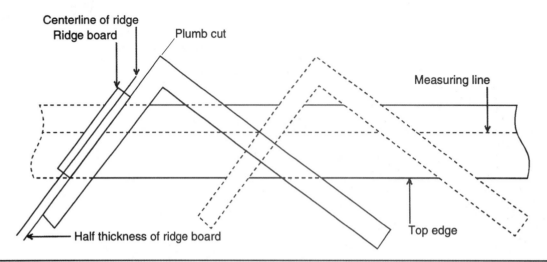

Figure 6-38
Allowance for ridge board

Applying the Roof Sheathing

After you nail the rafters in place, the next step is to apply the roof sheathing. The sheathing must be thick enough to carry the weight of the finish roofing between supports. Plywood or oriented strand board (OSB) is the most common kind of sheathing. Lay plywood or OSB panels so the long dimension is perpendicular to the rafters. Figure 6-40 shows how to apply the panels. Make end joints over the center of the rafter and stagger them by at least one rafter. Standard sheathing-grade panels are usually specified. In areas like open soffits, use interior grade with exterior glue. Then protect the edges against weather with metal drip cap at rake and eaves.

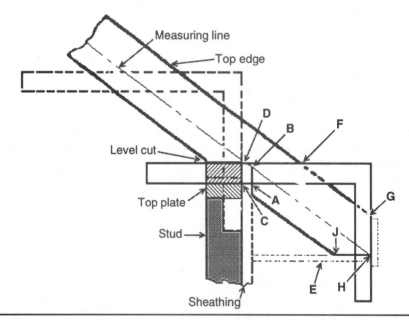

Figure 6-39
Tail cut for a box cornice

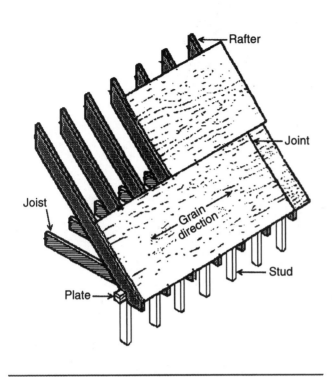

Figure 6-40
Installing plywood or OSB roof sheathing

Plywood thickness (inches)[2]	Plywood panel identification index[1]	Maximum span (inches)[3,4]
5/16	12/0	12
5/16	16/0	16
5/16	20/0	20
3/8	24/0	24
5/8	30/12	30
1/2	32/16	32
3/4	36/16	36
5/8	42/20	42
3/4	48/24	48

Notes:
(1) Applies to Standard, Structural I and II, and C-C grades only confroming to U.S. Commerce Dept. PS 1-66.
(2) Use 6d common smooth, ring-shank, or spiral-thread nails for 1/2-inch thick or less, and 8d common or 8d ring-shank or sprial-thread for plywood 1-inch thick or less.
(3) These spans shall not be exceeded for any load conditions.
(4) Provide adequate blocking, tongue-and-groove edges, or other suitable edge support such as metal fasteners. Use two metal fasteners for 48-inch or greater spans.

Figure 6-41
Plywood sheathing spans

Nail panels at each bearing, 6 inches on center along all edges and 12 inches on center along intermediate members. Unless the panels have an exterior glue line, the raw edges shouldn't be exposed to the weather at the gable end (rake) or at the cornice. Protect the edges with the trim or metal drip cap. Leave 1/8-inch edge spacing and 1/16-inch end spacing.

Apply 1/2-inch-thick plywood panels over rafters spaced 16 inches on center to make a solid decking for roofs covered with asphalt shingles, wood shingles, and shakes. Figure 6-41 shows allowable spans for plywood sheathing.

Sheathing with Solid Wood Decking

Instead of plywood, you might use 2-inch-thick wood roof planking or fiberboard roof decking on some flat or low-pitched roofs with post and beam construction. You can use 2-inch wood planking on spans up to 8 feet. Fiberboard decking 2 to 3 inches thick is limited to beam or purlin spacing of 4 feet. Face nail 2-by or fiberboard decking to beams, using only square-end-trimmed decking to insure a proper fit. Apply fiberboard or an expanded foamed plastic, in sheet form, to decking before you install it to increase the roof insulation.

Tongue-and-groove solid wood decking, such as the 3 x 6 or 4 x 6 sizes, is the best decking for post and beam construction when beams are spaced 8 to 10 feet. It's extremely important that you nail this solid wood properly. Toenail and face-nail the members directly to the beams. In addition, edge-nail the members to each other with long nails that you drive into predrilled holes. See Figure 6-42.

Experienced builders know that using wood with excessive moisture in it can create serious problems. Wood decking should have a moisture content of about 15 percent to keep joints from opening later. The greener the wood when you install it, the wider the joints will be when it dries.

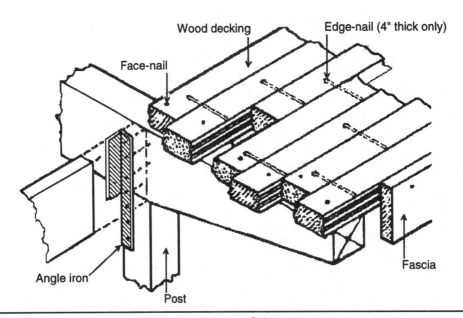

Figure 6-42
Post and beam framing with roof decking

Estimating Materials and Manhours

Figure 6-43 shows manhour estimates for joists, rafters and plywood roof sheathing.

Estimating Joists

Labor for framing ceiling joists and rafters is usually based on the board feet of lumber used. Suppose you're adding a 12 x 20 room. A 20-foot room will require 16 joists (20 x .75, plus 1). A 2 x 6 joist 12 feet long contains 12 board feet. The 16 joists contain a total of 192 board feet. It takes about 18 skilled and 7 unskilled manhours to install 1,000 board feet of 2 x 6 ceiling joists. Divide by 10 to find it takes 1.8 skilled and 0.7 unskilled hours for 100 board feet. Then multiply by 1.92 to find that 16 joists will require 3.5 skilled hours and 1.4 unskilled hour for a total of 4.9 manhours.

You can use a quick rule of thumb to find the manhours required to install ceiling joists. It works like this:

Multiply the square feet of the ceiling area by 1.2 minutes to determine manhours (²⁄₃ skilled, ¹⁄₃ unskilled).

Item	Manhours	
	Skilled	Unskilled
Joists (per 1,000 BF)		
2 x 4	20	8
2 x 6	18	7
2 x 8	16	6
2 x 10	15	5
Rafters (per 1,000 BF)		
Plain gable		
2 x 6 or 2 x 8	23	6
2 x 10	21	6
Hip, no gables or dormers	26	7
Hip, with gables & dormers	38	8
Plywood sheathing (per 1,000 SF)		
Plain gables	9	4
Hips	12	5

Figure 6-43
Manhours for joist and rafter framing

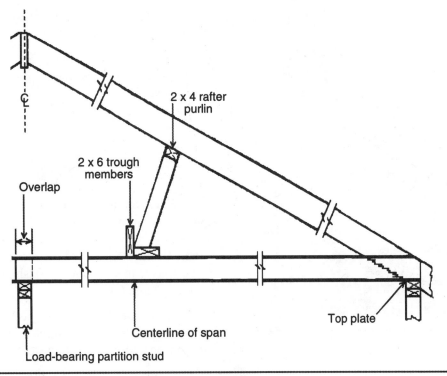

2 x 4 rafter
purlin

2 x 6 trough
members

Overlap

Top plate

Centerline of span

Load-bearing partition stud

Figure 6-44
Trough nailed to ceiling joist and braced to rafter purlin

For our sample 12 x 20 addition, it works out like this:

$$12 \times 20 = 240 \text{ SF}$$
$$240 \times 1.2 \text{ minutes} = 288 \text{ minutes}$$
$$288 \div 60 \text{ minutes} = 4.8 \text{ hours}$$
$$4.8 \times .66 \text{ (skilled)} = 3.16 \text{ hours}$$
$$4.8 \times .33 \text{ (unskilled)} = 1.58 \text{ hours}$$

Once the joists and rafters are in place, you have to stabilize the roof frame with purlins, troughs, and bracing as shown in Figure 6-44. Compute manhours for these tasks by adding 1 minute per square foot of ceiling area (divided between ⅔ skilled and ⅓ unskilled). For the 12 x 20 addition, this adds a total of 4 manhours.

Estimating Rafters

Labor is computed on a board-foot basis. Assume our 12 x 20 addition has a plain gable roof with a pitch of 5 in 12. The roof at the other end joins the gable end of the existing house.

From studying this chapter, you know the rafter run for the addition is 6 feet (half of the span). From your square, you know the length of the main rafter per foot of run is 13 inches. Multiply the run (6 feet) by 13 for a total of 78 inches or 6.5 feet for rafter length from ridge board to top plate. Assume there's a 1-foot overhang. A rafter length of 8 feet is required. A 20-foot addition with a 1-foot overhang at one end has a 21-foot roof. The number of rafters required for 16-inch on-center spacing is 21 multiplied by 0.75 or 15.75 (rounded to 16). Add 1 rafter for the end, for a total of 17.

A 2 x 6 rafter 8 feet in length has 8 board feet of lumber, and 17 rafters have 136 board feet.

We know from the Figure 6-43 that it takes about 23 skilled and 6 unskilled manhours to erect 1,000 board feet of 2 x 6 rafters. That's 2.3 skilled and 0.6 unskilled hours for 100 board feet. Multiply 2.3 and 0.6 by 1.36 to find that 3.13 skilled and 0.82 unskilled hours are required to put up 136 board feet of 2 x 6 rafters.

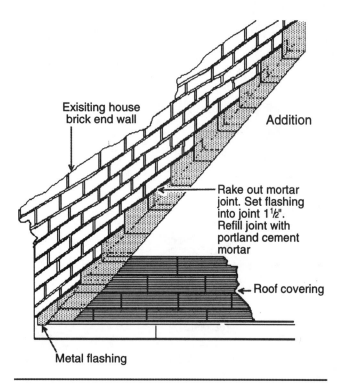

Figure 6-45
Joining an addition to a brick wall

Use this rule of thumb for estimating manhours on plain gable rafter framing 16 inches on center:

Multiply the square feet of roof area by 1.5 minutes to determine manhours (²⁄₃ skilled, ¹⁄₃ unskilled).

Add Manhours for Roof Tie-in

When you add to a house, it can take considerable amount of time to tie the roof to the existing house. Tie-in at brick walls will take you much more time than tie-in at gables with wood finish walls since you'll have to set the metal flashing cap into the brickwork (Figure 6-45).

Make sure the tie-in to wood siding and other finish materials is weather-tight. Figure 6-46 shows how to join an addition roof to a siding wall.

Estimate 1 skilled manhour per foot of rafter run for the tie-in at brick walls. Estimate 0.5 manhour per foot of rafter run for tie-in of wood finish walls.

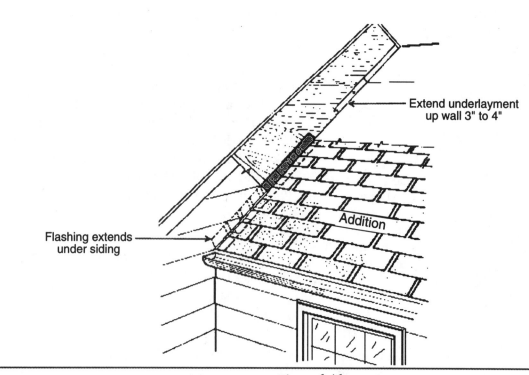

Figure 6-46
Joining an addition to siding wall

7

Easy Steps to Stair Construction

Few basements or attics that you'll convert to living space have stairways that are safe and usable. That means you'll often be called on to do some stair reconstruction. But stair construction isn't difficult once you learn the basic rules.

The two most common types of stairs in houses are main and basement stairs. *Main stairs* are any stairs in the house which don't go to the basement. You can assemble them from prefabricated parts, including housed stringers, treads, and risers. Main-stairway parts are usually made of oak, birch, or maple.

Basement stairs, sometimes called *service stairs*, are somewhat steeper than main stairs and are usually built with less-expensive materials. Basement stairs are usually made with plank treads of Douglas fir or southern pine and 2 x 12-inch carriages. You can also combine a hardwood tread with a softwood riser. In most basement conversions, you have to replace, or at least alter, the basement stairs.

Figure 7-1 shows the four types of stairway runs usually used in house construction. The winder is similar to the long "L" but it has steps instead of a landing where the stairway turns. Because winders aren't as convenient or safe as the long "L," some codes restrict them. Use a winder only if you don't have enough space for a more conventional stairway with a landing.

All stairs except the straight stairway have a change of direction. The long "L" stairs may have the short leg at the top or bottom. When at the bottom, it's often called a platform stairway. See Figure 7-2. The short leg generally extends into the room area.

A stairway may start as an open-stringer stair and change after a few steps to a closed-stringer stair. An open-stringer stair has a wall on one side and a handrail or baluster on the other or may be open on two sides

A Straight stairway run

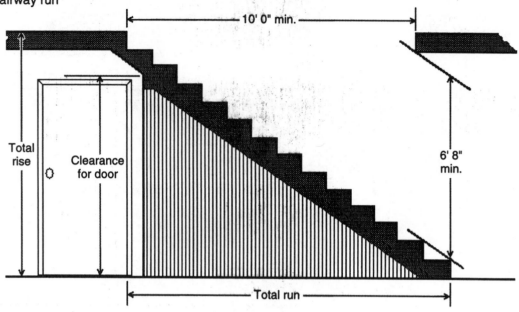

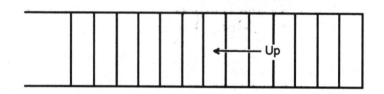

B Long "L" stairway run

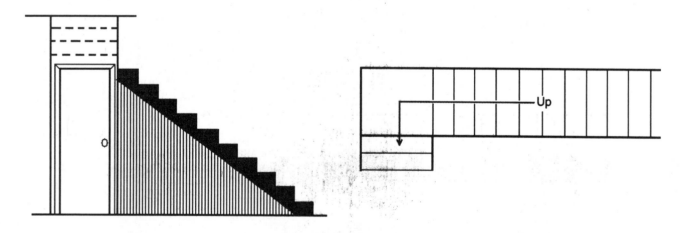

Figure 7-1
Four types of stairway runs

C Narrow "U" stairway run

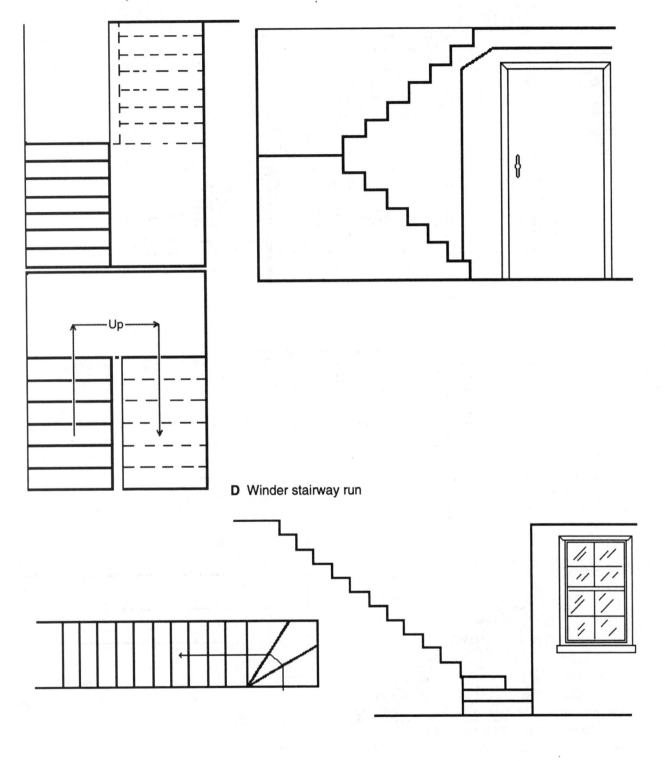

D Winder stairway run

Figure 7-1
Four types of stairway runs (continued)

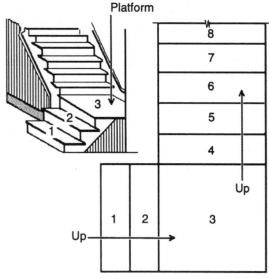

Figure 7-2
Platform stairway

Figure 7-3
Stairway with both open and closed stringers

with two balusters. A closed-stringer stair has a wall on each side. A stairway may start as an open stringer and change after a few steps to a closed-stringer stair. See Figure 7-3.

Stairway Code Requirements

Any stairway you build must follow the local building code regulations. Here are some typical building code rules:

♦ If you build a winder stairway, the winder tread width must be at least as wide as the minimum tread width on the straight run of the stairs. For example, if the straight-run tread is 10 inches wide, the winder tread has to be at least 10 inches wide at the 18-inch mark. Figure 7-4 A shows how to check this by measuring along a line 18 inches from the narrow end of the winder tread, and continuing up the stairs.

♦ If there's a landing at the top of a stair run and a door opens into the stairway, the landing must be at least 2'6" long. Landings in the middle of a flight of stairs must also be at least 2'6" long. See Figure 7-4 B.

♦ The clear vertical distance for main stairways must be at least 6'8" (in Figure 7-4 C). Basement stairs must have at least 6'4" clearance.

♦ Main stairs (inside of the handrail) should be at least 2'8" wide. In larger homes, main stairways are usually 3'6" between the centerlines of the enclosing side walls, so the stairway is about 3 feet wide. Split-level entrance stairs should be even wider. For basement stairs, the minimum clear width is 2'6".

♦ You must install a continuous handrail on at least one side of a stairway if there are more than three risers, and put protective railings on both sides of a stairway that's open on two sides.

A Winder tread width

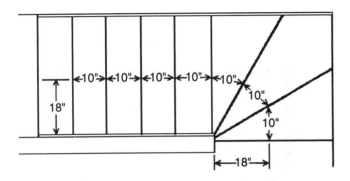

B Landing length

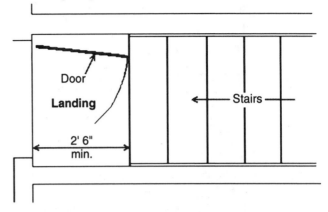

C Minimum headroom

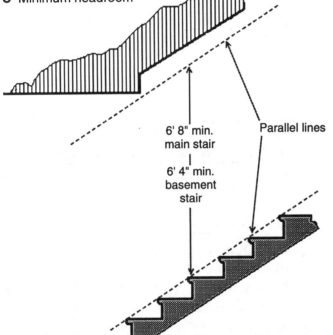

D Closed-stair tread width and riser height

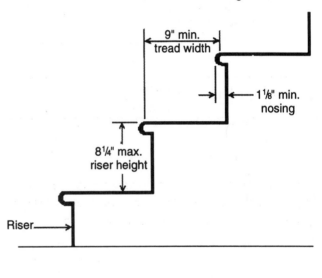

Figure 7-4
Stairway code requirements

Figuring the Tread Width and Riser Height

The minimum tread width on closed stairs inside a house is 9 inches, and the maximum riser height is $8\frac{1}{4}$ inches. See Figure 7-4 D. On exterior stairs, minimum tread is 11 inches, and the maximum riser is $7\frac{1}{2}$ inches. A comfortable step for most people is a riser height of $7\frac{1}{2}$ to $8\frac{1}{4}$ inches. Here's a good rule of thumb for the ratio between riser and tread:

Tread width (in inches) times the riser height (in inches) should equal 72 to 75.

The stairs shown in Figure 7-4 D follow this rule:

$9 \times 8\frac{1}{4} = 74\frac{1}{4}$

However, if the tread is 10 inches, the riser will be 7½ inches, which is a better layout better for most residential stairways.

Here's another rule you can use:

Tread width plus twice the riser height should equal about 25.

Use these rules and the ideal riser height (7½ to 8¼ inches) when you figure out the number of steps between the first and second floors. A first-floor 8-foot ceiling height plus the upper-story floor joists, sub-floor, and finish floor make a floor-to-floor distance of about 105 inches. And 105 divided by 14 is exactly 7½ inches, the height of each riser. If you use 15 risers for this height, the riser height would 7 inches.

Make sure each riser in a flight of stairs is the same height, no matter how many risers you use. Building inspectors are reluctant to pass stairs if the riser height varies more than a fraction of an inch.

Laying Out the Stair Carriage

Stair carriages anchor the treads and support the load on the stairs. There are two common types of stair carriages: notched and unnotched.

Figure 7-5 shows the dimensions for various heights of straight stairs, with riser height and tread width. Let's assume that you've already figured out the tread and riser dimensions. The next step is to set the carriage dimensions. Carriage dimensioning takes a lot of time. Don't waste it. Make sure you start with a piece of stock that's long enough to do the job.

Figure 7-6 shows the difference between the mathematical carriage length and the actual carriage length (which must be cut from a board somewhat longer, as explained below). You won't know the actual length until you complete the layout.

You can find the approximate carriage length with a steel square. On the body of the square, find the total run in feet. (Refer to the dimensions given in Figure 7-5.) On the tongue of the square, find the floor-to-floor height in feet. Measure the distance between these two points on the square. This will be the approximate carriage length.

Let's try an example. Suppose the total run is 12'6" and the floor-to-floor height is 9'6". The distance between 12'6" (on the body of the steel square) and

9'6" (on the tongue of the square) measures about 14'3". We have to use a 16-foot board for the carriage because the stock should be 18 to 20 inches longer than the carriage length.

Marking the Layout

Now you're ready to start the layout. Put the carriage board on a pair of sawhorses. The right-angle portion of the square should be toward you. On the body of the square, find the number representing the tread width (10 inches in our example). On the tongue of the square, find the number representing the rise height (7⅛ inches for our example).

Beginning at the end of the board, place the square so these two numbers intersect the top edge of the board. Mark a line along the outside edges of the square. Then move the square to the next step, as shown in Figure 7-7.

Continue laying out the steps until you've marked all treads and risers. The number of treads is always one less than the number of risers. In our example, there are 16 risers and 15 treads. Number each riser so you know you've laid out the correct number of risers.

Next, cut the carriage board along the marked lines. When you cut out the first step, allow for the thickness of one tread. If the treads are 1½ inches thick, cut 1½ inches from the bottom of the carriage so the entire stairway is 1½ inches lower. If you don't make this adjustment, the first step will be higher than the rest. See Figure 7-8.

Figure 7-8 also shows alternate methods of fastening the carriage board to the second-floor framing in the illustrations labeled A, B, and C. In illustration A, the carriage is attached to the framing at floor level with steel framing anchors (not shown). In illustration B, the carriage is attached at one riser dimension below the floor level with steel framing anchors (not shown). And in illustration C, the carriage is attached at floor level and supported by a ledger.

Framing a Stairway Opening

For a main stairway, the rough opening in the second floor is usually at least 10 feet long by 36 inches or more wide. For a basement stairway, the rough opening is usually about 9½ feet long by 32 inches wide.

Dimensions for straight stairs

Floor-to-floor height H	Number of risers	Riser height R	Tread width T	Total run L	Minimum headroom Y	Well opening U
8'-0"	12	8"	9"	8'-3"	6'-6"	8'-1"
8'-0"	13	7⅜"+	9½"	9'-6"	6'-6"	9'-2½"
8'-0"	13	7⅜"+	10"	10'-0"	6'-6"	9'-8½"
8'-6"	13	7⅞"−	9"	9'-0"	6'-6"	8'-3"
8'-6"	14	7⁵⁄₁₆"−	9½"	10'-3½"	6'-6"	9'-4"
8'-6"	14	7⁵⁄₁₆"−	10"	10'-10"	6'-6"	9'-10"
9'-0"	14	7¹¹⁄₁₆"+	9"	9'-9"	6'-6"	8'-5"
9'-0"	15	7³⁄₁₆"+	9½"	11'-1"	6'-6"	9'-6½"
9'-0"	15	7³⁄₁₆"+	10"	11'-8"	6'-6"	9'-11½"
9'-6"	15	7⅝"−	9"	10'-6"	6'-6"	8'-6½"
9'-6"	16	7⅛"	9½"	11'-10½"	6'-6"	9'-7"
9'-6"	16	7⅛"	10"	12'-6"	6'-6"	10'-1"

Dimensions shown under well opening are based on 6'6" minimum headroom. If headroom is increased well opening also increases.

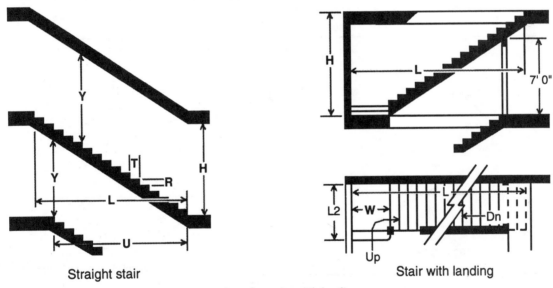

Straight stair   Stair with landing

Dimensions for stairs with landings

Floor-to-floor height H	Number of risers	Risers height R	Tread width T	Run		Run	
				Number of risers	L	Number of risers	L2
8'-0"	13	7⅜"+	10"	11	8'-4"+W	2	0'-10"+W
8'-6"	14	7⁵⁄₁₆"−	10"	12	9'-2"+W	2	0'-10"+W
9'-0"	15	7³⁄₁₆"+	10"	13	10'-0"+W	2	0'-10"+W
9'-6"	16	7⅛"	10"	14	10'-10"+W	2	0'-10"+W

Stairs with landings are safer and reduce the required stair space. The landing provides a resting point and a logical place for a right angle turn.

Figure 7-5
Stair dimensions

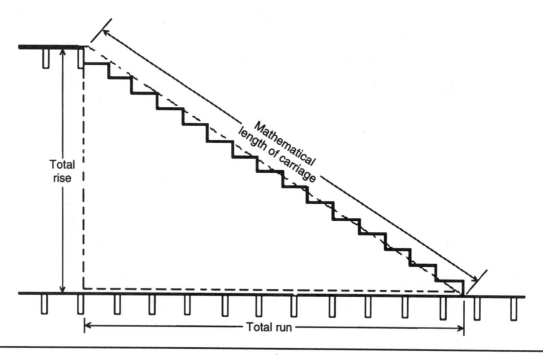

Figure 7-6
Mathematical length of carriage

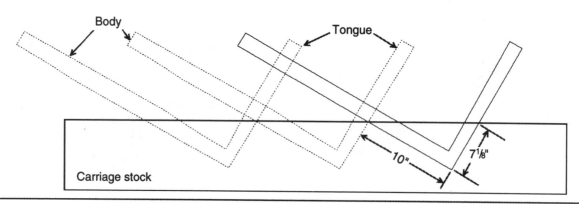

Figure 7-7
Using a steel square to lay out a stair carriage

The long dimension of a stair opening can be either parallel, or at right angles, to the joists. Figure 7-9 shows both. It's easier to frame a rough opening when the length runs parallel to the joists. You may need a short header for one or both ends.

When the length of a stair opening runs perpendicular to the joists, you need a long double-header. You can make construction easier if you have a load-bearing wall under part or all of the opening. Then the joists can bear on the top plate of the wall and you won't have to support them with joist hangers at the header. If you don't use a supporting wall, the maximum allowable header length is 10 feet.

You can frame a long "L" as shown in Figure 7-10. Nail the landing frame to the wall studs. The frame makes a nailing area for the subfloor and a support for the stair carriages.

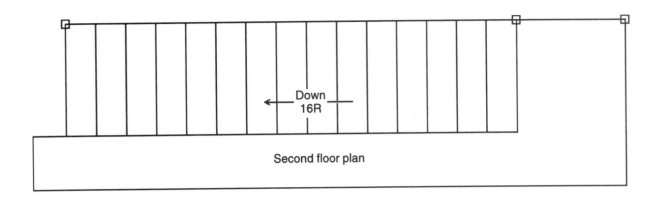

Second floor plan

Down
16R

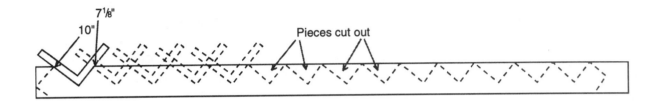

7⅛"
10"
Pieces cut out

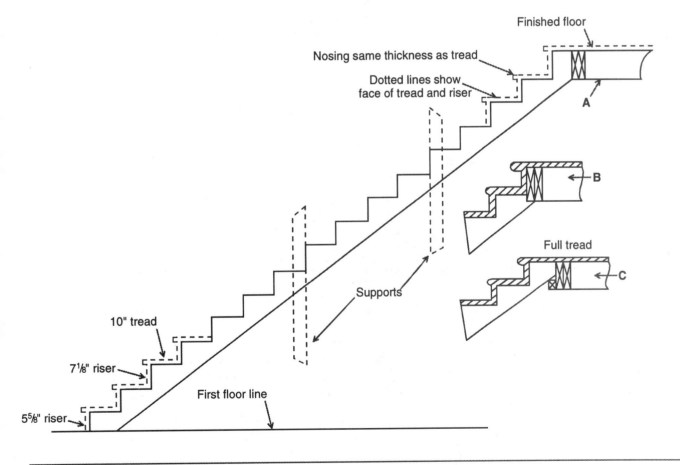

Finished floor

Nosing same thickness as tread

Dotted lines show
face of tread and riser

A

B

Full tread

C

Supports

10" tread

7⅛" riser

First floor line

5⅝" riser

Figure 7-8
Laying out a stairway

A Rough opening: length parallel to joists

B Rough opening: length perpendicular to joists

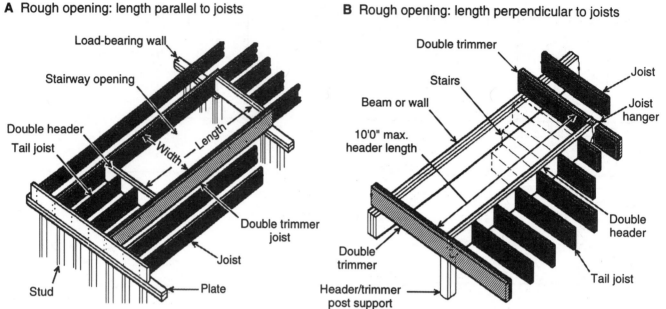

Figure 7-9
Framing a stairway

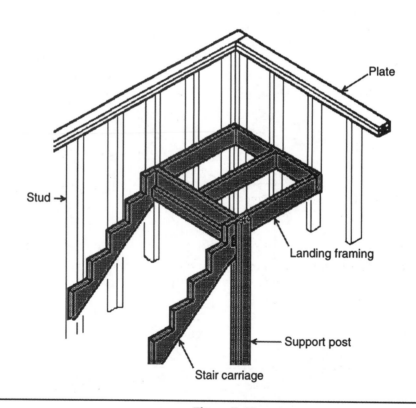

Figure 7-10
Framing a long "L" stairway

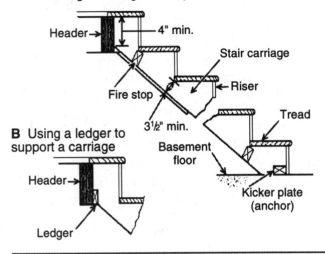

A Fastening a carriage to the joist header

B Using a ledger to support a carriage

Figure 7-11
Framing basement stairs

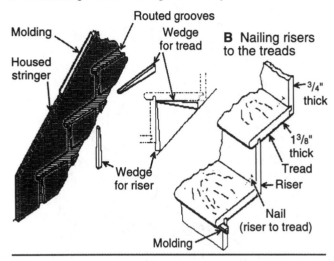

A Fastening housed stringers directly to the finish wall

B Nailing risers to the treads

Figure 7-12
Framing main stairs

Building Basement Stairs

You can usually build rough stair carriages made from notched 2 x 12 planks for basement stairs. The effective depth below the tread and riser notches must be at least 3½ inches, as shown in Figure 7-11. Cover the rough carriages with a white pine finish board.

Fasten the carriage to the joist headers at the top of the stairway (Figure 7-11 A) or support it with a ledger nailed to the header (Figure 7-11 B). Install an intermediate carriage at the center of the stairs if treads are 1¹/₁₆ inches thick and the stairs are wider than 2'6". You need three carriages if treads are 1⅝ inches thick and the stairs are wider than 3 feet. Of course, carriages can also be supported by adjacent walls.

The bottom of a stair carriage can rest on the basement floor. But it's better to use an anchored 2 x 4 or 2 x 6 treated kicker plate, as shown in Figure 7-11 A. Provide fire stops at the top and bottom of stairs, as shown.

You can also make basement stairs out of 1½-inch-thick plank treads without risers. Basement stairs made from 1⅛-inch finished tread material and nominal 1-inch boards for risers look better and they're more durable. Use finishing nails to attach the risers to the treads.

Building Main Stairs

On main stairways, the supporting members may be housed stringers. Route the stringers to fit both the tread and the riser. Fasten the housed stringers directly to the finish wall, as shown in section A of Figure 7-12. Assemble this type of stairway with hardwood wedges coated with glue, working from the underside of the stairway. Drive the wedges under the ends of the treads. Drive additional wedges behind the risers. Use nails to fasten the risers to the treads (Figure 7-12 B).

When you wedge and glue treads and risers into housed stringers, the maximum allowable stair width is 3'6". For wider stairs, make a notched carriage between the housed stringers.

If stairs are open on one side, you need a railing and balusters, as shown in Figure 7-13. Balusters are made with doweled ends that fit into drilled holes in the railing and in the treads. Fasten balusters to tread ends that have finished returns. The railing usually ends at a newel post. Use a stringer and appropriate moldings to finish the stairway trim.

Building Attic Stairs

A quality, fully-enclosed stairway is appropriate between the main or second floor and the attic conver-

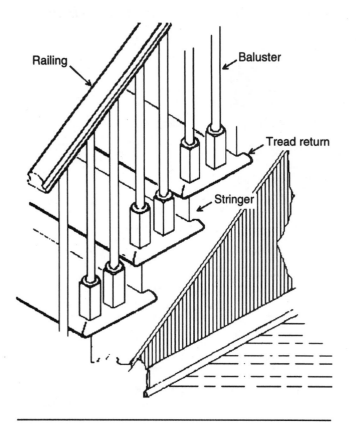

Figure 7-13
Open main stairs

sion. Due to limited space in most conversion projects, however, the attic stairs discussed here might be your best approach. Keep in mind that the owner will have to move furniture up the stairs.

One way to build a fully-enclosed stairway is to use a rough, notched carriage with a finish stringer, as shown in Figure 7-14 A. Fasten the stringers to the wall. Then install the carriages. Cut treads and risers to fit snugly between the stringers. Use finishing nails to secure the treads and risers to the carriages.

Figure 7-14 B shows another way to install a fully-enclosed stairway. Begin by nailing the rough carriages directly to the wall. Then notch the stringers to fit the carriages. Install treads and risers as described above.

Estimating Materials and Manhours

You can start estimating the materials when you know the stair dimensions. Use the checklist in Figure 7-15 as a guide to help you estimate the list of materials and labor costs.

Figure 7-16 gives average labor hours for building stairs. Use the chart as a guide only if you haven't compiled your own stairway construction manhour records.

A Using a rough, notched carriage with a finish stringer

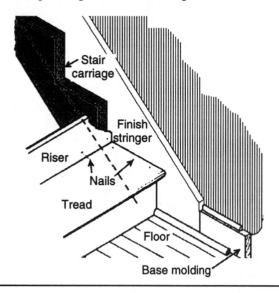

B Building attic stairs by nailing rough carriage directly to the wall

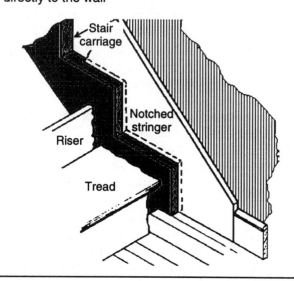

Figure 7-14
Building stairs for an attic conversion

Stair Checklist

1) The house is: ☐1-story ☐1½-story ☐2-story

2) Stairs required: ☐basement ☐main ☐attic ☐attic folding ☐exterior

3) Stair type: ☐long "L" ☐narrow "U" ☐landing ☐winders

4) Stair dimensions:

   ☐Floor-to-floor: _____   ☐Total run: _____

   ☐Number of risers: _____   ☐Minimum headroom: _____

   ☐Height of risers: _____   ☐Well opening: _____

   ☐Width of treads: _____

5) Number of carriages or stringers: ☐two ☐three

6) Number of handrails: ☐one ☐two

7) Main stairway is: ☐open ☐closed

8) Stairway has: ☐railing ☐balusters ☐newel post

9) Material costs:

   Carriages: (Size _____)   _____LF @ $_____LF = $_____

   Stringers: (Size _____)   _____LF @ $_____LF = $_____

   Treads: (Size _____)   _____LF @ $_____LF = $_____

   Risers: (Size _____)   _____LF @ $_____LF = $_____

   Handrail: _____LF @ $_____LF = $_____

   Newel posts: _____ea @ $_____ea = $_____

   Balusters: _____ea @ $_____ea = $_____

   Molding: _____LF @ $_____LF = $_____

   Nails: _____lbs @ $_____lb = $_____

   Framing and bracing: (Size _____)   _____LF @ $_____LF = $_____

   Other materials: _____   @ $_____LF = $_____

   (not listed above)

10) Labor costs:

   Skilled: _____hour @ $_____hour = $_____

   Unskilled: _____hours @ $_____hour = $_____

   Total = $_____

Figure 7-15
Stair checklist

Work element	Unit	Manhours per unit
Erecting stairwork, hours per 9' rise		
Building ordinary plain box stairs on the job	Each	8 to 16
Rails, balusters and newel post for above	Each	4 to 8
Erecting plain flight of stairs built up in shop	Each	6 to 8
Erecting two short flights	Each	10 to 12
Erecting open stairs	Each	10 to 12
Erecting open stairs with two flights	Each	12 to 16
Newels, balusters and hand rail for the above	Each	6 to 8
Erecting prefabricated wood stairs, hours per 9' rise		
Circular, 6' diameter, oak	Each	23.0
Circular, 9' diameter, oak	Each	31.0
Straight, 3' wide, assembled	Each	3.0
Straight, 4' wide, assembled	Each	3.2
Installing folding stairs (attic)	Each	2.5

Figure 7-16
Labor erecting stairs

8

Modular Construction

Modular construction means designing an addition by considering the dimensions of the materials you'll be using for the job. It can help you cut down on waste and enable you to make more competitive bids because you're making the best use of your materials and labor.

Let's look at an example. Say you're designing a room addition to use standard dimension materials efficiently. You'll use 48-inch width plywood, OSB, and insulation board. Now a wall that's 30 feet long isn't modular, but a wall that's 28 or 32 feet is. Let's see why. A 30-foot-long wall will take eight 4 x 8 panels (long side vertical) for a total of 32 feet. There will be 2 feet left over. A 28-foot wall will take seven 4 x 8 panels, with no overage. Or a 32-foot wall will take eight 4 x 8 panels, with no overage.

For another example, suppose you have a plan that uses a rafter length of 18'6". Now you'll need to cut the rafters from 20-foot stock. The 1'6" pieces left over are just waste. Say a 20-foot 2 x 6 piece of spruce lumber costs $8.00. That's $0.40 a foot. So each 1'6" piece you cut off and discard costs $0.60. A 28-foot room addition with rafters spaced 24 inches on center takes 15 rafters to the side, for a total of 30. So the waste amounts to $18.00. And it'll take extra labor to move the waste, cleanup, and so on. Double the rafter waste cost (to $1.20) to include labor costs caused by waste, and you have a total of $36.00. And this is just on the rafters! Add all the other wastes due to poor planning and you begin to get an idea of what you can save by using modular construction.

I've seen as much as 10 percent of the material delivered to a job site end up as waste because of lack of planning. Think of it this way: The builder could have built 10 percent more space with the same materials in a modular coordinated plan. Obviously, not every house or addition can be planned around modular sizes. But many can, and should be, to reduce construction costs.

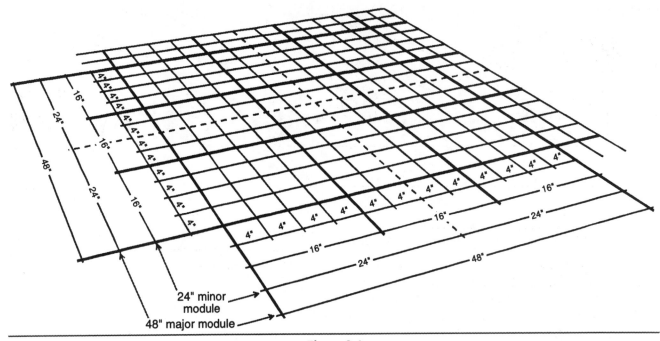

Figure 8-1
Modular planning grid

Planning for Modular Construction

Now take a look at Figure 8-1. Modular planning involves three dimensions — length, width, and height. The modular length and width dimensions form the base. You begin by dividing the horizontal plane or footprint of a house into units of 4, 16, 24, or 48 inches. Overall dimensions are in multiples of 4 inches.

The 16-inch dimension is a flexible unit for spacing windows and doors. You can use increments of 24 and 48 inches for the exterior dimensions of a house. The floor, ceiling, and roof also use these dimensions. A quick way to draw up your modular plans is to draw them on a grid like the one in Figure 8-1.

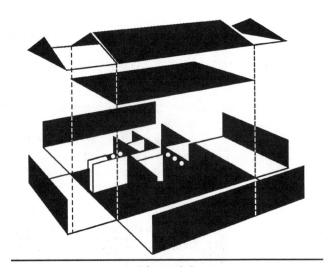

Figure 8-2
Dividing a house along its horizontal and vertical planes

Horizontal and Vertical Planes

Figure 8-2 shows the horizontal and vertical planes of a house, but it doesn't indicate the thickness of any part. You allow for wall thickness and tolerance based on fixed modular lines at the outside face of the studs, as shown in Figure 8-3. Fixed modular lines are the dimensions measured from the outside surface of the wall studs. The wall thickness is the stud width plus the thickness of the exterior and interior finish walls. If you use 2 x 4 studs, $\frac{1}{2}$-inch drywall and $\frac{5}{8}$-inch plywood exterior siding, the wall thickness is $4\frac{5}{8}$ inch. Exterior walls and partitions may have different thicknesses. Floor and roof construction can also vary in thickness, depending on structural requirements and types of framing and finish.

154

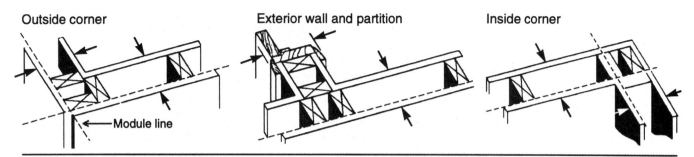

Outside corner

Exterior wall and partition

Inside corner

← Module line

Figure 8-3
Thickness and tolerance variables

Planning Exterior Walls, Doors, and Windows

Figure 8-4 shows how to separate exterior wall elements at natural division points. The overall room addition dimensions are based on 48-inch and 24-inch modules. For maximum flexibility in placing door and window openings, use a 16-inch module. Locating wall openings precisely on the 16-inch module will eliminate extra wall framing that's often required in non-modular construction.

Planning Roof Dimensions

Increments for house depths (width) are in 24-inch multiples. Figure 8-5 shows that a variety of modular house depths are available with 24-inch increments. Six 48-inch module depths and five 24-inch module widths fulfill most roof-span requirements.

Six 48-inch module depths:

6 x 48 inches = 288 inches
288 divided by 12 = 24 feet

Five 24-inch module depths:

5 x 24 inches = 120
120 divided by 12 = 10 feet

Standard roof slopes, combined with modular house depths, provide all the dimensions you need to design rafter, truss, and panel roofs. See Figure 8-6.

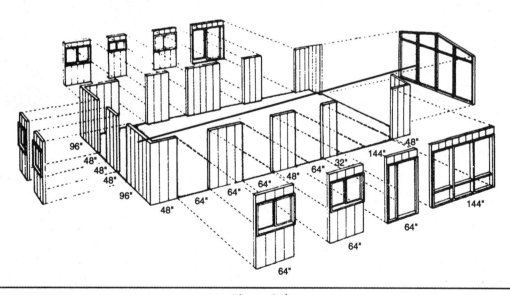

Figure 8-4
Exterior walls, doors and windows

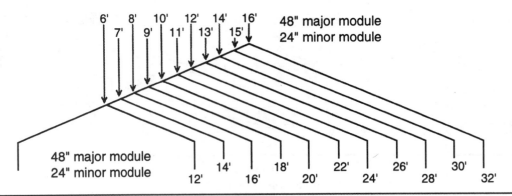

Figure 8-5
Modular house depths in 24" increments

The pivotal point shown in Figure 8-7 is the fixed point of reference in the modular line of an exterior wall. Always measure modular roof design and construction dimensions from this point.

Floor Framing

Floor framing can result in a lot of waste — sometimes as much as 5 to 15 percent. If the depth of the floor isn't evenly divisible by 4, you lose the maximum length of the floor joists. Figure 8-8 shows stan-

dard dimension material from floor joist to roof decking fitted without a lot of cutting and waste. When you plan a first-floor addition, think modular. If an addition is 13 x 25 feet, you're going to have a lot of waste. If possible, change the room to modular dimensions, such as 12 x 24 or 16 x 24.

Space floor joists 12, 16, or 24 inches on center, depending on the floor load. You can place the joists in a lapped or in-line position. Joist spacings of 13.7 inches and 19.2 inches are alternatives. They also divide the 8-foot length of a plywood or OSB subfloor panel into seven and five equal spaces, respectively. If you

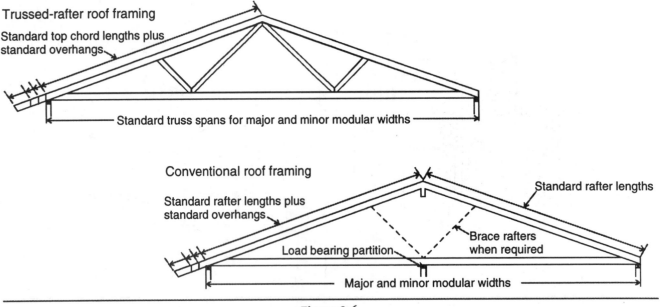

Figure 8-6
Standard roof slopes combined with modular house depths

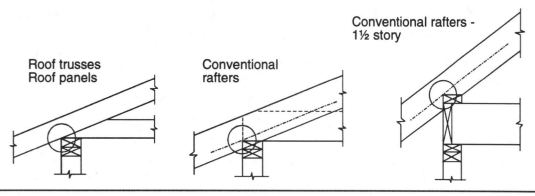

Figure 8-7
Pivotal point for modular roof planning

use a 48-inch module on house depths, you'll be able to use full 4 x 8 panels to minimize cutting and waste.

Joist material is sized in 2-foot increments. Joists 12 feet and longer usually are an extra ½ inch or more longer so you can trim a little to square the end without cutting it too short.

In conventional platform construction with lapped joists bearing on a center girder, the length of a joist is half the house depth. Note that the thickness of the band joist (1½ inches) and half the required overlap at the support (1½ inches) cancel each other out. See Figure 8-9.

Planning Room Depth

Joist lengths will correspond to standard lumber sizes if your addition depth is a multiple of 4 feet (12, 24, 28, or 32 feet). Look at Figure 8-10. It takes the same total linear footage of standard joist lengths to frame the floor of an addition that's 25 feet deep as one that's 28 feet deep. The same holds true for a 29-foot depth and a 32-foot depth. This applies to any joist spacing, in both in-line and lapped joists.

If joist spans are longer when you change to a 4-foot module, be sure to re-check the allowable span

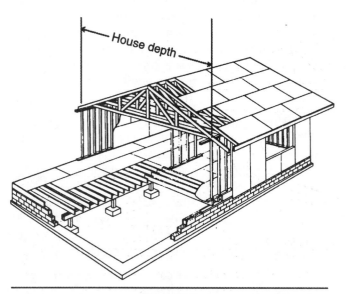

Figure 8-8
Measuring house depth

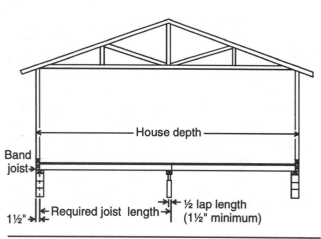

Figure 8-9
Required joist length

157

House depth feet	Joist required feet	Standard length feet	Linear feet		Board feet per square foot of floor area*			
			16" joist spacing	24" joist spacing	16" spacing		24" spacing	
					2 x 8	2 x 10	2 x 10	2 x 12
23	10½	12	72	48	1.14	1.43	.95	1.14
22	11	12	72	48	1.09	1.36	.91	1.09
23	11½	12	72	48	1.04	1.30	.87	1.04
24	12	12	72	48	1.00	1.25	.83	1.00
25	12½	14	84	56	1.12	1.40	.93	1.12
26	13	14	84	56	1.08	1.35	.89	1.08
27	13½	14	84	56	1.04	1.30	.86	1.04
28	14	14	84	56	1.00	1.25	.83	1.00
29	14½	16	96	64	1.10	1.38	.92	1.10
30	15	16	96	64	1.07	1.33	.89	1.07
31	15½	16	96	64	1.03	1.29	.86	1.03
32	16	16	96	64	1.00	1.25	.84	1.00

* Floor area = House depth times 4'

Figure 8-10
Required footage of joists per 4' of house length based on standard joist length

for the species and grade of lumber you're using. If the spans are shorter, you may be able to use a smaller-size joist.

Plan the layout of the subfloor panels using a 4-foot modular addition depth. Then you can use 48-inch-wide panels, without ripping, for the 24-, 28-, and 32-foot depths when you either lap or trim the joists for in-line placement. Figure 8-11 shows a panel layout option for the 28-foot addition depth with lapped joists. Similar layouts may be used with other lapped joist designs.

Planning Exterior Wall Framing

Figure 8-12 shows how you can cut exterior wall framing materials by as much as 25 percent with a modular layout. The size of both wall openings in the figure is the same, and they both use standard modular stud spacings. But the on-module unit uses 20 percent less material.

Figure 8-13 shows exterior wall framing which doesn't incorporate cost-saving techniques. Modular framing for the same walls is shown in Figure 8-14. As you can see, there are substantial savings possible when you use modular framing techniques.

Maybe you have a question at this point: But what about structural strength? There is, of course, a trade-off. The wall in Figure 8-14 isn't as sturdy as the one in Figure 8-13. But it's plenty sturdy enough to meet code requirements for single-story construction.

Stud Spacing

You can use 24-inch stud spacing in virtually any addition where exterior and interior facing materials can span 24 inches. Tests and structural analyses show that, for many installations, 24-inch spacing could even be used for walls supporting the upper floor and roof of two-story houses and additions if the code permitted.

Using 24-inch stud spacing will trim costs. For a 1,440 square foot one-story house, with standard door and window areas, you can save about 10 percent in wall framing costs if you use exterior wall framing that's 24 inches on center rather than 16. A 12-foot wall 8 feet high with studs spaced 16 inches on center requires 1.12 board feet per square foot of wall. If it's spaced at 24 inches on center, it takes 1.02 board feet per square foot. That's a difference of 10 board feet.

In many cases, you can use the same thickness exterior sheathing and exterior finish material. And there are additional savings in reduced labor for drywall, sheathing, insulation, and wiring installations.

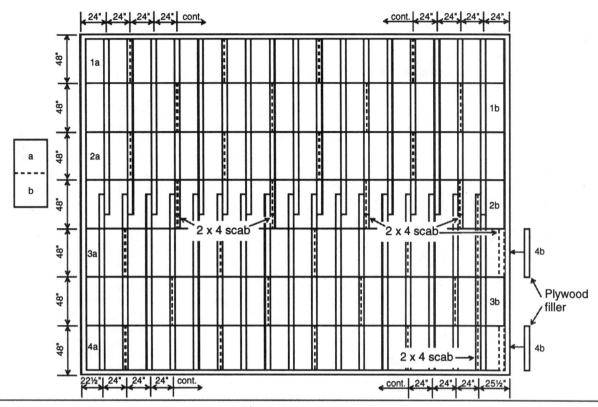

Figure 8-11
Subfloor panel layout for 28' house depth when joists are lapped over center support

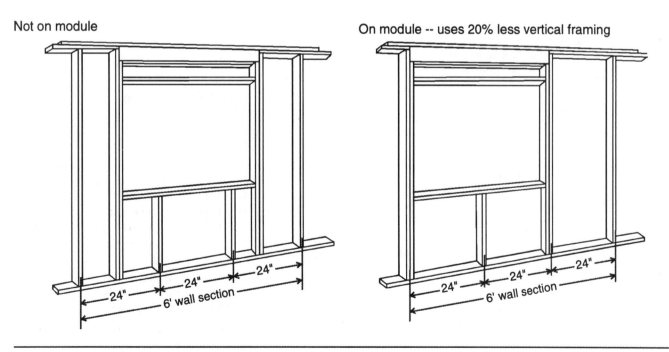

Figure 8-12
Windows located on module can save framing

A Single stud 16" oc
B Corner post - 3 studs and 3 spacer blocks
C & D Partition
E Door opening with jamb studs
F Window opening stud located off regular stud spacing

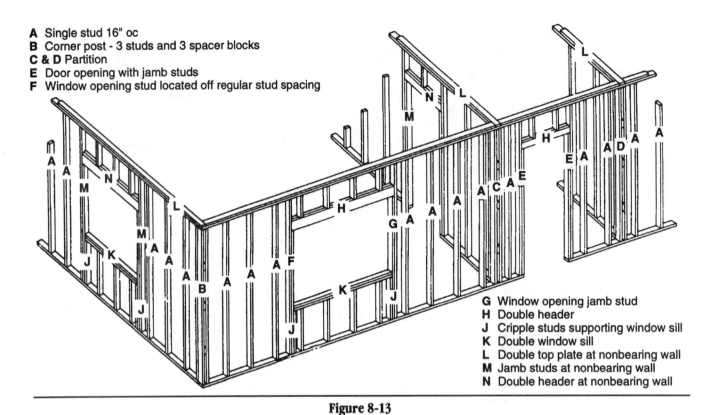

G Window opening jamb stud
H Double header
J Cripple studs supporting window sill
K Double window sill
L Double top plate at nonbearing wall
M Jamb studs at nonbearing wall
N Double header at nonbearing wall

Figure 8-13
Wall framing — not modular

A Single stud 24" oc
B Corner post - 3 studs without spacer blocks
C Partition intersection with 1 stud and cleats
D Partition intersection on regular stud location - 2 studs
E Door opening on regular stud location
F Window opening on regular stud location

G Window opening jamb stud
H Header at top plate location
J Short support studs eliminated at window sill
K Single member window sill
L Single member top plate
M Both sides of window opening on regular stud locations
N Single top plate

Figure 8-14
Modular wall framing

Where to Locate Openings and Intersections

Why use three 2 x 4s where one will do the job? Whenever possible, have one side of window and door rough openings fall on a regular stud position. You can see this in Figure 8-14 in the members labeled E, F, and M.

Choose windows and doors that have a rough-opening width that's a multiple of your stud spacing. When both sides are on the stud module, you need fewer studs and you can install sheathing and siding with a minimum of waste. Figure 8-14 shows how this can be done. For example, at the member labeled D, the partition joins the wall at a regular stud location, eliminating the need for a corner nailer on one side of the partition. Scrap plywood or boards can be used for back-up cleats for opposite-corner nailing.

Studs at Wall Corners and Intersections

Traditional framing methods for exterior corners and for intersections of partitions and walls use three studs. You can see this in Figure 8-13 and Figure 8-15 B and F. The space between the studs must be insulated before you apply the sheathing. One alternative, shown in Figure 8-15 A and E, is to use an extra stud to provide the desired insulation. While this is thermally effective, it's an expense that you can avoid.

A preferred three-stud arrangement is shown in Figure 8-15 C and G. This stud placement eliminates spacer blocks. It provides the same backup support for wall linings as the more traditional arrangement. You can install the insulation after you nail on the sheathing.

There's also another alternative (Figure 8-15 D). Here, you can leave out the studs that serve only as a backup for interior corner-nailing surfaces for finish materials by attaching backup cleats to the partition stud. Use 3/8-inch plywood or 1-inch lumber for the cleats. If you have some suitable scrap material, use it.

By using the three-stud exterior corner setup and backup cleats at all intersections of the partitions, you'll save 2 board feet at each corner by eliminating three spacer blocks 12 inches long, and 10 2/3 board feet at each partition intersection by eliminating two studs.

Framing Door and Window Openings

Traditional framing uses too much wood around openings. A window a few inches too wide or too narrow, or one that's located a few inches too far left or right, usually means that you need at least one extra stud. For example, Figure 8-13 shows doubled sills under windows, plus short support studs at the ends of the sill.

Figure 8-16 shows how the vertical loads at windows are transferred downward by the studs that support the headers. The sill and wall beneath the window are nonbearing. Figures 8-12 and 8-16 show how to eliminate the second sill and the two sill-support studs. The ends of the sill are supported by end-nailing through the adjacent stud. Using a single sill member at the bottom of all window openings, and eliminating all window sill support studs will save you about 6 board feet per standard-size window.

By moving the header beam up to replace the lower top plate, you can save even more (Figures 8-12 and 8-16). This requires longer support (jamb) studs. But it can eliminate most of the short fill-in studs (cripples) between the top plate and the header. Vertical loads aren't transferred to the top of the window opening. Cripples below the header are needed only when required to support the sheathing and finish materials.

If the sheathing or finish materials can span the distance between the header beam and the rough opening top plate, you won't need any cripples. In addition to saving in framing material and labor, you also save time on cutting and fitting insulation.

Apply the same principle to header beams across doorways. Install a single member top plate over a header, as shown in Figures 8-12 and 8-16.

Framing Nonbearing Walls

Not all exterior walls are load-bearing. Generally, there are two or more walls, parallel to the joists and roof trusses, which don't support much more than their own weight. End walls in a plain gable building are an example. You can frame nonbearing exterior walls the same way as interior partitions. Look at members labeled K, L, M, and N of Figure 8-14.

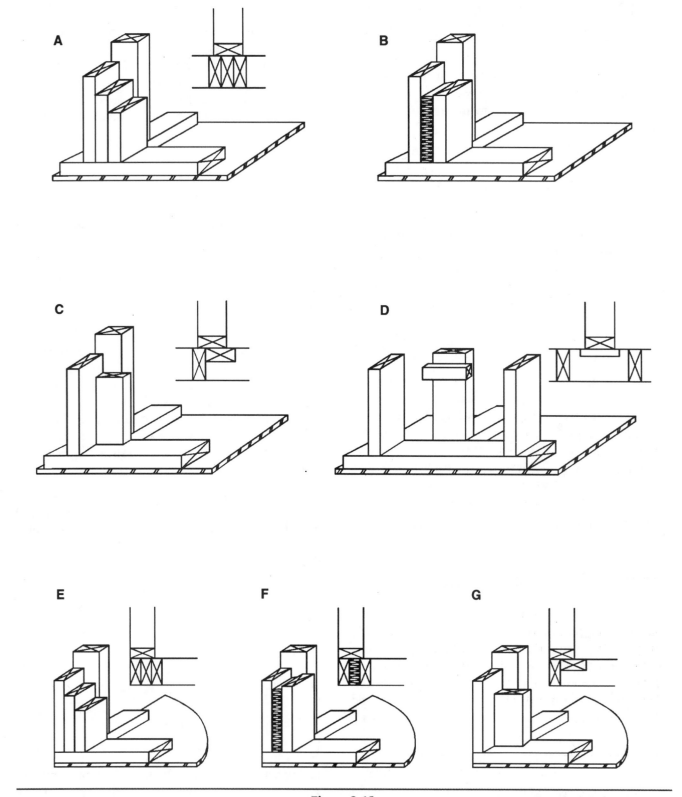

Figure 8-15
Framing alternatives at wall and partition intersections and exterior corners

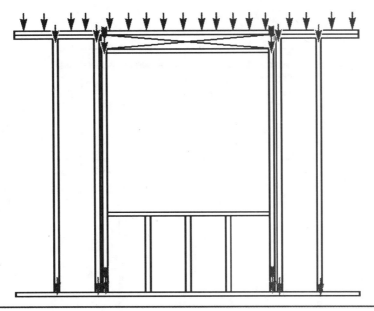

Figure 8-16
Load distribution through header and support
studs at opening in load-bearing wall

Since there are no loads to transfer, you can frame doors and windows with single members. A single top plate is enough if you use metal straps or plates to tie the top of the plates together at joints. Of course, if you use single top plates, studs must be 1½ inches longer. You can use regular precut studs for the load-bearing walls, and cut the studs on the job for the non-bearing walls.

Wall Blocking at Mid-Height

You don't usually have to block between wall studs at mid-height. Top and bottom plates provide adequate fire stopping, and ½-inch drywall applied horizontally doesn't need blocking for support if you space the studs 24 inches or less on center. Eliminating mid-height blocking will save you about 13 board feet per 24-foot wall.

Wall Racking Strength

Most codes require that exterior walls have a minimum racking strength for stability under wind loads. Racking strength is a structure's ability to withstand the direct or twisting forces of wind, earthquake or ground settling which tend to force a building or wall out of plumb or out of parallel.

Panel sheathing or siding provides enough racking strength so you won't need any additional let-in corner bracing. If you use a nonstructural sheathing, such as low-density fiberboard or gypsum board, you may need additional bracing. Use structural sheathing or siding panels at the corners of the addition, or use let-in 1 x 4 bracing.

Estimating Studding Requirements

Wall framing studs include cripples under and over openings, door and window jamb studs (also called jack or trimmer studs), window sill support studs, and the window sill, a 2 x 4 member forming the bottom member of the framed window opening.

For modular load-bearing walls, estimate 1 stud for every 2 feet, plus 2 studs for each window opening, and 2 studs for each door opening. Add 2 studs for each corner.

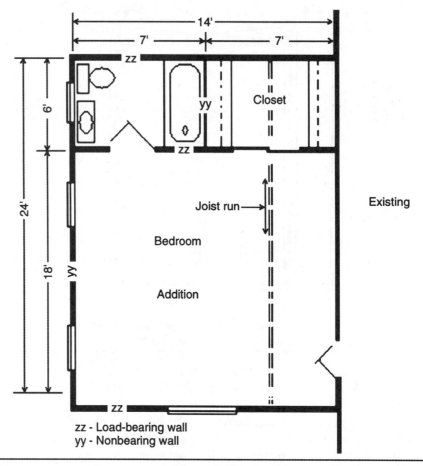

Figure 8-17
336-square-foot addition

For modular nonbearing walls, estimate 1 stud for every 2 feet, plus 1 stud for each window opening and 1 stud for each door opening. Add 2 studs for each intersection.

Figure 8-17 shows a 336-square-foot addition. Modular framing this addition, with studs spaced 24 inches on center, takes about 61 studs. Traditional framing, with studs spaced 16 inches on center, takes about 99 studs.

A rule of thumb for estimating studs spaced 16 inches on center using traditional wall framing methods is:

Estimate 1 stud for every 3 square feet of floor space.

A rule of thumb for estimating studs using modular wall framing methods is:

Estimate 1 stud for every 5 square feet of floor space.

9

Sheathing, Roofing and Cornices

Roof sheathing boards have about disappeared in most areas because plywood and OSB sheathing panels provide structural strength, a smooth surface, and take less time to install. But some builders still use spaced board sheathing with wood shingles and tin roofs.

Installing Roof Sheathing

If you're remodeling a house that has board roof sheathing and you're adding on at the roof's plane, you may want to use board sheathing. This is particularly true if there are open cornices that expose the board sheathing. If not, use plywood or OSB panels for a sturdy, fast installation.

Board Roof Sheathing

Lay board sheathing without spaces between the boards if it's under roofing that requires continuous support, such as strip shingles. I recommend seasoned fir, spruce, pine, redwood, hemlock or Western larch for board sheathing. Unseasoned wood will dry out and shrink, which can cause buckling or lifting of the shingles along the length of the board.

Install square-edged, matched or shiplapped boards with the ends staggered and positioned over the center of rafters. Use boards no wider than 8 inches to minimize shrinkage. A 6-inch-wide board is even better. The boards should be at least ³⁄₄ inch thick for rafter spacing of 16 to 24 inches on center. Install them with two 8d nails at each bearing.

Long boards at roof ends will provide good framing anchorage for gable roofs with a rake overhang or an unsupported fly rafter.

In damp climates, you can use spaced 1 x 4 boards when installing wood shingles or shakes. Space the boards the same distance on center as the shingles are to be laid to the weather. That is, shingles laid 5 inch-

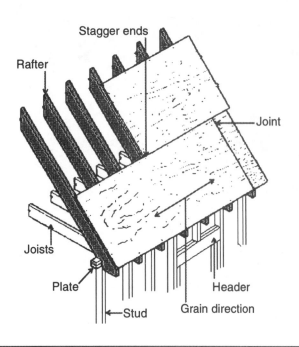

Figure 9-1
Applying plywood sheathing

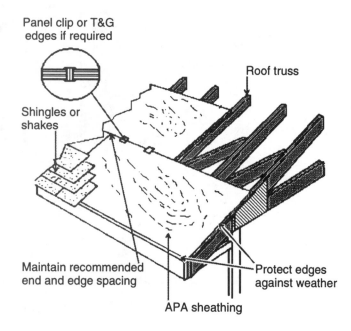

Figure 9-2
Applying APA panel roof sheathing

es to the weather can be applied to 1 x 4 boards spaced $1^3/4$ to $1^1/2$ inches apart. The spacing allows free air circulation under the shingles. That's essential for good drying.

Panel Roof Sheathing

Lay plywood roof sheathing with the face grain perpendicular to the rafters, as shown in Figure 9-1. You can usually use a standard sheathing-grade plywood, but in damp climates you'll need to use a standard sheathing grade with exterior glue. Make all end joints over the center of the rafters and stagger them by at least one rafter. Nail at each bearing, 6 inches on center along all edges and 12 inches on center along intermediate members. Unless plywood has exterior glue, don't let the raw edges be exposed to the weather at the gable end or at the cornice. Instead, protect it with trim or a metal drip edge.

APA Panel Roof Sheathing

APA-rated panel sheathing makes a good base under built-up roofing, asphalt or fiberglass shingles, tile roofing, or wood shingles or shakes (except in damp areas). APA-rated panel sheathing is marked with the span rating, which specifies the recommended rafter spacing for the panel thickness. Panels marked 24/0 are adequate for rafters spaced 24 inches on center. Sheathing panels with this span rating are available $^3/8$, $^7/16$, $^{15}/32$ and $^1/2$ inch thick. Install the panels continuously over two or more spans with the long dimension across the supports.

Figure 9-2 shows the typical APA panel roof sheathing procedure. For APA sheathing rated Exposure 1, Exposure 2, or Exterior, protect the exposed edges against weather or use an Exterior-rated panel starter strip. Leave $^1/8$ inch space at panel end joints and $^1/4$ inch space at edge joints unless the manufacturer has different instructions. Use felt under shingles and shakes if recommended by the manufacturer.

When you space roof trusses 24 inches on center, you can use $^3/8$-inch 24/0 plywood sheathing applied with panel clips to fasten the sheathing together. But it may be cheaper to use fewer supports with thicker panels. A good choice for long-span flat or sloped roofs is $^3/4$-inch 48/24 panels over framing 48 inches on center. Also, allowable live loads may have to be decreased for tile roofs with dead loads greater than 5

Panel span rating	Panel thickness (inches)	Maximum span (inches)		Nail size and type	Nail spacing (inches)	
		With edge support*	Without edge support		Panel edges	Intermediate
12/0	5/16	12	12			
16/0	5/16, 3/8	16	16			
20/0	5/16, 3/8	20	20	6d common		
24/0	3/8, 7/16, 1/2	24	20***			
24/16	7/16, 1/2	24	24			
32/16	1/2	32	28		6	12
32/16	5/8	32	28			
42/20**	5/8, 3/4, 7/8	42	32	8d common		
48/24**	3/4, 7/8	48	36		6	6

All panels will support at least 40 psf live load plus 5 psf dead load at maximum span, except as noted.
*Tongue-and-groove edges, panel edge clips (one between each support, exept two between supports 48 inches oc) lumber blocking or other.
**PS 1 plywood panels with Span Ratings of 42/20 and 48/24 will support 35 psf live load plus 5 psf dead load at maximum span. For 40 psf live load, specify Structural I.
***24 inches for 1/2-inch panels.

Figure 9-3
APA panel roof sheathing nailing recommendations

pounds per square foot. Nailing recommendations are given in Figure 9-3 and stapling recommendations in Figure 9-4. For special conditions, such as heavy concentrated loads, you may have to use thicker panels than those shown in Figure 9-3.

When support spacing exceeds the maximum length allowable without edge support, provide blocking, tongue-and-groove edges, or other edge support, such as panel clips. Panel clips provide edge support and assure panel spacing. When required, use one panel clip for spans less than 48 inches and two for spans that are 48 inches or more.

Panel thickness (inches)	Staple leg length (inches)	Staple spacing (inches)	
		Panel edges	Intermediate
5/16	1 1/4		
3/8	1 3/8	4	8
1/2	1 1/2		

Values are for 16-ga. galvanized wire staples with a minimum crown width of 3/8 inch.
For stapling asphalt shingles to 5/16 inch and thicker panels, use staples with a 3/4-inch minimum crown width and a 3/4-inch leg length. Space according to shingle manufacturer's recommendations.

Figure 9-4
APA panel roof sheathing stapling recommendations

Sheathing at Valleys, Hips and Chimney Openings

Install sheathing at valleys and hips so it provides a tight joint. Nail the sheathing securely to hip and valley rafters, spacing nails 6 inches on center. See Figure 9-5. This ensures a smooth, solid base for flashing.

Keep sheathing 3/4 inch from the finished masonry of a chimney extending through the roof. The 3/4-inch clearance is required on all sides. See Figure 9-6. Usually you need to leave a 2-inch clearance from the masonry to the rafters and headers around the opening for fire prevention. Your local code may have additional restrictions.

Installing Roof Coverings

Most homes are covered with asphalt shingles with either an organic or glass fiber base. There are 66 to 90 shingles to the square, depending on weight. A

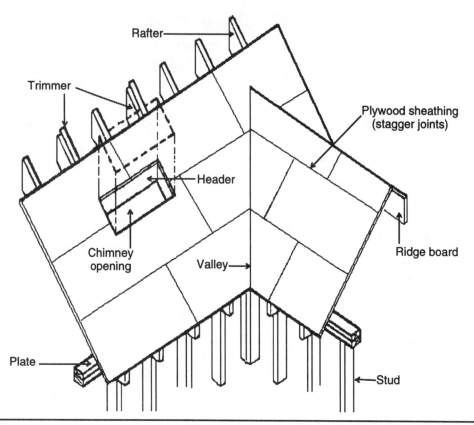

Figure 9-5
Valley sheathing

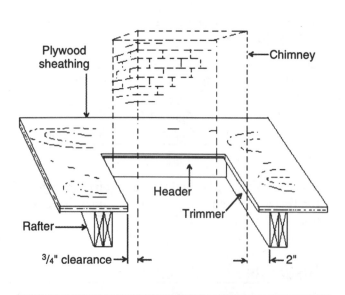

Figure 9-6
Chimney opening sheathing

square covers 100 square feet. Shingles are packed three to five bundles per square, depending on the type of shingle. Usually you lay strip shingles with a 4- to 6-inch exposure. Figure 9-7 gives information on typical asphalt shingles. Fiberglass shingles are equally serviceable and are available in most popular styles.

Cover the roof sheathing with 15-pound felt or, if required by local code, 30-pound felt. The felt is the underlayment for the shingles. Apply the felt when the deck is dry. Don't use coated felts, tar-saturated materials, or laminated waterproof papers. These could act as a vapor barrier to trap moisture or frost between the covering and the roof deck.

Laying Asphalt Shingles

The most popular strip shingle is a three-tab strip shingle. This shingle measures 12 to $13\frac{1}{4}$ inches wide and 36 to 40 inches long, depending on the weight.

Courtesy of Asphalt Roofing Manufacturers Association (ARMA)

Product	Configuration	Per Square			Size		Exposure	Underwriters Laboratories listing
		Approximate shipping weight	Shingles	Bundles	Width	Length		
Self-sealing random-tab strip shingle 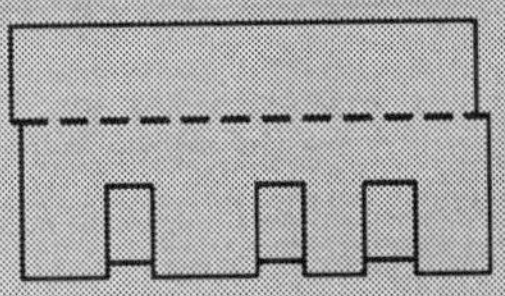 Multi-thickness	Various edge, surface texture and application treatments	285# to 390#	66 to 90	4 or 5	11½" to 14	36" to 40"	4" to 6"	A or C (Many wind-resistant)
Self-sealing random-tab strip shingle 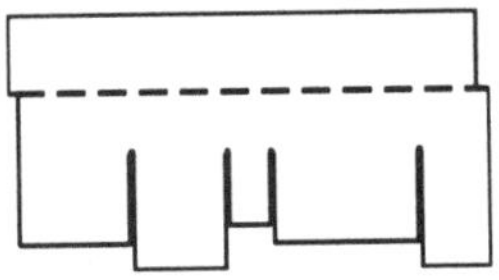 Single-thickness	Various edge, surface texture and application treatments	250# to 300#	66 to 80	3 or 4	12" to 13¼"	36" to 40"	5" to 5⅝"	A or C (Many wind-resistant)
Self-sealing square-tab strip shingle 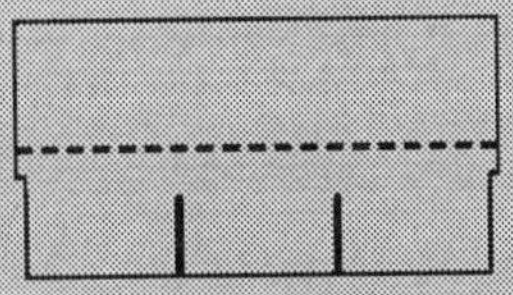 Three-tab	Two-tab or Four-tab	215# to 325#	66 to 80	3 or 4	12" to 13¼"	36" to 40"	5" to 5⅝"	A or C (All wind-resistant)
	Three-tab	215# to 300#	66 to 80	3 or 4	12" to 13¼"	36" to 40"	5" to 5⅝"	
Self-sealing square-tab strip shingle 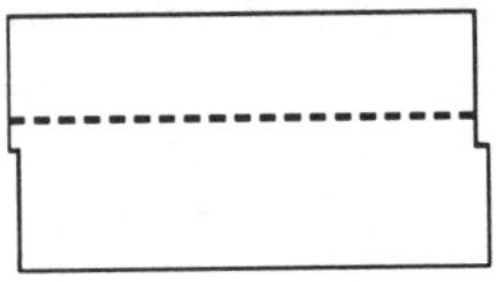 No-cutout	Various edge and surface texture treatments	215# to 290#	66 to 81	3 or 4	12" to 13¼"	36" to 40"	5" to 5⅝"	A or C (All wind-resistant)
Individual interlocking shingle 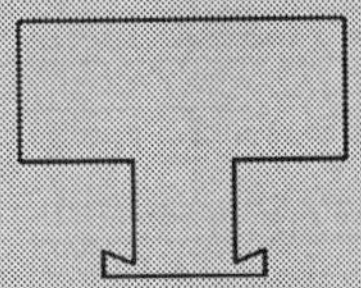 Basic design	Several design variations	180# to 250#	72 to 120	3 or 4	18" to 22¼"	20" to 22½"	—	C (Many wind-resistant)

Figure 9-7
Typical asphalt shingles

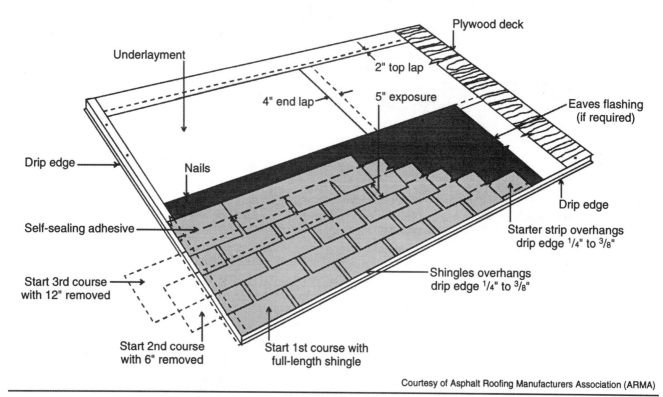

Underlayment

Plywood deck

2" top lap

5" exposure

4" end lap

Eaves flashing
(if required)

Drip edge

Nails

Drip edge

Self-sealing adhesive

Starter strip overhangs
drip edge ¹/₄" to ³/₈"

Shingles overhangs
drip edge ¹/₄" to ³/₈"

Start 3rd course
with 12" removed

Start 2nd course
with 6" removed

Start 1st course with
full-length shingle

Courtesy of Asphalt Roofing Manufacturers Association (ARMA)

Figure 9-8
6-inch method of laying shingles

Before laying the first course, you need to put down a starter strip. This strip protects the roof by filling in the spaces under the cutouts and joints of the first course of shingles. Use a row of shingles trimmed to the shingle manufacturer's recommendations, or a strip of mineral-surfaced roll roofing at least 7 inches wide. Let the starter strip overhang the eaves and rake edges ¹/₄ to ³/₈ inches, as shown in Figure 9-8.

Before starting to lay the shingles, snap a horizontal chalk line on the roof sheathing. To make sure the first course is straight, check the alignment often against this horizontal chalk line. You can snap several vertical chalk lines, aligned with the ends of the first-course shingles, to guide the cutout alignment in later courses.

Start the first course with a full shingle, and complete the course. But start succeeding courses with fractions of shingles, based on the kind of shingle and the pattern you want.

Choosing the Pattern and Exposure

There are three methods recommended for applying the three-tab strip shingles: the 6 inches, 5 inches, and 4 inches methods. The names refer to the amount you remove from the first shingle in each successive course to get the desired pattern. When you remove different amounts from the first shingle, the cutouts in one course of shingles won't line up directly with those in the course below. Figure 9-8 shows the 6-inch method, Figure 9-9 the 5-inch method, and Figure 9-10 the 4-inch method.

Save the pieces cut from the first shingle in each course after the first one. If they're full tabs, you can use them for finishing the opposite end of the course and for hip and ridge shingles.

To get the right exposure for square-tab strip shingles, align the butts with the top of the cutouts in the course below. For exposure for no-cutout shingles and

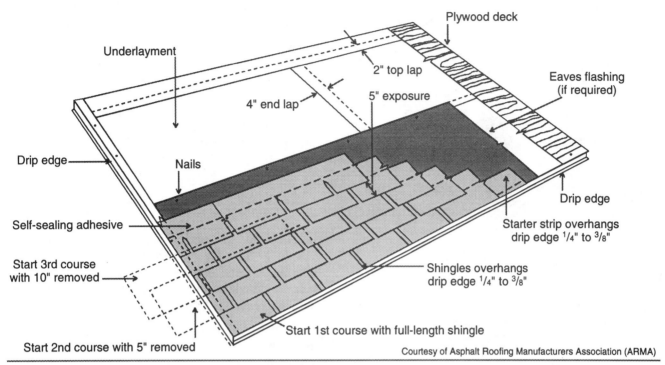

Figure 9-9
5-inch method of laying shingles

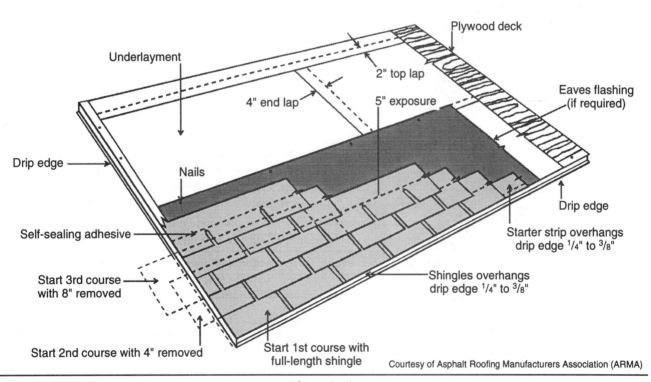

Figure 9-10
4-inch method of laying shingles

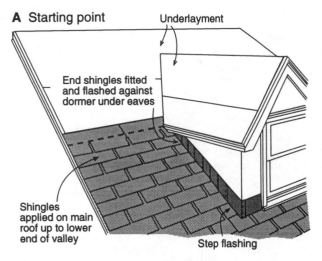

A Starting point

Underlayment

End shingles fitted and flashed against dormer under eaves

Shingles applied on main roof up to lower end of valley

Step flashing

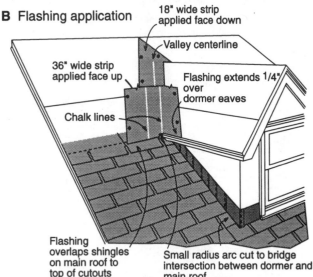

B Flashing application

18" wide strip applied face down

Valley centerline

36" wide strip applied face up

Flashing extends 1/4" over dormer eaves

Chalk lines

Flashing overlaps shingles on main roof to top of cutouts

Small radius arc cut to bridge intersection between dormer and main roof

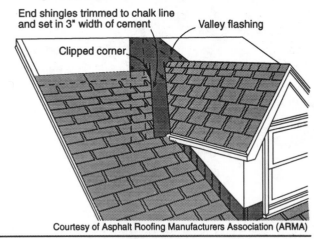

C Shingle application

End shingles trimmed to chalk line and set in 3" width of cement

Valley flashing

Clipped corner

Courtesy of Asphalt Roofing Manufacturers Association (ARMA)

Figure 9-11
Applying open valley flashing at dormer roof

those with variable butt lines, follow the manufacturer's directions printed on the bundle wrapper.

An alternate method for applying shingles is called *stacking*. With this method, you apply the shingles beginning at the eave and working up the roof, laying a 3- or 6-foot-wide section. The problem with this method is that shingles with a different color shade will all be applied in a block up the roof. You can easily spot this difference in color shades from the curb.

Nailing the Shingles

Align and nail each shingle carefully. Drive nails straight so the edge of the nail head doesn't cut into the shingle. And make sure the nail heads are flush with the shingle surface, not sunk into it. Finally, don't nail into, or above, factory-applied adhesives.

Start nailing from the end nearest the shingle last laid, then work across. This prevents buckling. Keep cutouts or end joints less than 2 inches from a nail in an underlying course. Don't try to realign a shingle by shifting the free end after two nails are in place. Remove the second nail and then position the shingle properly.

Flashing a Valley

A valley is formed where sloping roof planes join at an angle. The sloping planes direct water toward the valley, where it drains along the joint. To make a roof leakproof, you have to flash the valleys properly. Finish the valley flashing before you put on the shingles, except for the open valleys around dormers. There, you have to lap the valley flashing over the top courses of shingles along the dormer sidewalls. Figure 9-11 shows how to install flashing around a dormer.

The popular methods of flashing valleys are open, woven, and closed cut. Woven or closed-cut valleys are the best treatment for strip shingles.

Open Valley Method

Use 90-pound mineral surface roll roofing for open valley flashing. Choose a color that either matches the shingles or is neutral, because the flashing will

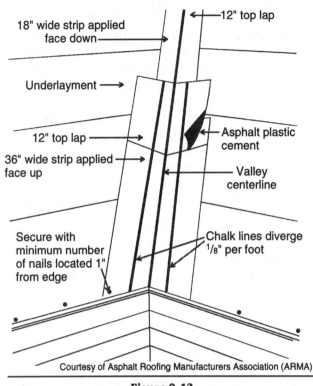

Courtesy of Asphalt Roofing Manufacturers Association (ARMA)

Figure 9-12
Open valley flashing with 90-pound roll roofing

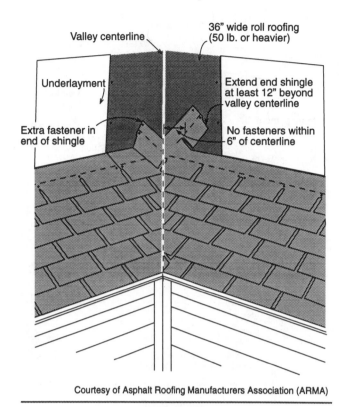

Courtesy of Asphalt Roofing Manufacturers Association (ARMA)

Figure 9-13
Applying woven-valley shingles

show. Apply the valley flashing in two layers. See Figure 9-12 for details.

Center the first layer, 18 inches wide, in the valley, with the mineral surfacing down. Trim the lower edge flush with the eaves' drip edge. Install this first layer up the entire length of the valley. If you need two or more strips of roll roofing, lap the upper piece over the lower so water flows over the joint. Overlap the top layer at least 12 inches and bond it with asphalt plastic cement. Nail along a line 1 inch from each edge. Use only enough nails to hold the strip in place. Start at one edge and work all the way up. Now return to nail the other side, pressing the flashing strip firmly into the valley at the same time.

After you've nailed the 18-inch strip, center a second strip 36 inches wide in the valley over the first strip. This time place the mineral surface facing *up*. Nail the strip in place just as you did the first strip. Make overlaps at least 12 inches and seal with asphalt plastic cement. The valley will be completed as you apply the shingles.

Woven and Closed-Cut Valley Method

Cover both types of valleys with 36-inch-wide mineral- or smooth-surfaced roll roofing, 50 pounds or heavier. Center the strip in the valley, over the underlayment. Use only enough nails to hold it in place. Nail the strip along a line 1 inch from the edges, first on one edge all the way up, then on the other, while pressing the flashing strip firmly and smoothly into the valley. Make laps 12 inches and cement. The valley will be completed as you apply the shingles.

Figure 9-13 shows how to apply shingles in the woven-valley method. Figure 9-14 shows the closed-cut method.

Finishing a Roof at the Ridge

Figure 9-15 shows three ways to finish a roof at the ridge if you don't use a ridge vent.

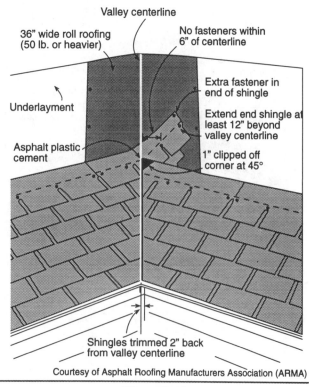

Valley centerline

36" wide roll roofing
(50 lb. or heavier)

No fasteners within
6" of centerline

Extra fastener in
end of shingle

Extend end shingle at
least 12" beyond
valley centerline

1" clipped off
corner at 45°

Underlayment

Asphalt plastic
cement

Shingles trimmed 2" back
from valley centerline

Courtesy of Asphalt Roofing Manufacturers Association (ARMA)

Figure 9-14
Applying closed-cut valley shingles

Flashing at Chimneys

A chimney's ground weight is concentrated in a small area, so the chimney and house seldom settle at the same rate. To prevent problems due to uneven settling, build chimneys on a separate foundation from that of the main structure. This won't eliminate possible differences in settling between the chimney and the main structure, but it'll free the chimney from the stresses and distortions that would occur if both were on the same foundation.

Because of the difference in settling, you have to apply the flashing around the chimney so it can move without damaging the water seal. To do this, fasten the base flashing to the masonry of the chimney. Then, if movement occurs, the counter flashing slides over the base flashing without affecting the water runoff. You'll find more on counter flashing later in this chapter.

Install a cricket (or wood saddle) where the back face of the chimney and the roof deck meet. The cricket is important for the life of the flashing. It keeps ice and snow from building up at the rear of the chimney and diverts water runoff around the chimney.

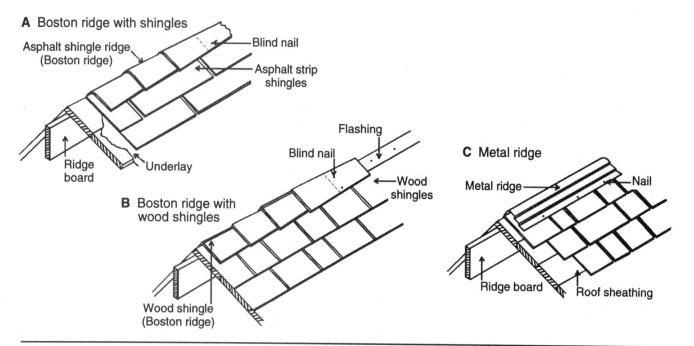

A Boston ridge with shingles

Asphalt shingle ridge
(Boston ridge)

Blind nail

Asphalt strip
shingles

Ridge
board

Underlay

Flashing

Blind nail

Wood
shingles

C Metal ridge

Metal ridge

Nail

B Boston ridge with
wood shingles

Wood shingle
(Boston ridge)

Ridge board

Roof sheathing

Figure 9-15
Ridge finishing

Apply shingles up to the front edge of the chimney before installing any flashing. Apply a coat of asphalt primer on the chimney's brickwork to seal the surface. The primer will also improve the adhesion of the asphalt plastic cement you'll apply later.

Base Flashing

Start with 26-gauge corrosion-resistant metal base flashing between the chimney and the roof deck on all sides. Apply the base flashing to the front first, as shown in Figure 9-16.

A Pattern for cutting flashing

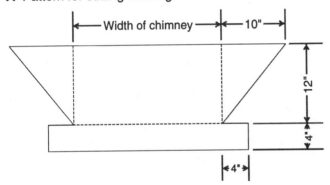

B Flashing

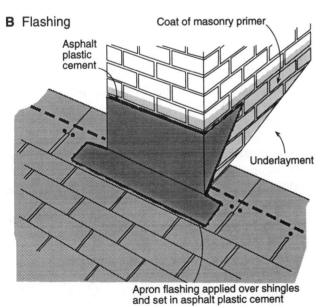

Apron flashing applied over shingles and set in asphalt plastic cement

Figure 9-16
Base flashing at front of chimney

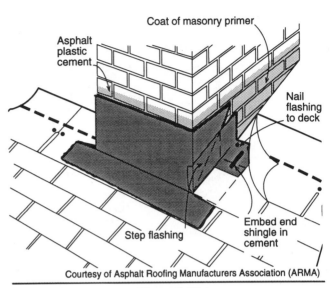

Figure 9-17
Base flashing at side of chimney

Bend the base flashing so the lower section extends at least 4 inches over the shingles and the upper section extends at least 12 inches up the face of the chimney. Work the flashing firmly and smoothly into the joint between the shingles and chimney. Set both the roof and chimney overlaps in asphalt plastic cement placed over the shingles and on the chimney face. Drive one or two nails into the mortar joints to hold the flashing against the chimney until the cement sets.

Use metal step flashing for the sides of the chimney. Place the pieces as shown in Figure 9-17. Secure each flashing piece to the masonry with asphalt plastic cement and to the deck with nails. Embed the end shingles of each course that overlaps the flashing in asphalt plastic cement.

Place the rear base flashing over the cricket and the back of the chimney, as shown in Figure 9-18. Cut and bend the metal base flashing to cover the cricket and extend onto the roof surface at least 6 inches. Also extend the flashing at least 6 inches up the brickwork and far enough around to lap the step flashing on the sides.

Cover the cricket with shingles if it's big enough. Otherwise, apply the rear base flashing first, and then bring the end shingles in each course up to the cricket and cement them in place.

A Base flashing at corner

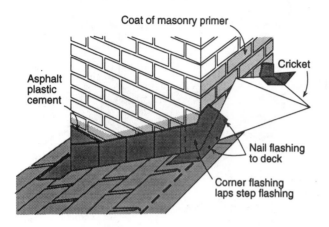

B Base flashing over cricket

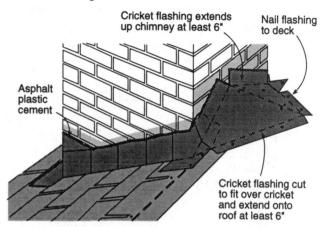

Courtesy of Asphalt Roofing Manufacturers Association (ARMA)

Figure 9-18
Base flashing at rear of chimney

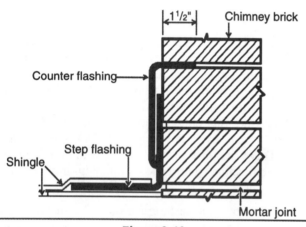

Figure 9-19
Applying counter flashing

Counter Flashing

Counter flashing fits over all the base flashing to keep water out of the joints. Begin by setting the metal counter flashing into the brickwork, (Figure 9-19).

Rake out a mortar joint to a depth of 1¹/₂ inches and insert the bent edge of the flashing into the cleared joint. Since it has a little spring tension, the flashing won't come out easily. Refill the joint with mortar. Finally, bend the flashing down so it covers the base flashing and lies snug against the chimney.

Use one continuous piece of counter flashing on the front of the chimney, as shown in Figure 9-20 A. On the sides and back of the chimney, use several pieces of similar-sized flashing, trimming each to fit the particular location of brick joint and roof pitch (Figure 9-20 B). Start the side pieces at the lowest point and overlap each at least 3 inches.

Laying Wood Shingles

No. 1 grade wood shingles are the most common residential wood shingles. They're all-heartwood, all-edge-grain, and tapered. Second-grade shingles make good roofs for secondary buildings and excellent side-walls for main buildings. Western cedar, cypress, and redwood are the main commercial shingle woods. The heartwood of all these species has high decay-resistance and low shrinkage.

Shingles come in random widths, the narrower shingles being in the lower grades. Four bundles of 16-inch shingles laid with 5 inches exposed (or "to the weather") will cover 100 square feet. Recommended exposures for the standard shingle sizes are shown in Figure 9-21.

Even if you subcontract your roofing jobs, you still need to know something about wood shingles and shakes. Figure 9-22 shows the correct way to install

A At front and side of chimney

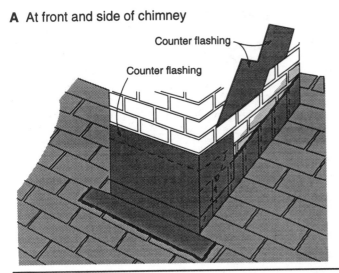

Counter flashing

Counter flashing

B At side and rear

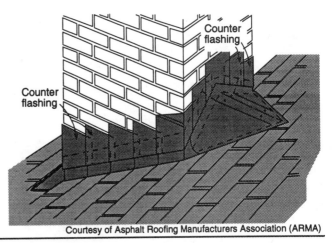

Counter flashing

Counter flashing

Courtesy of Asphalt Roofing Manufacturers Association (ARMA)

Figure 9-20
Counter flashing around chimney

wood shingles. You only need underlayment or roofing felt for protection in ice-dam areas. In damp areas, it's best to use spaced roof boards under wood shingles. In other areas, spaced or solid sheathing is optional.

Guidelines for Applying Wood Shingles

1. Extend shingles about 1½ inches beyond the eave line and about ¾ inch beyond the gable (rake) edge.

2. Drive two rust-resistant nails in each shingle. Space the nails about ¾ inch from the edge and 1½ inches above the butt line of the next course. Use 3d nails for 16- and 18-inch shingles and 4d nails for 24-inch shingles. Use a ring-shank (threaded) nail if plywood roof sheathing is less than ½ inch thick.

3. Double the first course of shingles. Allow a ⅛- to ¼-inch space between each shingle for expansion when wet. The joints between shingles should be offset at least 1½ inches from the joints in the course below. Also space the joints in succeeding courses so they don't line up with joints in the second course below.

4. On a hip roof, shingle away from the valleys, selecting and precutting wide valley shingles.

Shingle length (inches)	Shingle thickness (green)	Maximum exposure	
		Slope less[1] than 4 in 12 (inches)	Slope 4 in 12 and over (inches)
16	5 butts in 2"	3¾	5
18	5 butts in 2¼"	4¼	5½
24	4 butts in 2"	5¾	7½

[1] Minimum slope for main roofs — 4 in 12. Minimum slope for porch roofs — 3 in 12.

Figure 9-21
Recommended exposures for wood shingles

5. A metal edging along the gable end will help guide water away from the sidewalls.

6. When laying No. 1 all-heart, edge-grained shingles, you don't have to split wide shingles. Top-quality wide shingles are less likely than lower-quality shingles to split due to normal expansion and shrinkage.

Laying Wood Shakes

Shakes are longer than shingles so they have greater exposure, usually 7½ inches for 18-inch shakes, 10 inches for 24-inch shakes, and 13 inches for

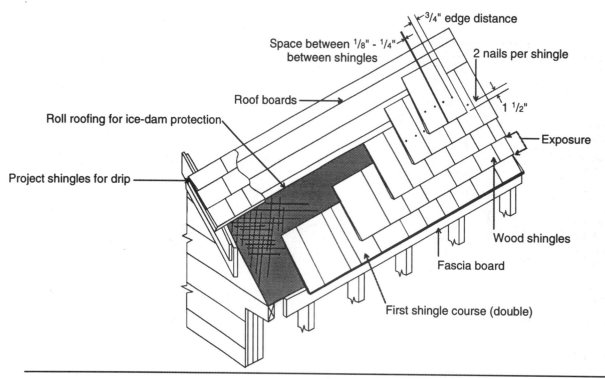

Figure 9-22
Applying wood shingles

32-inch shakes. Since shakes have thicker butts, you'll need to use long galvanized nails. However, you apply wood shakes about the same way as wood shingles. If you want to create a rustic appearance, lay the butts unevenly.

Shakes aren't smooth on both sides, so in areas with wind-driven snow, you'll need to build in some extra protection. Use solid sheathing under the shakes and apply underlayment between each course. Put a 36-inch wide starting strip of 30-pound asphalt felt at the eave line. Use an 18-inch-wide layer of the felt between each course. Put the bottom edge of the felt above the butt edge of the shake at a distance equal to double the weather exposure.

Material and Manhour Estimates for Roofing Materials

Plywood and OSB roof sheathing for a plain gable roof takes about 9 skilled and 4 unskilled hours per 1,000 square feet. The steeper the roof, the more man-

hours required. Suppose you're building an addition that's 24 feet long and 14 feet wide (from ridge to end of rafter). That's 336 square feet for one side of the roof. Both sides total 672 square feet. So it'll take about 6 skilled manhours and 2.7 unskilled manhours to install the sheathing. Here's a rule of thumb for estimating manhour requirements for installing plywood sheathing on a plain gable roof:

Multiply the number of 4 x 8-foot panels required to cover the roof by 30 minutes. About $^2/_3$ of the total will be for skilled labor and $^1/_3$ will be for unskilled labor.

Figure 9-23 lists the labor and materials for various types of asphalt roofing applied to new decks and reroofing. Use the same guidelines for fiberglass shingles. Figure 9-24 shows slope limitations for asphalt roofing materials. Figure 9-25 shows coverage and labor and material estimates for wood shingles. Figure 9-26 gives the coverage for shakes. Estimate installation labor for shakes the same as for wood shingles.

Types of roofing	Shingles per 100 SF	Nails per shingle	Length of nail*	Nails per 100 SF	Pounds per 100 SF (approximate)		Manhours per 100 SF
					12 ga. by $^7/_{16}$" head	11 ga. by $^7/_{16}$" head	
Roll roofing on new deck	—	—	1"	252**	0.73	1.12	1.0
Roll roofing over old roofing	—	—	$1^3/_4$"	252**	1.13	1.78	1.25
19" selvage over old shingles	—	—	$1^3/_4$"	181	0.83	1.07	1.0
3 tab sq. butt on new deck	80	4	$1^1/_4$"	336	1.22	1.44	1.5
3 tab sq. butt reroofing	80	4	$1^3/_4$"	504	2.38	3.01	1.85
Hex strip on new deck	86	4	$1^1/_4$"	361	1.28	1.68	1.5
Hex strip reroofing	86	4	$1^3/_4$"	361	1.65	2.03	2.0
Giant American	226	2	$1^1/_4$"	479	1.79	2.27	2.5
Giant Dutch lap	113	2	$1^1/_4$"	236	1.07	1.39	1.5
Individual hex	82	2	$1^3/_4$"	172	.79	1.03	1.5

*Length of nail should always be sufficient to penetrate at least $^3/_4$" into sound wood. Nails should show little, if any, below underside of deck.
**This is the number of nails required when spaced 2" apart.

Figure 9-23
Labor and materials for asphalt roofing

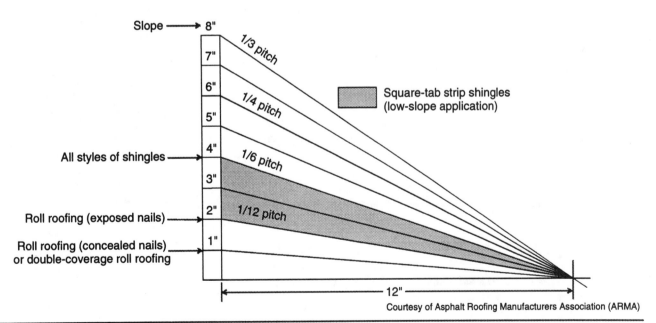

Figure 9-24
Slope limitations for asphalt roofing materials

A Wood shingle coverage

Shingle length	Minimum thickness	Approximate SF coverage of 1 square (4 bundles) shingles based on these weather exposures:							
		4"	4½"	5"	5½"	6"	6½"	7"	7½"
16"	5 in 2"	80	90	100	110	120	130	140	150
18"	5 in 2¼"	72½	81½	90½	100	109	118	127	136
24"	4 in 2"	—	—	—	—	80	86½	93	100

B Material and labor

Laid to weather	Material per 100 SF			Nails per 100 SF*		Manhours per 100 SF*
	Shingles	Waste	Shingles (with waste)	3d nails (pounds)	4d nails (pound)	
4"	900	10%	990	3¾	6½	3¾
5"	720	10%	792	3	5¼	3
6"	600	10%	660	2½	4¼	2½

Nails based on using 2 nails per shingle. Increase time factor 25% for hip roofs.

Figure 9-25
Estimating wood shingles

Handsplit and resawn	Approximate SF coverage of 1 square of handsplit shakes based on these weather exposures:						
	5½"	6½"	7"	7½"	8"	8½"	10"
18" x ½" to ¾"	55*	65	70	75**	80	85	—
18" x ¾" to 1¼"	55*	65	70	75**	80	85	—
24" x ½" to ¾"	—	65	70	75*	80	85	100**
24" x ¾" to 1¼"	—	65	70	75*	80	85	100**
32" x ¾" to 1¼"	—	—	—	—	—	—	100*

Recommended maximum weather exposure for 3-ply roof construction.
**Recommended maximum weather exposure for 2-ply roof construction.*

Figure 9-26
Handsplit shake coverage

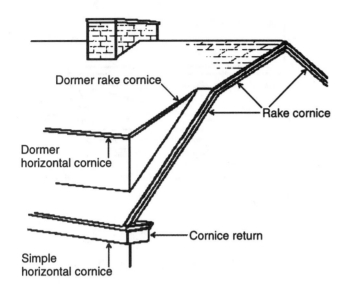
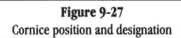

Figure 9-27
Cornice position and designation

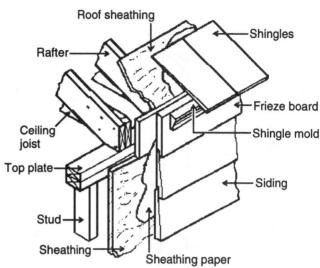

Figure 9-28
Simple cornice

Types of Cornices

Cornice work deserves careful attention because it stands out as a finish trim. The cornice you build on an addition should be the same design and type as the cornices on the existing structure. Besides serving a decorative function, a cornice is an overhang or "umbrella" that diverts water away from the walls of a house, cutting painting and maintenance costs. All dormers must have cornices.

Cornices fall into two broad categories: open and closed. The *open cornice* has exposed rafter tails and the *closed cornice* has enclosed rafter tails. There are many variations of each type.

The cornice of a building where the lower edge of the roof meets the wall line is called a *horizontal cornice*. A cornice extending up the slope of a roof is called a *rake cornice*. These are shown in Figure 9-27.

Simple or Close Cornice

A simple or close cornice merely "kills" the juncture where the roof meets the wall. There's no overhang or umbrella. Figure 9-28 shows a simple cornice. It uses a single strip called a frieze board that's beveled on the top edge to fit closely under the eave overhang. The frieze board is often rabbeted on the bottom to overlap the upper edge of the top course of the siding. A crown or shingle molding is used to give the eave line a finished look.

Open Cornice

In an open cornice, the rafters extend beyond the wall line the distance of the overhang (Figure 9-29). To make an attractive open cornice, nail a fascia board

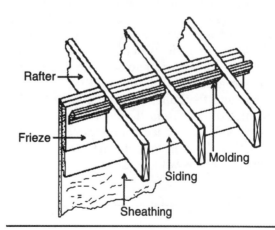

Figure 9-29
Open cornice

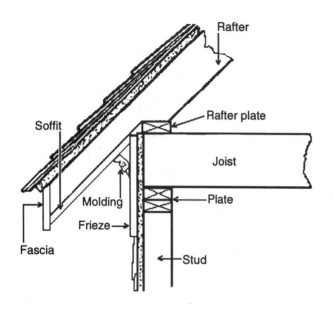

Figure 9-30
Closed cornice

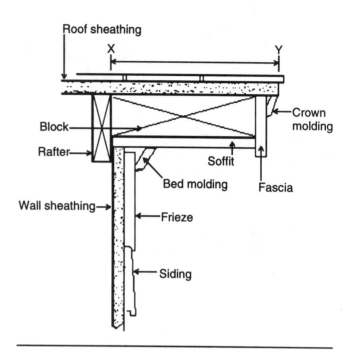

Figure 9-31
Rake with closed cornice

to the plumb or square cut of the rafter ends. If you need a firm nailing base for installing gutters, use a fascia board. The open cornice saves materials and labor and fits in nicely with the overall design of many styles of homes.

In cold climates where snow accumulates on the roof, the open cornice can present the same problem as that of a closed cornice with no soffit ventilation. If the building isn't properly insulated, heat will escape through the roof and melt the snow there. This causes water to drain from the roof surface until it reaches the overhang. But because the overhang is exposed to the cold on the underside, the water freezes again. This accumulated ice causes water to back up underneath the shingles to a point inside the wall line where it usually seeps into the building. If a building is adequately insulated, heat from the interior won't melt snow on the roof, and the ice dam doesn't become a problem. A little later in this chapter we'll look at ways to avoid problems with ice dams.

Closed Cornice

There's only one difference between an open and closed cornice: the closed cornice has a soffit to cover

the bottom of the rafter tails. Figure 9-30 shows a closed cornice.

You build this cornice on extended common rafters. Nail the fascia to the plumb cut at the end of the rafter tail. Fit the soffit to the back of the fascia and nail it to the bottom edge of the rafter. Extend the soffit up the rafter to the top edge of the frieze. Install molding at the intersection of the soffit and the frieze to cover the joint. Use the same materials for the return up the gable.

Install the roof sheathing to project beyond the outside common rafter (at the gable end) the distance of the thickness of the frieze, plus the width of the soffit, plus the thickness of the fascia. See Figure 9-31, line X-Y. If you're installing crown molding at the rake, extend the sheathing the thickness of the crown mold used.

Nail blocks every 4 feet to the underside of the sheathing, along the rake. Use blocks with the proper thickness to bring the bottom face of the rake soffit in line with the bottom face of the horizontal soffit, as shown in Figures 9-31 and 9-32.

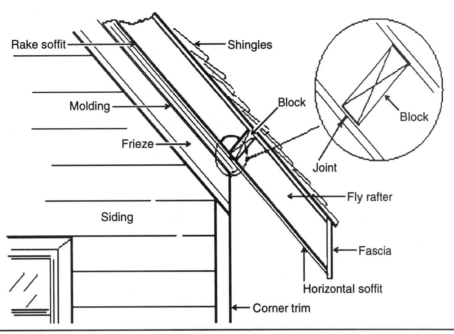

Rake soffit · Shingles · Molding · Block · Block · Frieze · Joint · Siding · Fly rafter · Fascia · Horizontal soffit · Corner trim

Figure 9-32
Horizontal and rake soffit joint

Box Cornice

The box cornice gives a more finished look to a house. The wide box cornice offers more protection for walls, windows, and doors. In a narrow box cornice, the rafter serves as a nailing surface for the soffit as well as for the rough or finish fascia (Figure 9-33). The rafter extension may vary between 6 and 12 inches, depending on the roof slope. A wide box cornice normally requires additional framing for fastening the soffit. Toenail lookouts to the wall or nailing header, and face nail to the ends of the rafter tails, as shown in Figure 9-34.

Use care in selecting your soffit material. The key is to avoid material that's too thin for the job. The distance between supports should determine the thickness of the material. The greater the distance, the thicker the material should be. You can use lumber, plywood, paper-overlaid plywood, hardboard, or medium-density fiberboard. Special soffit materials such as aluminum and vinyl are also available, and often come with ventilation panels.

Use $3/8$-inch plywood or OSB, or $1/2$-inch fiberboard for 16-inch rafter spacing. Use $5/8$-inch plywood for spacing up to 48 inches. A rough fascia installed at the end of the rafters makes a firm nailing base for a soffit and a finish fascia board. You can eliminate the rough fascia in a moderate cornice extension if you use a rabbeted fascia.

For ventilation in soffit areas, you can install inlet ventilators, usually narrow continuous slots covered with screen wire. This type of ventilator works particularly well in hip roofs.

You can't extend a box cornice very far on a steep roof. Be sure to allow space for a narrow frieze board or molding above the tops of windows. In a wide box cornice, a steep slope and a wide projection will bring the soffit too low unless the design calls for "framing-out" the window within the cornice run. Plan to use a narrow box cornice in steep-roof construction. Of course, your final guide in addition work is the cornice used in the existing structure.

Rake Cornice

The rake section is an extension of a gable roof beyond the end wall of a structure. The extension may vary from 6 to 24 inches or more. If the rake extension (overhang) is 6 to 8 inches, you can nail the fascia and

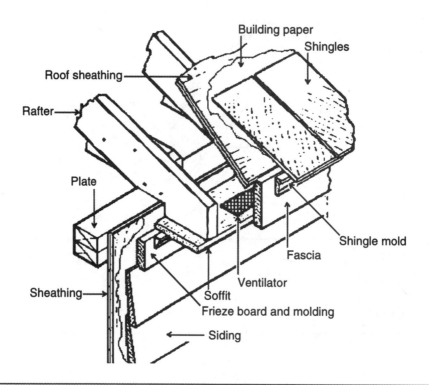

Figure 9-33
Narrow box cornice

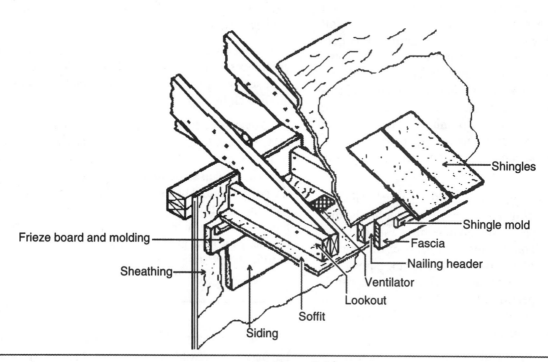

Figure 9-34
Wide box cornice

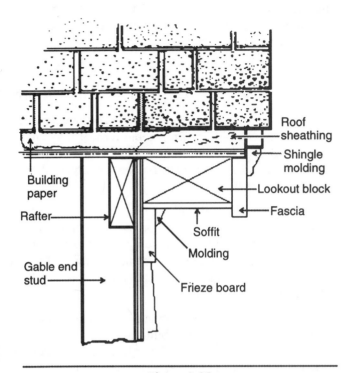

Figure 9-35
Moderate gable overhang

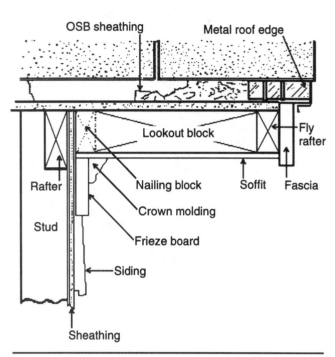

Figure 9-36
Extended gable overhang

soffit to a series of short lookout blocks, as shown in Figure 9-35. Make the fascia more secure by nailing through the projecting roof sheathing. Complete the construction with a frieze board and molding.

In an overhang of up to 20 inches, both the extended roof sheathing and a fly rafter support the rake section, as shown in Figure 9-36. The fly rafter extends from the ridge board to the rough fascia (nailing header) at the tail end of the rafters. Extend the roof sheathing from inner rafters to the end of the gable projection to provide rigidity and strength. Nail the roof sheathing to the fly rafter and to the lookout blocks. This helps support the rake section.

A close rake usually has no extension beyond the end wall other than the frieze board and moldings. To provide additional protection and overhang, use a 2 x 3- or 2 x 4-inch fascia block over the sheathing instead of a frieze board, as shown in Figure 9-37. The fascia block acts as a frieze board you can butt the siding against. The fascia, commonly a 1 x 6, provides the trim. Install metal roof-edging along the rake section.

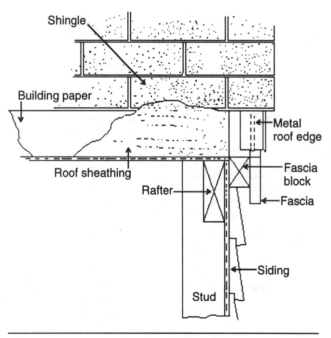

Figure 9-37
Close rake

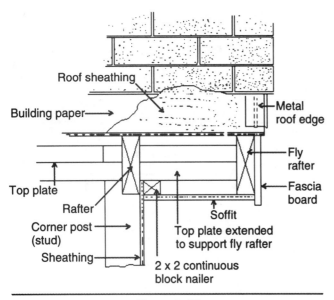

Figure 9-38
Boxed return for supported fly rafter

Where the rake overhang has a supported fly rafter, the extension can be 30 inches or more. Nail the sheathing to the rafter in the conventional manner. Fasten the soffit at the gable end to a continuous or

block nailer. See Figure 9-38. The cornice-end finish board completes the joint where the eave box cornice joins the rake box cornice.

The Cornice Return

On a hip roof, the cornice usually continues all the way around a building. On a gable roof, it may cover two sides of a building, and return a short distance around the ends. This is called a cornice return, shown back in Figure 9-27.

The type of detail you use depends on the type of cornice and how far the roof projects beyond the end wall. The cornice return in Figure 9-39 is usually used on more expensive homes and some commercial institutions. But you may occasionally find a return like this on a home you remodel.

When the soffit is horizontal, you can build the cornice return against the building at the gable end. The rake cornice at the roof line has the same design as the cornice at the eaves. The rake doesn't miter with the eave cornice members, but ends on top of the eave cornice return.

A narrow box cornice has a boxed return when the rake projects (Figure 9-40). Carry the fascia board of

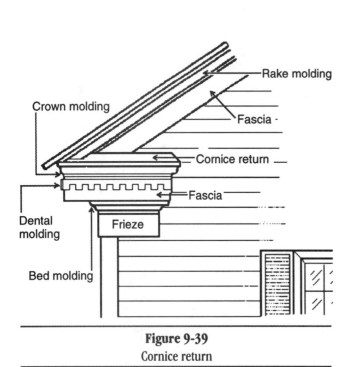

Figure 9-39
Cornice return

Figure 9-40
Narrow box cornice with boxed cornice return

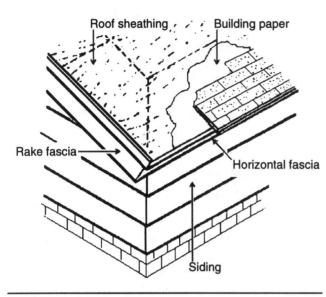

Figure 9-41
Wide box cornice with sloping rake and horizontal soffits

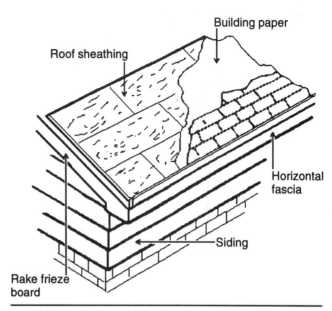

Figure 9-42
Narrow box cornice with close rake

the horizontal cornice around the corner of the rake projection. For a wide box cornice with no horizontal lookout members, the rake soffit is at the same slope as, and coincides with, the horizontal soffit. Look at Figures 9-32 and Figure 9-41. Use this simple system if there are wide overhangs at both the sides and ends of a house.

You can use a close rake (a gable end with little projection) with a narrow box cornice or a simple or closed cornice. The rake frieze board joins the frieze board or fascia of the horizontal cornice as shown in Figure 9-42.

Basic Cornice Construction

To make cornice construction easier, install a rough fascia board to the ends of the rafters before you nail on the roof sheathing. Use a 2-by that's *wider* than the height of the rafter tail ends, lined up with the bottom of the rafter tail end so it extends above the rafter the thickness of the sheathing. This serves two purposes. It lets you adjust the ends of the rafters if any of them are out of line horizontally and makes a straight, solid nailing base for the finish fascia board.

Use a taut string to straighten a rough fascia (Figure 9-43). Tack a ¾-inch block at each end of the fascia board as a gauge. You can use a third ¾-inch gauge block to determine where a fascia board is out of alignment by gauging at various points along the

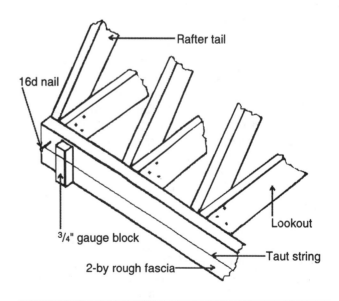

Figure 9-43
Using a rough fascia to straighten the rafter ends

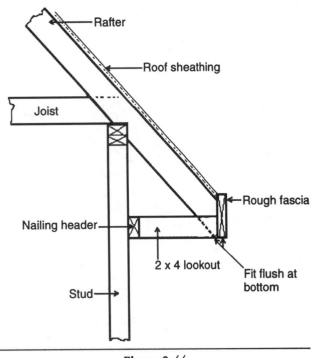

Figure 9-44
Nailing a lookout to nailing header, rafter tail and fascia

string. Tap out and wedge the board where necessary to align it. It might be necessary to trim off a portion of a rafter tail that's too long.

I prefer to secure lookouts to a nailing block (nailing header) that's attached to a wall, as shown in Figure 9-44. The nailing block also provides a nailer for the soffit or, in the case of brick veneer, for the frieze board and molding.

To install a nailing header, mark a point at both ends of the wall level with the bottom of the rough fascia board installed at the rafter ends. Snap a chalk line across these points to mark the bottom of the header. Install the header with 16d nails at each stud. Install the lookout members at each rafter with 10d or 12d nails. Make the bottom of the lookout flush with the bottom of the header and the rough fascia board.

In some areas, you'll have to take special precautions to prevent ice dams. Figure 9-45 shows ice dams and how to prevent them. Lay smooth roll roofing, 50 pounds or heavier, on the roofing over the overhang area, and up the roof for 36 inches. That should eliminate seepage, even if snow on the roof melts and re-freezes. Install ventilators in open cornice construction to prevent attic heat buildup (Figure 9-46).

You build the cornice treatment on a brick veneer just like you do on siding. But there's one difference. It's generally best to finish most of the cornice work before laying the brick. The mason "lays to" the finished carpentry (soffit). Once the masonry sets up, install the frieze and crown molding. Figure 9-47 shows two cornice treatments on brick veneer.

Estimating Manhours for Cornice Trim Work

The manhours needed for cornice trim work depend on the type of horizontal cornice and rake cornice treatments, and whether the addition is a one- or two-story structure. Estimate lookout members and

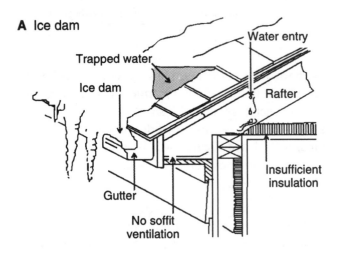

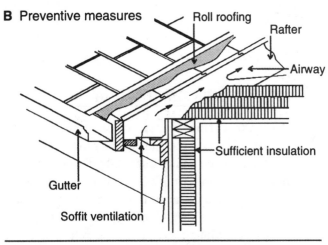

Figure 9-45
Cornice cold-weather protection

other rough framing components shown in Figures 9-34 and 9-36 on the basis of 50 skilled manhours per 1,000 board feet. Allow an additional 10 skilled manhours per 1,000 board feet for two-story work. Allow 4 hours per 100 linear feet if you'll finish off the gable end of a building with a fascia as shown in Figure 9-39.

When estimating manhours, list the linear feet of each item and establish a unit cost per 100 linear feet for each member. Here's a chart which shows the approximate manhours needed to install 100 linear feet of cornice trim work:

Skilled Manhours

Trim	Per 100 LF
2-member closed cornice	8
3-member boxed cornice	12
Molding	3
Barge board (verge) or separate frieze board	4

You have to work from a ladder or scaffolding to build cornices, and relocating these takes time. Be sure to take this into consideration when you make an estimate.

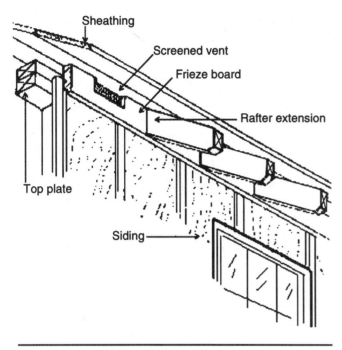

Figure 9-46
Installing frieze ventilator in open cornice

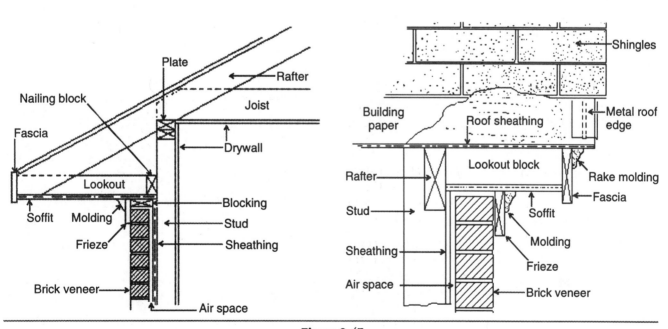

Figure 9-47
Cornice treatment on brick veneer structure

10

Finishing Exterior Walls

In residential construction, masonry walls are usually made of brick, concrete block, or stone. Of these, brick is the most common. Since you'll deal with it the most, we'll start with brick veneer.

Brick Veneer Construction

Brick veneer construction is usually a nominal 3- or 4-inch-thick exterior brick wythe. It's tied to a sheathing-covered stud wall or a concrete block wall, generally supported by a poured concrete footing. Brick veneer construction is designed to carry only its own weight, not a vertical load.

It's almost impossible to match original brick, except the most common red, gray and white, which may be close enough in color and texture to get by with. The owner may want to use an alternative, contrasting exterior finish like board and batten instead of using an imperfectly-matched brick. Or you can use a brick the same size and texture as the originals, and paint the whole house so the color differences don't matter.

Here are six requirements for doing a professional job of installing brick veneer:

1. Adequate foundation

2. Strong, rigid, well-braced backup system

3. Proper attachment of the veneer to the backup system

4. Neat, attractive detailing

5. Good quality materials

6. Professional workmanship in construction

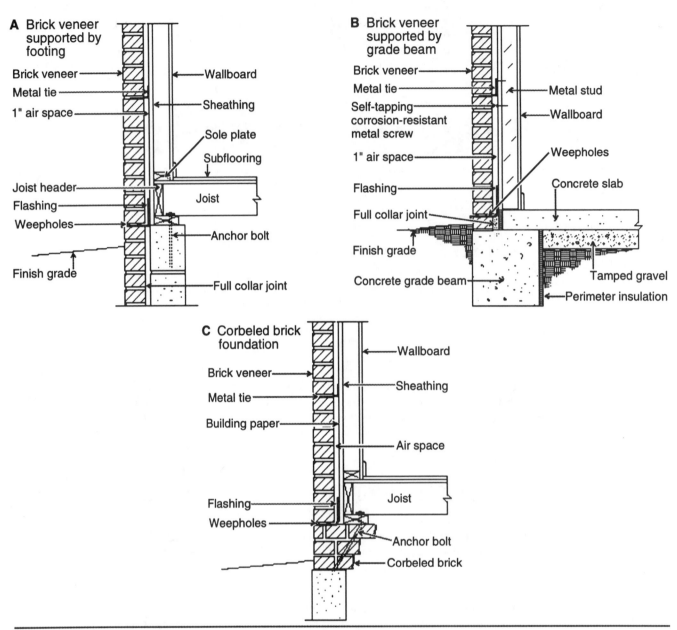

Figure 10-1
Typical foundation details for brick veneer construction

The Foundation

The first requirement for brick veneer is a solid foundation. Figure 10-1 shows three typical foundation details for brick veneer construction. Make the foundation, or foundation wall, that supports the brick veneer at least as thick as the total thickness of the brick veneer wall assembly. Check your local building code on this. Many building codes permit a nominal 8-inch foundation wall under single-family housing constructed of brick veneer, provided the top of the foundation wall is corbeled as shown in Figure 10-1 C. The total projection of the corbel can't exceed 2 inches, and individual corbels can't project more than $1/3$ of the thickness of the unit, or $1/2$ the height of the unit. The top corbel course shouldn't be higher than the bottom of the floor joist, and it must be a full header course.

The Materials

For veneer construction, select brick that meets the standards in ASTM C 62 or C 216. Select Grade SW (severe weather) if you're laying the brick in a freezing climate.

Use portland cement-lime mortar for brick veneer because it performs better and more predictably than masonry cement mortars. Type N mortar is suitable for most brick veneer. Use Type M where the brick veneer is in contact with the ground (sidewalks), and for below grade work (foundations and retaining walls). Choose Type S where extra strength is required, such as when the mortar is the sole bonding agent between the veneer and the masonry backing wall. Type S mortar provides a strong bond for brick walls.

Anchors and Ties

Use metal ties to tie brick veneer to a backup wall to provide lateral support for the veneer wall. Leave a 1-inch clear space between the veneer and the backup wall so rainwater will drain completely. Brick veneer will settle over time. And wind blowing against brick veneer causes pressure and movement. The ties you use must allow for all this movement and still provide the necessary stability. Select the ties based on the backup system you use them with.

Figure 10-2 shows various ties you can use for brick veneer. Let's look at ties that are appropriate for different backup systems.

Ties for Wood-Frame Backup

Use corrosion-resistant corrugated metal ties, 22 gauge, $7/8$ inch wide, 6 inches long, to attach brick veneer to wood-frame construction (Figure 10-2 A). Fasten the ties to the studs with corrosion-resistant nails that penetrate the sheathing. Drive the nail at least $1^{1}/_2$ inches into the studs.

Ties for Metal Stud Backup

Use corrosion-resistant wire ties, 9 gauge, to attach brick veneer to metal studs. You can use the wire ties shown in Figures 10-2 C and D to attach brick veneer to metal studs. Use the wire tie shown in Figure 10-2 F for structural steel.

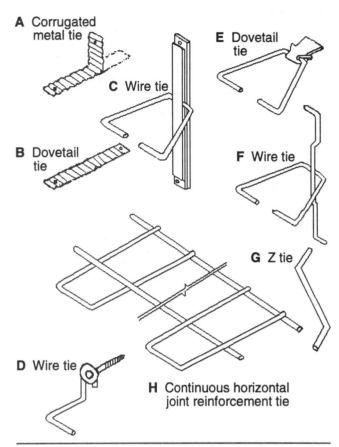

Figure 10-2
Ties for brick veneer

Ties for Concrete Backup

Use a corrosion-resistant wire or flat bar dovetail anchor to tie brick veneer to concrete. Use at least 6 gauge wire anchors that are 4 inches wide with the wire looped and closed. Use flat bar dovetail anchors that are at least 16 gauge and $7/8$ inches wide. Turn the end of the anchor up $1/4$ inch and embed it in the masonry. Embed dovetail anchors at least 2 inches into the bed joint of the veneer. Anchor them to dovetail slots in the concrete. Dovetail anchors are shown in Figures 10-2 B and 10-2 E.

Ties for Masonry Backup

Install Z ties (Figure 10-2 G) to attach brick veneer to masonry backup walls. Don't use Z ties with hollow blocks. Use a continuous horizontal joint reinforcement with tabs (Figure 10-2 H) on concrete masonry backup walls.

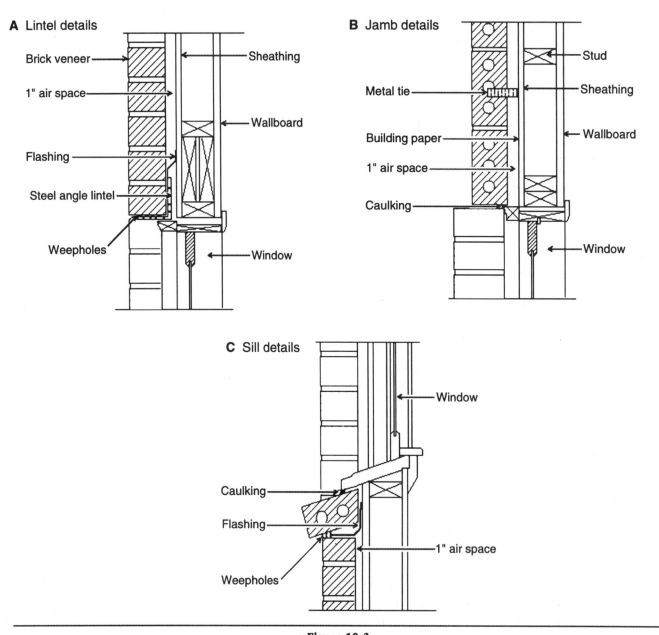

A Lintel details

Brick veneer
1" air space
Flashing
Steel angle lintel
Weepholes
Sheathing
Wallboard
Window

B Jamb details

Metal tie
Building paper
1" air space
Caulking
Stud
Sheathing
Wallboard
Window

C Sill details

Window
Caulking
Flashing
Weepholes
1" air space

Figure 10-3
Tie system construction details for brick veneer

Installing the Ties

Figures 10-1 and 10-3 show construction details for the various tie systems. Install one tie for every 2²/₃ square feet of wall area, a maximum spacing of 24 inches on center. For one- and two-family wood-frame construction, the tie spacing may be one tie for each 3¹/₄ square feet of wall area with a maximum spacing of 24 inches on center. Embed the tie a minimum of 2 inches into the bed joints of the veneer. Place the ties so they are surrounded by the mortar.

Flashing and Weepholes

Replacing flashing in brick veneer construction is difficult and expensive. That's the best reason to use only good quality materials in your walls. Sheet metals, bituminous membranes and plastics, or combinations of these three, make good flashing materials. Don't use asphalt-impregnated felt. It's not as good for this purpose.

Form weepholes 24 inches on center by omitting mortar from all or part of the head joint when you lay the bricks. You can also form weepholes by putting a well-oiled rod in the mortar and then taking it out just before the mortar sets. This leaves an unobstructed opening in the mortar so the wall will drain properly. Or you can leave "weepers" such as plastic tubing or rope wicks in the mortar.

Locate flashing and weepholes above grade, but as close to grade as possible, at the bottom of a wall and at all openings. Space the weepholes no more than 24 inches on center. Locate holes immediately above all flashing. Place weepholes formed with wick materials a maximum of 16 inches on center. If veneer continues below flashing at the base of a wall, grout the space between the veneer and the backup up to the height of the flashing. Fasten the flashing securely to the backup wall and extend it through the face of the brick veneer. See Figures 10-1 and 10-3.

Install flashing with care to prevent punctures or tears. Seal the joints where flashing overlaps.

Caulking and Sealants

There are good caulks and sealants, and there are poor ones. This isn't the place for cost-cutting. The good ones cost more, but they're well worth it. The success of your brick job depends on using the best of them. You want a flexible and durable seal, not one that will dry out or shrink in a few months. Use only good grades of polysulfide, butyl, or silicone rubber sealants. Don't use an oil-based caulking because most of them lack flexibility and durability.

Make the exterior caulking joints at exterior doors and windows no less than 1/4 inch wide, and no greater than 3/8 inch. Clean the joints for a depth of 3/4 inch. Fill all joints completely with an elastic caulking compound or sealant, using a pressure gun to force it into place. Prime all joints before caulking. Pack compressible backer rope materials into joints that are deeper than 3/4 inch, or wider than 3/8 inch.

Masonry Joints

The best joints to use with brick veneer are the concave, V, and grapevine joints. Other joints aren't resistant enough to moisture penetration. With a jointer, tool the joints as soon as the mortar has become slightly hard (thumbprint hard) to firmly compact the mortar against the edges of the adjoining brick. Here's a point important enough to repeat: Keep the 1-inch space between the veneer and the backup wall clean and free of all mortar droppings. If you don't, the wall assembly won't drain as it should. Mortar blocking the air space makes a bridge for water to travel to the interior.

Protecting Masonry

While masonry will last centuries *after* construction, you've got to protect the materials *before* and *during* construction. Store brick, block, and all masonry materials off the ground. This keeps polluted surface water, mud, and dust from contaminating them. Cover materials to protect them from the elements.

A partially-completed masonry wall that's exposed to rain may become so saturated with water that it'll take months to dry out. Such prolonged saturation can cause efflorescence. To prevent saturation, cover all walls at the end of each workday, and before all shutdown periods. Use a strong, weather-resistant membrane which overhangs the brickwork at least 36 inches. Attach the cover securely.

Estimating Masonry Materials

Here's a rule of thumb for roughly estimating the number of bricks required for veneer on an addition with normal window and door openings:

♦ Allow 6.5 bricks per square foot of wall (without deducting window and door areas). This rule allows for normal waste and the mason's tendency to break a whole brick in half to fit a space even when he's surrounded by previously-broken halves.

♦ Allow 5 or 6 bags of portland cement-lime mortar to lay 1,000 bricks. A common mix uses 1 bag of masonry cement and 3 cubic feet of sand.

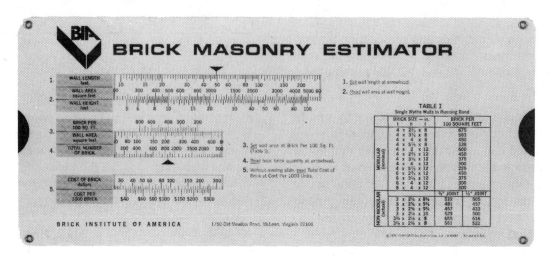

Courtesy of Brick Institute of America

Figure 10-4
Brick masonry estimator

A more accurate way to estimate masonry is to calculate the units required and use the Brick Masonry Estimator shown in Figure 10-4. It's very inexpensive and small enough to carry in your pocket. If you know the length and height of the walls, the size and cost of the brick, it'll give you the brick cost. The Estimator includes data for 19 modular and non-modular brick sizes. It also helps with mortar estimates. After you've determined the brick quantities, use the Estimator to find the quantity of portland cement, lime, and sand for four types of mortars: M, S, N, and O. You can order an Estimator from:

Brick Institute of America
11490 Commerce Park Drive
Reston, Virginia 22091
(703) 620-0010

Figure 10-5 provides brick equivalent factors for modular brick. Figure 10-6 gives material and labor for brickwork per 100 square feet of wall.

Wood and Manufactured Wood Siding

Manufactured and natural wood sidings come in many patterns and textures. APA Sturd-I-Wall, plywood paneling, plywood lap siding, hardboard lap siding, hardboard paneling, hardboard shakes, and wood siding all are exterior finishes.

A finished wall should be flat, but when you install plywood siding, that's sometimes hard to achieve. If the studs are straight, it makes it easier to apply the siding. Leave $1/8$ inch between the panel edges and ends for expansion, unless otherwise recommended by the manufacturer.

Unit designation	Nominal dimensions (inches)	Brick equivalents[1]
Standard Modular	4 x 2²/₃ x 8	1.0
Engineer	4 x 3¹/₅ x 8	1.2
Economy or Jumbo Closure	4 x 4 x 8	1.5
Double	4 x 5¹/₃ x 8	2.0
Roman	4 x 2 x 12	1.13
Norman	4 x 2²/₃ x 12	1.5
Norwegian	4 x 3¹/₅ x 12	1.8
Economy 12 or Jumbo Utility	4 x 4 x 12	2.25
Triple	4 x 5¹/₃ x 12	3.0
SCR	6 x 2²/₃ x 12	2.25
6" Norwegian	6 x 3¹/₅ x 12	2.7
6" Jumbo	6 x 4 x 12	3.38
8" Jumbo	8 x 4 x 12	4.5

[1] Based on nominal face dimensions only.

Figure 10-5
Brick equivalent factors for modular brick

Mortar joint	Wall thickness	Material				Labor 100 SF wall	
		Brick		Wall ties per 100 SF	Mortar CF per 100 SF	Mason	Laborer
		100 SF wall	SF per 1000 brick				
1/4	4"	698	143	100	4.48		
3/8	4"	655	153	93	6.56		
1/2	4"	616	162	88	8.34	6½ hours average	5 hours average
5/8	4"	581	172	83	10.52		
3/4	4"	549	182	78	12.60		

Note: Mortar includes 20% waste for all bead and bed joints.

Figure 10-6
Brickwork material and labor

The nailing sequence can affect the appearance of a finished wall. Install the first panel flush at a corner so you don't compress the other panels. Plumb it with a level. Then position the second panel, leaving the recommended space between the edges. Lightly tack the panel at each corner. Drive in the first row of nails along the edge nearest the preceding panel. Nail from top to bottom. Remove tacking nails. Now nail along the first intermediate stud. Continue by nailing at the second intermediate stud, and then along the outside edge. Complete the installation by nailing the siding to the top and bottom plates.

Since wood siding hasn't changed much over the years, you can usually match the original siding. The exception might be a very old home with custom-made siding.

Plywood Siding

The general term plywood siding includes APA Sturd-I-Wall, plywood panel siding, and plywood lap siding.

APA Sturd-I-Wall Siding

APA Sturd-I-Wall (SIW) uses APA 303 plywood panel siding. You can install it directly to studs or over non-structural sheathing materials such as fiberboard, gypsum, or rigid foam insulation sheathing. "Non-structural" means that the sheathing material doesn't

meet the bending and racking strength requirements required by building codes. A single layer of SIW is strong and rack-resistant. It eliminates the need for separate structural sheathing and diagonal wall bracing.

Be careful when you install foam sheathing. It's a highly-effective vapor barrier, but when you install it on a wall exterior, the vapor barrier is on the wrong side of the studs. The vapor barrier goes on the warm (in winter) side of the wall. If you use foam sheathing under plywood siding, install either a polyethylene vapor barrier or foil-backed gypsum wallboard on the warm side of the wall. This helps prevent condensation in the wall cavity. When you use rigid foam insulation sheathing, install 1/2-inch gypsum wallboard on the inside surface of the wall. Building codes generally require this gypsum board installation for fire protection.

Normally you install SIW vertically, as shown in Figure 10-7. You can also install it horizontally, as shown in Figure 10-8. For horizontal application, install 2 x 4 blocking at the horizontal joints. Maximum stud spacing for both vertical and horizontal applications is shown in Figure 10-9.

When you install SIW panel siding over rigid foam sheathing, drive nails flush with the siding surface. Don't overdrive the nails or you'll dimple the panel and compress the foam sheathing. Back all panel edges with framing or blocking. Use corrosion-resistant nails to prevent staining.

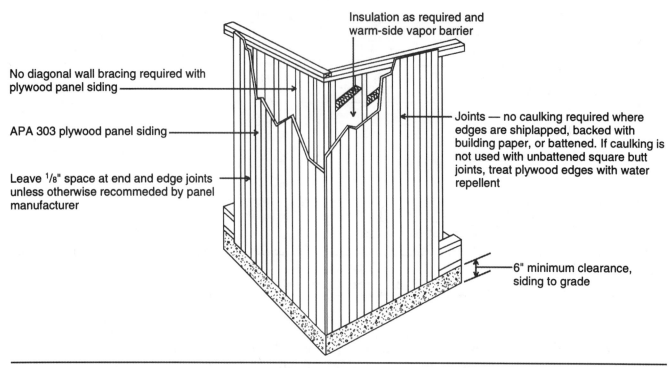

No diagonal wall bracing required with plywood panel siding

APA 303 plywood panel siding

Leave ⅛" space at end and edge joints unless otherwise recommeded by panel manufacturer

Insulation as required and warm-side vapor barrier

Joints — no caulking required where edges are shiplapped, backed with building paper, or battened. If caulking is not used with unbattened square butt joints, treat plywood edges with water repellent

6" minimum clearance, siding to grade

Figure 10-7
APA Sturd-I-Wall (vertical application)

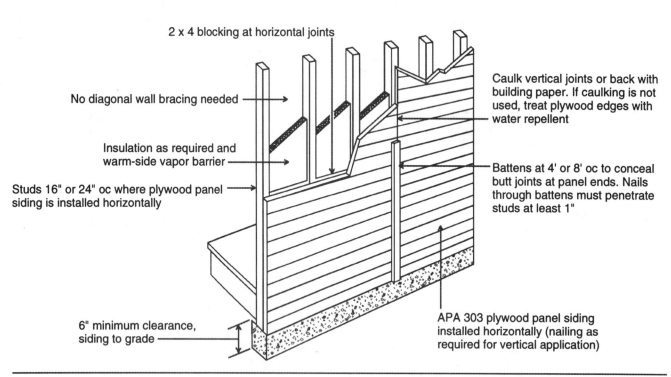

2 x 4 blocking at horizontal joints

No diagonal wall bracing needed

Insulation as required and warm-side vapor barrier

Studs 16" or 24" oc where plywood panel siding is installed horizontally

Caulk vertical joints or back with building paper. If caulking is not used, treat plywood edges with water repellent

Battens at 4' or 8' oc to conceal butt joints at panel ends. Nails through battens must penetrate studs at least 1"

6" minimum clearance, siding to grade

APA 303 plywood panel siding installed horizontally (nailing as required for vertical application)

Figure 10-8
APA Sturd-I-Wall (horizontal application)

Plywood panel siding description (all species groups)	Nominal thickness (inches)	Maximum stud spacing (inches)		Nail size*	Nail spacing (inches)	
		Face grain vertical	Face grain horizontal		Panel edges	Intermediate
APA MDO EXT	¹¹/₃₂ & ³/₈	16	24	6d for panels ¹/₂" thick or less, 8d for thicker panels	6***	12
	¹/₂ & thicker	24	24			
APA 303 siding — 16 oc EXT (including T1-11)	¹¹/₃₂ & thicker	16	24			
APA 303 siding — 24 oc EXT	¹⁵/₃₂ & thicker**	24	24			

Recommendations apply to siding direct to studs and over sheathing other than structural panels or lumber.

* *If siding is applied over sheathing thicker than ¹/₂ inch, use next regular nail size. Use nonstaining box nails for siding installed over foam insulation sheathing.*

Hot-dipped or hot-tumbled galvanized steel nails are recommended for most siding applications. For best performance, stainless steel nails or aluminum nails should be considered. APA tests also show that electrically or mechanically galvanized steel nails appear satisfactory when plating meets or exceeds thickness requirements of ASTM A641 Class 2 coatings, and is further protected by yellow chromate coating. Note: Galvanized fasteners may react under wet conditions with the natural extractives of some wood species and may cause staining if left unfinished. Such staining can be minimized if the siding is finished in accordance with APA recommendations, or if the roof overhang protects the siding from direct exposure to moisture and weathering.

** *Only panels ¹⁵/₃₂" and thicker which have certain groove depths and spacings qualify for 24 oc Span Rating.*

*** *For braced wall section with ¹¹/₃₂" or ³/₈" siding applied horizontally over studs 24" oc, space nails 3" oc along panel edges.*

Figure 10-9
APA Sturd-I-Wall construction

Plywood Panel Siding and Lap Siding

Most plywood siding is installed over sheathing. Figure 10-10 gives installation recommendations for APA 303 plywood panel and lap siding. Figures 10-11 and 10-12 show how to install these materials. Install lap siding with the face grain horizontal — across the supports. Stagger the siding joints so they don't line up with each other.

The joints don't have to fall on a stud if you use nailable panel or lumber sheathing under the siding. Nailable sheathing includes:

♦ Nominal 1-inch boards with studs spaced 16 or 24 inches on center.

♦ Rated sheathing panels with a span rating of 24/0 or greater, and the long dimension parallel to or perpendicular to studs spaced 16 or 24 inches on center. If you install 3-ply plywood panels to studs spaced 24 inches on center, put the long dimension across the studs. Check your code on this.

Hardboard Siding

Hardboard is made from wood chips and sawmill by-products. It comes in many designs and patterns. It's one of the least expensive siding materials. And it's fairly easy to install and requires no special tools. Hardboard is also free of knots and is uniform in thickness, density, and appearance.

Hardboard has to be maintained just like any other wood, and kept free of termites. And it's important that you protect hardboard from the elements before you install and prime it. You can store hardboard siding outside, but keep it off the ground. Protect the top and sides with a waterproof cover. But don't seal the bundle. Adequate ventilation is important. Protect it from dirt, grease, and rough handling. Stack hardboard flat to avoid warping.

Cut hardboard siding with a fine-toothed hand saw — or a power saw with a combination blade if you don't mind the dust. If you use a hand saw, put the finish side face up while sawing. With a power saw, the finish side goes face down.

199

	Plywood siding description (all species groups)	Nominal thickness (inches)	Maximum stud spacing		Nail size*	Nail spacing (inches)	
			Face grain vertical	Face grain horizontal		Panel edges	Intermediate
Panel siding	APA MDO EXT	$^{11}/_{32}$ & $^{3}/_{8}$	16	24	6d for panels $^{1}/_{2}$" thick or less, 8d for thicker panels	6	12
		$^{1}/_{2}$ & thicker	24	24			
	APA 303 Siding - 16 oc EXT (including T1-11)	$^{11}/_{32}$ & thicker	16	24			
	APA 303 SIDING - 24 oc EXT	$^{15}/_{32}$ & thicker**	24	24			
Lap siding	APA MDO EXT	$^{11}/_{32}$ & thicker	--	24	6d for siding $^{3}/_{8}$" thick or less, 8d for thicker siding	4d @ vertical butt joints; 6d along bottom edge	8d (if siding wider than 12")
	APA 303 SIDING	$^{11}/_{32}$ & thicker	--	24			

If siding is applied over sheathing thicker than $^{1}/_{2}$ inch, use next regular nail size.

Hot-dipped or hot-tumbled galvanized steel nails are recommended for most siding applications. For best performance, stainless steel nails or aluminum nails should be considered. APA tests also show that electrically or mechanically galvanized steel nails appear satisfactory when plating meets or exceeds thickness requirements of ASTM A641 Class 2 coatings, and is further protected by yellow chromate coating. Note: Galvanized fasteners may react under wet conditions with the natural extractives of some wood species and may cause staining if left unfinished. Such staining can be minimized if the siding is finished in accordance with APA recommendations, or if the roof overhang protects the siding from direct exposure to moisture and weathering.

** Only panels $^{15}/_{32}$" and thicker which have certain groove depths and spacings qualify for 24 oc Span Rating.

Figure 10-10
APA 303 plywood siding over nailable panel or lumber sheathing

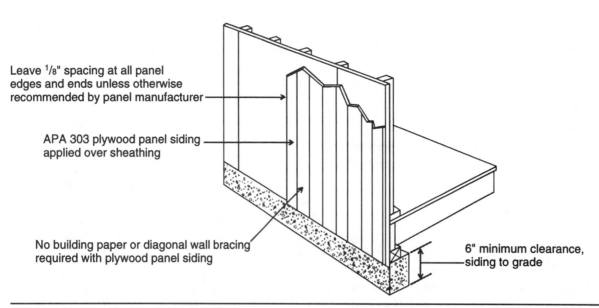

Leave $^{1}/_{8}$" spacing at all panel edges and ends unless otherwise recommended by panel manufacturer

APA 303 plywood panel siding applied over sheathing

No building paper or diagonal wall bracing required with plywood panel siding

6" minimum clearance, siding to grade

Figure 10-11
APA 303 plywood panel siding over nailable panel or lumber sheathing

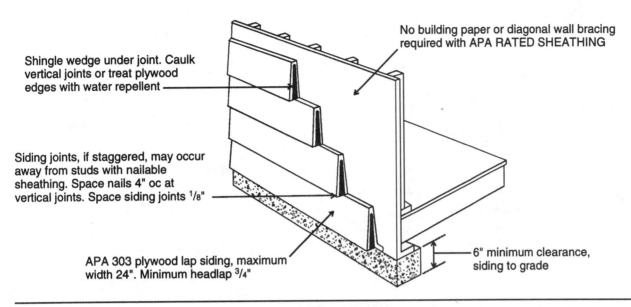

Shingle wedge under joint. Caulk vertical joints or treat plywood edges with water repellent

No building paper or diagonal wall bracing required with APA RATED SHEATHING

Siding joints, if staggered, may occur away from studs with nailable sheathing. Space nails 4" oc at vertical joints. Space siding joints 1/8"

APA 303 plywood lap siding, maximum width 24". Minimum headlap 3/4"

6" minimum clearance, siding to grade

Figure 10-12
APA 303 plywood lap siding over nailable panel or lumber sheathing

Never apply hardboard siding to green concrete, plaster, or framing materials. Give the concrete or framing time to dry thoroughly before you start applying any hardboard.

The two most common types of hardboard siding are lap and panel siding.

Hardboard Lap Siding

If your local code permits it, you can install hardboard lap siding directly to the studs. But you may wind up with wavy siding. To minimize waviness, install the siding over plywood or board sheathing. Whether you apply the siding directly to studs or over sheathing, the maximum stud spacing is 16 inches on center. The wall framing must be properly braced.

Apply a layer of building paper under siding, even when you apply it over plywood or board sheathing. The paper acts as a wind barrier.

Begin installation with a wood starter strip measuring 7/16 inches x 1 1/2 inches, or use a strip of lap siding cut down to 2 inches wide. Level and nail it along the bottom edge of the sill plate. See Figure 10-13A.

Nail the first course of siding so it extends at least 1/4 inch (but not more than 1 inch) below the starter strip. Drive a nail every 16 inches on center, at each stud location. Allow at least an 8-inch clearance between the siding and the finish grade. See Figure 10-13 B.

Lap subsequent courses at least 1 inch, but not more than 1 1/2 inches. Use corrosion-resistant nails with a 3/16-inch head diameter. Shim behind the siding over doors or windows, or apply a drip cap. Leave a 1/8-inch space between the siding and the window or door frame. Also leave a 1/8-inch space between the siding and the corner boards. Caulk these spaces with a quality caulk after you've finished installing the siding.

Figure 10-14 shows application details for hardboard siding. All butt joints must be staggered and centered over a stud. See Figure 10-14 B. Nail the siding at the top and bottom of the butt joint, and also on both sides of the joint, using nails 1 to 1 1/8 inches long. Consider using the primed aluminum "H" expansion molding shown in Figure 10-13 A, or use the 1-inch butt-joint cover shown in Figure 10-14. "H" molding allows for the natural expansion and contraction caused by changes in temperature and humidity. It

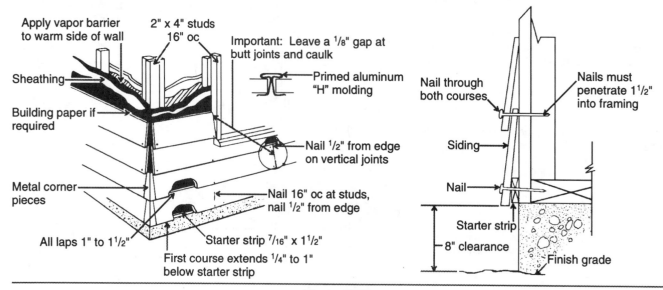

A Siding installation details

Apply vapor barrier to warm side of wall

2" x 4" studs 16" oc

Important: Leave a 1/8" gap at butt joints and caulk

Sheathing

Primed aluminum "H" molding

Building paper if required

Nail 1/2" from edge on vertical joints

Metal corner pieces

Nail 16" oc at studs, nail 1/2" from edge

All laps 1" to 1 1/2"

Starter strip 7/16" x 1 1/2"

First course extends 1/4" to 1" below starter strip

B Siding nailing details

Nail through both courses

Nails must penetrate 1 1/2" into framing

Siding

Nail

Starter strip

8" clearance

Finish grade

Figure 10-13
Hardboard lap siding application

also hides the gaps that often occur at butt joints. If you don't use "H" molding or joint covers, caulk the gaps. A 1/8-inch gap is essential at all butt joints. If you don't leave a gap for expansion, the siding tends to buckle and "wrinkle" when it expands.

At inside and outside corners, use wood corner boards, as shown in Figure 10-14 C and D. Or use formed metal corners.

If you apply hardboard lap siding over foam sheathing, set the nails flush with the surface of the hardboard. If you overdrive the nails, it'll dimple the board and give the siding a wavy appearance. Drive the nails at least 1 1/2 inches into each stud. Otherwise, the foam sheathing may cause the siding to "hang out" from the wall as much as 1 inch. With time, the siding may begin to sag. For 1/2-inch lap siding and 1-inch foam sheathing, use a 4-inch (20d) nail.

As with plywood, use a vapor barrier on the interior side of the wall when you apply hardboard siding over foam sheathing.

Hardboard Panel Siding

You can apply grooved panel siding with shiplap joints over sheathed or unsheathed walls with studs

spaced no more than 16 inches on center. You can apply nongrooved panels over sheathed or unsheathed walls with studs spaced up to 24 inches on center. Apply hardboard panel siding (to wall framing without corner bracing) directly to studs, and nail it as recommended in Figure 10-15, to get a good racking resistance and meet the FHA racking strength requirements.

To apply nongrooved panel siding (square edges) as shown in Figure 10-16 A:

1. Apply panels parallel to framing. Cover the sill and the top plates.

2. All panel edges must fall on studs or other nailing members. Don't force panels into place. Leave a 1/8-inch space where siding butts against trim. Caulk the gap.

3. You can apply square-edge panels directly to studs spaced 24 inches or less without having to use corner bracing. Nail as recommended in Figure 10-15.

4. Begin nailing at the middle of a panel and work toward the edges.

5. Apply a quality sealant to vertical joints, at windows, and at doors.

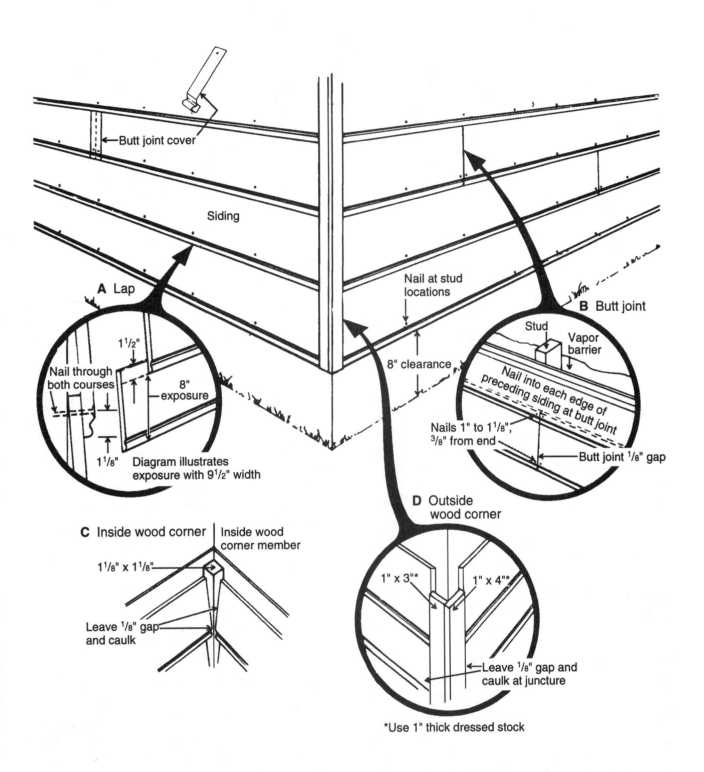

Butt joint cover

Siding

Nail at stud
locations

8" clearance

A Lap

Nail through
both courses

1 1/2"

8"
exposure

1 1/8"

Diagram illustrates
exposure with 9 1/2" width

B Butt joint

Stud

Vapor
barrier

Nail into each edge of
preceding siding at butt joint

Nails 1" to 1 1/8",
3/8" from end

Butt joint 1/8" gap

C Inside wood corner | Inside wood
corner member

1 1/8" x 1 1/8"

Leave 1/8" gap
and caulk

D Outside
wood corner

1" x 3"*

1" x 4"*

Leave 1/8" gap and
caulk at juncture

*Use 1" thick dressed stock

Figure 10-14
Hardboard lap siding application details

Edge detail	Grooves	Substrate	2 x 4 framing, maximum spacing inches oc	Nail size	Nail spacing		Joint gap	Gap around openings
					Siding only*	Racking strength**		
Shiplap or square edge	No	Direct to studs	24	6d	6" oc edges 12" oc intermediate	4" oc edges 8" oc intermediate	$1/16$"	$1/8$"
Shiplap or square edge	No	Over sheathing	24	8d	6" oc edges 12" oc intermediate	4" oc edges 8" oc intermediate	$1/16$"	$1/8$"
Shiplap	Yes	Direct to studs	16	6d	6" oc edges 12" oc intermediate	4" oc edges 8" oc intermediate	$1/8$"	$1/8$"
Shiplap	Yes	Over sheathing	16	8d	6" oc edges 12" oc intermediate	4" oc edges 8" oc intermediate	$1/8$"	$1/8$"

*Racking resistance per FHA Circular No. 12 provided by sheathing or corner braces
**Racking resistance provided by siding

Figure 10-15
Hardboard panel siding nail size and spacing requirements

6. Install battens over all vertical joints. Make battens from wood or strips of siding cut to the desired width. Install battens only where there's an adequate nailing base. Nail through the panels and into the framing. Space nails 12 inches on center.

7. Intermediate battens can also be applied if there's an adequate nailing base.

8. Nail outside wood corner boards 12 inches on center.

9. Apply quality sealant to any butt joints at inside corners. Install a 1 x 1 inside wood corner post. Nail every 12 inches on center.

When you apply grooved panel siding (shiplap edges), you don't need any battens. Just apply the panels directly to studs without using sheathing paper or corner bracing. Where there's no corner bracing, the maximum stud spacing is 16 inches on center. See Figure 10-16 B. Follow the same application instructions as for panels without grooves, but omit the batten and don't caulk the vertical shiplap joints. When field-cut butt joints are made, butter the edges with sealant before installation. Remove the excess sealant.

Hardboard Shakes

Hardboard shakes provide a durable exterior. You can usually install shakes over sheathing or directly to studs. You won't need building paper over vertical sheathing unless it's required by your code. Select shakes that match the existing ones in size, thickness, texture and wood species.

You can apply shakes to walls that slope as much as 15 degrees from vertical, as long as you apply sheathing to the framing and cover the sheathing with paper.

Corner bracing is required when hardboard shakes are installed directly over studs, or when non-structural sheathing is used. When shakes are applied over sheathing, corner bracing requirements depend on the type of sheathing.

You'll want to use quality, non-hardening caulks where siding meets windows, doors, and trim. Don't seal shiplap edges. If the siding rests on a wood or concrete sill, there must be enough slope for drainage. Use a non-hardening, permanent sealant at the joint between siding and sill.

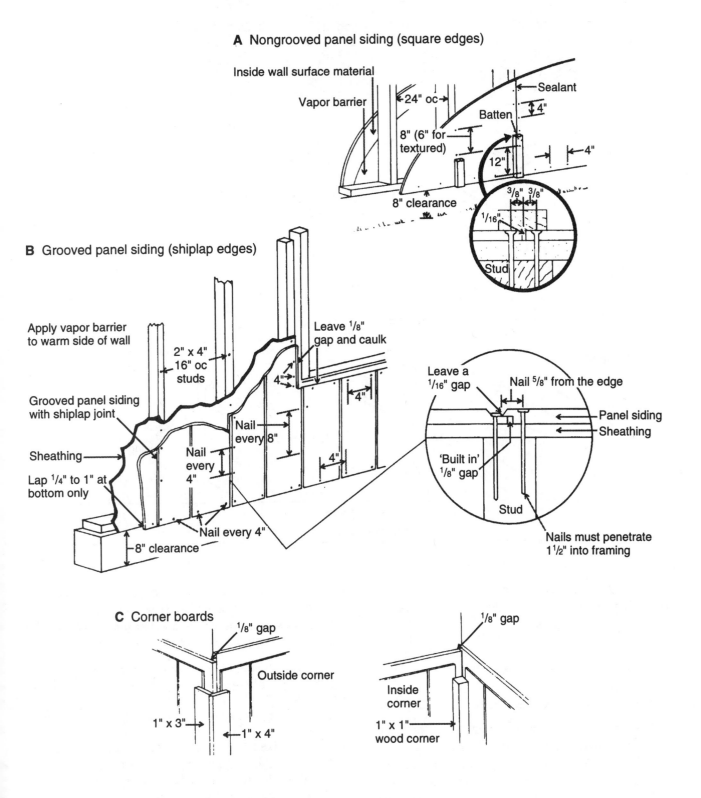

A Nongrooved panel siding (square edges)

Inside wall surface material

Vapor barrier

Sealant

24" oc

Batten

4"

8" (6" for textured)

12"

4"

8" clearance

3/8" 3/8"

1/16"

Stud

B Grooved panel siding (shiplap edges)

Apply vapor barrier to warm side of wall

2" x 4" 16" oc studs

Leave 1/8" gap and caulk

4"

4"

Grooved panel siding with shiplap joint

Nail every 8"

Nail every 4"

Sheathing

4"

Lap 1/4" to 1" at bottom only

Nail every 4"

8" clearance

Leave a 1/16" gap

Nail 5/8" from the edge

Panel siding

Sheathing

'Built in' 1/8" gap

Stud

Nails must penetrate 1 1/2" into framing

C Corner boards

1/8" gap

Outside corner

1" x 3"

1" x 4"

1/8" gap

Inside corner

1" x 1" wood corner

Figure 10-16
Hardboard panel siding application details

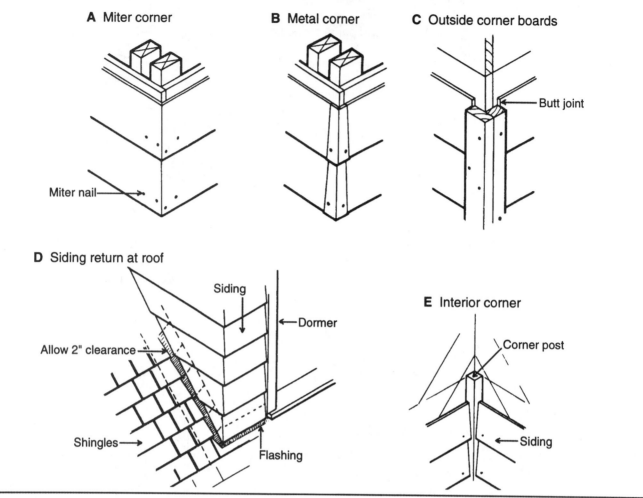

A Miter corner   **B** Metal corner   **C** Outside corner boards

Miter nail

Butt joint

D Siding return at roof

Siding

Dormer

Allow 2" clearance

Shingles

Flashing

E Interior corner

Corner post

Siding

Figure 10-17
Corner treatments for horizontal siding

Always leave a slight gap at joints and openings. Never spring panels into place. Keep the siding at least 8 inches above finish grade.

Wood Siding

Wood siding has been the mainstay in housing construction where aesthetics and durability are concerned. It's more expensive than hardboard siding, but it's still used on quality homes throughout the country. Wood siding is generally easy to work with and shouldn't warp. If you plan to paint the siding, it should be reasonably free of knots, pitch (resin) pockets, and tapered edges. Cedar, eastern white pine,

sugar pine, western white pine, cypress, and redwood have these properties. Other species used for siding include western hemlock, ponderosa pine, spruce, yellow poplar, Douglas fir, western larch, and southern pine.

Vertical-grain lumber makes the best siding because it doesn't expand and contract very much with changes in temperature and humidity. Redwood and western red cedars are usually available in vertical-grain and mixed-grain grades. The moisture content of siding should be 10 percent to 12 percent when you install it. In the dry southwestern states, however, an 8 to 9 percent moisture content is preferable.

Ideally, you should give siding a 3-minute dip in a water-repellent preservative before you install it. This will prolong paint life and help the wood resist mois-

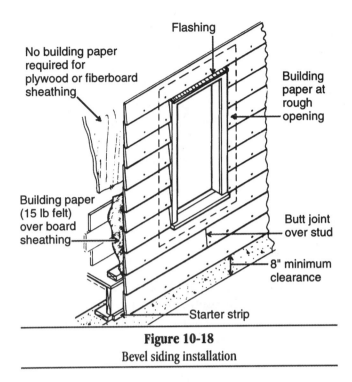

Figure 10-18
Bevel siding installation

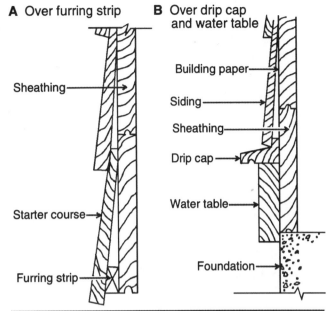

Figure 10-19
First course of bevel siding

ture-entry and decay. Brush-treat freshly-cut ends on the job.

How to Nail Wood Siding

Use corrosion-resistant galvanized nails when you install wood siding. Aluminum and stainless steel nails cost more, but they prevent the rust-spotting that can occur when the paint surface begins to deteriorate.

Finishing nails and siding nails are two types of nails commonly used with wood siding. Finishing nails have a small head. Siding nails have a larger, flat head. Small-head finishing nails are set about 1/16-inch below the face of the siding. Fill the nail hole with putty after the prime coat has been applied. Flat-head siding nails are driven flush with the face of the siding and then painted. Don't overdrive flat-head siding nails because it leaves hammer marks and can split or crush the wood. This is especially important on wood siding with a prefinished surface or overlay.

When you're installing wood siding in the Deep South, and you want it to "weather" naturally, use annular-threaded or helical-threaded shank nails. I don't know exactly what causes it, unless it's the heat and humidity, but smooth-shank nails will "pop" out

after a few years. I've seen 8d nails come out as much as 1/2-inch in a five-year period. It's better, as a matter of course, to use modified shank nails in all your wood siding installations since they stay in the wood better.

Common wire nails will rust in a short time and leave an ugly stain on the face of the siding. Small-head wire nails may even show rust spots through the putty and paint. Use galvanized nails. Most lumber-yards carry them.

Fasten siding that's going to have a "natural finish" (a water-repellent preservative or stain) with stainless steel or aluminum nails. Some types of prefinished sidings come with nails that are color-matched to the siding.

Some wood siding patterns are only used horizontally. Others are applied only vertically. Some can be used either way if enough nailing area is available. Figure 10-17 shows corner treatments for horizontal siding.

Figure 10-18 shows typical installation for bevel siding. Figure 10-19 shows how to use a furring strip or a drip cap and water table with the first course of bevel siding. Finally, look at Figure 10-20 for nailing standards for bevel siding, drop siding and matched paneling.

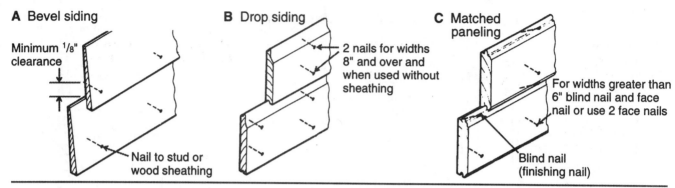

Figure 10-20
Nailing bevel and drop siding and match paneling

How to Make a Material Transition

If an existing house uses two types of siding, or both vertical and horizontal sidings of the same type, or different siding for gable ends and walls, then your room addition should probably follow the same pattern. Whatever you do, the joints between the two types of siding must provide good drainage.

Figure 10-21 shows two ways to make the material transition. For example, if vertical board-and-batten siding is used at the gable ends, and horizontal siding is used on the walls below, you need a drip cap or similar molding (Figure 10-21 A). Use flashing above the drip cap so that moisture will fall clear of the joint between the two types of siding.

Here's another way to make the material transition. Extend the plate and studs of the gable end out from the wall a short distance. The gable siding will project beyond the wall siding and provide good drainage. See Figure 10-21 B.

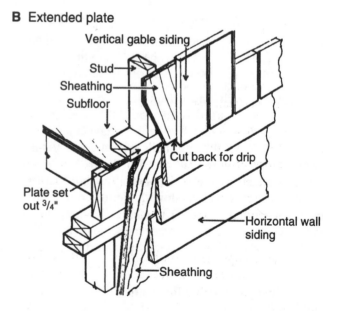

Figure 10-21
Making a material transition

Size	Material				
	Exposed to weather	Add for lap	SF of siding per 100 SF of wall	Lbs. nails per 100 SF	Manhours per 100 SF
Bevel siding					
$1/2$" x 4"	$2^3/4$	46%	151	$1^1/2$	3.2
$1/2$" x 5"	$3^3/4$	33%	138	$1^1/2$	2.5
$1/2$" x 6"	$4^3/4$	26%	131	1	1.9
$1/2$" x 8"	$6^3/4$	18%	123	$3/4$	1.7
$5/8$" x 8"	$6^3/4$	18%	123	$3/4$	1.8
$3/4$" x 8"	$6^3/4$	18%	123	$3/4$	1.8
$5/8$" x 10"	$8^3/4$	14%	119	$1/2$	2.1
$3/4$" x 10"	$8^3/4$	14%	119	$1/2$	2.2
$3/4$" x 12"	$10^3/4$	12%	117	$1/2$	2.1
Drop siding					
1" x 6"	$5^1/4$"	14%	119	$2^1/2$	2.0
1" x 8"	$7^1/4$"	10%	115	2	1.9

Quantities include 5% for end cutting and waste. Deduct for all openings over ten square feet.

Figure 10-22
Calculating labor and materials for bevel and drop siding

How to Finish Installed Siding

You can treat plywood siding with a water repellent or wood preservative. The treatment gives the siding more durability and a nicer finish. Watch preinstallation treatment, however. If a panel isn't dry when you install it, the solvent may react chemically with any foam sheathing you've used.

Siding comes both factory-primed and unprimed. Paint and stain are the two most common finishes. To finish factory-primed siding, paint it within 60 days after you install it. If it's exposed for a longer time, reprime the siding with a quality exterior-grade primer compatible with the existing finish. Prime and paint all cut edges.

To finish unprimed siding, prime it within three days after you install it with a quality exterior-grade primer. Then paint with a finish coat within 30 days of installation.

Always use a good-quality exterior acrylic, acrylic latex, latex, or oil-base paint, following the manufacturer's recommendations. Avoid flat alkyd-type house paints. They don't look good and they don't last.

Textured siding looks good when it's stained. Use a quality, opaque exterior acrylic latex stain on primed or unprimed textured sidings. This will provide a finish with good color and durability. For a top-grade appearance, use two coats of stain. Carefully follow the application procedure recommended by the stain manufacturer. Properly stained (or painted) quality siding will last a long time. But hardboard siding isn't intended to be left unpainted or to "weather."

Estimating Siding Labor and Materials

If you don't have good records of your own, use Figure 10-22 to estimate labor and materials for bevel and drop siding. Use Figure 10-23 to calculate coverage for tongue-and-groove and shiplap boards. For plywood siding, estimate 14 manhours per 1,000 square feet for 4' x 8' x $3/8$" siding and 16 manhours per 1,000 square feet for 4' x 8' x $5/8$" siding.

Measured size (inches)	Finished width (inches)	Add for shrinkage (percent)	Quantity required (multiply area by)	SF of lumber required per 100 SF
1 x 2	$1^3/_8$	50	1.50	150
1 x $2^3/_4$	2	$42^1/_2$	1.425	$142^1/_2$
1 x 3	$2^1/_2$	$38^1/_3$	1.383	138
1 x 4	$3^1/_4$	28	1.28	128
1 x 6	$5^1/_4$	20	1.20	120
1 x 8	$7^1/_4$	16	1.15	115
$1^1/_4$ x 3	$2^1/_4$	$38^1/_3$	1.73	173
$1^1/_4$ x 4	$3^1/_4$	28	1.60	160
$1^1/_4$ x 6	$5^1/_4$	20	1.50	150
$1^1/_2$ x 3	$2^1/_4$	$38^1/_3$	2.08	208
$1^1/_2$ x 4	$3^1/_4$	28	1.92	192
$1^1/_2$ x 6	$5^1/_4$	20	1.80	180
2 x 4	$3^1/_4$	28	2.60	260
2 x 6	$5^1/_4$	20	2.40	240
2 x 8	$7^1/_4$	16	2.32	232
2 x 10	$9^1/_4$	13	2.25	225
2 x 12	$11^1/_4$	12	2.24	224
3 x 6	$5^1/_4$	20	3.60	360
3 x 8	$7^1/_4$	16	3.48	348
3 x 10	$9^1/_4$	13	3.39	339
3 x 12	$11^1/_4$	12	3.36	336

This data applies to most dressed and matched lumber. Waste allowance shown includes width lost in dressing and lapping.

Add 5% for end-cutting and matching.

Figure 10-23
Calculating coverage for T&G and shiplap boards

Finishing Walls and Ceilings

No matter how imaginative your design or solid your rough framing, your competence (or lack of competence) as a builder will be judged by the interior finish. The floors, walls, and ceilings should be as close to perfection as possible. Strive for smooth, even surfaces. Plaster, drywall, stone and brick walls shouldn't have any dips, humps, or waves. Since most interior walls are drywalled, we'll start there.

Hanging Drywall

Drywall is an engineered building panel made of gypsum (hydrated calcium sulfate) and other materials. It's finished on both sides with special paper to provide a smooth and attractive wall finish. It's noncombustible, nontoxic, dimensionally stable, and resists sound transmission. And it's the least expensive wall-surfacing material offering these advantages. The most common sheet sizes are 4 x 8 and 4 x 12, either $1/2$ or $5/8$ inch thick, but other sizes are also available.

Having done it both ways, I prefer to subcontract the job of hanging and taping drywall. I find that if I sub the job at a fixed cost per square foot I usually save money and time. But whether you do the job yourself or subcontract it out, you'll still need to know how the job should be done.

Use $1/4$-inch drywall over old walls and ceilings. Install $3/8$-inch drywall for single-layer application over framing members that are spaced no more than 16 inches on center. Framing should be 16 inches on center when you install $1/2$- and $5/8$-inch drywall vertically (with the long dimension parallel to the framing). Maximum framing-member spacing is 24 inches on center when you install drywall horizontally (with the long dimension at right angles to the framing).

If a ceiling has to support insulation, or if you're going to spray it with a water-base textured coating, install $1/2$- and $5/8$-inch drywall. Apply $1/2$-inch panels horizontally over framing members spaced 16 inches on

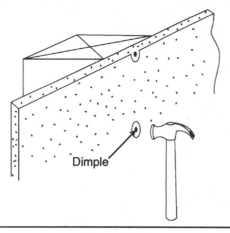

Figure 11-1
Nail set with hammer

center. You can apply ⁵/₈-inch panels horizontally over framing spaced at 16 or 24 inches, or vertically over framing spaced at 16 inches. Coat the drywall with a pigmented primer-sealer before you put on the textured coating.

A finish wall is only as smooth and straight as the framing behind it. Any 2 x 4 or larger framing can support drywall. Closet walls may be 2 x 2s. If you've used only dry, straight lumber for the framing, alignment shouldn't be a problem. Green lumber, however, will shrink as it ages. This can make nails pop out of

the drywall. Green lumber also has a tendency to bow. Bows can seriously distort the wall or ceiling finish.

Dampness and high humidity are drywall's worst enemy. You'll need special protection, such as an exhaust fan, if drywall is exposed to continuous moisture or high humidity in laundry rooms and bathrooms. Install backerboard in these rooms.

Drywall delivered to the job site should be dry. Stack it in a dry place. Apply drywall finishes only when the air temperature is above 55 degrees F for at least 24 hours before you install it. Provide adequate ventilation if the humidity is high.

Nailing Drywall

You should dimple all the nails you put in drywall. Drive the nails so that the heads are set slightly below the panel surface. Use a drywall hammer, not a nail set. The hammer will make a dimple. See Figure 11-1. But don't break the paper face of the panel. Fill nail dimples with joint compound. When the compound is dry, sand it smooth. Repeat with a second coat of compound if the patch isn't level.

Figure 11-2 shows the recommended nails for applying drywall. You can single or double nail the panels. Figure 11-3 shows the single nailing method and Figure 11-4 shows double nailing. Double nailing

GWB-54 annular ring, .098 diameter. Maximum ¹⁹/₆₄ head.		Smooth bright. ¹/₄" diameter head.		Coated, 13 guage. ¹/₄" cupped head.	
Drywall thickness	Length of nail	Drywall thickness	Length of nail	Drywall thickness	Length of nail
¹/₄"	1¹/₈"	¹/₄"	1¹/₄"	¹/₄"	1¹/₄"
³/₈"	1¹/₄"	³/₈"	1³/₈"(4d)	³/₈"	1¹/₄"
¹/₂"	1³/₈"	¹/₂"	1⁵/₈"(5d)	¹/₂"	1³/₈"
⁵/₈"	1³/₈"	⁵/₈"	1⁷/₈"(6d)	⁵/₈"	1¹/₂"

Note: When Parkerhead-type nails are used, follow manufacturer's recommendations.

Figure 11-2
Nails recommended for drywall installation

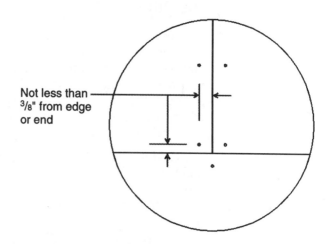

Not less than ³/₈" from edge or end

Space nails a maximum of 7" oc on ceilings, and a maximum of 8" oc on walls

Figure 11-3
Drywall single nailing schedule

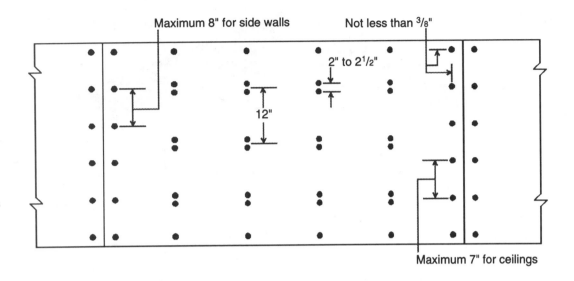

Figure 11-4
Drywall double nailing schedule

minimizes nail pops. Start nailing *from the center of the panel* and work toward the edge, nailing the panel at intermediate studs 12 inches on center. Allow about 2 inches between each pair of nails as shown in Figure 11-4. Nail as usual around the panel edges.

Glue-Nailing Drywall

Glue-nailing is a combination of nailing and gluing. It takes fewer nails than just nailing alone. Begin by applying adhesive to studs and joists. Let the glue set for the manufacturer's recommended amount of time. Then place the panel in position. Drive in just enough nails to hold the panel in place until the glue dries. For wall applications, space nails 24 inches on center. Space nails in a ceiling 16 inches on center. Figure 11-5 shows some patterns you can use when you apply the glue.

Using Floating Angles

"Floating angles" can prevent damage to wall and ceiling finish materials caused by building settlement. To create floating angles, you omit some of the nails at the interior corners where the ceiling and side walls meet, and where side walls intersect. Then you nail as

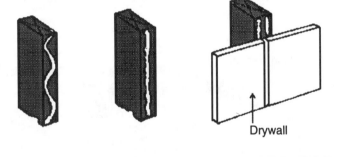

Figure 11-5
Adhesive application patterns

usual for the rest of the ceiling and wall area. Always install the ceiling panels first. Fit the drywall snugly into all corners. See Figure 11-6.

When installing ceiling drywall across the joists, nail as usual where the panel ends meet the wall intersection. On the long edges of the panel, set the first row of nails back about 7 inches from the wall intersection.

When you hang ceiling drywall with the long edges parallel to the joists, it's just the opposite. Nail as usual where the long edges meet the wall intersection. Set the first row of nails back about 7 inches where the panel ends meet the wall intersection.

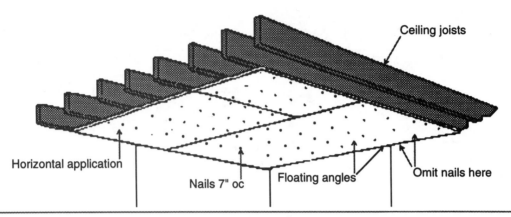

Figure 11-6
Drywall ceiling installation details

That 7-inch nail-free border on each panel "floats" freely against the side walls. Any expansion or contraction of the structure is absorbed at this joint.

Side wall drywall must be in firm contact with the ceiling panels to help support them. Along the wall-ceiling intersection, omit nails directly below the ceil-

ing angle. See Figure 11-7. Don't drive any nails within 7 inches of the ceiling intersection.

Where side walls intersect, omit corner-nailing on panels you apply to the first of the two intersecting walls. Don't drive any nails within 7 inches of the corner. Then hang the panels on the adjoining wall. Butt

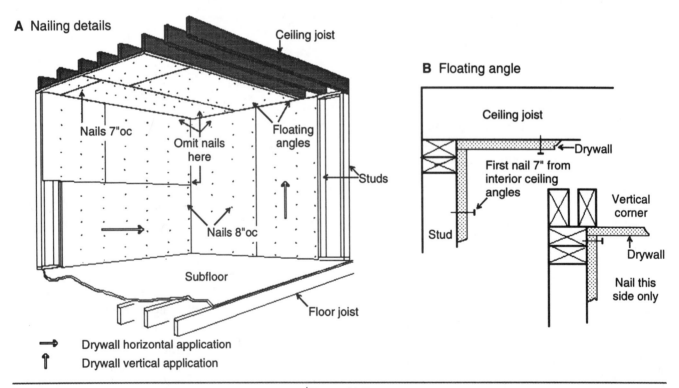

Figure 11-7
Side wall installation details

the first panel against the corner, overlapping the panels you just installed. Nail this panel the usual way, spacing nails 8 inches on center.

Using Wood Furring

Many builders find it almost impossible to get a level ceiling finish when nailing drywall or other wallboard directly to ceiling joists. Let's face it — framing lumber just isn't as straight as we'd like it to be. So how do you hang flat drywall on not-so-straight joists? You'll have to use furring, and shim or trim the joists as required to even them up. Figure 11-8 gives the board feet of furring strips and pounds of nails you'll need. A carpenter should cut and install 350 to 400 linear feet of furring in 8 hours.

When you fasten drywall to wood furring strips on ceilings, the furring should be at least nominal 1 x 3-inch boards spaced no more than 24 inches on center. It's better to use 1 x 4-inch boards. You can get these at most supply houses. Space framing members no more than 16 inches on center if insulation is going to rest on the ceiling panels. Apply drywall panels at right angles (horizontal application) to the framing.

How to "Mud" and Tape Joints on Drywall

Once the drywall is up, you've got to smooth and level it with joint compound (mud) and tape. Figure 11-9 shows how to tape a joint. Here are the steps:

1. Starting at the top of the wall, use a 5-inch-wide spackling knife and spread the mud into the tapered edges at the joint.

2. Press tape into the recess of the panel joints with the same spackling knife until the mud is forced through the tape perforations.

3. Spread mud over the tape and feather the edges.

4. When the mud is dry, apply a second coat. Feather the edges to extend beyond the edges of the first coat. A steel trowel works best for the second coat. If you apply a third coat be sure to spread and feather it beyond the edges of the second coat.

5. When the joint is dry, sand it smooth. *Don't* sand the paper face of the panel.

Size of strips (inches)	Spacing of furring (inches)	BF per SF of wall	Nails per 1000 BF (lbs.)
1 x 2	12	.18	55
	16	.14	
	20	.11	
	24	.10	
1 x 3	12	.28	37
	16	.21	
	20	.17	
	24	.14	
1 x 4	12	.36	30
	16	.28	
	20	.22	
	24	.20	

Figure 11-8
Materials required for furring

Finish interior joints with either tape or molding. If you use tape, fold a strip of tape down the center so it forms a sharp angle, as shown in Figure 11-10. Apply mud at the corner. Press the tape into place, and finish the corner with mud. When it's dry, sand it smooth. Repeat the procedure with a second coat.

Figure 11-11 shows an interior corner finished with molding. If you use molding, you can omit the taping. Use metal corner beads on outside corners to protect them from damage. Install the metal corner bead directly over the drywall with nails and cover it with mud.

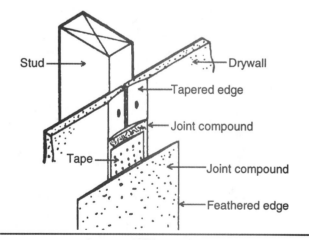

Figure 11-9
Compounding and taping joint

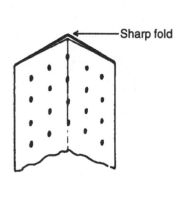

Figure 11-10
Taping interior corner

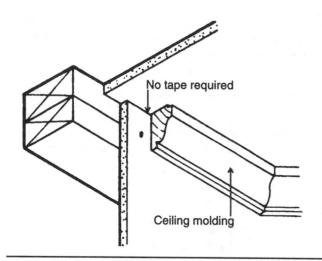

Figure 11-11
Molding at interior corner

Backerboard Gypsum Wallboard

There's a specially-formulated backerboard you can use as a base for applying ceramic, metal, and plastic wall tile to a surface with an adhesive. Use it in areas which get a lot of moisture, like shower stalls and tub enclosures. Backerboard is made of an asphalt-treated core covered with a heavy water-repellent back paper and an ivory face paper that doesn't require a surface sealant before you put the tile on.

You also don't have to tape the joints. But don't use this material in a ceiling or soffit except as a base layer for other finish material.

Install furring around the tub enclosure and shower stall so the inside face of the fixture lip is flush with the face of the backerboard. The top of the furring should be about even with the upper edge of the tub or shower pan, as shown in Figure 11-12.

If you're going to install ceramic tile over $5/16$ inch thick on studs spaced more than 16 inches, place a row

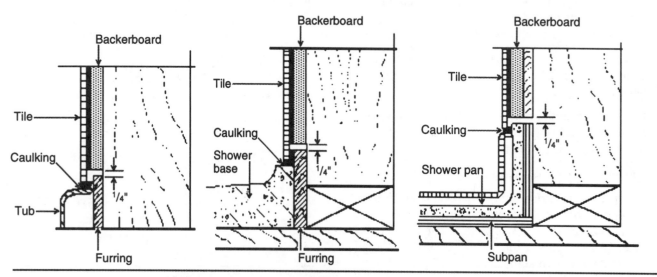

Figure 11-12
Backerboard application details

of blocking about 1 inch above the top of the tub or shower receptor. Put another row midway between the fixture and the ceiling.

Install headers or supports for the tub, plumbing fixtures, soap dishes, grab bars, and towel racks. Set the tub and shower receptor or pan before installing the wallboard. Tubs and shower receptors or pans should have an upstanding lip or flange that's 1 inch higher than the water drain or threshold of the shower. Reinforce the interior angles with supports to provide rigid corners.

Install backerboard horizontally to eliminate butt joints. Allow a $1/4$-inch space between the lip of the fixture and the paper-bound edge of the board. Space nails at 8 inches and screws at 12 inches unless you're using ceramic tile thicker than $5/16$ inch. Then space the nails at 4 inches and screws at 8 inches. Dimple the nail heads. Don't tear or break the face paper.

Treat joints and angles with a waterproof tile adhesive in areas you're going to tile. Don't use regular joint compound and tape. Caulk openings around pipes and fixtures with a waterproof nonsetting caulk.

Apply the tile down to the top edge of the shower floor surfacing material, and to the return of the shower pan, or over the tub lip, as shown in Figure 11-12. Grout all joints completely and continuously. Fill the space between fixtures and tiles with nonsetting caulk or tile grout compound.

Paneling

Because of its low cost and ease of installation, prefinished plywood paneling is commonly used in room additions and conversions. Here are a few tips for a professional-looking job. First, expose plywood paneling to the conditions of the room for at least 24 hours before you install them. Then spot the panels around the room before you install them. Check the panels for continuity of color. It's not unusual to find that the panels don't match. If a panel is too dark or too light, don't use it. All the panels in a room should be the same color.

Use $1/4$-inch-thick panels for studs spaced at 16 inches. Drive color-matched panel nails about every 8 inches. The nailing-edge distance should be at least $3/8$ inch. Butt panels together lightly. You can also glue

the panels to the framework. Follow gluing instructions issued by the manufacturer.

Cut plywood panels with the finish side up when you're using a handsaw. With a power saw, cut with the back side up. If you must cut into the panel face with a power saw, first score the saw line with a knife. This reduces splintering. Keep the saw blade on the waste side of the line.

When measuring for window and door openings, hold the panel in position and have a helper mark the opening on the back of the panel with a pencil. Return the panel to the workbench and adjust the saw line, allowing for jamb thickness. Then cut.

For wall outlets and switch boxes, mark along the edges of the box with a pencil or chalk. Place the panel in position and tap it against the box with your hand. This will mark the correct position of the box on the back of the panel. Return the panel to the bench, back side up, and saw out the opening. Some carpenters drill holes at each corner of the box and saw out the opening with a keyhole or saber saw. Others will merely cut along the marked outline with a power saw. This is faster, but be careful not to saw over the lines.

When installing panels where room corners are true, you can butt them to the corner and omit the corner molding. If you don't use inside corner molding, install the panels with the sawed edge butted against the stud. Butt the mill edge of the panel on the adjoining wall to this panel, covering the sawed edge. Sometimes the edge of a panel won't exactly fit the edge of the adjoining panel, leaving the stud showing through the gap. Before installing the panel, use a black felt marker or pencil to draw a thick line down the stud where the panel butts. If there's a gap between the panels, it won't be as visible as it would if the light-colored stud were showing through.

Hardboard and Fiberboard Paneling

Hardboard and fiberboard are generally less expensive than plywood paneling. You can install hardboard that's $1/4$ inch thick over studs spaced at 16 inches. But fiberboard (in tongue-and-groove plank or sheet form) must be $1/2$ inch thick over studs at 16 inches. Use $3/4$-inch-thick fiberboard on studs at 24 inches. Use casing or finishing nails slightly longer than you'd use for $1/4$-inch plywood or hardboard panels.

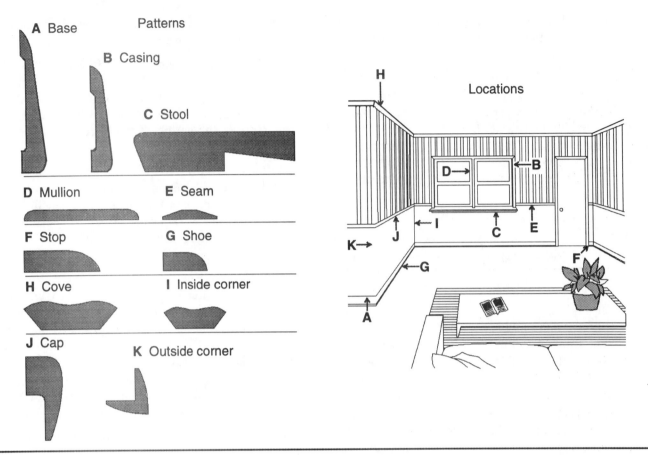

Figure 11-13
Molding patterns and locations

If your client wants the advantages of a sound-absorbing ceiling without paying for suspended ceiling grids, fiberboard might be the answer. You can use fiberboard as acoustic tile on ceilings by nailing it to furring strips fastened to the ceiling joists.

Trim

Installing the trim work is called *trimming out* — and it's your key to a professionally-completed project. If it's done right, that is. Use your best finish carpenter on your trim work to make sure you get a good job. Make sure each piece is carefully fit to form perfectly-mitered corners on all trim.

You'll generally use unfinished softwood moldings of cedar, fir, pine, or hemlock ripped from kiln-dried boards up to 16 feet in length. There are about 30 different stock patterns or profiles. Each profile is designed for a specific purpose, but most have many secondary uses as well. Figure 11-13 shows standard molding patterns and the places where they're commonly used.

For installation of base molding, look at Figure 11-14. Figure 11-15 shows how to install ceiling molding. Cutting and fitting molding takes practice. Unfortunately, it isn't a skill all carpenters have. Figure 11-16 is a general overview of how to cut molding. Most molding joints are cut on a 45-degree angle (Figure 11-16 A). To make the cut, set your miter box or saw at 45 degrees and trim (at opposite angles) each of the two pieces to be mated. When mitering cove molding for ceiling trim, place the molding in the miter box so the molding is upside down and end-reversed to the way you're going to install it.

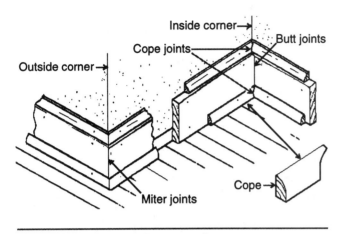

Figure 11-14
Base molding installation joints

When you're coping the molding, place it in the miter box and position it upright against the backplate. Cut at a 45-degree angle. The cut exposes the profile of the molding. With the profile as a template, use the coping saw and follow along the profile (Figure 11-16 C). Trim away a wedge at another 45-degree angle. This duplicates the pattern so that it fits over the face of the adjoining molding.

You can finish softwood molding with any wood finish such as enamel, stain, paint, lacquer, varnish, or shellac. Before applying the finish, fill nail holes with wood putty. Then sand and smooth the wood with the grain, using #00 or finer sandpaper. Prime before you apply paint or enamel. Or you can get prefinished moldings in many wood-grain color tones.

Estimating Wallboard Material and Labor

To reduce drywall installation manhours, use the longest panels possible and install the panels horizontally whenever possible. Many drywall subcontractors also apply spray-on ceiling texture finish. This costs less than other finishes when it's applied at the same time as the drywall. If you hang the drywall yourself, the cost will be somewhat higher for texture spray. It's

Use both glue and nails to make a tight joint. To figure how much molding you need for mitering, add the width of the molding to the length of each miter. If your molding is 3 inches wide and you have two miters, add 6 inches.

When splicing two lengths of molding, as shown in Figure 11-16 B, place the molding flat on its backside in the miter box. Miter the ends to be joined at a 45-degree angle. This will be an identical cut. When the ends are butted together in their correct position, you get a neat match without any unevenness.

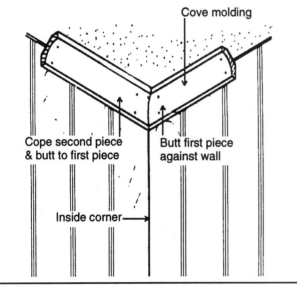

Figure 11-15
Installing ceiling molding

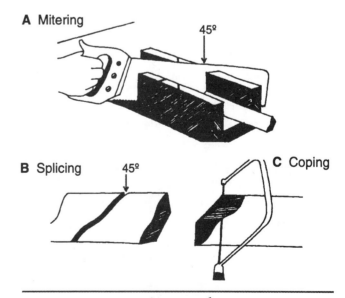

Figure 11-16
Cutting molding

Work element	Manhours per 100 SF	Gypsum wallboard types
Drywall on one face of metal or wood studs or furring		
1 layer, ³/₈"	1.8	
1 layer, ¹/₂"	1.9	**Regular** is available in several thicknesses for both new and remodeling construction.
1 layer, ⁵/₈"	2.1	
2 layers, ³/₈", mastic	2.7	**Fire rated** is designed especially for fire resistance. Major additives are vermiculite and
2 layers, ¹/₂", mastic	3.0	fiberglass.
2 layers, ⁵/₈", mastic	3.4	**Sound deadening board** is usually applied in combination with other wallboard products
Drywall for columns, pipe chases or fire partitions		to achieve higher sound and fire ratings.
1 layer, ³/₈", nailed	4.4	**Tile backerboard** is recommended as a base for adhesive application of ceramic, metal or plastic tile for interior areas where moisture and humidity are a
1 layer, ¹/₂", nailed	4.5	problem. (Direct, continuous contact with moisture should be avoided.)
1 layer, ⁵/₈", nailed	4.6	**Sheathing** is for exterior applications. Used as a substrate for siding, masonry, brick veneer
2 layers, ¹/₂", mastic	8.5	and stucco.
2 layers, ⁵/₈", mastic	8.9	**Backerboard** is recommended for backing paneling and other multi-layered applications.
3 layers, ¹/₂", mastic	12.5	Adds strength and fire protection. Also can be used effectively with ceiling tile.
3 layers, ⁵/₈", mastic	13.0	**Vinyl-surfaced wallboard** resists scuffs, cracks and chips. Ideal for commercial and
1 layer, 1¹/₂", coreboard	4.0	institutional use.
Drywall for beams and soffits		**Tapered edge** inclines into the board from the long edge. With joint finishing, results in a
1 layer, ¹/₂"	3.9	smooth, monolithic wall.
1 layer, ⁵/₈"	4.0	**Square edge** is used where an exposed joint is desired.
2 layers, ¹/₂"	7.3	**Tapered, round edge** is for the same applications as tapered-edge board. Designed to
2 layers, ⁵/₈"	8.0	reduce beading and ridging problems often associated with poorly
Drywall, glued		finished joints.
1 layer, ¹/₂"	1.9	**Beveled edge** is used where a "panel" effect is desired. In this application the joints are left
1 layer, ⁵/₈"	2.0	exposed.
Screwed drywall		**Tongue and groove** is available in 24" wide sheathing and backerboards.
1 layer, ¹/₂"	1.9	
1 layer, ⁵/₈"	2.2	**Modified beveled edge** needs no special joint finishing, though matching batten strips
Additional time requirements		may be used if desired.
Add for ceiling work	.6	**Thickness:** ¹/₄", ³/₈", ¹/₂", ⁵/₈". (Not all products are available in all thicknesses.)
Add for walls over 9' high	.5	**Width:** 4'.
Add for resilient clip application	.4	
Add for vinyl covered drywall	.4	**Length:** 6' through 16'.
Add for thincoat plaster finish	1.4	
Deduct for no taping, finish or sanding	.9	

Time includes move on and off site, unloading, stacking, installing drywall, taping, joint finishing, sanding, repair and cleanup as needed.
Suggested crew: 1 applicator and 1 laborer

Figure 11-17
Labor installing gypsum wallboard

Room areas, square feet — 4 walls (W) and ceiling (C)													
Linear ft. per wall	6	8	10	12	14	16	18	20	22	24	26	28	30
6	C 36 / W 192	C 48 / W 224	C 60 / W 256	C 72 / W 288	C 84 / W 320	C 96 / W 352	C 108 / W 384	C 120 / W 416	C 132 / W 448	C 144 / W 480	C 156 / W 512	C 168 / W 544	C 180 / W 576
8	C 48 / W 224	C 64 / W 256	C 80 / W 288	C 96 / W 320	C 112 / W 352	C 128 / W 384	C 144 / W 416	C 160 / W 448	C 176 / W 480	C 182 / W 512	C 198 / W 544	C 224 / W 576	C 240 / W 608
10	C 60 / W 256	C 80 / W 288	C 100 / W 320	C 120 / W 352	C 140 / W 384	C 160 / W 416	C 180 / W 448	C 200 / W 480	C 220 / W 512	C 240 / W 544	C 260 / W 576	C 280 / W 608	C 300 / W 640
12	C 72 / W 288	C 96 / W 320	C 120 / W 352	C 144 / W 384	C 168 / W 416	C 192 / W 448	C 216 / W 480	C 240 / W 512	C 264 / W 544	C 288 / W 576	C 312 / W 608	C 336 / W 640	C 360 / W 672
14	C 84 / W 320	C 112 / W 352	C 140 / W 384	C 168 / W 416	C 196 / W 448	C 224 / W 480	C 252 / W 512	C 280 / W 544	C 308 / W 576	C 336 / W 608	C 364 / W 640	C 392 / W 672	C 420 / W 704
16	C 96 / W 352	C 128 / W 384	C 160 / W 416	C 192 / W 448	C 224 / W 480	C 256 / W 512	C 288 / W 544	C 320 / W 576	C 352 / W 608	C 384 / W 640	C 416 / W 672	C 448 / W 704	C 480 / W 736
18	C 108 / W 384	C 144 / W 416	C 180 / W 448	C 216 / W 480	C 252 / W 512	C 288 / W 544	C 324 / W 576	C 360 / W 608	C 396 / W 640	C 432 / W 672	C 468 / W 704	C 504 / W 736	C 540 / W 768
20	C 120 / W 416	C 160 / W 448	C 200 / W 480	C 240 / W 512	C 280 / W 544	C 320 / W 576	C 360 / W 608	C 400 / W 640	C 440 / W 672	C 480 / W 704	C 520 / W 736	C 560 / W 768	C 600 / W 800
22	C 132 / W 448	C 176 / W 480	C 220 / W 512	C 264 / W 544	C 308 / W 576	C 352 / W 608	C 396 / W 640	C 440 / W 672	C 484 / W 704	C 528 / W 736	C 572 / W 768	C 616 / W 800	C 660 / W 832
24	C 144 / W 480	C 182 / W 512	C 240 / W 544	C 288 / W 576	C 336 / W 608	C 384 / W 640	C 432 / W 672	C 480 / W 704	C 528 / W 736	C 576 / W 768	C 624 / W 800	C 672 / W 832	C 720 / W 864
26	C 156 / W 512	C 198 / W 544	C 260 / W 576	C 312 / W 608	C 364 / W 640	C 416 / W 672	C 468 / W 704	C 520 / W 736	C 572 / W 768	C 624 / W 800	C 676 / W 832	C 728 / W 864	C 780 / W 896
28	C 168 / W 544	C 224 / W 576	C 280 / W 608	C 336 / W 640	C 392 / W 672	C 448 / W 704	C 504 / W 736	C 560 / W 768	C 616 / W 800	C 672 / W 832	C 728 / W 864	C 784 / W 896	C 840 / W 928
30	C 180 / W 576	C 240 / W 608	C 300 / W 640	C 360 / W 672	C 420 / W 704	C 480 / W 736	C 540 / W 768	C 600 / W 800	C 660 / W 832	C 720 / W 864	C 780 / W 896	C 840 / W 928	C 900 / W 960

Note: Based on wall height of 8'0".

Figure 11-18
Room area chart

probably less expensive to paint the ceiling. But it's the homeowner who'll decide which one you use.

If you don't have records based on your own work, use the average manhour figures shown in Figure 11-17.

To estimate how much wallboard you need, figure the square footage of walls and ceilings in each room, closet, hall, and stairway. Figure 11-18 gives the square footage for walls and ceilings of rooms with 8-foot ceilings and even wall lengths. Figure 11-19 gives the square footage for all standard size wallboard panels.

Let's figure out how much wallboard you'll need for a 14 x 20 room addition with a standard 8-foot ceiling. Using Figure 11-18, you find that the walls total 544 square feet and the ceiling is 280 square feet for a total of 824 square feet. Suppose you choose 8-foot panels. Look at Figure 11-19. Find the 4 x 8 foot column and follow down it until you come to 824, or the figure nearest to 824. It's 832. Follow the line to the left until you come to the Pieces column. You need 26 sheets of wallboard for the addition.

Suppose you need the wallboard requirements for the walls only. Use Figure 11-20 to find the number of

Wallboard (square feet)										
Pieces	4' x 6'	4' x 7'	4' x 8'	4' x 9'	4' x 10'	4' x 12'	4' x 14'	4' x 16'	2' x 8'	2' x 10'	2' x 12'
2	48	56	64	72	80	96	112	128	32	40	48
4	96	112	128	144	160	192	224	256	64	80	96
6	144	168	192	216	240	288	336	384	96	120	144
8	192	224	256	288	320	384	448	512	128	160	192
10	240	280	320	360	400	480	560	640	160	200	240
12	288	336	384	432	480	576	672	768	192	240	288
14	336	392	448	504	560	672	784	896	224	280	336
16	384	448	512	576	640	768	896	1,024	256	320	384
18	432	504	576	648	720	864	1,008	1,152	228	360	432
20	480	560	640	720	800	960	1,120	1,280	320	400	480
22	528	616	704	792	880	1,056	1,232	1,408	352	440	528
24	576	672	768	864	960	1,152	1,344	1,536	384	480	576
26	624	728	832	936	1,040	1,248	1,456	1,664	416	520	624
28	672	784	896	1,008	1,120	1,344	1,568	1,792	448	560	672
30	720	840	960	1,080	1,200	1,440	1,680	1,920	480	600	720
32	768	896	1,024	1,152	1,280	1,536	1,792	2,048	512	640	768
34	816	952	1,088	1,224	1,360	1,632	1,904	2,176	544	680	816
36	864	1,008	1,152	1,296	1,440	1,728	2,016	2,304	576	720	864
38	912	1,064	1,216	1,368	1,520	1,824	2,128	2,432	608	760	912
40	960	1,120	1,280	1,440	1,600	1,920	2,240	2,560	640	800	960
42	1,008	1,176	1,344	1,512	1,680	2,016	2,352	2,688	672	840	1,008
44	1,056	1,232	1,408	1,584	1,760	2,112	2,464	2,816	704	880	1,056
46	1,104	1,288	1,472	1,656	1,840	2,208	2,576	2,944	736	920	1,104
48	1,152	1,344	1,536	1,728	1,920	2,304	2,688	3,072	768	960	1,152
50	1,200	1,400	1,600	1,800	2,000	2,400	2,800	3,200	800	1,000	1,200
52	1,248	1,456	1,664	1,872	2,080	2,496	2,912	3,328	832	1,040	1,248
54	1,296	1,512	1,728	1,944	2,160	2,592	3,024	3,456	864	1,080	1,296
56	1,344	1,568	1,792	2,016	2,240	2,688	3,136	3,584	896	1,120	1,344
58	1,392	1,624	1,856	2,088	2,320	2,784	3,248	3,712	928	1,160	1,392
60	1,440	1,680	1,920	2,160	2,400	2,880	3,360	3,840	960	1,200	1,440
62	1,488	1,736	1,984	2,232	2,480	2,976	3,472	3,968	992	1,240	1,488
64	1,536	1,792	2,048	2,304	2,560	3,072	3,584	4,096	1,024	1,280	1,536
66	1,584	1,848	2,112	2,376	2,640	3,168	3,696	4,224	1,056	1,320	1,584
68	1,632	1,904	2,176	2,448	2,720	3,264	3,808	4,352	1,088	1,360	1,632
70	1,680	1,960	2,240	2,520	2,800	3,360	3,920	4,480	1,120	1,400	1,680
72	1,728	2,016	2,304	2,592	2,880	3,456	4,032	4,608	1,152	1,440	1,728
74	1,776	2,072	2,368	2,664	2,960	3,552	4,144	4,736	1,184	1,480	1,776
76	1,824	2,128	2,432	2,736	3,040	3,648	4,256	4,864	1,216	1,520	1,824
78	1,872	2,184	2,496	2,808	3,120	3,744	4,368	4,992	1,248	1,560	1,872
80	1,920	2,240	2,560	2,880	3,200	3,840	4,480	5,120	1,280	1,600	1,920
82	1,968	2,296	2,624	2,952	3,280	3,936	4,592	5,248	1,312	1,640	1,968
84	2,016	2,352	2,688	3,024	3,360	4,032	4,704	5,376	1,344	1,680	2,016
86	2,064	2,408	2,752	3,096	3,440	4,128	4,816	5,504	1,376	1,720	2,064
88	2,112	2,464	2,816	3,168	3,520	4,224	4,928	5,632	1,408	1,760	2,112
90	2,160	2,520	2,880	3,240	3,600	4,320	5,040	5,760	1,440	1,800	2,160
92	2,208	2,576	2,944	3,312	3,680	4,416	5,152	5,888	1,472	1,840	2,208
94	2,256	2,632	3,008	3,384	3,760	4,512	5,264	6,016	1,504	1,880	2,256
96	2,304	2,688	3,072	3,456	3,840	4,608	5,376	6,144	1,536	1,920	2,304
98	2,352	2,744	3,136	3,528	3,920	4,704	5,488	6,272	1,568	1,960	2,352
100	2,400	2,800	3,200	3,600	4,000	4,800	5,600	6,400	1,600	2,000	2,400
200	4,800	5,600	6,400	7,200	8,000	9,600	11,200	12,800	3,200	4,000	4,800
300	7,200	8,400	9,600	10,800	12,000	14,400	16,800	19,200	4,800	6,000	7,200
400	9,600	11,200	12,800	14,400	16,000	19,200	22,400	25,600	6,400	8,000	9,600
500	12,000	14,000	16,000	18,000	20,000	24,000	28,000	32,000	8,000	10,000	12,000
600	14,400	16,800	19,200	21,600	24,000	28,800	33,600	38,400	9,600	12,000	14,400
700	16,800	19,600	22,400	25,200	28,000	33,600	39,200	44,800	11,200	14,000	16,800
800	19,200	22,400	25,600	28,800	32,000	38,400	44,800	51,200	12,800	16,000	19,200
900	21,600	25,200	28,800	32,400	36,000	43,200	50,400	57,600	14,400	18,000	21,600
1000	24,000	28,000	32,000	36,000	40,000	48,000	56,000	64,000	16,000	20,000	24,000

Figure 11-19
Wallboard footage table

How to figure a room	
Determine the perimeter. This is merely the total of the widths of each wall in the room. Use the conversion table to figure the number of panels needed.	
Perimeter	**No. of 4' x 8' panels needed**
36'	9
40'	10
44'	11
48'	12
52'	13
56'	14
60'	15
64'	16
68'	17
72'	18
92'	23
Deductions	
Door	1/2 panel
Window	1/4 panel
Fireplace	1/2 panel

Figure 11-20
Figuring wallboard panels by room perimeter

Work element	Unit	Manhours per unit
Baseboard		
Two member, ordinary work	100 LF	4 to 6
Two member, hardwood, first class work	100 LF	6 to 8
Three member, ordinary work	100 LF	5 to 7
Three member, first class or difficult work	100 LF	7 to 9
Cove molding		
Ordinary work	100 LF	2.7 to 3
Hardwood, first class or difficult work	100 LF	4 to 5
Closets (2 x 5)		
Shelving, hook strips, hooks, and poles	Each	2 to 4

Figure 11-21
Manhours for installing trim

4 x 8 panels needed. First, add the total of the four walls to find the perimeter of the room. For the 14 x 20 addition you get 68 feet. Now look up the number of panels you need in the conversion table in Figure 11-20. You need 17 panels, minus the allowance for doors, windows and fireplaces.

You'll need more than just drywall panels to complete the job. Be sure you include these materials in your estimate:

1. Five pounds of $1^3/_8$-inch annular ring nails per 1,000 square feet of wallboard if you're using adhesives (12 pounds if you're not).

2. One tube of adhesive per 500 square feet of wallboard.

3. One roll of tape (250 feet long) per 600 square feet of wallboard.

4. Five gallons (one can) of joint compound per 1,000 square feet of wallboard.

5. Five gallons per 400 square feet for texture-finished ceilings using joint compound.

6. One 8-foot metal corner bead (for an 8-foot ceiling) for each outside corner.

7. One 8-foot inside corner molding for each inside corner.

Estimating Trim Materials and Labor

You estimate trim by the linear foot. For example, there's 68 linear feet of wall in the 14 x 20 addition (14 + 14 + 20 + 20). You'll need enough cove molding to trim 68 feet. Deduct openings to find how much base molding you'll need. Many carpenters figure a 10 percent waste factor when trimming out a room.

Use Figure 11-21 to estimate labor for trim.

Finish Floor Coverings

Wood Flooring

Wood flooring is made of both softwood and hardwood. Softwood is less expensive, but doesn't stand up like hardwood in heavy traffic areas. You may even have trouble getting softwood flooring in some areas. Softwood flooring is usually made from southern pine, but you can also find Douglas fir, western hemlock, and larch in various lengths and thicknesses. The most common size boards are $2^1/4$ inches wide and $^5/32$ inches thick. The underside of each tongue-and-groove board is grooved to help reduce warping.

Most hardwood flooring is made from oak and maple, but hickory, beech, birch, and a few other hardwoods are available. It comes in thicknesses of $^3/8$, $^1/2$, and $^{25}/32$ inches and widths ranging from $1^1/2$ to $3^1/4$ inches. The most common hardwood flooring is tongue and groove $2^1/4$-inch-wide strip flooring with grooved undersides. The boards or strips come in lengths ranging from 2 to 16 feet. Each board end is end-matched (tongue and groove).

In both softwood and hardwood, vertical-grain flooring is more wear-resistant than flat-grain flooring. Vertical-grain (also called edge-grain) is lumber that has been sawed so that the wide surfaces of the board form approximately a right angle to the annual growth rings. Flat-grain lumber has been sawed parallel to the pith and approximately tangent to the growth rings. A board is flat-grain when the annual growth rings make an angle less than 45 degrees with the surface of the board.

You can nail the boards down on firm subfloor, either underlayment or an existing floor. Most builders install 15-pound felt building paper over a subfloor before laying flooring. In new construction, lay the boards crosswise to the floor joists. If you're installing the boards over an existing wood floor, lay them crosswise to the old flooring. It's easier to lay flooring if you use a floor hammer.

Figure 12-1 shows the common types of wood-strip flooring. The tongue-and-groove strip in Figure 12-1 A is the most popular. But the

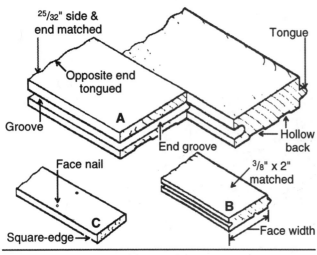

Figure 12-1
Wood-strip flooring types

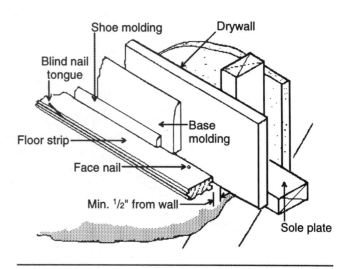

Figure 12-2
Installing first flooring strip

square-edge strip flooring (Figure 12-1 C) is sometimes used. It's usually $^3/_8$ inch thick and 2 inches wide. Unlike tongue-and-groove boards which you nail at an angle through the tongue, you face nail square-edge boards.

Start the first strip at least $^1/_2$ inch from the wall to allow for expansion. See Figure 12-2. Nail the board in place at a point that will later be covered by the base or shoe mold. Then nail through the tongue. Don't face nail the other courses, just tongue nail them. Slant tongue nails at about a 45-degree angle. If you use a floor hammer, you won't have to worry about the angle because the hammer does that for you.

Stagger the board butts so the ends don't fall in line. Discard crooked or bent boards because they just cause trouble. Face nail the last course the same way you did the first course, with a $^1/_2$-inch expansion joint between the board and the wall.

Wood Block Flooring

Wood block flooring is made in a number of patterns. The blocks vary in size from 4 x 4 inches to 9 x 9 inches or larger. Block thicknesses can be $^1/_8$ inch thick (when made of stabilized veneer) to $^{15}/_{32}$ inch (when made of laminated blocking or the plywood block tile shown in Figure 12-3). The thicker tile has tongue-and-groove edges.

Solid wood tile is also available as shown in Figure 12-3. It may be made of narrow strips of wood that are splined or keyed together.

Apply the $^1/_8$-inch block flooring with adhesive recommended by the flooring manufacturer, using the instructions on the adhesive container. Nail the $^{15}/_{32}$ T&G block through the tongue to a wood subfloor, or apply with an adhesive to a concrete slab. You'll usually get the best results from laying the blocks with the grain directions alternating, making a checkerboard effect. Divide the room into four equal parts and pro-

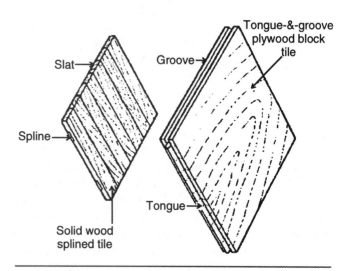

Figure 12-3
Wood block flooring

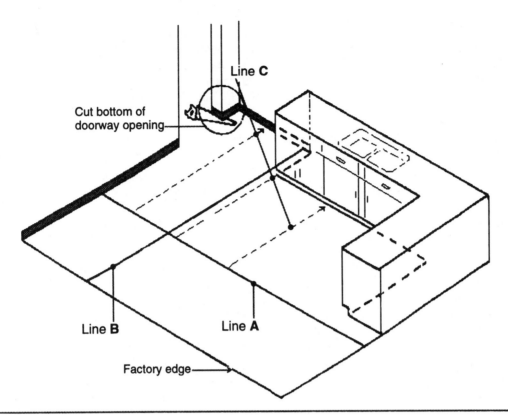

Line **C**

Cut bottom of
doorway opening

Line **B**

Line **A**

Factory edge

Figure 12-4
Establishing reference points

ceed according to the directions for laying vinyl tile given later in this chapter. Leave a ¹/₂-inch space between the tile and the wall for expansion.

Many block floor coverings are prefinished. Once the floor is installed, all you have to do is wax it to give it a final finish.

Sheet Vinyl Flooring

Polyvinyl chloride (PVC) is the main ingredient of vinyl flooring, which also contains resin binders with mineral fillers, plasticizers, stabilizers, and pigments. Vinyl can be clear or filled. The clear has a layer of opaque particles or pigments covered with a wearing surface of clear vinyl bonded to a durable backing. It's highly resistant to wear. Filled vinyl is made of colored vinyl chips immersed in a clear vinyl base, bonded by heat and pressure.

Vinyl flooring is ideal for kitchens, playrooms, and bathrooms. With normal household traffic and regular care, quality vinyl can still look good 20 years down the road.

Preparing to Install Sheet Vinyl

Begin by taking out everything in the room that isn't nailed down. Sweep and vacuum the floor clean. You don't want bits of sawdust or discarded tacks or nails under the vinyl. Look for any obstructions that will show through the vinyl, such as protruding nail heads. Drive the nails flush with the subfloor. Unroll the sheet vinyl, preferably in another room.

If you didn't allow for the thickness of the flooring when you put in the doors, cut the bottom of doorway moldings so the flooring slips under them easily. Use a handsaw to make the cut. Hold the saw flat on a piece of cardboard or folded building paper that's the same thickness as the vinyl. See Figure 12-4.

Find and Mark Reference Points

There are several different ways to install sheet vinyl. Here's a step-by-step method you can follow for a one-piece installation:

1. It's best to put the factory edge along the longest straight wall. Pick which wall you can put one factory edge against. (Factory edges run the entire length of the vinyl, not the width of the roll.)

2. Measure out the same distance, from either end of this wall, to about the center of the room. Snap a chalk line through these two points to make a line like the one shown in line A, Figure 12-4. This is your first reference line.

3. Mark a second line at a 90-degree angle to the first line at a point where the second line can run the entire width of the room. This is your second reference line, and it must be exactly perpendicular to the first line. It's shown as line B, Figure 12-4. You use both of the reference lines to mark and cut the vinyl.

4. On graph paper, draw the two reference lines from the floor. Roughly sketch the room (to scale) around the intersection of the two lines. Draw all cabinets and closets.

5. Measure from the reference lines on the floor out to the walls or cabinet every 2 feet around the room, including at least two measurements for every offset. Don't get careless. Walls are seldom exactly straight so take the time to measure every 2 feet. See line C, Figure 12-4.

How to Transfer the Measurements

Now position your floor-plan sketch on the flooring material so that your first reference line is parallel to a factory edge of the flooring. Using the measurement written on your floor plan, measure in from the factory edge on the vinyl the distance from your first reference line to the wall. Mark this distance at both ends on the vinyl, and snap a chalk line through the points.

To establish the second reference line on the flooring, measure along the first reference line from the edges to where the floor plan indicates the reference lines intersect. Snap a chalk line through the points at an exact 90-degree angle to the first line. This second line should run the entire width of the floor.

Now the vinyl is marked with reference lines that match those in the room. Measure out from these lines to all walls and cabinets at the same places on the floor plan on the graph paper. Connect these marks with a chalk line. These outside lines are the cut lines. See Figure 12-4.

How to Cut Sheet Vinyl

This isn't the time to rush the job. It always pays to recheck your measurements to make sure you transferred them correctly. When you're satisfied the measurements are correct, use a straight-blade utility knife and cut along all outside cut lines. I recommend you use a straightedge as a guide for the knife. If you're cutting over a concrete floor, place a piece of plywood, OSB panel, or cardboard under the cut lines before you cut.

Steps for Adhering and Stapling

After trimming the flooring to fit, fasten it down and complete the following steps within two hours after you cut and fit the flooring. If you wait longer than that, the flooring can lose its elasticity. That will make it more difficult to fix any fitting mistakes. If you act soon enough, you can usually fix minor fitting mistakes by stretching the edge of the flooring and fastening it down.

Depending on the type of subflooring, you can fasten the perimeter of the flooring with adhesive, staples, or a combination of the two. Use adhesive on concrete or tempered hardboard. Some floor coverings require staples, others a combination of staples and adhesives. You obviously can't staple areas like the toe-kick overhang on the front of cabinets.

To fasten the perimeter of the flooring with adhesive, apply a 3-inch band of adhesive around the perimeter and all fixtures. Don't apply more than the recommended amount — and don't get the adhesive on the face of the material. A slight "picture frame" effect may occur after installation, but this will disappear within about 24 hours.

1. Fold back the flooring along one wall. Starting 1 foot past the corner, use a trowel to spread a 3-inch-wide band of adhesive along the edge of the floor to within 1 foot of the next corner, as shown in Figure 12-5. Leave the adhesive off this area so you can fold the flooring back from the next wall.

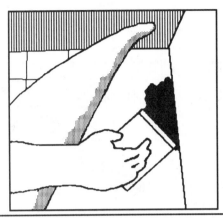

Figure 12-5
Spread adhesive at edges

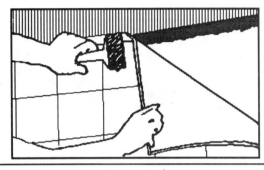

Figure 12-6
Press covering firmly in adhesive

2. Firmly press the flooring onto the fresh adhesive with a hand roller as shown in Figure 12-6. Fold back the flooring on the next wall and spread the 3-inch-wide band of adhesive along the 1 foot you left bare. Continue spreading around the corner and along the edge to within 1 foot of the next corner. Again, roll the edge of the flooring onto the adhesive. Continue adhering and rolling in this manner until you've fastened the entire perimeter of the flooring with adhesive.

An Alternate Method for Installing One Piece of Sheet Vinyl

1. Unroll and position the piece of vinyl, allowing any excess to extend up the walls and cabinets. Allow enough material to cover the floor in every offset. Whenever possible, line up the floor's pattern with the longest unobstructed wall.

2. Cut and fit the corners first. To fit the inside corners, press the excess flooring into the corner's wall and floor juncture. Using a straight-blade utility knife, punch through the flooring at the base of the corner and cut upward through the excess material as shown in Figure 12-7.

3. To fit the outside corners, lay the flooring back at the base of the corner so the fold runs diagonally across it. See Figure 12-8. Hold the flooring against the corner, punch your knife through at the base, and cut upward through the excess flooring.

4. To fit the walls, press a steel carpenter's square into the wall/floor juncture firmly, and cut off the

excess material with a utility knife at a 45-degree angle as shown in Figure 12-9. When you trim flooring for a doorway, cut the edge so it'll be directly under the closed door. Cover exposed edges with a metal threshold molding.

5. Roll the vinyl up, face side in, so it'll roll out into the room with the factory edge against the longest straight wall. Roll out enough flooring to see that it's in the correct position, but don't force it under offsets or cabinets. Fold half of the flooring back onto itself, being careful not to move the other half out of position or to crimp the fold.

6. Now spread the adhesive. Follow the manufacturer's instructions on the container. Spread the adhesive evenly, using a trowel with notches $1/16$ inch wide, $1/16$ inch deep, and $3/32$ inch apart. Don't let

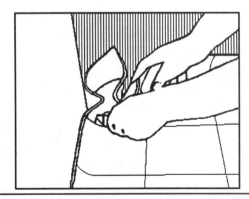

Figure 12-7
Fit and trim corners

Figure 12-8
Fit and trim outside corner

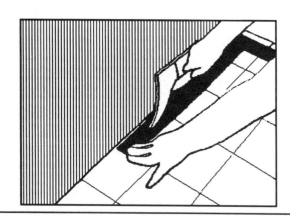

Figure 12-9
Trim at walls for fit

the adhesive dry more than 15 minutes before you lay the floor covering.

7. Fold back the other half of the flooring and repeat the process. Roll the flooring from the center out toward the edges, using a heavy roller to make a good bond and remove any air pockets. Cap doorways and openings with a metal threshold strip.

Installing Two Pieces of Sheet Vinyl

If the room has a side larger than 12 feet, you'll need to use two pieces of flooring. There are two methods you can follow. For the first, follow the procedures for one-piece installation with the following exceptions:

1. Overlap the two pieces at the seam area before transferring measurements onto the sheet vinyl flooring. Make sure the pattern is matched at the overlap. Place strips of masking tape across the overlap to hold the pieces together.

2. Now transfer your measurements onto the flooring and cut the flooring to the size and shape of the room. Don't cut overlap seams.

3. Untape the seams before you move the flooring to the room you're putting it in. Move and position both pieces in place. Do one piece at a time.

4. Fold back the top piece halfway and draw a pencil line on the subfloor along the edge of the second piece (at the seam area). Fold back the second piece and spread adhesive to within 12 inches of either side of the line as shown in Figure 12-10.

5. Put the flooring on the adhesive and roll to make a good bond, avoiding the overlap area.

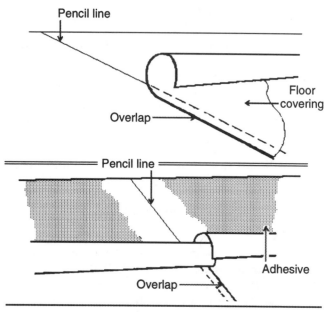

Figure 12-10
Steps for two-piece installation

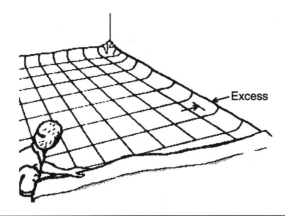

Figure 12-11
Extend excess up walls

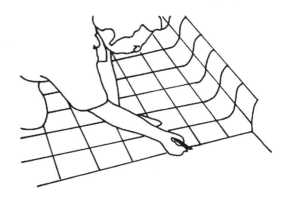

Figure 12-12
Mark the underlayment

6. Cut through both pieces where they overlap. Use a straight-blade utility knife and a metal straight-edge as a guide.

7. Fold back both seams, spread adhesive, and place the flooring into position.

The last step is to seam seal the flooring. There are some floor coverings, however, that you put in by seam sealing first. Find out from the supplier and follow the manufacturer's instructions. Follow the seam sealing instructions on the sealer container.

Here's another way to install two pieces of sheet flooring:

1. Unroll and position the first piece of the flooring so the excess goes up the walls and the cabinets. See Figure 12-11. Don't forget to allow enough material to cover the floor in every offset.

2. With the first piece in position, draw a pencil line on the floor from one wall to the other along the factory-cut edge of the flooring. This is where you'll seam the two pieces together. See Figure 12-12.

3. Place the second piece of flooring in position. Allow the excess to extend up the walls and cabinets. Don't move the first piece you just positioned. See Figure 12-13.

4. Overlap the two pieces of flooring where the seam is by matching up the pattern at the center as

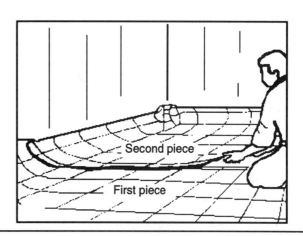

Figure 12-13
Positioning the second piece

shown in Figure 12-14. When possible, use one of the simulated grout lines (a straight recessed line in the surface design of the flooring) as an overlap matching point.

5. Cut and remove a wide U-shaped piece of the excess flooring at both ends of the seam. See Figure 12-15. The bottom of the U should form a perfect fit along the wall base. This lets both ends of the seam lie flat on the floor instead of extending up the base of the walls. Check your pattern match at the seam. You don't want to lose the match at the seam while you make the U cuts.

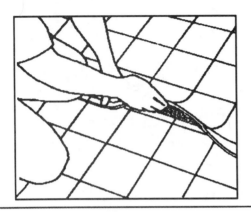

Figure 12-14
Match the pattern at overlap

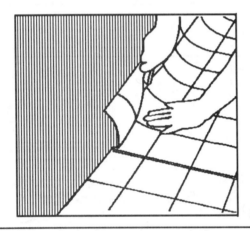

Figure 12-15
Remove the excess material

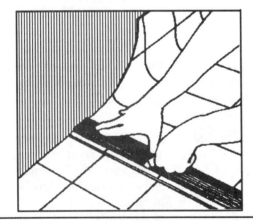

Figure 12-16
Cut the overlap

6. Using a metal straightedge and a straight-blade utility knife, cut along the overlapped grout lines (whenever possible) in the flooring's design. Cut from one wall to the other, being sure to cut neatly through both layers of flooring as shown in Figure 12-16. Some installers get in a hurry at this point, and the end result is a crooked or ragged cut which you can see when you look closely.

7. Remove both strips of flooring scrap created by the pattern-matching cut. See Figure 12-17. The two pieces of flooring are now pattern-matched and cut to fit each other. *Don't move the two pieces out of position.* When the seam edges are butted together, the pattern should flow evenly and uniformly.

8. Gently fold back both edges of the seam and apply a 3-inch band of adhesive under the seam as shown in Figure 12-18. Lay one piece of material onto the adhesive, then slowly lay the second piece onto the adhesive, making sure that the seam is tight and the pattern matched. Firmly press the flooring onto the fresh adhesive using a hand roller as shown in Figure 12-19.

9. Apply seam sealer with the applicator bottle, moving the bottle from one end of the seam to the other as you squeeze out the seam adhesive. See Figure 12-20. You don't need to remove small amounts of excess sealer on the surface of the seam because they'll gradually match the gloss level of the vinyl surface. After the seam surface is sealed, begin the cutting and fitting sequence of the floor's perimeter.

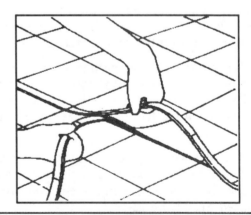

Figure 12-17
Remove both scrap pieces

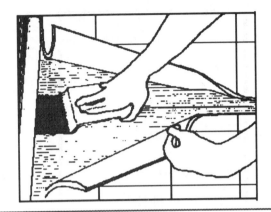

Figure 12-18
Spread 3-inch band of adhesive under seam

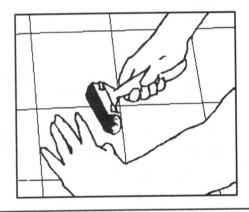

Figure 12-19
Press the flooring for firm contact

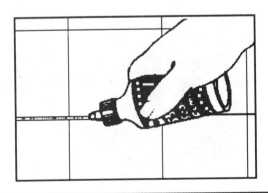

Figure 12-20
Apply seam sealer to seam

Installing Vinyl Tile

Vinyl tile is made from polyvinyl chloride resins, pigment, and clay-based inert fillers. It comes in various patterns and textures in 9 x 9 and 12 x 12 inch squares that are $1/16$, $3/32$, or $1/8$ inch thick. Vinyl tile resists grease, alkaline substances, oils, and some acids. Some are available with a peel-and-stick backing.

You can install the tiles on slabs below grade, but they always require a rigid subfloor. Prepare the subfloor for vinyl tiles just like you would for vinyl sheet flooring.

Border tiles on both sides of a room should be the same width. The same rule applies to the border tiles at both ends of the room. They should be the same size. That takes planning.

To lay the starter runs, first find the center of the room by marking the center of each wall. Snap a chalk line on the subfloor across the center of the room from one wall to the opposite wall. Then do the same thing for the other two walls. You should have two intersecting lines like the ones in Figure 12-21.

Then lay a row of loose tiles along the chalk line from the center point to one side wall and one end wall as shown in Figure 12-22.

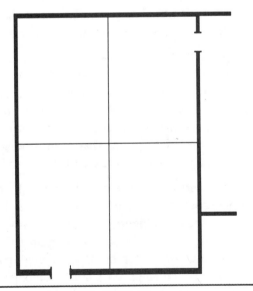

Figure 12-21
Divide the room into 4 equal parts.
Snap chalk line on underlayment

233

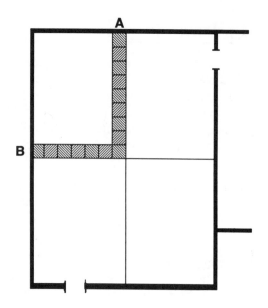

Figure 12-22
Lay a row of loose tiles

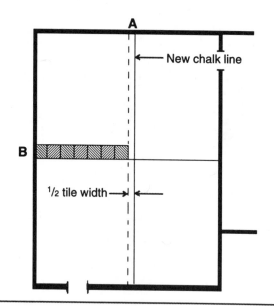

Figure 12-23
Shift tiles to new chalk line which is
half of a tile width from old chalkline

Measure the distance between the wall and the last full tile at B. If this space is less than half a tile width, snap a new line half a tile width closer to the opposite wall. Follow the same procedure for row A. See Figure 12-23. You want to make sure that each row ends with at least half a tile.

Lay the A-B rows first, then the rest of the quarter section. Lay the next quarter, starting at the established chalk line and work toward the walls.

Apply self-sticking tiles directly to the underlayment without adhesives. For plain tile, apply a thin coat of adhesive. Be very careful here. It's easy to get too much adhesive on the floor. Follow the manufacturer's instructions. Place each tile straight down — don't slide them into place. That makes the adhesive pile up at the joint. Make sure the tile is flat and firm.

To cut and fit the tile next to the wall, place a loose tile squarely on top of the last full tile closest to the wall as shown in Figure 12-24, tile A. Now place a third tile, tile B, on top of A and against the wall. Using the edge of the top tile B as a guide, mark the tile under it, A, with a pencil. Cut tile A along the pencil line. You can use the same method to mark and cut tiles for corners and irregular shapes. See Figures 12-25 A and B.

Wood Subfloors for Vinyl Flooring

You can apply most sheet vinyl directly over almost any type of structurally sound subfloor such as plywood or particleboard. Use particleboard underlayment that's approved for that purpose by the National Particleboard Association (NPA). You can also put it over concrete, whether the concrete is above, on, or below grade.

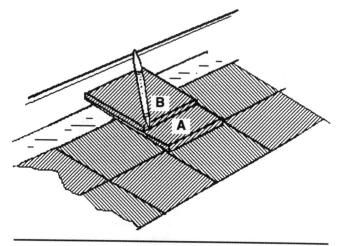

Figure 12-24
Steps for measuring wall border tile to fit

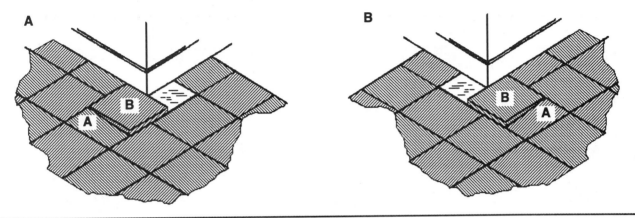

Figure 12-25
How to measure tile for a corner fit

Use exterior plywood or plywood bonded with exterior glues for subflooring in a kitchen, bathroom, mud-room, entryway, or laundry room where a lot of water can be spilled.

Resilient flooring requires a smooth, firm base. Whether you use sheet vinyl, vinyl tile, or linoleum, any bulge, crack, protruding nail head, or hole will show through.

In basement conversions, don't install tempered hardboard or resilient flooring over "sleeper" constructed subfloors, on or below grade, that don't have a proper vapor barrier. If you're putting tempered hardboard over any crawl spaces, make sure the crawl spaces are at least 18 inches high and properly ventilated.

Before you begin finishing a basement floor, make sure it was properly constructed with gravel fill and a vapor barrier. It's a good idea to put a vapor barrier directly on top of the floor. Use 6-mil polyethylene. Overlap the seams at least 6 inches and seal the seams. Install sleepers directly on the vapor barrier. You can use pressure-treated 1 x 4s or 2 x 4s spaced 16 inches on center as sleepers. See Figure 12-26.

Concrete Subfloors for Vinyl Flooring

Keep a concrete subfloor free of expansion joints, depressions, and scale. Clean and fill all cracks, expansion joints, and score marks with latex underlay-

ment mastic. The slab should be dry, dense, and smooth. Remove wax, oils, paints, and varnishes. A good grime remover for concrete subfloors is trisodium phosphate (TSP) and hot water. Oakite and Climalene also work well. For paints you'll have to use grinding or sanding to remove the finish.

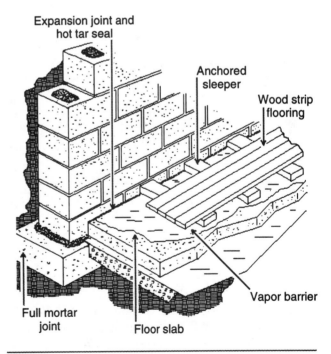

Figure 12-26
Installing sleepers on a concrete floor

235

Length feet	12 ft. SY	15 ft. SY	Length feet	12 ft. SY	15 ft. SY	Length feet	12 ft. SY	15 ft. SY	Length feet	12 ft. SY	15 ft. SY
2	2.67	3.33	27	36.00	45.00	52	69.00	86.67	77	102.67	128.33
3	4.00	5.00	28	37.33	46.67	53	70.67	88.33	78	104.00	130.00
4	5.33	6.67	29	38.67	48.33	54	72.00	90.00	79	105.33	131.67
5	6.67	8.33	30	40.00	50.00	55	73.33	91.67	80	106.67	133.33
6	8.00	10.00	31	41.33	51.67	56	74.67	93.33	81	108.00	135.00
7	9.33	11.67	32	42.67	53.33	57	76.00	95.00	82	109.33	136.67
8	10.67	13.33	33	44.00	55.00	58	77.33	96.67	83	110.67	138.33
9	12.00	15.00	34	45.33	56.67	59	78.67	98.33	84	112.00	140.00
10	13.33	16.67	35	46.67	58.33	60	80.00	100.00	85	113.33	141.67
11	14.67	18.33	36	48.00	60.00	61	81.00	101.67	86	114.67	143.33
12	16.00	20.00	37	49.33	61.67	62	82.67	103.33	87	116.00	145.00
13	17.33	21.67	38	50.67	63.33	63	84.00	105.00	88	117.33	146.67
14	18.67	23.33	39	52.00	65.00	64	85.33	106.67	89	118.67	148.33
15	20.00	25.00	40	53.33	66.67	65	86.67	108.33	90	120.00	150.00
16	21.33	26.67	41	54.67	68.33	66	88.00	110.00	91	121.33	151.67
17	22.67	28.33	42	56.00	70.00	67	89.33	111.67	92	122.67	153.33
18	24.00	30.00	43	57.33	71.67	68	90.67	113.33	93	124.00	155.00
19	25.33	31.67	44	58.67	73.33	69	92.00	115.00	94	125.33	156.67
20	26.67	33.33	45	60.00	75.00	70	93.00	116.67	95	126.67	158.33
21	28.00	35.00	46	61.33	76.67	71	94.67	118.33	96	128.00	160.00
22	29.33	36.67	47	62.67	78.33	72	96.00	120.00	97	129.33	161.67
23	30.67	38.33	48	64.00	80.00	73	97.33	121.67	98	130.67	163.33
24	32.00	40.00	49	65.33	81.67	74	98.67	123.33	99	132.00	165.00
25	33.33	41.67	50	66.67	83.33	75	100.00	125.00	100	133.00	166.77
26	34.67	43.33	51	68.00	85.00	76	101.33	126.67	—	—	—

Figure 12-27
The carpet yardage calculator

You can smooth a rough concrete floor with clean, sharp, white sand and a terrazzo grinder. Keep the sand and concrete wet while grinding to prevent dust. Don't soak the floor because it must be dry before you lay the flooring. Use a latex underlayment mastic to smooth out the floor if it's too rough for grinding.

If a concrete floor froze before setting up, it will be scaly and cracked. The solution is to add a top coat of concrete at least $1\frac{1}{2}$ inches thick or install a "sleeper" joist system and install a new subfloor.

You'll have to neutralize concrete floors that have been treated with alkali before you lay the floor tile.

Use a mixture of 1 part muriatic acid to about 8 parts of water. Close off the basement from the rest of the house and ventilate it as much as possible. Spread the solution over the floor and leave it there for about an hour before rinsing it off with clear water. Let the floor dry completely before you put down the new floor covering.

Carpeting

Carpet is available in indoor, outdoor, indoor/outdoor and artificial grass. All carpets have a surface pile and a backing material. The surface pile may be wool, cotton, nylon, acrylic, polyester, or polypropylene. Each fiber has its advantages and disadvantages. Consult a reputable dealer for the type and grade of carpet best suited for your particular addition or conversion.

Most carpets are 12 or 15 feet wide. Wall-to-wall carpeting is usually sold by the square yard. To find approximately how many square yards you'd need for a room, multiply the length of the room, in feet, by the width, in feet, and divide by 9. Or you can use the carpet yardage chart in Figure 12-27. Simply find the appropriate length in feet in one the vertical columns, and follow across to the width in feet (12 or 15 feet) in the headings at the top of the table. For example, a room that's 20 feet long and 12 feet wide will require about 27 yards of carpet (rounded up from 26.67).

Padding extends carpet life, increases sound reduction, and adds comfort underfoot. Common types of padding are soft- and hard-backed vinyl foam, sponge-rubber foam, latex (rubber), and felted cushions made either of animal hair or a combination of hair and jute. Latex and vinyl foams are probably the most practical. They have a waffled surface that helps to hold the carpet in place. Standard padding is $4\frac{1}{2}$ feet wide.

One-piece and cushion-backed carpeting need no extra padding or underlay. Foam rubber-backed carpeting is popular. It's mildew-proof and unaffected by water. You can lay it in basements and below grade on concrete floors that are protected by a water sealant. The backing is non-skid. Since it's a heavy material, it stays in place without being glued or tacked. But some installers prefer to apply an adhesive band at the perimeter or even over the entire floor.

Size	BF per 100 SF	SF per 1000 BF	Nails, lbs. per 100 SF
$^{25}/_{32}$ x 2	142.5	701.8	3.0
$^{25}/_{32}$ x $2\frac{1}{4}$	138.3	723.0	3.0
$^{25}/_{32}$ x $3\frac{1}{4}$	129.0	775.2	2.3
$^{3}/_{8}$ x $1\frac{1}{2}$	138.3	723.0	3.7
$^{3}/_{8}$ x 2	130.0	769.2	3.0

Figure 12-28
Estimating material for wood strip flooring

Indoor/outdoor carpeting works well over concrete and tile floors. The carpet's backing is made of a closed-pore vinyl or latex foam that keeps out moisture.

If a basement you convert already has a vinyl or asbestos floor covering, you can't install carpeting unless you remove the old flooring. Otherwise it'll accumulate moisture under the new carpet. The moisture soaks through into the carpet and eventually causes a musty odor and mildew stains.

Installation charges are often included in carpeting square yard costs. The cost for installation is usually reasonable — probably less than it would cost you to install it yourself. Let trained workers do the installation for a professional-looking but inexpensive job.

Estimating Materials and Manhours

Estimate underlayment material requirements the same way as plywood subflooring requirements. Allow 5 percent waste for cutting and fitting. Use Figure 12-28 to estimate materials required for wood strip flooring.

Strip flooring takes about 12 manhours per 1,000 BF of $^{25}/_{32}$ x $2\frac{1}{4}$-inch boards, and 1,000 BF will cover 723 square feet. For attic floors, add 25 percent for a total of 3 additional manhours.

To find out how much wood block or resilient tile you'll need for a room, divide the area of the room, in square inches, by the area of a block or tile, in square inches. Add 10 percent for cutting and waste.

Here's an example for a 20 x 20 foot room using 9 x 9 inch tiles:

Area of the room in square feet = 20 x 20 = 400 SF
Area of the room in square inches = 400 x 144
= 57600 SI
Area of a piece in square inches = 9 x 9 = 81 SI
Area of room / area of one piece = 57600 ÷ 81 = 711
10 percent of 711 = 71
Number of pieces needed = 711 + 71 = 782

If you use 12 x 12 inch block or tile, you need 400 pieces (plus 10 percent for cutting and waste) for a total of 440.

If you don't have good records of your own, use these figures to estimate labor for laying 100 square feet of blocks or tile: For laying 12 x 12-inch wood block, 2 manhours. For 9 x 9-inch vinyl tile, 1.5 manhours. And for 12 x 12-inch vinyl tile, 1.3 manhours. Add 25 percent to these figures for attic work.

Sheet vinyl comes in 6- and 12-foot widths. Figure how much material you need based on the room size and cut-outs for obstructions such as cabinets. A 20 x 20 foot room with no obstructions will require 400 SF of sheet vinyl plus about 2 inches at each wall to allow for any adjustments due to irregularities in a room, such as off-square or uneven walls.

Sheet vinyl installation manhours depend on the thickness of the flooring. Estimate 100 square feet of 0.070-inch-thick vinyl at 1.8 manhours; 0.090-inch vinyl at 2 manhours; and 0.125-inch vinyl at 2.3 manhours. Again, add 25 percent for attic work.

Building a Bathroom

Every bathroom design should be both attractive and functional. That's not a difficult combination to achieve if you have plenty of space to work with. But if floor space is limited, it takes care and imagination to plan the arrangement of the bathroom fixtures. And most bathrooms for conversions and additions are "extra" baths — they're seldom spacious.

Designing a Bathroom for a Small Space

Figure 13-1 shows how you might place fixtures in a small bathroom where the plumbing is limited to a common wall or two adjacent walls. Figure 13-2 shows some other possible designs for a small bathroom. If you can't find room for a full bath, there's probably space for a half bath. A 3 by 5½-foot space can accommodate a half bath as shown Figure 13-3.

If you crowd bathroom fixtures, they'll be awkward to use. Figures 13-4 and 13-5 show the minimum and recommended spacing to be able to use the fixtures comfortably. The minimum space for a full bathroom with a bathtub is 5 by 7 feet.

There are special problems when you're building a bathroom in an attic or basement. Place an attic bathroom over the bathroom on the lower floor whenever possible. And the drain pipe for a basement bathroom must be below the bath or you'll have to install a pump to lift the discharge up to the drain.

If the bathroom doesn't have a window, install an exhaust fan. The fan pulls out excess moisture and odors, protecting the walls and ceilings. In attic bathrooms that don't have a window, you can install a vented skylight in the ceiling.

Colored fixtures, ceramic tile, and marble are permanent so be sure your clients are completely happy with the colors you're going to install. For fixtures and countertops, use colors that will blend with several

A Bathroom with fixtures on one wall

B Fixtures on two walls — lavatory pipes run under vanity

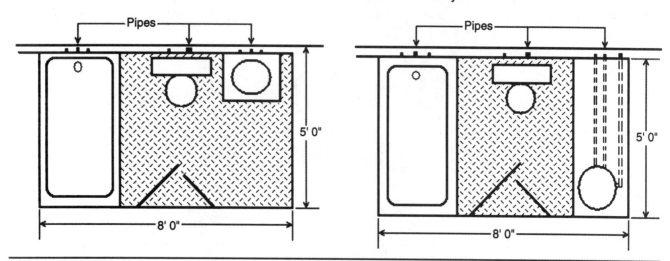

Figure 13-1
Bathrooms with common wall plumbing

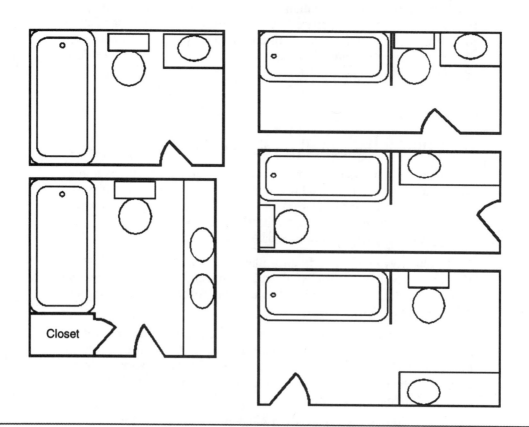

Figure 13-2
Designs for small bathrooms

styles and color schemes. That way the homeowners can keep the bath looking modern without a major remodeling.

It's essential that you carefully consider every part of a bathroom design *before* beginning construction. Work out all the plumbing and electrical problems during the design and layout stages. You may want to get help from your plumbing and electrical subs, not only for design advice, but also to be sure your estimate is accurate. There are several potential problems that could affect your profit if you aren't careful. Get good advice from your subs on such items as:

- Adding a new soil stack
- Connecting to lead pipe or removing old pipe
- Relocating old plumbing or extending drain and water lines
- Bringing old plumbing up to code requirements, such as installing fixture cut-off valves
- Mating new pipe to old
- Adding electrical circuits, switches, and outlets
- Relocating ductwork and electrical lines

If space is no problem, go for a luxury design. Figure 13-6 shows some more dramatic possibilities.

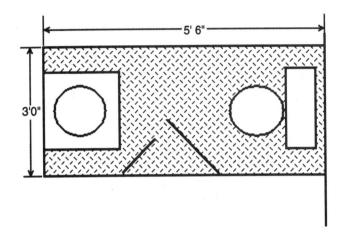

Figure 13-3
Fitting a half-bath into a small space

Pick Components to Fit the Design

Once the basic layout is done, it's time to consult with the clients on the types of fixtures and accessories that will make the bathroom as attractive as it is functional. Even a small bathroom can be a source of pride if it's charming, with accents that match the decor.

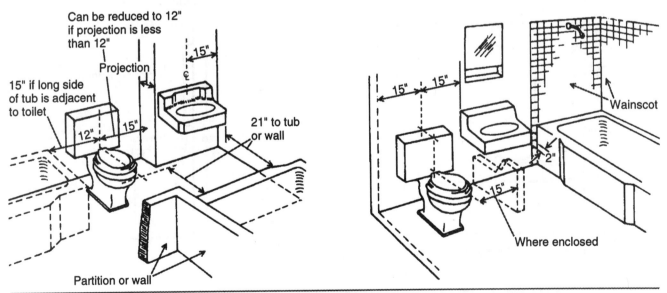

Figure 13-4
Minimum dimensions for bathroom fixture spacing

Lavatories

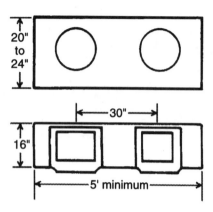

Toilet

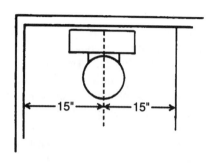

Towel bar

Face towels - 18"
Bath towels - 24"

Allow 27" rod space per person.
Install 36" to 42" above floor.

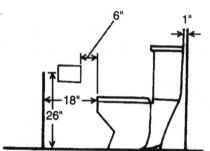

Allow 1" from back wall, 15" to the center of
the bowl from side wall, and 18" from facing
wall for knee room. When facing door, allow
space for door swing. Center of paper should
be 26" from floor, 6" from front of bowl.

Shower and tub

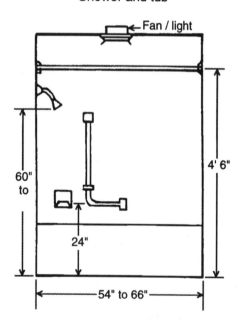

Medicine cabinet

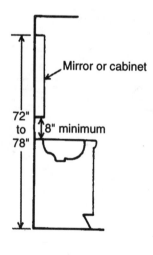

Figure 13-5
Recommended space requirements for bathroom fixtures

A His and her bathroom

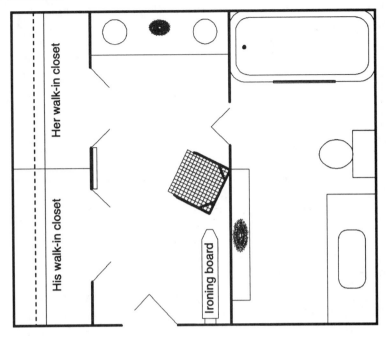

B Utilizing odd-shaped space for luxury

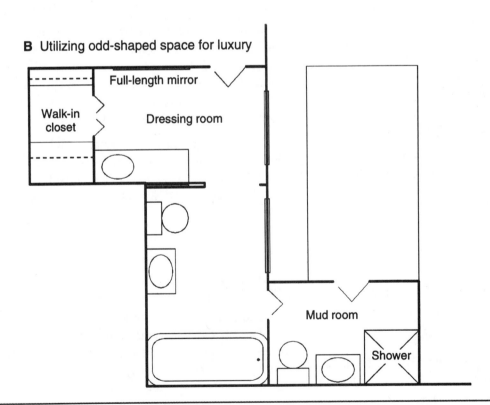

Figure 13-6
Luxury bathroom

A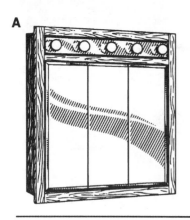

B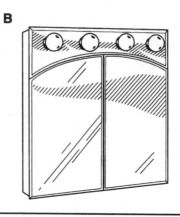

C

Courtesy of Nutone®

Figure 13-7
Lighting must be functional as well as decorative

Faucets and Accessories

Your client, with your advice, should pick the style of faucets and accessories best suited for the new bathroom during the planning and designing stage. The hardware should complement the design. If the design is elegantly modern, the hardware should be the same. If your client prefers old-fashioned charm, use faucets and accessories to highlight that period. Consult manufacturer's catalogs and brochures to find what's available. The faucets and accessories you choose will play a key role in a bathroom design.

Lighting and Electrical Outlets

Make sure the bathroom has enough light and electrical outlets. A bathroom needs special lighting in specific areas and general or decorative lighting for the entire room. Here are some of the available bathroom fixtures:

♦ Waterproof lights for showers and tubs

♦ Heat and sun lamps for a quick warm-up

♦ Luminous ceiling lights to brighten an entire room

♦ Indirect lighting from bulkheads for a softer look

♦ Special theatrical lights for a vanity area

Figure 13-7 shows some of the fixtures for lighting wall cabinets. Windows and skylights can also provide natural light during the day.

Be sure to put in enough ground-fault circuit interrupter (GFCI) receptacles for all the small appliances

people use in today's bathrooms. Keep outlets above the vanity or lavatory level for easy access. Always consider safety and don't install switches or receptacles within reach of the shower or tub.

Vanities, Cabinets, and Bathroom Storage

Bathroom vanities come in as many styles as kitchen cabinets: modern, Mediterranean, early American, and many others. The vanity treatment — color, trim, doors, and hardware — is virtually unlimited. You can use wood stains, veneers or paint to create cabinets in any color scheme or style.

Try to design each bathroom to include as much closet and drawer space as possible. There's no such thing as too much storage space considering all the small appliances and supplies stored in today's bathrooms.

Bathtubs

The standard rectangular bath tub is 5 feet long, but you can also get rectangular tubs in lengths of 4 to 6 feet and widths of 30 inches or more. They also come in a variety of shapes and sizes, including squares, ovals, and triangles that fit into a corner. You can even get a metal tub with one finished end that you can use in a corner with the finished end completing a three-sided enclosure.

Tubs may be cast iron, steel, acrylic, fiberglass, or even teak wood. Cast iron tubs, although fairly expensive, are the most durable and retain heat the longest. The porcelain finish on a quality tub is about $^1/_{16}$-inch thick. With proper care, a cast iron tub can last a lifetime. But there's one disadvantage: The tub can weigh as much as 500 pounds. That's clearly not appropriate for an attic conversion unless you reinforce the floor joists.

Steel tubs aren't as expensive as cast iron and weight only about 100 pounds — which makes them a good alternative for an attic. Although steel tubs aren't as rugged as cast iron, they offer excellent service.

Most American homes have a rectangular metal tub recessed into a tub compartment or niche with walls finished in a waterproof material. Ceramic tile is the most popular choice, but many homes have modular fiberglass tub/shower combinations. They come in large one-piece units, or an easier-to-handle two-piece unit. The combination units are large, and may not fit through the passage to the attic or basement. Tub and shower modules eliminate the need for waterproof finishes in the tub compartment. ABS plastic wall surrounds also provide the same advantage, but they scratch easily and need frequent cleaning.

Today, most metal tubs are built with non-skid bottom surfaces for safety's sake. Tub enclosures should include grab bars and hand grips that are properly positioned and firmly secured. Glass enclosures should always be made of safety glass.

Installing a Bathtub

There are many ways of installing a bathtub. No two building projects are exactly the same and few builders do things just the same way. So we'll show you one way to install a regular cast iron tub (Kohler's K-790-S). The tub's specifications are shown in Figure 13-8. You'll need conventional woodworking tools and:

♦ Arch pliers or 14-inch pipe wrench

♦ Screwdriver

♦ Rule

♦ Pliers

♦ Level

♦ Plumber's putty

♦ Square

♦ Water-resistant sealer

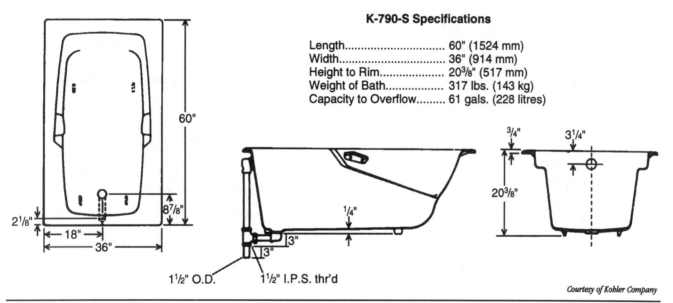

K-790-S Specifications

Length.............................. 60" (1524 mm)
Width................................ 36" (914 mm)
Height to Rim.................... 20⅜" (517 mm)
Weight of Bath................. 317 lbs. (143 kg)
Capacity to Overflow........ 61 gals. (228 litres)

Courtesy of Kohler Company

Figure 13-8
Tub specifications

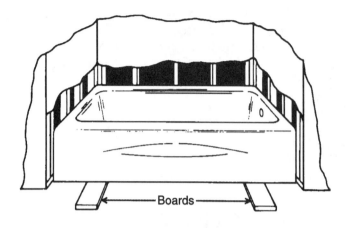

Figure 13-9
Use board skids to remove or install tub

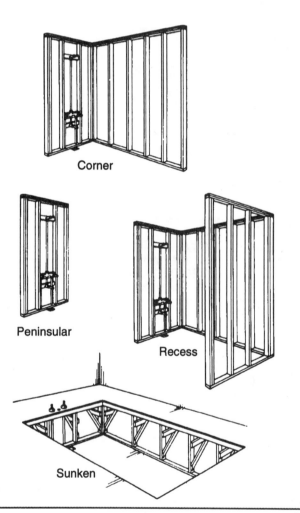

Figure 13-10
Framing for various tub installations

A cast iron tub is heavy, so you should slip boards under it when you move it in or out of place. See Figure 13-9. It's also a good idea to wear safety shoes when handling the tub. Let your end of a cast iron tub slip out of your hand onto your foot and you'll know exactly why I recommend this.

Any tub needs a frame, but the type of frame you should build for it will depend on what position you're installing the tub in. Is it in a recess, corner, peninsular, or sunken position? Figure 13-10 shows types of tub framing you can use. Be sure you provide enough support for a tub under its legs — not just at its rim.

How to Install the Tub Drain

There are several types of tub drains, and each one is installed a different way. In every case, read and follow the instructions packed with the drain. In this installation, we're going to use Kohler's Clearflo drain. Follow along on Figure 13-11. The letters in parentheses refer to the illustrations in that figure.

1. Apply a bead of plumber's putty about ¼ inch thick under the lip of the strainer flange (A). Insert the strainer through the drain hole of the tub. Place the black, flat gasket over the strainer from the underside of the tub.

2. Attach the strainer firmly to the drain ell. The drain ell tube should face the overflow hole. Tighten the strainer into the drain ell with the handle of your pliers (B). Be sure there's a complete putty seal around the strainer body. Remove any excess putty. Don't reposition the drain after you tighten the strainer or you'll break the putty seal.

3. Assemble the coupling nuts and tapered gaskets on the overflow and drain ell tubes (C). Notice the position of the tapered gasket on the tube. Align the parts with the tee as shown in the illustration. Insert each tube completely into the tee. Align and hand tighten the coupling nuts.

4. Thoroughly lubricate (with grease) the two O-rings provided with the overflow ell. Slide them into the grooves on the overflow ell tube (D and E).

5. Apply a bead of RTV sealant to the overflow ell. Attach the black gasket to the overflow ell (F). The gasket is tapered. Make sure you place the thickest part of the gasket at the bottom.

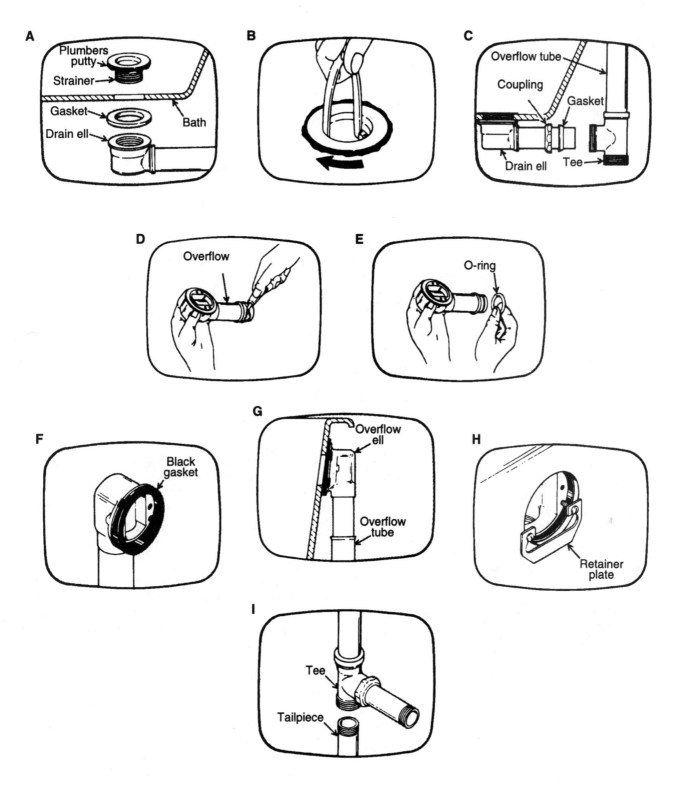

Figure 13-11
Installing a Clearflo tub drain

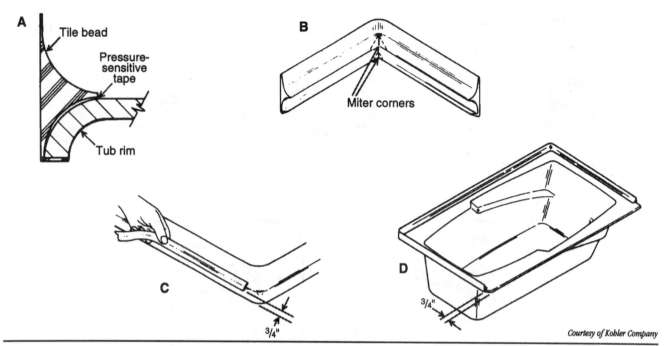

Figure 13-12
Vinyl tiling-in bead installation

6. Insert the overflow ell into the overflow tube. Align the overflow ell with the overflow hole in the tub. Apply a bead of RTV sealant between the gasket and the tub. The tapered gasket will fit snugly into the tub's contour (G).

7. From inside the tub, attach the retainer plate to the overflow ell with the two screws provided. Tighten the screws securely (H).

8. Tighten all the coupling nuts on the tee to secure the assembly. Attach the tailpiece to the tee (I) and tighten it securely. You may need to cut the tailpiece so it'll fit properly. There should only be 1 to 2 inches of tailpiece inside the trap.

How to Install Vinyl Tiling-in Bead

Before positioning a tub in place, apply vinyl tiling-in bead to the sides of the tub which contact the wall. The vinyl bead keeps water from seeping between the tub and the wall. Use it for a water-tight installation. The vinyl bead comes in a kit (K-1179) and contains 14 feet of bead, enough for three sides of the tub. The kit also has 14 feet of pressure-sensitive tape, which you need to seal the vinyl bead to the tub. See Figure 13-12 A.

1. Before you install the vinyl bead, clean all the dust, grease, and foreign material off the tub. Don't install vinyl bead or pressure-sensitive tape when the temperature's below 40 degrees F.

2. Temporarily position the bead around the edge of the tub, measuring for correct installation. (Don't use the sealing tape until you're ready to put it permanently in place.) Bend the bead and clip the excess material from the corners to form a miter joint (Figure 13-12 B). Be careful not to cut through the bead when you miter the corners.

3. When you have a good fit with the bead, apply the pressure-sensitive tape to the tub rim. Using the bottom edge of the rim as a guide, place the tape 3/4 inch in from the edge of the rub rim (Figure 13-12 C). Leave the paper backing on. Cut the excess material from the corners to form a miter joint.

4. Now remove the paper backing from the tape. Start the vinyl bead 3/4 inch in from the edge of the

rim as you did with the tape. Position the bead around the tub. Figure 13-12 D shows bead installation for a recessed tub enclosed by three walls. Press the bead firmly in place with heel of your hand to seal it properly. Continue to work the bead firmly in place until you reach the opposite end. After you've secured the bead in place, you can install the tub.

How to Level and Set a Bathtub

The tub must be level and resting on all four feet when you complete the installation.

1. To position the tub, slide it into place and insert the tailpiece into the trap. Check for level along the sides and across the drain end as shown in Figure 13-13 A.

2. You may need to shim under the tub feet with solid shims (Figure 13-13 B). If you can't reach the feet from the back or side, move the tub in and out of the recess area until it's properly shimmed.

3. When the tub is level and secure, connect the drain into the trap (Figure 13-13 C). You may have to remove the tailpiece and cut it to fit the trap.

4. If you haven't already done so, construct an access panel on the drain-end wall to simplify future maintenance. Remove any finish wall material and frame an opening about 12 inches wide and 36 inches high. Cover the opening with a removable panel. Access may be required by code.

Installing Finish Wall Material

When you install a tub, you'll need finish material to protect the wall from moisture. Figure 13-14 shows how to protect the tub area from water damage.

Cover the framing and walls with water-resistant drywall or other material appropriate for the wall finish you're using. Install the wall finish on the subwall. Seal the joints under the tub rim between the tub and finish wall with a water-resistant sealer.

Protect the tub from damage while installing finish wall materials.

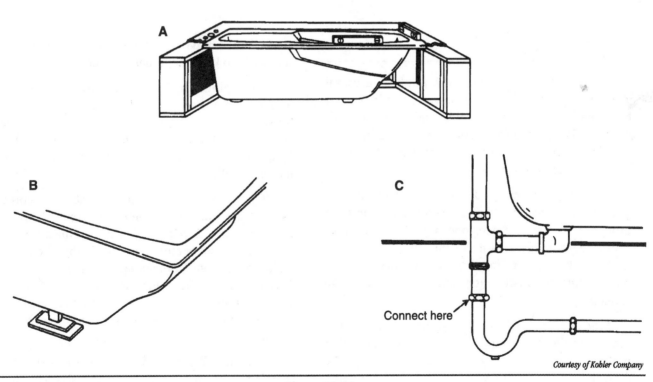

Courtesy of Kohler Company

Figure 13-13
Leveling and setting a tub

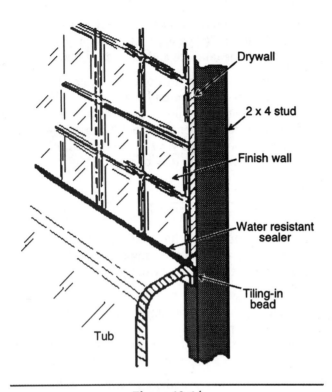

Figure 13-14
Finish wall installation

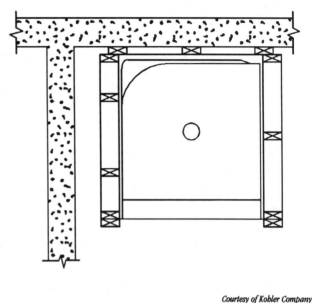

Courtesy of Kobler Company

Figure 13-15
Construct a separate wall to access plumbing

Installing a Shower

A shower cove, separate from a tub, is a useful alternative to the usual tub/shower combination if there's enough space for it. Molded units come in various sizes. The most popular units are from 32 by 36 by 72$\frac{1}{2}$ inches to 48 by 36 by 72$\frac{1}{2}$ inches. Most sizes can hold a glass shower door.

A shower cove is easy to install and takes up less space than a larger tub/shower module. The unit fits through most standard door openings. However, take careful measurements to make sure the unit fits into the area where you're installing it. You may have to move it into the installation area before you finish framing.

Protect fiberglass units before and after installation. Keep the unit wrapped in protective packaging until you're ready to install it. During installation, the shower floor protector will prevent abrasions and scratches on the finish. If you must store a unit outdoors, place it upside down to protect it from the ele-

ments. When moving a shower cove, avoid flexing the side walls to keep the radius from cracking.

If the plumbing is adjacent to a masonry wall (probably in a basement), build a separate wall at least 6 inches in from the masonry wall. You can access connections through this space. See Figure 13-15. Install furring if the back of the unit is against the masonry wall.

If you're installing a unit on a slab at the corner of two outside walls, make plumbing connections at the accessible end. If you install a unit in the attic or anywhere drain connections are accessible from below, make connections from underneath. For a shower cove adjacent to a vertical duct or chase, install fire-rated drywall around the unit. Whenever a fire-rated wall is specified, you must have it in place before installing the unit.

Since the fiberglass shower cove is a single unit, there's no need for hot mopping or a shower pan. You don't need any additional support under the basin area as long as you nail the unit securely into the recess.

How to Frame a Fiberglass Shower Cove

A shower unit made of polypropylene or fiberglass requires special framing. Follow the instructions here and the illustrations in Figure 13-16 and you can't go wrong.

1. Construct the framing as shown in the illustration. The frame must be square and plumb. If you're installing grab bars, provide 2 x 6 bridging for their attachment. (See Step 10, below, for grab bars.)

2. The illustrations show drain installations for both wood and concrete flooring. Locate the rough plumbing for the shower cove drain according to the dimensions specified in the manufacturer's instructions. Notice the opening required in the subfloor for the drain fittings. The 2-inch waste pipe extends $7/8$ inch above the subfloor or slab. In slab construction, you must have a pocket to accommodate the drain fitting.

3. Position the rough plumbing for the supply, but don't strap it. Where you have limited access to supply fitting connections, consider using soft copper tubing as a riser between the valve and supply line. Connect the supply fitting and riser before positioning the unit. The soft tubing can be bent into position for the supply fitting and shower arm after the unit is in place. Install the shower drain fitting in the unit's drain outlet using a non-hardening mastic sealant that meets code requirements.

4. On the outside of the unit, lay out the location of all fitting holes. Using a quarter-inch drill, make the pilot holes from the outside of the unit.

5. Working from the finished face of the unit, enlarge the pilot holes with a keyhole saw.

6. Clean the framed recess thoroughly and set the unit squarely into the pocket of the subfloor or slab. Make sure it fits evenly over the drain pipe extension. Plumb the front and side nailing-in flanges and level the rim of the unit. You may need to shim the unit to level it. Shower cove units are plumb and level when you install them properly. You may need to make some framing adjustments due to variations in the cove widths or framing.

Before nailing, make sure the nailing flanges are pressed firmly against the wall studs. This will help prevent the unit from moving while you nail it into place.

Using No. 6 large-head galvanized nails, fasten the top back wall nailing flange to the wall studs. Attach the top side wall nailing flanges the same way. Then nail the front vertical nailing flanges to the studs on 8-inch centers. Be careful to avoid damaging the unit. Predrill the holes in the flange before nailing to prevent buckling.

7. Caulk and seal the drain. Plug it and test for leaks.

8. Apply $1/8$-inch-thick furring strips to the studs to insure your drywall installation is true and level. Next, apply a water-resistant sealer to the nailing flange. Install the drywall horizontally. The factory (paperbound) edge should be no more than $1/4$ inch above the horizontal finished surface of the unit. Extend the drywall out at least as far as the next stud on each side of the unit.

    Fur the vertical nailing flanges. Then seal the drywall to the nailing-in flange. Mud, tape, and finish the drywall true and level. After applying the finish, seal the area between the paper-bound edge of the drywall and the unit with a water-resistant sealer.

9. Strap the supply fittings. Caulk all the openings around the fittings and shower arm with a water-resistant sealer.

10. Install the finish trim. You can install the grab bars or towel bars through the cove walls and fasten them directly to the bridging. Secure the grab bars with the proper screws, bolts, and backing. You may attach the grab bars directly to the shower cove, but be sure to use the fastening device suggested by the manufacturer. Always follow the manufacturer's guidelines when installing grab bars.

    Install the shower rod above the unit and position it so the shower curtain will hang inside the dam. Follow the manufacturer's installation instructions if you're putting in a shower enclosure. Shower heads are usually placed 60 inches or more above the shower floor.

251

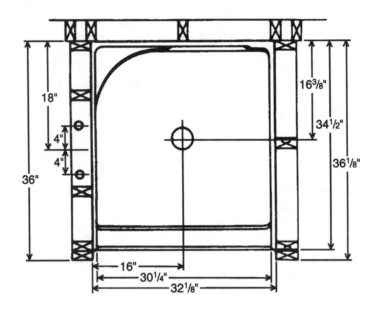

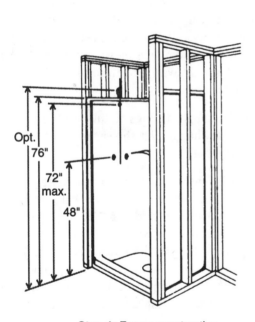

Step 1: Frame construction

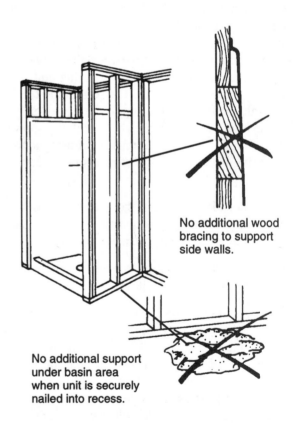

No additional wood
bracing to support
side walls.

No additional support
under basin area
when unit is securely
nailed into recess.

Figure 13-16
Installing a shower cove unit

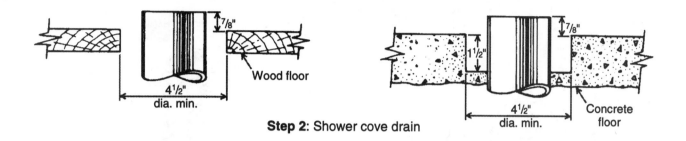

Step 2: Shower cove drain

7/8"

Wood floor

4 1/2"
dia. min.

1 1/2"

7/8"

4 1/2"
dia. min.

Concrete
floor

Step 3: Rough plumbing

Step 4: Lay out and drill pilot holes

Step 5: Enlarge pilot holes

Step 6: Place unit in frame

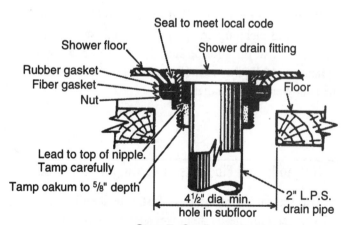

Seal to meet local code

Shower floor

Shower drain fitting

Rubber gasket

Fiber gasket

Nut

Floor

Lead to top of nipple.
Tamp carefully

Tamp oakum to 5/8" depth

4 1/2" dia. min.
hole in subfloor

2" L.P.S.
drain pipe

Step 7: Caulk and lead drain

Figure 13-16 (continued)
Installing a shower cove unit

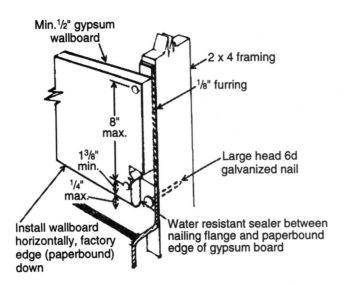

Min. ½" gypsum wallboard

2 x 4 framing

⅛" furring

8" max.

1⅜" min.

¼" max.

Large head 6d galvanized nail

Install wallboard horizontally, factory edge (paperbound) down

Water resistant sealer between nailing flange and paperbound edge of gypsum board

Step 8: Install wallboard

Step 9: Caulk openings

Courtesy of Kobler Company

Figure 13-16 (continued)
Installing a shower cove unit

Clean-Up

Use warm water and a liquid detergent to clean the surface of the shower cove. Don't use abrasive cleaners. Remove stubborn stains, paint, or tar with turpentine or paint thinner. Remove plaster by scraping with a wood edge. Don't use metal scrapers, wire brushes or other metal tools. Use a powdered detergent and a damp cloth to take off residual plaster.

Restore the finish to dulled areas by rubbing them with a liquid cleaning compound. Use the same kind you would use on auto bodies. Follow with a light application of liquid wax. Figure 13-17 shows a finished shower cove installation.

How to Install Fiberglass Tub and Shower Units

Use the same procedure to install a fiberglass tub and shower module as a shower alone. Figure 13-18 shows installation details for framing and installing the module. Provide an access panel to the drain connections and water supply pipes for servicing. Figure 13-19 shows a unit installed flush with the wall.

Courtesy of Kobler Company

Figure 13-17
The shower cove installed

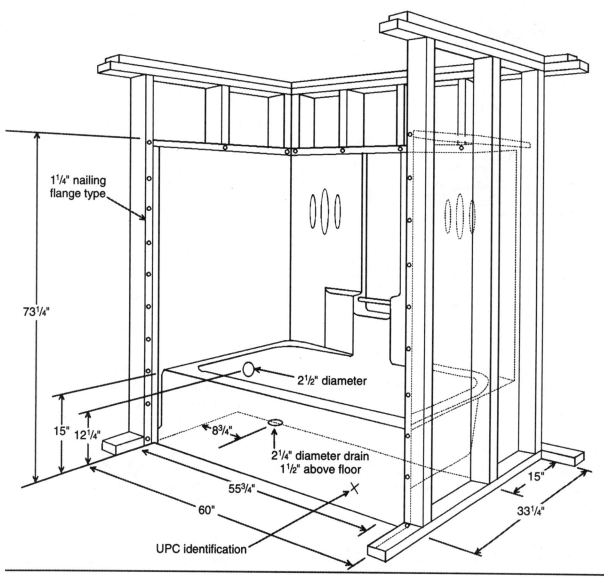

1¼" nailing flange type

73¼"

2½" diameter

15" 12¼"

8¾"

2¼" diameter drain
1½" above floor

55¾"

60"

UPC identification

15"

33¼"

Figure 13-18
Framing and installation of a tub/shower unit

Toilets and Bidets

A good toilet is expensive but usually worth the extra cost. A poor quality toilet is likely to overflow, leak, or drip. Install toilets with non-overflow features and vacuum breaker safeguards against back siphonage. A good quality toilet should have a sturdy seat and strong hinges. Plastic toilet seats, though not as sturdy as the heavier wood, often last longer because the paint on wood seats chips off.

There are several types of toilets. The close-coupled (two-piece) type is standard. But the modern one-piece, low-silhouette design is becoming the most popular. There's also a wall-mounted toilet that's easy to clean under. If your clients are interested in water conservation, install toilets with siphon vortex flushing action which will flush with only 3.5 gallons of water.

If you're building a bathroom in a basement with concrete slab floors, there's a rear outlet close-coupled

Courtesy of Kohler Company

Figure 13-19
Unit installed flush with wall

toilet designed especially for installation on concrete slab. The rear outlet lets you install the drain pipe in the wall instead of the floor.

The bidet (pronounced be-day) has been a standard in European bathrooms for many years. They're becoming a popular addition to the modern American bathroom. The bidet is usually installed next to the toilet. Follow the manufacturer's instructions for installing the bidet.

Installing a Toilet

Use care when installing any vitreous china product. It might break or chip if you overtighten the bolts or handle it carelessly. Here are the tools and supplies you'll need to install a toilet:

♦ 10-inch adjustable wrench
♦ 12-inch pipe wrench
♦ Metal file (fine cut)
♦ Tape measure
♦ Level
♦ Tubing cutter
♦ Hacksaw
♦ Putty knife
♦ Screwdriver

♦ Toilet setting compound
♦ Toilet gasket
♦ Toilet seat
♦ Toilet T-bolts (2)
♦ Toilet supply shut-off valve

Suppose you're installing a Kohler low-profile, one-piece toilet (Model K-3397-EB). This toilet needs a full $1/2$-inch ID water supply. The water supply tubing should be $2^5/8$ inches above the floor and $6^1/2$ inches to the left of the centerline. The toilet needs 25 psi of running pressure at the shut-off valve. See Figure 13-20 A for installation dimensions. You can use the following steps to install the toilet, but be sure to check your local plumbing code and follow all its regulations.

1. Install T-bolts as shown in Figure 13-20 B. Temporarily set the toilet over the closet flange. Align the T-bolts with the holes at the base of the toilet.

2. Place a retainer and washer over each bolt as shown in Figure 13-20 C. Hand tighten the nuts. Mark the bolts $1/4$ inch from top of the nut. Remove the nuts, washers, retainer, and toilet from the closet flange. Remove the T-bolts and thread the nuts onto them. Cut the bolts off at the mark and file the rough edges. Once again, remove the nuts. Replace the T-bolts in the closet flange.

3. Place the toilet upside down on a pad. Firmly place a gasket on the toilet outlet, as in Figure 13-20 D. If you use a gasket with an integral plastic sleeve, make sure you position the gasket with the sleeve facing away from the toilet.

4. Place a bead of toilet-setting compound, about $1/8$ inch thick, evenly around the base of the toilet. See Figure 13-20 E.

5. Carefully lower the toilet onto the closet flange, aligning the holes in the base with the T-bolts, as shown in Figure 13-20 F. Be sure the toilet sits squarely over the closet flange and both holes. If you have to lift the toilet off the floor to realign it, you'll have to apply a new gasket to ensure an adequate seal.

6. Apply your full body weight to the rim of the toilet to set the seal (Figure 13-20 G). Don't rock the toilet — that would break the watertight seal.

A Installation dimensions

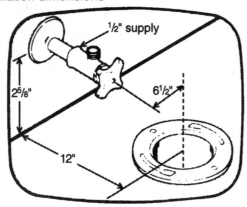

B Install T-bolts

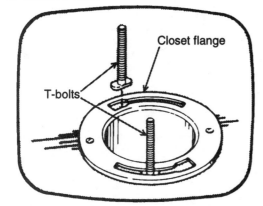

C Trim the bolts

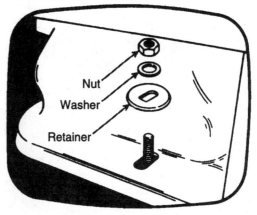

Figure 13-20
Toilet installation

7. Assemble the retainers, washers, and nuts over the exposed T-bolts (look back to Figure 13-20 C). Hand tighten the nuts, then tighten them a half-turn more with a wrench.

8. Remove the excess setting compound from around the base. Wipe off any wax, setting compound, or dirt from the area around the bolts. Then snap on the caps. See Figure 13-20 H.

9. To connect the water supply, remove the coupling nut from the supply shank. Carefully bend the tubing to fit between the supply shank and the shut-off valve. Using a tubing cutter, cut the tube $1/4$ inch longer than the connecting distance. Remove any burrs from inside the tubing. Slip the coupling nut, compression nut, and ferrule onto the tubing. Insert the cut end of the tubing into the shut-off valve and the other end into the supply shank. Tighten the coupling nut first, but don't overtighten. Don't use pipe sealant on the supply shank. Complete the assembly by tightening the compression nut. (Figure 13-20 I shows this procedure.)

10. Turn the shut-off valve on and check for leaks. If the pipe connections are squarely assembled, you can just slightly retighten the nuts to stop any leaks.

You can also get flexible hose with factory-assembled fittings for easy water supply hookups. It's good for both hot and cold lines, and requires no cutting or flaring. It comes in various lengths for toilet, lavatory, and sink installations.

D Place gasket

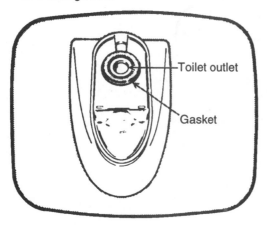

Toilet outlet

Gasket

E Place compuond

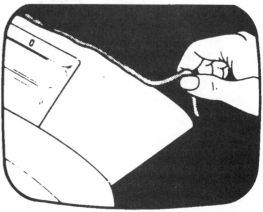

F Align toilet on bolts

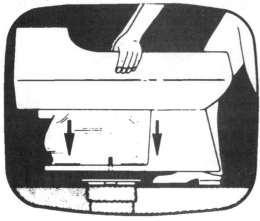

G Set the seal

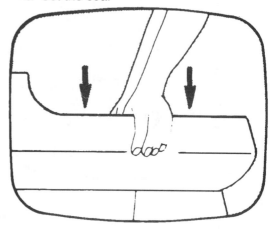

H Attach to bolts

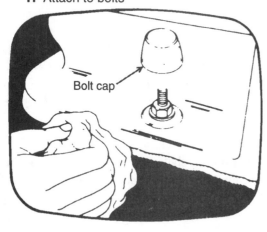

Bolt cap

I Connect the water supply

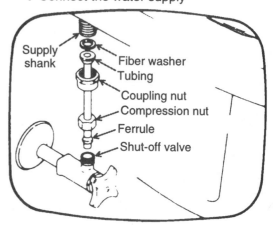

Supply shank

Fiber washer

Tubing

Coupling nut

Compression nut

Ferrule

Shut-off valve

Courtesy of Kohler Company

Figure 13-20 (continued)
Toilet installation

Figure 13-21
Pedestal lavatory

Courtesy of Kobler Company

Figure 13-22
Corner lavatory installation

Courtesy of Kobler Company

Lavatories and Vanities

Lavatories come in all shapes and colors, made from cast iron, steel, or vitreous china. They may also be formed as part of a vanity top in Corian, cultured marble, or other materials. The pedestal lavatory shown in Figure 13-21 is a popular modern fixture available in many styles and materials. If you design a bathroom using a pedestal lavatory, you lose the storage space in the vanity cabinet. You'll have to provide more storage somewhere else in the bathroom.

Lavatories may be self-rimming, rimless, or under-counter models, and molded in rectangular, oval, round, or square shapes. Sizes are also available for narrow or odd-shaped countertop installations.

Before you install a lavatory, make sure it fits correctly into the vanity cabinet. Cabinet drawers and doors should open and close freely. Figure 13-22 shows a self-rimming lavatory installed in a corner vanity.

Molded one-piece vanity tops are available in several popular lengths, with single or double bowls. The bowls come in several sizes and can be located in several positions in the countertop. Units are available with standard pre-drilled faucet holes. Most units are shipped with installation instructions and hole-drill templates. A separate $2^7/8$-inch backsplash is also available.

Cultured marble integral vanity tops and bowls are available in most areas. They come with a molded backsplash and pre-drilled faucet and drain holes.

Installing a Lavatory

Let's see how to install a self-rimming lavatory. Here are the tools and materials you'll need:

A Cut the template

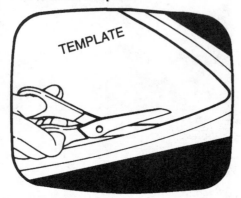

B Trace template on countertop

C Cut out the opening

D Position and mark the lavatory

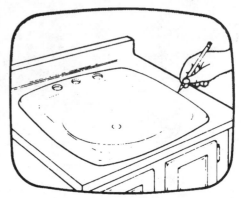

Figure 13-23
Lavatory installation

♦ Putty knife

♦ 10-inch adjustable wrench

♦ Saber or keyhole saw

♦ 12-inch pipe wrench

♦ Tubing cutter

♦ Screwdriver

♦ Hacksaw

♦ Rule

♦ Drill

♦ ½-inch drill bit

♦ Scissors

♦ Polyseam seal

♦ Plumber's putty

♦ Faucet unit

♦ Shut-off valves

Follow these steps:

1. You'll need a template as an aid in making the cutout for the lavatory. Templates are commonly shipped with the lavatory. Follow the designated line for that particular lavatory to cut the template to the size required for the opening, as shown in Figure 13-23 A.

2. Trace the template onto the countertop using a soft lead pencil (B, in Figure 13-23). Templates have the centerlines marked to help align the opening.

E Assemble the faucet and drain

F Apply the seal

Guideline

G Position and place the lavatory

H Remove exess seal

I Connect water supply lines

J Connect the drain pipe

Courtesy of Kobler Company

Figure 13-23 (continued)
Lavatory installation

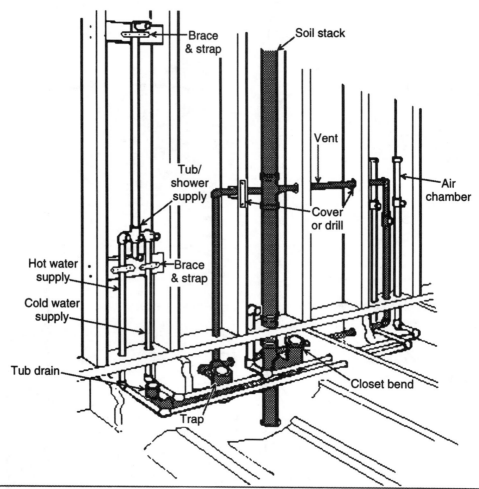

Figure 13-24
Typical second-story bathroom plumbing

3. Before making a cutout in a countertop, use a $\frac{1}{2}$-inch drill to make a pilot hole. Then use a saber or keyhole saw to cut out the opening. Carefully follow the pencil line traced from the template (C).

4. Temporarily place the lavatory in the opening and adjust it for exact positioning. Lightly trace a pencil line around the outside edge of the lavatory (D). This line will be your guide when you apply the polyseam seal. Then remove the lavatory from the countertop.

5. Assemble the faucet and drain to the lavatory, following the manufacturer's instructions (E).

6. Apply two ribbons of polyseam seal on the countertop, between the edge of the opening and the guideline you just traced. Spread the seal evenly with a putty knife (F). Polyseam sets up in a few minutes, so spread it quickly.

7. Carefully place the lavatory in the countertop opening. Use the guide line to position it properly (G). Press it firmly into the polyseam seal.

8. Immediately remove the excess polyseam seal with a damp cloth (H). Fill any voids in the joint.

9. Allow the polyseam seal to set 30 minutes before connecting the supply lines and drain. When you connect the lines and drain, be careful not to move the lavatory out of position. Connect the water supply lines the same way as described in step 9 for the toilet installation. Your complete connections should look like Figure 13-23 I.

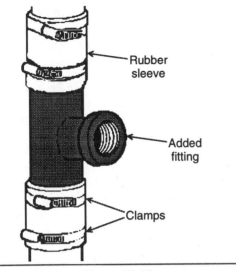

Figure 13-25
Inserting fittings in existing soil stack

10. Connect the drain pipe and trap to the fixture and the wall outlet (J). Turn the tailpiece into the drain body. Align the trap inlet with the tailpiece and insert the tailpiece into the trap. You may have to cut the tailpiece to fit; it should extend only 1 to 2 inches into the trap.

11. Turn on the water and check for leaks at the supply and drain connections. Tighten the nuts to stop any leaks.

12. Clean up after you finish installation, but don't use abrasive cleaners on new fixtures. Use only warm water and a nonabrasive liquid detergent to clean a new lavatory.

Second-Story Bathrooms

It's usually a good idea to put a second-story bath near first-story piping if you can. Figure 13-24 shows basic plumbing for a three-fixture bathroom.

You can tie into an existing soil stack by cutting out a section of the stack and adding a tee, Y, or tee-Y component. Use a flexible connector such as a rubber sleeve and clamp the sleeve in place. See Figure 13-25.

Give special consideration to framing the floor under a bathtub. A cast iron tub will weigh about 500 pounds. Fill it with water and you've placed a lot of weight on the floor. Figure 13-26 shows a simple method for reinforcing the floor under the tub.

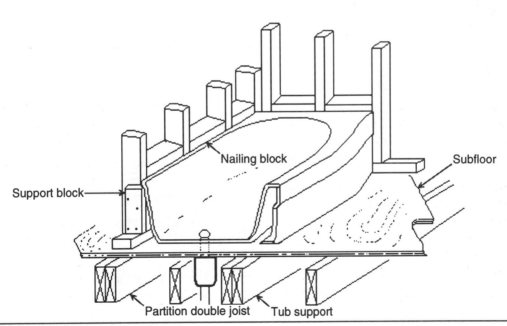

Figure 13-26
Framing under tub

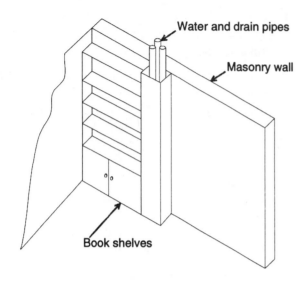

Figure 13-27
Boxed-in pipes

What do you do when the only place to run the pipes to a second floor add-on bathroom is through a lower-story partition wall that's made of concrete block? One method is to run the water and drain pipes down on the outside of the wall and box the pipes in. You can even use the run to an advantage by making the box part of book shelves or a shallow storage closet as shown in Figure 13-27.

Bathroom Wall and Floor Coverings

The most common choice for bathroom walls and floors is ceramic tile. Many other materials are also available to the builder with imagination. Combinations of wood, stone, brick, paneling, wallpaper, and mirrors will give your designs a distinct look. The way you use the materials will make the difference between an ordinary bathroom and a showplace. Unless you're a tile setter, sub out tile work. Special tools and experience are essential for a professional job.

Here's one important tip: Always use floor tile on the floor and wall tile on the walls. Wall tiles are available in various sizes, with the $4^{1}/_{4}$-inch and 6-inch square wall tiles the most popular.

Glazed wall tiles on a floor can be dangerously slick, especially in an area where people will be walking in stocking feet. Mottled or crystalline glazed tile is better for floors. Floor tile comes in a variety of shapes, including large and small squares, rectangles, hexagons, and octagons.

A good alternative to ceramic tile is quarry floor tile. Quarry tile makes a durable and attractive floor. It's available in different shades of red, brown, and tan. The 6 x 6 x $^{1}/_{2}$ inch and $3^{7}/_{8}$ x 8 x $^{1}/_{2}$ inch tiles are most popular. A patterned wall tile in a similar or contrasting shade makes a striking combination with quarry tile floors.

Sheet vinyl is another popular choice for floor covering. It comes in 6 foot and 12 foot widths. Use the narrow width for small bathrooms and the 12 foot width for larger rooms. Try to avoid seams when installing sheet vinyl in bathrooms.

For a plush atmosphere in a bath, use carpeting or a combination of carpeting and tile or marble. But consider this: Installed carpeting isn't a practical choice for a bathroom used by children. A loose-laid carpet that a homeowner can take up, dry, and replace is always a better choice.

For more information on floor covering, see Chapter 12.

Estimating Manhours

Figure 13-28 shows guidelines you can use when estimating manhours to install bathroom fixtures.

Work element	Manhours per unit
Standard cast iron bathtub	7.8
One-piece toilet	4.0
Two-piece toilet	4.5
Lavatory, self-rimming in cutout	4.5
Integral vanity top and bowl	5.0

Figure 13-28
Manhours for installing bathroom fixtures

Attic Conversions and Lofts

Some builders won't do attic conversions. Others will tackle the job only if there's no other work available. It takes a lot of know-how to negotiate the complexities of the job. But there are some who specialize in turning attics into well-designed, comfortable living areas.

Old houses with high attics are the best candidates for conversion because they were built with conventional (stick) construction. That leaves plenty of open space in the attic. Attics in modern hip roof structures are usually low, and too short to convert to living areas.

A house with a truss roof requires a different approach. Trusses are engineered components, with each piece critical to the overall structural strength of the span. To understand the difference in conventional (stick) construction and truss construction, compare Figures 14-1A and 14-1B. It's difficult to convert a trussed attic economically unless the trusses were designed for attic space. So we'll just cover conventional attic conversions in this book.

The Attic Inspection

Don't try to convert an attic without first looking at it carefully to see how it was built. You'll also need to figure out just how you're going to get building materials into the attic. Unless you think the job through before you do the estimate, it may take many more manhours than you anticipated.

The most important thing to inspect is the height of an attic. How much headroom is there? In many areas, a 7-foot minimum headroom is required in habitable attic space. See Figure 6-7, Chapter 6, for recommended ceiling heights. How much reinforcing will you need for the floor joists? Are the joists supported by a load-bearing wall?

Does the homeowner want dormers in the attic? If so, can you use the dormer opening to pass building materials into the attic?

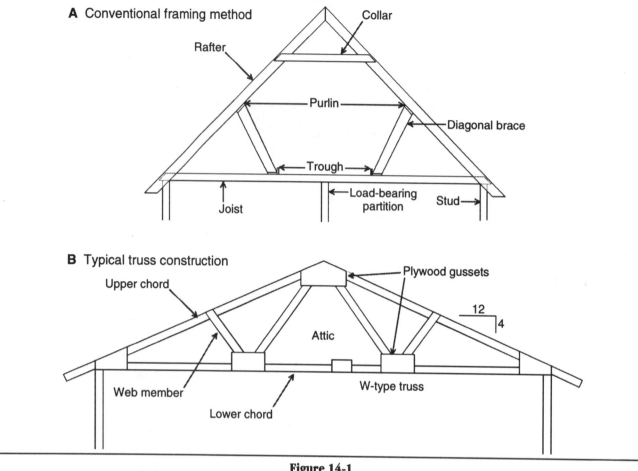

Figure 14-1
Conventional vs. truss construction

Is there a stairway to the attic? Will you have to design and build one? How much work will it take to change the floor in the story below to make room for the stairs?

If a bathroom is part of the conversion, where are the plumbing pipes in the story below the attic? Where will you run the lines?

And what about electrical circuits?

If you have to build an outside entrance to the attic, where should you put it? Is it best to build a stairway first, or later? Do you have to go around a chimney or some soil stacks? How will you do this?

Figure 14-2 is an attic inspection checklist to use as a guide during your inspection.

Design Considerations for an Attic Conversion

Before you can design the conversion, you have to answer one critical question: Can you convert it without taking the roof off the house and adding another story?

Here are some things to consider when you design a conversion.

Standard or Spiral Staircases

Fold-down stairs don't do the job. If there isn't space for a standard staircase, use a spiral staircase. Chapter 7 covered building standard stairs. You can order spiral stairs through most building supply houses.

Attic conversion checklist

Owner's name:_____

Address:_____

Telephone:_____

Type of construction

_____ Gable (Pitch:_____)

_____ Hip (Pitch:_____)

Structural components

_____ Conventional

_____ Truss _____ Type

Floor joists

_____ 2 x 6   16" oc

_____ 2 x 6   24" oc

_____ 2 x 8   16" oc

_____ 2 x 8   24" oc

_____ Other (Specify:_____)

Load-bearing wall

_____ None

_____ Number

　　　Location:

　　　_____ Center of attic

　　　_____ Rear portion

　　　_____ Front portion

Flooring

_____ None

_____ Boards

_____ Plywood

_____ OSB

(Note: Flooring must be removed if joist reinforcement is required.)

Floor insulation

_____ Type

_____ Thickness

Rafters

_____ 2 x 6   16" oc

_____ 2 x 6   24" oc

_____ 2 x 8   16" oc

_____ 2 x 8   24" oc

_____ Other (Specify:_____)

Roof sheathing

_____ Board

_____ Plywood

_____ OSB

Roofing

_____ Asphalt shingles

_____ Wood shingles

_____ Metal

_____ Other (Specify:_____)

Bracing

_____ Diagonal (Spacing_____)

_____ "Trough"

_____ Purlin

_____ Collar (Spacing_____)

_____ Other (Specify:_____)

Figure 14-2
Attic conversion checklist

Windows

_____ Number (Size:_____)

_____ Located at each gable end

_____ Located one gable end

Vents

_____ Type

_____ Size

Location:

_____ Gables

_____ Ridge

_____ Soffit

Dormers

_____ Number

_____ Gable type

_____ Shed type

_____ Located at front

_____ Located at rear

_____ Ceiling height (headroom)

_____ Width

Attic headroom

_____ To collar

_____ To ridge board

_____ To proposed ceiling

Knee wall data

Knee wall recommended height:

_____ 5' _____ 4'6" _____ 4'

Available floor space:

With 5' knee wall _____

With 4'6" knee wall _____

With 4' knee wall _____

Stairway

_____ None

_____ Inadequate

_____ Adequate

_____ Outside entrance

Location:

_____ Center of attic

_____ Near lower end of attic

_____ Near upper end of attic

_____ From outside at gable end

_____ Other (Specify:_____)

_____ Framing required for new stairway

Chimney

_____ None

_____ Number

_____ Masonry Size:_____

_____ Metal Size:_____

Location:

_____ Center of attic

_____ Lower end of attic

_____ Upper end of attic

_____ Other (Specify:_____)

Ductwork

_____ None

_____ Air/heat

Size:_____

Type:_____

Location:_____

Figure 14-2 (continued)
Attic conversion checklist

Plumbing pipe

_____None

_____Water lines

_____Soil stack

Location:

_____Center of attic

_____Lower end of attic

_____Upper end of attic

_____Attic bathroom/kitchen can be tied into plumbing

_____Attic bathroom can be located over bathroom below

Electrical

_____Attic has_____(number) electrical circuit(s)

Wire size:_____

_____Attic has no electrical circuit

_____Number of light fixtures

Type: (Specify_____)

_____Wall receptacles

_____Wall switches

_____Cable runs on top of structural components (on top of joists or on ceiling side of rafters) and must be rerouted

_____Circuits will have to be added to attic conversion

Contractor:_____

Address:_____

Telephone:_____

Inspected by:_____

Date:_____

How will I get building materials to the attic?

_____By outside stairway enterance

_____Through window from scaffolding

_____Through new opening cut in gable end

_____Through new opening cut in roof (possible when planning to add a dormer)

Can a truck delivering materials get close enough to the house to hoist materials to attic level?

_____Yes

_____No

Note: Don't operate trucks or heavy equipment within 10 feet of any basement area.

Scaffolding required for job

_____No

_____Yes

Number of jacks (units)_____

Rental cost_____per day

Ventilation equipment required for job

_____No

_____Yes

Type_____

Rental cost_____per day

Figure 14-2 (continued)
Attic conversion checklist

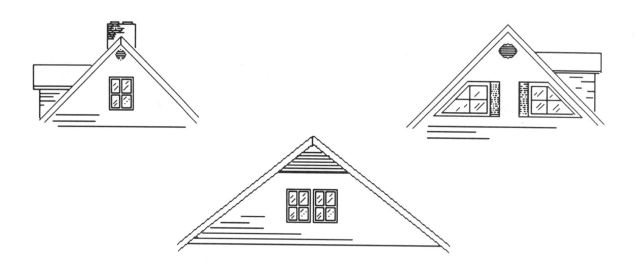

Figure 14-3
Providing light and ventilation in an attic conversion

Heating and Cooling

The existing heating and cooling system was designed for the floor space below. It won't take care of a converted attic. So you'll have to provide the conversion with its own heating and cooling system. It's generally a good idea to use an individual unit for the conversion. And there's one more thing to consider. Design the conversion so it can be heated (or cooled) only when it's occupied, not all the time. The homeowners should be able to close off the attic area completely so it doesn't affect the main heating/cooling unit.

Light and Ventilation

Few attics have large windows. When you convert an attic to a living area, you'll probably have to put in windows that open for natural light and ventilation. The code requires a living unit to have 8 percent of its floor area as windows that provide natural light. Even on mild days, an attic can get very warm. It'll need 4 percent of its floor area as windows that open to provide natural ventilation. For air to move, there must be an inlet and outlet. In other words, you have to provide two openings. See Figure 14-3 for some possibilities.

Skylights

Skylights offer many decorative and illuminating possibilities in attic conversions. Many attics have only a small window at each gable end, hardly enough glazing area to provide adequate natural light and ventilation. I recommend adding a ventilating skylight for attic rooms. To provide enough daylight under most conditions, plan for 1 square foot of skylight for each 20 square feet of floor. A 24 inch x 24 inch unit provides 4 square feet, which is sufficient for an 80 SF area. Many skylights come equipped with blinds or shades to control light and energy flows.

Skylights can save electricity too. Low-E units have high-performance glass with a thin metallic coating that reflects radiant heat back to its source. This means that heat is reflected out of a home on warm days, and into it on cold days.

When it comes to reducing heat loss, low-E glass (compared with uncoated glass) is rated 72 percent better than single-glazing, 36 percent better than double-glazing, and 14 percent better than triple-glazing. In direct sunlight, low-E glass cools 28 percent better than single-glazed uncoated glass, and 19 percent better than double-glazed. It also reduces fading on furniture, draperies, and carpeting.

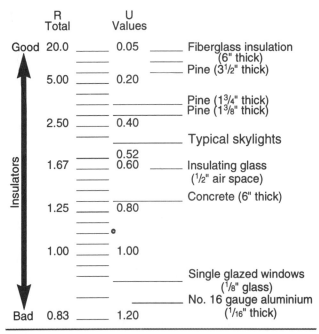

Figure 14-4
Insulating values

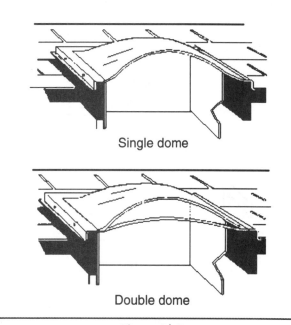

Single dome

Double dome

Figure 14-5
Single- and double-dome skylights

With some units, a solid, continuous "weather boot" molded to the frame makes a barrier that wind and rain can't get through. It's easy to install vented and fixed units because they come fully assembled and you don't need to caulk them.

If you don't use low-E units, use double-dome skylights. The double-domed units have a dead air space between the dome and diffuser which creates a thermal insulation barrier, cutting down on heat or cold passing through the unit. Figure 14-4 shows comparative insulating values.

Skylights come with clear, frost, and bronze domes and with combinations of these in multi-dome units. The clear dome has a clear inner dome that gives maximum lighting and visibility if you want the most intense light. A clear dome with a white diffusion panel is a good choice to light a larger area with no harsh glare. The bronze skylight eliminates harsh glare, and colors the area below it with slightly tinted light. Figure 14-5 shows single- and double-dome skylights.

Rafter spacing is a main consideration when adding skylights. Units are available to fit roofs with rafters 16 and 24 inches on center. Usually, the higher up on a roof that you install a skylight, the more it spreads light into a room. Units installed high in the ceiling can be opened or adjusted with the extendible operating rod available with the unit. See Figure 14-6.

Dormers

One builder who specializes in attic conversions made an interesting statement: The only trouble with dormers is you have to cut a hole in the roof. What does that mean? If you're considering dormer construction, pay particular attention to the structural strength of the roof. When you have to cut two or more rafters, use temporary supports until the framing is finished. Also, your dormer design must blend in with the design of the house. If you locate dormers at the wrong place, the balance of the house is thrown off. If a dormer is too small or too large, it spoils the appearance of a house. If the dormers are too high or too low, the roof and house look awkward.

Bathrooms

Always try to connect the plumbing in a new attic bathroom to the bathroom directly below it. Put the attic plumbing (water lines and waste pipes) in a wall or closet directly above the wall below. This cuts conversion costs.

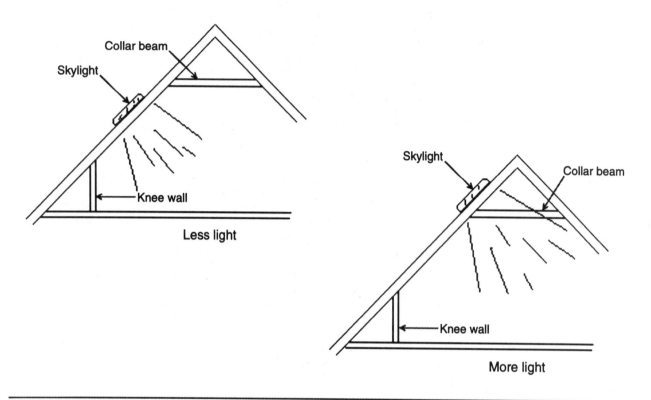

Figure 14-6
Locate a skylight high in the ceiling for greater illumination

Exits

Every living area must have emergency exits. An attic conversion is no exception. In fact, some local codes may require two means of exit, such as a second stairway. In any event, sleeping rooms without a door to the outside need a window that's big enough for an adult to exit through it to the outside. It's got to have a clear openable area of 5.7 square feet with a minimum 24-inch height dimension and 20-inch width.

A basic attic conversion design for two bedrooms and a bathroom with a standard staircase is shown in Figure 14-7. Figure 14-8 shows how to convert an attic into a recreation room with a half bath. Figure 14-9 shows a possible design for making an income-producing apartment with an outside entrance.

When you've finished the design, it's time to do the work. The first step is to strengthen the floor system if it's needed to support the additional weight.

Adding Floor Joists

If the attic you're converting has a floor, take it out before you begin installing extra floor joists. You may also have to remove the braces and trough. Use temporary bracing to support the rafters until you can build the knee walls. The diagonal or trough braces can often be removed permanently after the knee wall is constructed. But be sure to check the local building code before you take out any roof brace. In most high-wind or heavy-snow areas, you can't remove any braces until after you've put the knee walls in place.

Adding floor joists in an attic is like reinforcing first floor ceiling joists for a second story addition. We covered that in Chapter 6. In that chapter you learned that you could add wider members (2 x 8s, for example) to strengthen a 2 x 6 floor system. But in an attic, height is often at a premium. If you add wider joists, it makes the ceiling height lower. For a 2 x 6 or wider

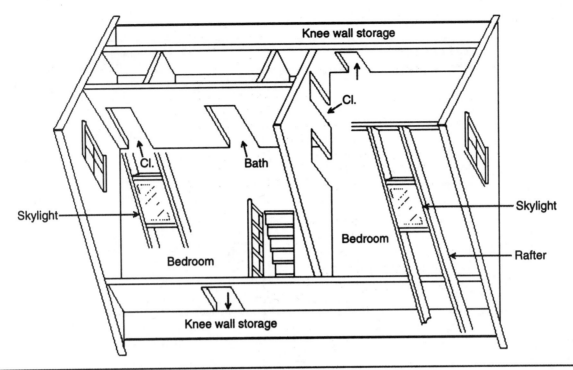

Figure 14-7
Two bedroom and bathroom attic conversion

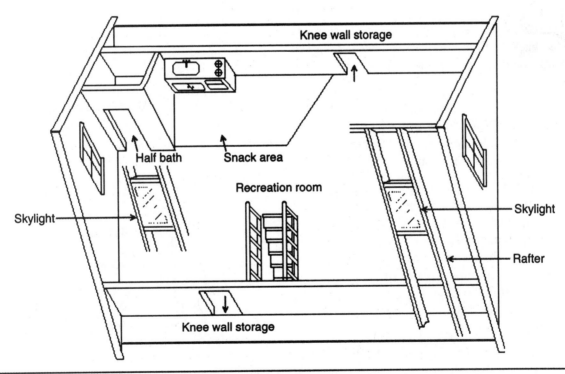

Figure 14-8
Recreation room and half-bath attic conversion

Plan view

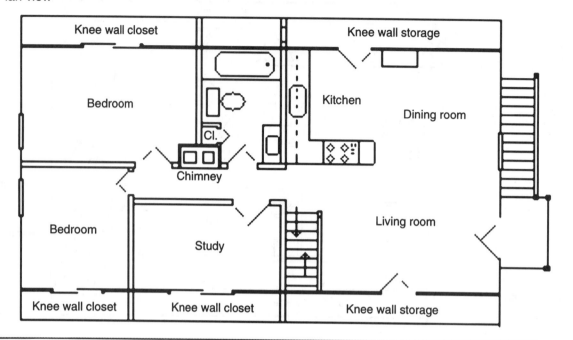

Figure 14-9
Converting an attic to an income apartment

joist system, it's better to use the same-size joist member. Refer back to Figure 4-5 in Chapter 4 for span limitations for different species and sizes of floor joists.

Figure 14-10 shows three ways you can reinforce a conventional floor joist system for an attic conversion. You can double the joists, add larger joists, or add new joists between the existing joists.

Whichever method you use, cut the ends of all joists to fit under the roof decking. They should bear fully on the top plate. When you add a joist against an existing joist, stagger 12d nails 16 inches on center along the span. If there's only a narrow space between the roof decking and the top plate, you won't be able to toenail the joist to the plate. In that case, toenail the joist to the top plate of the load-bearing wall with 8d nails (Figure 4-11).

When you nail to existing joists, be careful that you don't damage the ceiling underneath. It's a good idea to brace the existing joist with your foot as you nail into it.

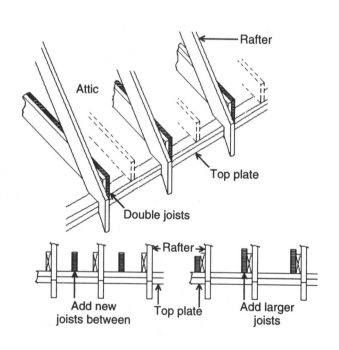

Figure 14-10
Reinforcing attic floor joists

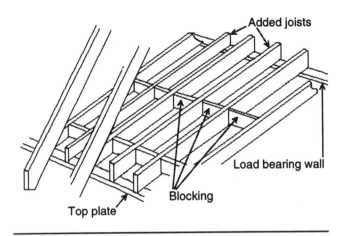

Figure 14-11
Blocking added joists

Installing Knee Walls

After the floor joists are reinforced, you can install the knee walls. Even if the knee walls aren't in the same place as the original braces, they do support the roof. While you can build a knee wall as low as 4 feet, I recommend building a knee wall anyplace the ceiling height is less than 5 feet. (Look back to Figure 6-7 in Chapter 6.)

For each knee wall, snap a chalk line perpendicular to the run of the rafters for the sole plate. Nail the 2 x 4 plate to each joist with 12d or 16d nails.

Figure 14-12 shows how to install the knee wall top plate and nailers. Cut the studs at the same pitch as the rafter cuts so they fit into the angle formed by the top plate. Nail the studs directly under the rafters. As you build the knee wall, install floor sheathing behind it. You may not be able to put down the subfloor behind the knee wall after you've nailed all the studs in place. Butt the subflooring against the rafter and floor joist juncture at the eave to minimize gaps. With sturdy subflooring, the knee wall area is usable storage space.

If you space the added joist between existing joists, nail in 2 x 4 or same-size blocks as shown in Figure 14-11. Locate one block as close to the side walls as possible and the second block half the distance (or 8 feet on center) to the load-bearing wall. Then replace any disturbed insulation.

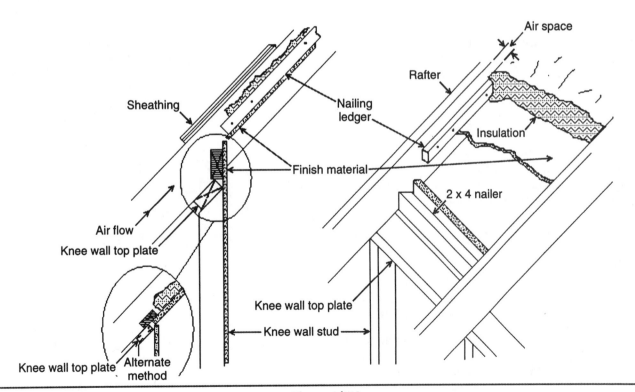

Figure 14-12
Knee wall top plate and nailer

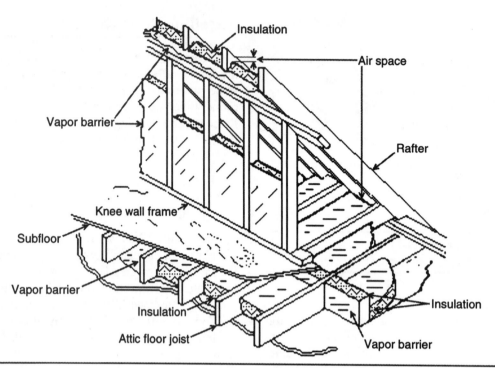

Figure 14-13
Attic conversion insulating techniques

As shown in Figure 14-12, your finish ceiling treatment will determine the location of the nailing blocks and ledgers. You can either install the finish ceiling between the rafters or against the rafters.

Insulating Knee Walls

Figure 14-13 shows how to insulate an attic conversion. Put insulation batts, with the vapor barrier facing down, between the joists from the outside wall plate to the knee wall. Fill up the entire joist space directly under the knee wall with insulation, with the vapor barrier on the warm side of the attic space. When you put the insulation batt at the junction of rafter and exterior wall, allow an airway for attic ventilation. Insulate the knee wall with blanket or batt insulation, either with integral vapor barrier or a separate vapor barrier on the side facing into the attic.

Place batt or blanket insulation between the rafters at the sloping portion of the room. Always leave at least a 1-inch clear space between the top of the insulation and the roof sheathing at each rafter space. Air must be able to flow behind the knee wall and vent out at the ridge as shown in Figure 14-14.

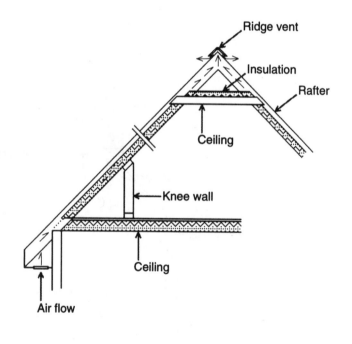

Figure 14-14
Minimum 1" clearance for air flow

Subflooring an Attic

Once you've marked a cutout for the stairway, lay plywood or OSB sheathing over the remaining attic. Stagger the panel ends at least the distance of two floor joists to strengthen the floor. Space and fasten the panels as discussed in Chapter 4 on subflooring. Glue-nail the subflooring so you don't disturb the finished ceiling below.

Attic Partition Walls and Rafter Collar Beams

It's a good idea to put a double floor joist directly under a partition wall sole plate that runs parallel to the floor joists. For attic partition walls which extend to the rafters, you can nail them directly to the rafters. If the partition wall is located between rafter runs, you'll have to install blocking to nail into, as shown in Figure 14-15.

Locate 2 x 4 blocking 24 inches on center between the rafters, nailing it in place with 16d nails through the rafters. Then nail the 2 x 4 top plate to the blocking using 12d or larger nails. Cut the studs to fit the angle. Position partition wall studs 16 or 24 inches on center.

Rafter collar beams are a key element in the structural strength of a roof. The beams may be 1 x 6 planks, 2 x 4s, or 2 x 6s. These beams help tie the rafters together, so they won't spread apart.

Different builders use different techniques to install collar beams. You can find collar beams installed in the "high" or "low" range compared to the relative height of the attic and pitch of the roof. You also may find that the beams are not all positioned the same height from the floor, or one end is slightly lower or higher than the opposite end. I prefer to use 1 x 6s in the upper third of the attic space, installed level, all at the same height.

You can make minor adjustments in existing collar beams. If they're fairly low, you can move them to a higher position, making the ceiling higher. Of course, if they aren't installed evenly, you should correct the problem by changing them so they're all even.

Don't remove the collar beams. Use them as ceiling joists for the attic ceiling. That'll give you more airspace or attic space above the conversion. Of course, if the beams are 1 x 6 planks you'll want to replace them with 2 x 4s or larger, depending on the span. The 1 x 6s aren't adequate to support the finish ceiling you'll nail to them. See Figure 14-16.

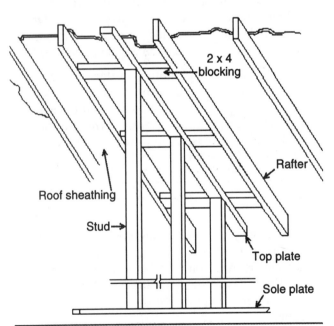

Figure 14-15
Partition installed with blocking between rafters

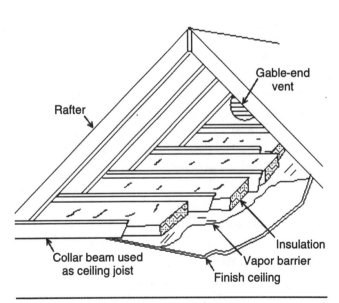

Figure 14-16
Small attic created above conversion

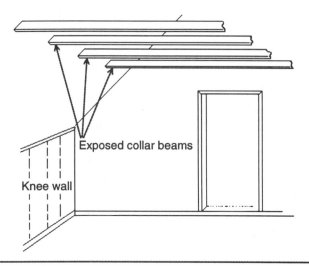

Figure 14-17
Utilizing collar beams in a vaulted ceiling

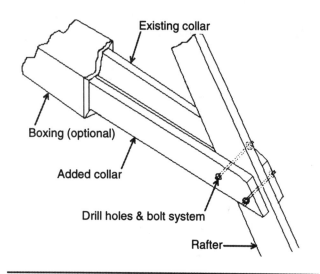

Figure 14-18
Collar treatment choices for vaulted ceiling

The small attic created above the collar beams should have a free ventilating area of 1/300, or greater, of the attic floor area. I like to use at least 1 square inch of screened ventilator to 1 square foot of attic floor. Don't forget that the screen (or louvers if you use louvered ventilators) reduces the ventilating area. Keep this in mind when you pick which size ventilator to use. Some manufacturers list the free ventilating area of their vents.

Working Around Obstructions in an Attic

Converting an attic poses special problems that you'll have to solve. You'll have to work around existing structural elements, including collar beams, chimneys, and the mechanical ducts and wiring. Let's take them one at a time.

Exposed Collar Beams

Exposed collar beams can be worked into almost any conversion design, especially if you're using a vaulted or cathedral-type ceiling. If rafters are spaced 16 inches on center, collar beams are usually spaced every third or fourth rafter. This spacing is more

attractive in exposed beams. Figure 14-17 shows how you can use exposed collar beams in a vaulted ceiling.

Exposed collar beams look more massive — and more impressive — if you box them. I recommend adding a same-size 2-by on the opposite side of the rafter and box as shown in Figure 14-18. This increases the strength of the collar. To add more strength to the structure, bolt the collar to the rafter with two $3/16$-inch bolts. Tack the added collar to the rafter. Drill a $3/16$-inch hole through the added collar, the rafter, and the opposing collar. Use a wide washer at both collars.

Instead of adding another collar, you can use shims or blocks spaced 16 or 24 inches on center along the beam to fur out the boxing and increase the size of the beam. Whichever method you use, paint or stain the beam to finish it, or cover it with material to match the vaulted ceiling finish.

Chimneys

A chimney isn't something you can knock down and move just because it gets in the way of your conversion plans. And you can't tap into a chimney to use it as a flue unless it's got an extra flue. Here's the rule: If you can't move it, you can cover it, paint it, or leave it alone.

If possible, work the chimney into your design as a room separator. That solves the problem neatly. You

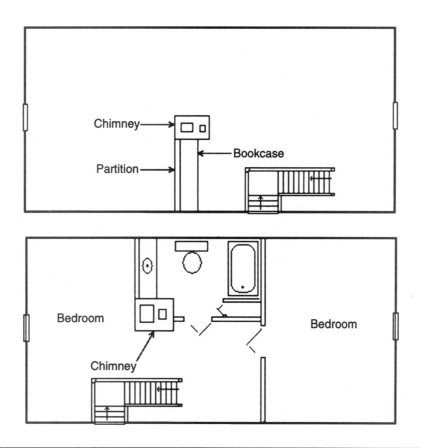

Figure 14-19
Making chimney part of partition wall

can also make the chimney part of a partition wall. Figure 14-19 shows both solutions. If you enclose a chimney, be sure to leave a minimum 2-inch space between the masonry and framing materials. This is a code requirement to prevent a fire hazard.

Often, the masonry finish on a chimney that's hidden in an attic isn't smooth. Sometimes, it doesn't even look professional. You'll have to box in the chimney with a finish that will add to, instead of detract from, the room.

Ducts, Vent Pipes and Wires

Try to conceal ducts and vent (soil) pipes coming up through an attic in walls or closets. If there's a bathroom in the conversion, try to design it so the bathroom uses the existing vent and you can enclose the pipe within a bathroom wall. If this isn't practical, try building a partition to enclose the pipe or duct. As a last resort, relocate them if you have to. But the less you have to relocate, the lower the costs for the homeowner, and the more chance you have of making a profit on the job.

Electrical Wires

Concealing wires isn't normally a problem because most attics are only wired for a pull-chain light, or a light and switch. If wires to light fixtures in the ceiling below run over the top of the ceiling joists (which will be your attic floor joists), you'll have to reroute these wires before beginning the conversion. Figure 14-20 shows three ways to do it. Where the ceiling joists are furred, run the wire between the finish ceiling and the joists. If the finish ceiling is nailed directly to the joist, run the wire through holes drilled in the center of the joists or beside the joists.

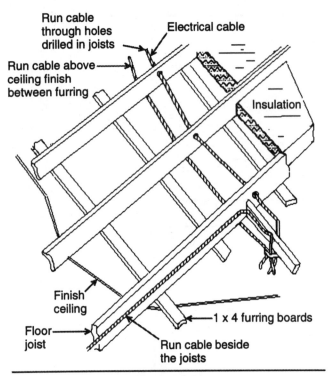

Figure 14-20
Rerouting electrical cable under attic floor

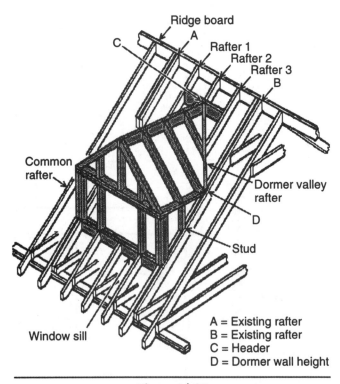

A = Existing rafter
B = Existing rafter
C = Header
D = Dormer wall height

Figure 14-21
Positioning a gable dormer and cutting the existing rafters

Dormer Construction

A dormer is a framed structure projecting from the roof surface, which can provide natural light, ventilation, space, and headroom. You can build it up from the level of the main roof plate, or from a point above the plate as shown in Figure 14-21. The front wall of the dormer may be flush with the main building line or behind it.

To keep it from looking "tacked on," it's usually best to slope the dormer's roof at the same pitch as the main roof. Also make the dormer walls at least 6 inches wide on each side of the window. If the dormer is just for natural light and ventilation, not living space, you can make the ceiling lower than the ceiling of the room.

Most houses look better if you add two gable dormers rather than one, especially in the front of the house where looks count the most. Complete the balanced look by spacing the dormers the same distance from the ends of the roof. But a tall, narrow house may look good with one large dormer in the center of the roof. If the addition is in the back of the house, you can often use a shed instead of a gable dormer.

Before you can start to build any dormer, you've got to determine its exact location and ceiling height. Draw a plan of the dormer with dimensions. From inside the attic, locate and mark these dimensions on the underside of the roof. Drive a nail through the roof at these points. Go out on the roof and snap a chalk line from nail to nail to mark the dormer opening. Then remove the shingles and cut out the roof sheathing in the dormer opening. Be prepared to cover the opening with waterproof membrane and supports to protect against the weather.

Gable Dormers

Let's get down to the details of framing a gable dormer. We'll use a dormer ceiling height of 8 feet for this example. Follow along on Figure 14-21. First you have to cut the existing rafters (labeled 1, 2, and 3 on the illustration). Remember to provide the necessary temporary support. You can cut rafter 2 at the point even with the conversion's vaulted ceiling height, plus

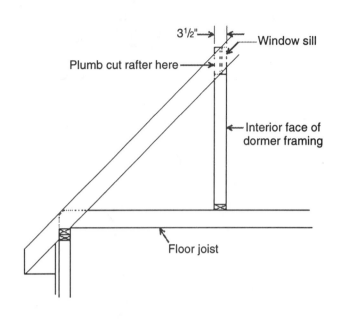

Figure 14-22
Cutting lower end of rafters

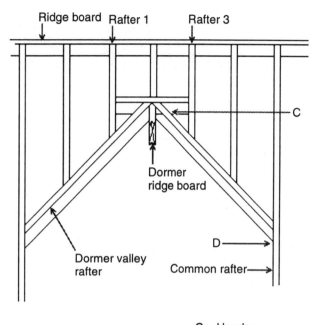

C = Header
D = Dormer wall height

Figure 14-23
Making plumb and miter cuts for a dormer

an additional 1¹⁄₂ inches for the thickness of the header (C). Use your carpenter's level to make this a plumb cut.

To figure out where you cut the lower end of rafters 1, 2, and 3, mark the interior face of the framing of the front wall as shown in Figure 14-22. With your level, mark a plumb line on rafter 2. Add 3¹⁄₂ inches for the thickness of the window sill and mark the plumb cut. Cut rafters 1 and 3 at the same point.

Point D in both Figure 14-21 and Figure 14-23 is the dormer wall height (from floor to top of dormer top plate). Snap a plumb chalk line from point D to the juncture of header C and the dormer ridge board position as shown in Figure 14-23. This gives the miter cut for rafter 3. Use a level to mark a plumb cut at the miter line. Repeat these steps to find the miter and plumb cuts for rafter 1. If there are more rafters, follow same procedure. The valley rafter will fit flush against the cut.

Figure 14-21 shows a dormer constructed between rafters A and B, which covers the distance of four rafters spaced 16 inches apart. That makes the dormer

width 62¹⁄₂ inches. Allowing 6 inches for wall space on each side of the window leaves a 50¹⁄₂-inch window space.

Always plan your dormer width to fit between existing common rafters. Double the rafter at each dormer side wall as shown in Figure 14-21 to give added structural strength to the roof and dormer. Rest the side studs and the short valley rafters on the double rafters. The alternate method for studding is to carry the side studs past the rafter to rest on the sole plate nailed to the framing and subfloor.

Follow the steps covered in Chapter 6, Ceiling and Roof Framing, for installing dormer rafters. If the dormer ceiling is vaulted, tie the dormer rafters with collar beams just as you do in conventional rafter construction.

Shed Dormers

Figure 14-24 shows a finished shed exterior. Determine the dormer ceiling height for shed dormers the same way as for gable dormers. Mark the existing house rafters at the dormer header position for a verti-

Figure 14-24
Shed dormer

cal (plumb) cut. Before cutting rafters for a dormer opening, install temporary braces to support the roof. When using wood shingles on shed dormers, give the rafters a 6-inch rise per foot to properly shed rain and snow.

Measure and cut the lower rafter end (at front dormer wall) for shed dormers the same as for gable dormers. Install a header as shown in Figure 14-25. Use a double header on spans greater than 48 inches.

Now you're ready to frame the dormer:

1. Build the front wall section of the dormer. Frame and erect the studs, plates, and window openings as an outside wall. If the attic subfloor is in place, build the wall horizontally. Space the studs so the lower rafter ends will fit against the sides of the studs as shown in Figure 14-25. After you raise the wall and plumb it into place, nail the sole plate to the floor joists through the subflooring. Face nail the rafter ends to the studs with 12d or larger nails.

2. Lay out and cut the required number of dormer rafters.

3. Install the rafters. Toenail the rafters to the dormer top plate (front wall) with 10d nails or secure them with rafter ties. Secure the dormer rafters to the header you installed on the main rafters.

4. Double the main common rafters on each side of the dormer.

5. Angle cut the dormer side wall studs to fit on top of the double rafter and under the dormer end rafter as shown in Figure 14-25. The alternate method is to extend the stud from the sole plate to the rafter, face nailing the stud to the rafter at the point of contact. Space side wall dormer studs 16 or 24 inches on center.

6. If you use ceiling furring, nail it with 8d nails at each dormer rafter.

7. Apply roof and wall sheathing.

8. Apply roof covering.

9. Complete dry-in by installing the window.

Installing Skylights

Most skylight installations require a shaft connecting the ceiling to the skylight. A straight shaft works well for a direct, overhead unit. To distribute the light over a broader area, change the angle of the shaft. This gives a softer, more diffused light. See Figure 14-26.

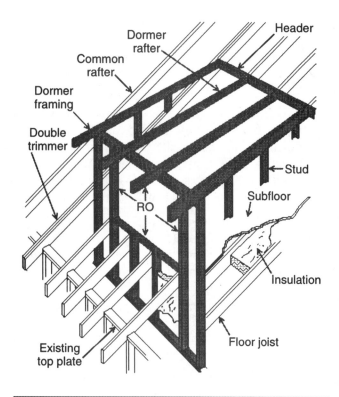

Figure 14-25
Shed dormer framework

Rough opening	1' 8⁹/₁₆"	2' 4⁹/₁₆"	2' 11³/₁₆"	3' 9³/₁₆"
Frame	1' 8¹/₁₆"	2' 4¹/₁₆"	2' 10¹¹/₁₆"	3' 8¹³/₁₆"
Glass	19¹/₄"	27¹/₄"	33⁷/₈"	44"

Rough opening 2' 4¹⁵/₁₆" | **Frame** 2' 4⁷/₁₆" | **Glass** 27¹/₄"

19 x 27   27 x 27   33 x 27

Rough opening 3' 9⁵/₁₆" | **Frame** 3' 8¹³/₁₆" | **Glass** 44"

19 x 44   27 x 44   33 x 44   44 x 44

Rough opening 6' 2⁹/₁₆" | **Frame** 6' 2¹/₁₆" | **Glass** 73¹/₄"

19 x 73   27 x 73   33 x 73

Figure 14-28
Typical skylight rough openings

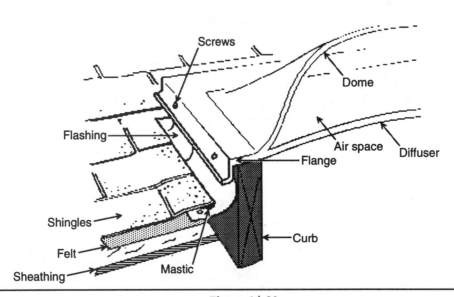

Figure 14-29
Curb-mount installation

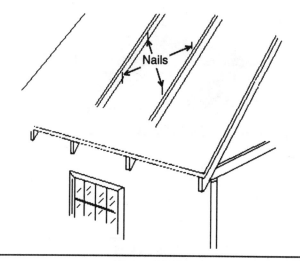

Figure 14-30
Locate rafter position

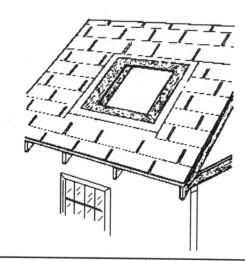

Figure 14-31
Cutting through the roof

Figure 14-32
Framing the opening

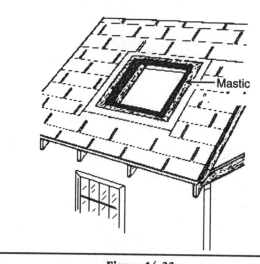

Figure 14-33
Applying asphalt roofing cement

Begin the installation by driving a 3-inch nail up through the roof (from underneath) at each corner of the proposed opening as shown in Figure 14-30.

Go up on the roof and locate the nails you drove through the roof. Remove the roofing material back about 12 inches all around the skylight area. Be careful with the roofing material so you can reuse it. Cut the hole through the sheathing at the location marked by the nails. It should look like Figure 14-31.

Frame the inside of the roof opening at the top and bottom as in Figure 14-32. If a rafter runs through the opening, cut it out. Frame the opening with the same size lumber as the existing rafters.

Spread asphalt plastic roofing cement around the opening, about $1/4$ inch thick. Make sure you cover all exposed wood and felt. See Figure 14-33.

Build the curb with 2 x 6-inch lumber. Make the inside dimensions the same as the opening in the roof.

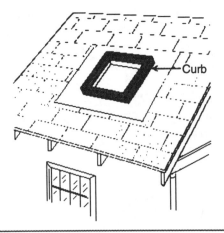

Figure 14-34
Constructing the curb

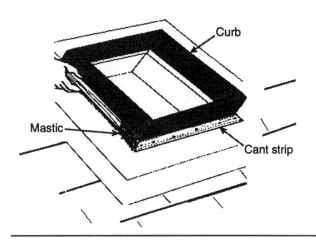

Figure 14-35
Sealing the outside curb

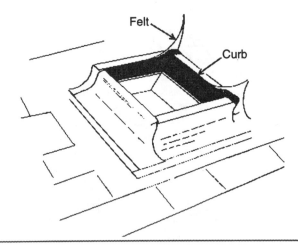

Figure 14-36
Applying 15-pound felt

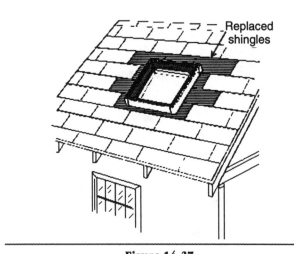

Figure 14-37
Replacing the shingles

Use roofing cement to seal all joints. Figure 14-34 shows your progress to this point.

Apply roofing cement on the outside of the curb at the bottom on all four sides. Nail the cant strip in place as shown in Figure 14-35.

Now cover the entire outside of the curb with roofing cement. Then immediately apply 15-pound roofing felt in the soft roofing cement. Put down the bottom strip at the low side of the skylight first, then the sides, and finally the strip at the top of the skylight.

Be sure to apply roofing cement where the felt overlaps. Cover exposed seams with roofing cement as in Figure 14-36. Then replace the shingles as shown in Figure 14-37.

Spread a bead of clear mastic weatherstripping around the top edge of the curb, and press the skylight down into place. Drill small holes for the screws and secure the flange around the edge about every 3 inches (Figure 14-38). Figure 4-39 shows a cross-section view of the finished installation.

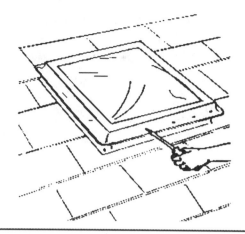

Figure 14-38
Tightening the skylight screws

Self-Flashing Skylights

You can install a self-flashing skylight directly on a pitched roof. Because it doesn't have a curb, the unit has a low profile and is less conspicuous. Attach the unit directly to the roof and flash it as described for curb-mounted units. Figure 14-40 shows this type of installation.

You locate, mark, and cut for a self-flashing skylight the way same as a curb-mounted skylight. Place the dome in a 1/4-inch-thick bead of roofing cement and nail in predrilled holes. Most units come with special nails and rubber washers to secure the unit. See Figure 14-41.

Apply a thick coat of roofing cement over the edge of the skylight up to the bubble. Cut strips of roofing felt wide enough to go from the bubble to overlap the felt on the deck. Put the side pieces on first. Brush more cement over these strips at the top and apply the top strip of felt. Don't put a strip at the bottom. See Figure 14-42.

Spread mastic over the felt strips and replace the asphalt shingles. After you've got the shingles in place, apply roofing cement across the bottom of the skylight as shown in Figure 14-43. Figure 14-44 shows a cross-section view of the finished installation.

Adding a Second-Story Loft

For another type of conversion, take a look at Figure 14-45. This plan provides additional first-floor space as well as a loft. The 4/12 pitch roof is extended

Figure 14-39
Cross-view of curb-mounted skylight installation

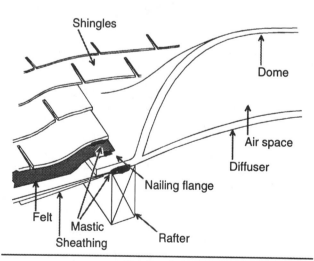

Figure 14-40
Self-flashing skylight

Figure 14-41
Nailing down the skylight

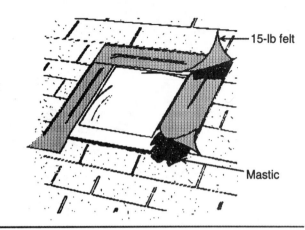

Figure 14-42
Applying mastic and felt

up to meet the 12/12 pitch roof. While it's usually done on the back, you can add this extension on the front of the house as long as it stays within the setback required by code. A skylight provides natural light for the loft area. The addition has a vaulted ceiling with exposed beams, and a straight stairway leading to the loft.

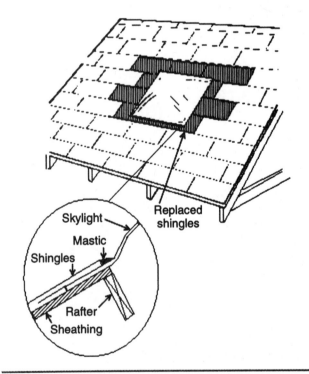

Figure 14-43
Replacing shingles

This addition creates two attic spaces — and they both need ventilation. Access to the lower attic is through a door at the back of the loft closet.

The only shingles you have to remove with this addition are the ones under members that butt into the roof. These include sole plates for partitions and a plate the rafters are nailed to. Cut off the ends of the existing rafters flush with the outside surface of the exterior wall.

Figure 14-46 shows an elevation and a plan view of an alternative plan with stairs that have a landing. This loft space includes a bunk area, bookcase, and closet or storage. Stairway construction is covered in detail in Chapter 7.

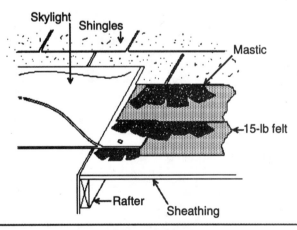

Figure 14-44
Cross-view of self-flashing skylight installation

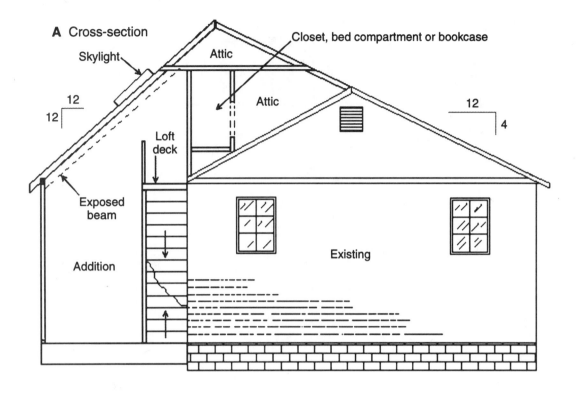

A Cross-section

Skylight

Attic

Closet, bed compartment or bookcase

Attic

12 / 12

Loft deck

Exposed beam

Addition

Existing

12 / 4

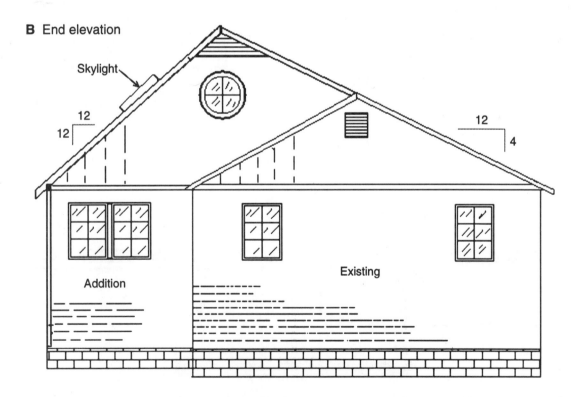

B End elevation

Skylight

12 / 12

12 / 4

Addition

Existing

Figure 14-45
A room addition with a second-story loft

A Elevation

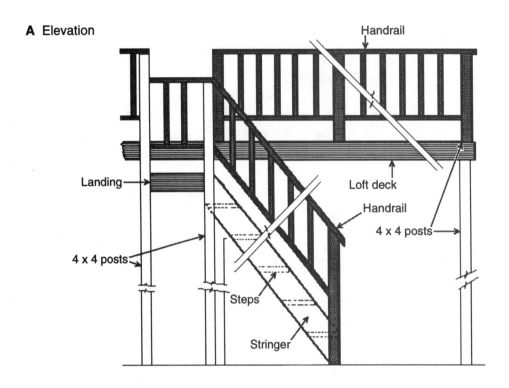

B Plan view

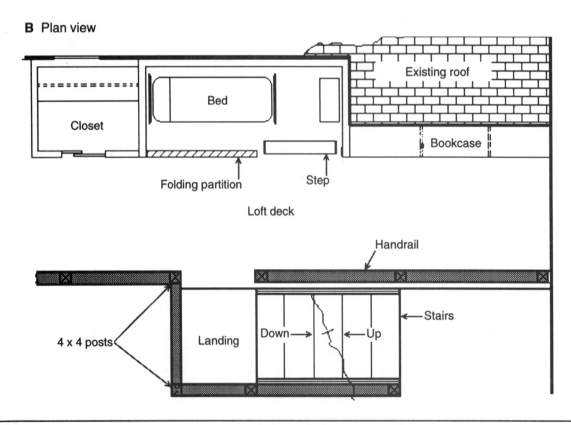

Figure 14-46
Loft staircase and deck

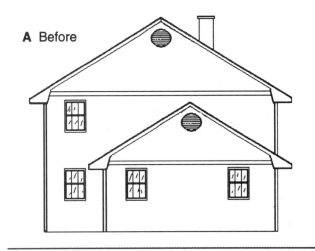
A Before

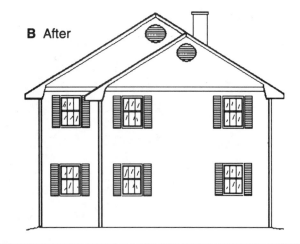
B After

Figure 14-47
Adding a second-story room

The loft approach gives you a lot of possibilities. You can extend the first floor living space and make a second floor over the existing house without demolition work. And the normal activities of the occupants in the rooms below won't be interrupted too much as you work on the addition.

Look at Figure 14-47 for a different type of loft addition. This figure shows an addition for a homeowner who wants to add a second story to the one-story wing of his house to include a master bedroom and bath. You'll need to remove the existing roof on this one. Begin by removing the shingles, the roof sheathing and the roof framing. The sheathing and framing members are reusable materials that can help reduce the cost of the project.

Since the 2 x 6 ceiling joists span 16 feet (there is no interior load-bearing partition) you'll need to reinforce the joists. Let's suppose you decide to double the joists using 2 x 8s as shown in Figure 14-48. Install ½-inch plywood floor sheathing on top of the reinforced joist and proceed with sole plate and framing.

When there's a load-bearing partition as shown in Figure 14-49, you can double every second or third first-floor ceiling joist, depending on the span. In any event, double with the same-size member whenever you can.

Estimating Manhours

Attic conversion is never a simple process and estimating manhours can be perplexing. Give this some thought:

1. To get large size building materials such as 12 foot or longer 2-bys, 4' x 8' sheathing panels, prehung doors, etc., you'll need a fairly large opening — something at least 4 feet high, wide, or diagonal to the outside. Few attics will have such an opening.

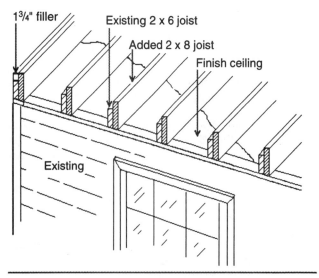

Figure 14-48
Reinforcing first-floor ceiling joists for second-floor addition

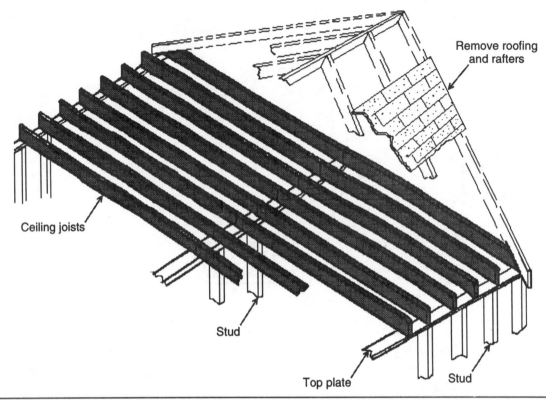

Figure 14-49
Preparing one story for second-story addition

2. How will you get the material up to the attic level? Hoist? Handling by workers standing on scaffolding? Some builder supply houses have delivery trucks equipped with hydraulic lifts that can raise the bed of the delivery truck to unload materials at a second-story level. Can you use this type of truck?

3. If not, will you have to build temporary outside stairs and an entrance door?

4. Or will you measure and cut materials outside on the ground and pass the pieces up to the attic? That takes a lot of manhours. Your saw man will either stay on the ground (wasting a lot of hours) or he'll have to be constantly climbing up and down.

If you have records of manhours on attic conversions you've done, use them. If not, use the estimates given in earlier chapters in this book for each part of the job, and add 25 percent. After all, it will take longer to build a wall, a stairway or a bathroom in an attic conversion than to build a similar wall, stairway or bathroom for a room addition on the ground. For some builders, the 25 percent addition may be too much. For others, it may be too little. Every attic conversion job is different. Carefully consider the difficulties you'll face for each particular job before you estimate manhours.

Manhours for Skylight Installation

Here's how to estimate skylight installation:

Unit size	Framing	Manhours per unit
14" x 24"	16" x 24"	2.5
14" x 36"	16" x 36"	3.0
30" x 36"	32" x 36"	3.5

Estimate interior trim at 1 manhour per 8 linear feet.

15

Building Fireplaces and Chimneys

There are two basic types of fireplaces: masonry and prefabricated. The prefabricated fireplace is an "engineered furnace" designed for energy efficiency. It's easy to install, and can be finished with the same mantel, hearth, and chimney as a masonry fireplace. Most manufacturers of prefabricated fireplaces provide installation instructions with their units. That's all you need to provide a safe, efficient fireplace.

The masonry fireplace is about as old as civilization and the current design evolved through trial and error. Today, it's probably valued more for the esthetics of an open fire than its heating capability. In this chapter we will take a look at constructing masonry fireplaces.

Masonry Fireplace Design

The key to an efficient, workable fireplace is the design. To perform properly, a fireplace must be more than a firebox and a flue. A fireplace must be designed and built to withstand high temperatures over extended periods of time without leaking smoke into the room.

There are two important factors in sizing the fireplace. First, each part of a fireplace should be compatible with its other parts, so it works efficiently. Second, the size of the fireplace should complement the size of the room it's in. For example, a fireplace in the 12-foot long wall of a 12 x 20 room should have a 32- to 36-inch wide opening. If it's in the 20-foot wall, a 36- to 40-inch wide opening is appropriate. A 36-foot wall can handle a 48- or 50-inch wide fireplace. On a square-foot basis, a 30-inch wide fireplace will serve 300 square feet of floor area.

Location is important too, both for appearance and for efficient operation. A fireplace with a too-small opening might not warm the room even though it works perfectly. With a too-large opening, a properly-made fire might be too hot for the room. It also would need a larger flue area. And it would use a lot of interior air, unless you provide exterior combustion air.

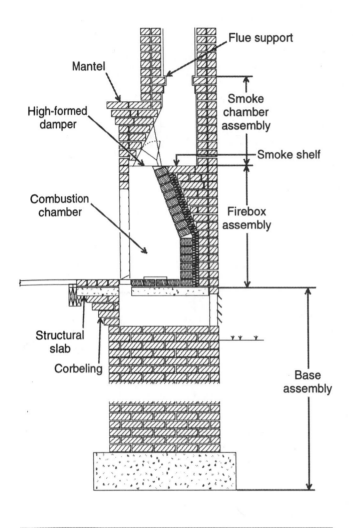

Figure 15-1
Typical fireplace section

conform to ASTM C 216. Building brick should conform to ASTM C 62. Or, use hollow brick (ASTM C 652) with vertical reinforcement. Use grade SW brick in exposed areas. It's more durable. It might be more economical to use Grade MW or NW brick in areas not exposed to weather and dirt. Three other general requirements, found in many building codes, are:

♦ Firestop all spaces between masonry fireplaces and wood or other combustible materials. Use a 1-inch thickness of noncompressible, noncombustible material, such as fibrous insulation, in these places.

♦ No combustible material is permitted within 6 inches of the fireplace opening.

♦ Combustible material within 12 inches of the fireplace opening can only project $1/8$ inch (or less) for each inch of distance from the opening. For instance, wood trim that is $3/4$ inch thick must be at least 6 inches from the opening.

You should fill all *nonfunctional* empty areas in a fireplace — from the foundation through the chimney — solidly, with masonry mortared in place. Filling these areas makes the fireplace work better, less likely to leak, and last longer.

The *functional* empty areas are the air passageway, the ash pit, the 1-inch airspace between the combustion chamber and surrounding brickwork, and the smoke chamber. Don't fill in these spaces. Tool all exposed mortar joints. Concave jointing is best.

Figure 15-1 shows a typical fireplace section with the parts labeled.

Most of the heat from a fireplace is radiated heat. The more surface there is to radiate heat, the better. A fireplace with a shallow firebox and flared sides and back radiates the most heat. Add a glass screen at the opening for maximum all-round energy performance. That will give the most radiated heat, with the least air infiltration.

Every energy-efficient fireplace has an exterior air supply. The air supply has to be the right size, and in the right place. You also have to make sure the dampers fit tightly.

Most building codes require you to build a fireplace with solid bricks. You can use face brick, stone, tile, or marble to face the fireplace. Face brick should

Types of Fireplaces

While there are several popular residential fireplace designs and many variations of each style, the basic principles are the same. Let's look at two: the single-face and the multiface.

Single-face fireplaces can be efficient heating units. Our ancestors learned that the more brick masonry surface that can be exposed to a fire, the better. The actual burning of the wood can do little more than take the chill off a room. The mass of the brick in the combustion chamber radiates and reflects more heat even after the fire is out. Figure 15-2 shows a section, plan, and front elevation of a single-face fireplace.

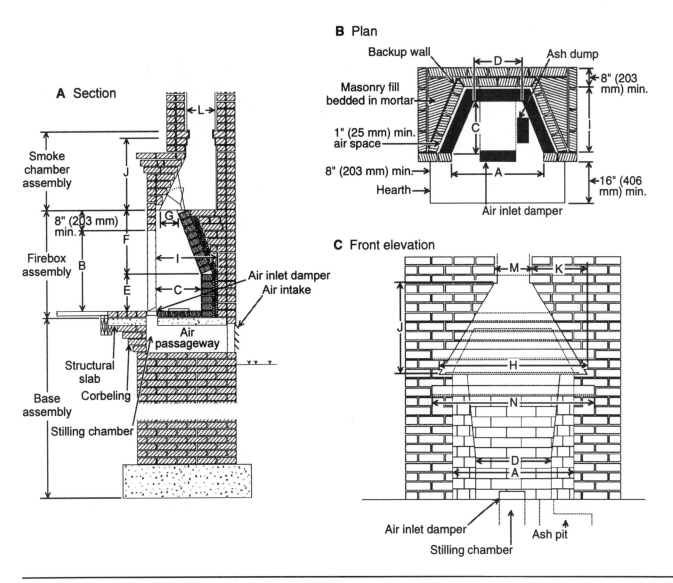

A Section

Smoke chamber assembly

8" (203 mm) min.

Firebox assembly

Air inlet damper
Air intake

Air passageway

Structural slab

Corbeling

Base assembly

Stilling chamber

B Plan

Backup wall

Ash dump

8" (203 mm) min.

Masonry fill bedded in mortar

1" (25 mm) min. air space

8" (203 mm) min.

Hearth

16" (406 mm) min.

Air inlet damper

C Front elevation

Air inlet damper

Stilling chamber

Ash pit

Figure 15-2
Single-face fireplace

The Rumford fireplace is a single-face fireplace. It has widely-splayed sides, a shallow back, and a high opening. Figure 15-3 shows a section, plan, and front elevation of a Rumford fireplace, and how it's built. The size and shape of the firebox opening determine the design of the rest of the fireplace components. Figure 15-4 gives the sizes of the dimensions (marked with letters) in Figures 15-2 and 15-3. It shows which fireplace opening sizes you should use to build the most attractive and efficient fireplace. The dimensions in Figure 15-4 are critical. Don't make any more than minor changes or you'll be asking for trouble.

We often think of a multiface fireplace as contemporary, but it's really an old design. Consider, for example, the corner fireplace with its two adjacent open sides. It has been used in Scandinavia for centuries. Multiface fireplaces may have adjacent, opposite, three, or even all faces open. But multiple faces present design problems which can result in insufficient draw, external draft requirements, and excessive smoking. Consult a qualified technician or architect when planning a multiface fireplace. The design and construction information I'm presenting is for single-face fireplaces.

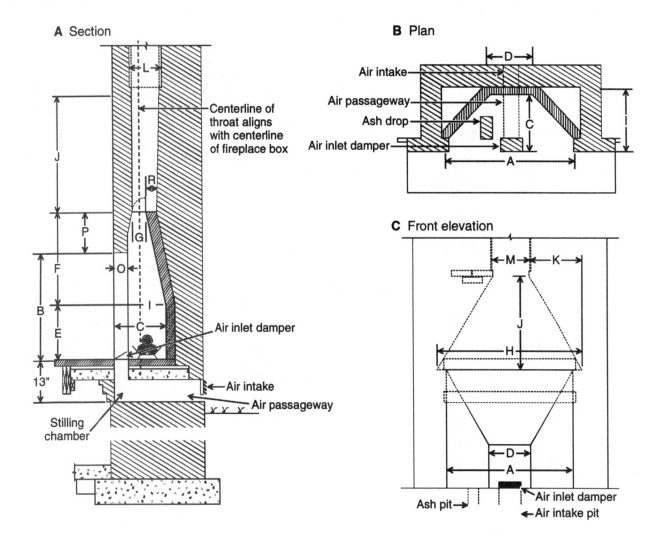

A Section   **B** Plan   **C** Front elevation

For maximum heat radiation from a Rumford fireplace:

1) The width of the firebox (D) must equal the depth (C).
2) The vertical portion of the firebox (E) must equal the width (D).
3) Thickness of the firebox (I minus C) should be at least $2^{1}/_{4}$".
4) Area of fireplace opening (A x B) must not exceed 10 times the flue opening area.
5) The width of the fireplace opening (A), and its height (B) should each be 2 to 3 times the depth of the firebox (C).
6) Opening height (B) should not be larger than width (A).
7) The throat (G) should be no less than 3" or more than 4".
8) Centerline of the throat must align with the centerline of the firebox base.
9) The smokeshelf (R) should be 4" wide.
10) The width of the lintel (O) should be no less than 4" nor more than 5".
11) Vertical distance from lintel to throat (P) must be at least 12".
12) A flat plate damper is required at the throat, and must open towards the smokeshelf.

Figure 15-3
Rumford fireplace with exterior air supply system

Single-face fireplace dimensions (inches[a,d])													
Finished fireplace opening							Rough brickwork				Flue size[b]		Steel angle[c]
A	B	C	D	E	F	G	H	I	J	K	L M		N
24	24	16	11	14	18	8¾	32	21	19	10	8 x 12		A - 36
26	24	16	13	14	18	8¾	34	21	21	11	8 x 12		A - 36
28	24	16	15	14	18	8¾	36	21	21	12	8 x 12		A - 36
30	29	16	17	14	23	8¾	38	21	24	13	12 x 12		A - 36
32	29	16	19	14	23	8¾	40	21	24	14	12 x 12		A - 42
36	29	16	23	14	23	8¾	44	21	27	16	12 x 12		A - 42
40	29	16	27	14	23	8¾	48	21	29	16	12 x 16		A - 48
42	32	16	29	14	26	8¾	50	21	32	17	16 x 16		B - 48
48	32	18	33	14	26	8¾	56	23	37	20	16 x 16		B - 54
54	37	20	37	16	29	13	68	25	45	26	16 x 16		B - 60
60	37	22	42	16	29	13	72	27	45	26	16 x 20		B - 66
60	40	22	42	16	31	13	72	27	45	26	16 x 20		B - 66
72	40	22	54	16	31	13	84	27	56	32	20 x 20		C - 84
84	40	24	64	20	28	13	96	29	61	36	20 x 24		C - 96
96	40	24	76	20	28	13	108	29	75	42	20 x 24		C - 108

[a]*Adapted from The Donley Brothers Company,* Book of Successful Fireplaces — How to Build Them
[b]*Flue sizes conform to modular dimensional system*
[c]*Angle sizes: A — 3" x 3" x ³/₁₆"   B — 3¹/₂" x 3" x ¹/₄"   C — 5" x 3¹/₂" x ⁵/₁₆"*
[d]*SI conversion: mm = in. x 25.4*

Figure 15-4
Single-face fireplace dimensions

How to Construct a Residential Fireplace

All fireplaces have these three basic parts:

♦ Base assembly
♦ Firebox assembly
♦ Smoke chamber assembly

Let's look at these parts in some detail.

Base Assembly

The base assembly shown in Figure 15-5 has two parts: the foundation and the hearth support. No rule says you must always use both of these components. In slab-on-grade construction, for example, the slab can act as both foundation and hearth support.

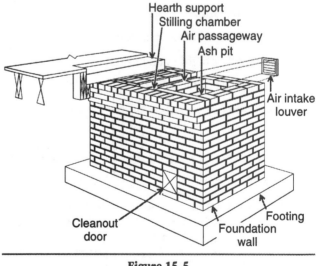

Figure 15-5
Base assembly

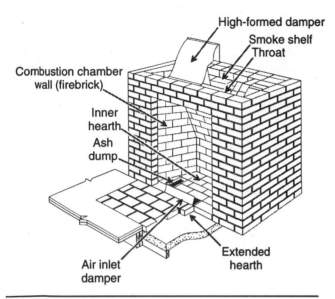

Figure 15-6
Firebox assembly

The foundation supports the whole fireplace and chimney assembly. It must be heavy enough to carry the load. Footings support either foundation walls or a structural slab. Most building codes, however, don't let you support other parts of the building on the fireplace/chimney assembly. It's not a structural element.

When designing the foundations, consider soil type and condition. Undisturbed or well-compacted soil will usually be adequate. But some types of soil, or some conditions of the soil, may need more analysis. Consult your local code or building authority, or increase the size of the footings if you encounter:

♦ Inorganic clays of high plasticity

♦ Peat and other highly organic soils

♦ Organic clays of medium to high plasticity

♦ Organic silts or silty clays of low plasticity

♦ Fat clays

♦ Elastic silts

♦ Inorganic silty soils

Build footings on undisturbed or properly-compacted soil. Make concrete footings at least 12 inches thick. Extend them at least 6 inches past the fireplace walls on each side. Footings should go below the frost line. Footings in a basement, or other area that won't freeze, don't need to penetrate the frost line.

Build foundation walls of masonry or concrete. Most building codes call for a minimum thickness of 8 inches. In brick foundation walls, solidly fill the voids (except the ash pit and external air ducts). Use brick bedded in mortar.

When the fireplace is on a slab-on-grade, you'll need to thicken the slab under the fireplace at least 12 inches. It has to support all loads from the fireplace and chimney.

There are several ways to support the hearth, including corbeled brickwork, structural slab, and cantilevered reinforced brick masonry. Codes for corbeling usually limit the individual maximum projection. No unit can project more than half its height. No unit can project more than a third its thickness. When corbeling from walls, limit the overall horizontal projection to half the wall thickness, unless reinforced. Your local code and foundation design may also limit the maximum horizontal projections, both overall and individual. Figure 15-2 shows a hearth supported by corbeling and a structural slab.

The Firebox

The firebox assembly consists of the firebox opening and hearth, the combustion chamber, the throat, and the smoke shelf. Figure 15-6 shows a typical firebox.

Firebox Opening and Hearth

You also have to support the brickwork above the fireplace opening, which is called the soffit. To do this you can use brick arches, reinforced brick masonry lintels, or steel angle lintels:

1. With brick arches, you usually don't need steel lintels. When figuring the height of an opening, use the maximum height of the arch soffit.

2. Reinforced brick masonry lintels also don't require steel lintels. They have a brick soffit, without any exposed steel angle.

3. Steel angle lintels are the most common.

Figure 15-4 gives steel angle dimensions for fireplaces. As a general rule, steel angle lintels should be at least $1/4$ inch thick. They should have a horizontal leg at least $3^1/2$ inches long, when used with a (nominal) 4-inch thick brick face wall. And they should have a horizontal leg of $2^1/2$ inches, when used with a

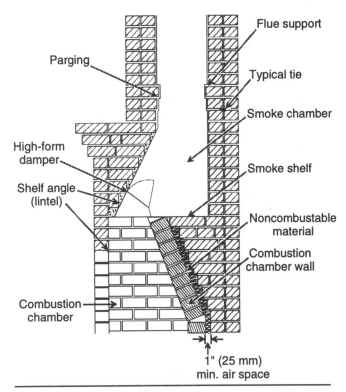

Figure 15-7
Combustion chamber and smoke chamber

(nominal) 3-inch thick face wall. The minimum bearing length is 4 inches. Use corrosion-resistant steel (ASTM A 36) for lintels. The maximum clear spans might be limited by the fire-protection requirements in some building codes.

A fireplace hearth has an inner hearth and an extended hearth. The inner hearth is the floor of the combustion chamber. The fire is above it. The inner hearth should be of noncombustible material at least 4 inches thick. This 4 inches includes both the inner hearth and the noncombustible hearth support.

The extended hearth is the part that projects into the room. It should also be noncombustible. Most building codes require the extended hearth to project at least 8 inches on each side of the opening, and 16 inches in front of it. If the opening's area is 6 square feet or more, some building codes require the hearth to project 12 inches on each side of the opening and 20 inches in front of it.

An extended hearth may be raised or flush with the floor. Figure 15-6 shows a fireplace hearth that's flush with the floor.

The Combustion Chamber

The shape and depth of the combustion chamber are important. They determine the draft and the air needed for combustion. They also determine how much heat is reflected into the room. Figure 15-7 shows the combustion chamber and smoke chamber. Look back at Figures 15-2 and 15-3 for plan views of the combustion chamber, and Figure 15-4 for recommended dimensions.

The sides of the combustion chamber are vertical. So is the lower part of the back. Above the vertical part in the back, the brick slopes forward toward the opening. The top of this slope will support the damper. For maximum heating of a room, make this sloped part flat, not concave. If it's concave, the heat reflects back into the fire, not into the room. Splayed, rather than vertical, sides also reflect more heat into the room.

The combustion chamber must be laid out correctly. It's inside the firebox assembly but isolated from it. Figure 15-8 shows one way to locate the combustion chamber.

Your first step is to choose the dimensions from Figure 15-4. Then locate the front wall (facing) of the fireplace. Line A-A marks the inside face position. Next, find Point I. It's at the center of Line A-A. Now, square from Point I back into the combustion chamber. Mark the chamber's depth. This is Point II. Line B-B connects Points I and II. From Point II, square two perpendiculars to line B-B, one in each direction. The length of each perpendicular is half the width of the rear chamber wall. Points c and d are at the ends of these perpendiculars. Now, from Point I on Line A-A, measure half the fireplace opening dimension, in each direction. You've now located Points a and b. Finally, connect the four points (a, b, c, and d) for the outline of the inside face of the combustion chamber.

Make the combustion chamber of brick 4 inches or more thick. Firebrick (ASTM C 64) is best. It's the most resistant to heat and temperature changes. You can lay it with any face exposed, but it's best as a stretcher course. Use fireclay mortar (ASTM C 105). Make mortar joints no thicker than $3/16$ inch. The mortar only has to be thick enough to fill irregularities in the firebrick. Use the "pick and dip" method for thin mortar joints by dipping the brick into a soupy mix of fireclay mortar, and then immediately putting it in place.

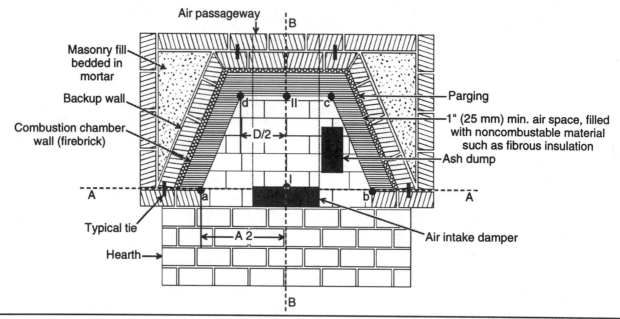

Figure 15-8
Sizing the combustion chamber

Or you can build the combustion chamber of Grade SW brick (ASTM C 62, or ASTM C 216). Use Type N or Type O, portland cement-lime mortar (ASTM C 270). These high-lime mortars are more heat-resistant than high-portland cement mortars. Also, you can use these mortars with the firebrick discussed above. Because it's not as durable as firebrick, only lay grade SW brick as a stretcher course. Make the mortar joints no more than $3/16$ inch thick. They'll be less likely to crack and deteriorate.

You can build the surrounding brickwork while you're building the combustion chamber or after you complete the combustion chamber. Either way, build a backup wall — a full course of masonry surrounding the combustion chamber. Make this wall at least 4 inches thick to support the smoke chamber and chimney above it. For high chimneys, build a thicker wall. The backup wall and combustion chamber together make up the fire box assembly. See Figure 15-8.

Leave an airspace of at least 1 inch between the combustion chamber wall and the backup wall. This is expansion space for the heated combustion chamber. Wrap a compressible, noncombustible material like fibrous insulation around the combustion chamber. This assures that the air space won't be filled with

mortar droppings. The air space isolates the combustion chamber, reducing stress from thermal expansion.

Use wall ties at all intersections where the wall isn't masonry bonded, except in the combustion chamber walls. Use wire ties (ASTM A 82 or ASTM A 185), at least 9 gauge, and corrosion-resistant. Space the ties no more than 16 inches apart vertically. Embed the ties at least 2 inches into the bed joints of the brick masonry.

Horizontal joint reinforcement is a good idea. Use it at the corners of adjacent wythes and in the wythe (backup wall) surrounding the combustion chamber walls. This reinforcement will reduce cracking.

Make sure you instruct the homeowners to wait 30 days after construction to build a fire. The mortar needs moisture to cure; fires built too soon dry the masonry out too fast.

The Throat

Because it affects the draft, design the fireplace throat carefully. Put it at least 8 inches above the highest point of the fireplace opening. Column G in Figure 15-4 gives the dimensions. Details are shown in Figures 15-2 and 15-3.

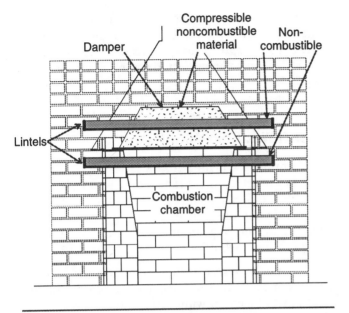

Figure 15-9
Lintel and damper installation with
allowances for thermal expansion

Use the same mortar as in the combustion chamber. This seat also seals against gas and smoke leakage.

The damper assembly shouldn't touch any masonry, other than what it bears on. So make sure it's seated. Then wrap the damper with a compressible, noncombustible material, taking care not to cover the opening. See Figure 15-9. This material provides space for thermal expansion and space for damper movement during fireplace use.

The Smoke Shelf

The smoke shelf is directly under the flue as shown in Figure 15-7. Design the smoke shelf to provide a uniform flow of air. It should also cause any downdrafts to eddy, then drift upward. The smoke shelf is level and on an even horizontal plane with the base of the damper. It can be flat or curved to blend with the rear wall of the smoke chamber. See Figure 15-10.

Use a metal damper that's as wide as the opening in the throat. The valve plate should open toward the back of the fireplace. This plate, when open, will deflect downdrafts.

There are many damper designs. The high-formed damper is a good choice; it extends the throat. It also forms a critical part of the smoke chamber. This damper style also lessens the chance of masonry blocking the damper's valve plate. A high-formed damper is shown in the fireplace throat in Figure 15-6.

Don't embed the damper in mortar. Just seat it on a thin setting bed of mortar, just thick enough for a seat.

The Smoke Chamber Assembly

The smoke chamber assembly forms the chimney flue support, as shown in Figures 15-1 and 15-11. The smoke chamber is above the throat and smoke shelf. It supports the flue lining on all sides. The back wall of the chamber is vertical. The side walls slope evenly toward the center. The front wall above the throats is also sloped. The dimensions of L, M, H and J in

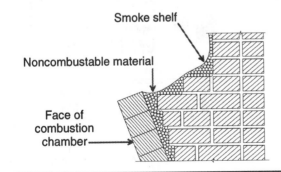

Figure 15-10
Optional smoke shelf configuration

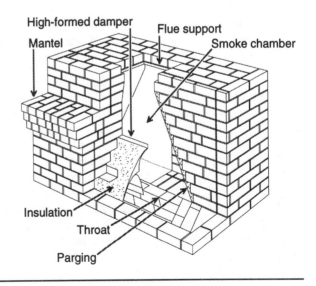

Figure 15-11
Smoke chamber assembly

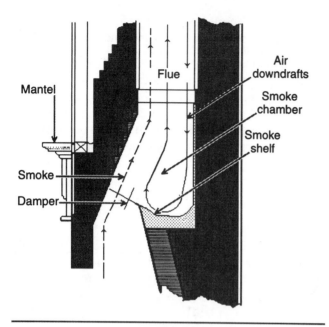

Figure 15-12
Downdrafts and smoke shelf

Figure 15-4 give the size of the smoke chamber. The points of measurements are in Figure 15-2, A and C.

A steel lintel supports the front wall above the throat. Don't use the damper for this purpose. Put a noncombustible, compressible material between the masonry and the damper and steel lintel. Figure 15-9 shows how. This permits both the damper and the lintel to expand.

Give the smoke chamber a smooth slope. For the required size, corbel each course of brick. Parge the inside of the smoke chamber to reduce friction and prevent smoke leakage.

Starting at the smoke shelf, corbel in the front and sides of the smoke chamber. Build the rear wall vertically. This ensures that the entire edge of the flue liner will be supported. The usual limitations for corbeling walls don't apply in the smoke chamber. Here, the fireplace's configuration determines the limitations. The corbels are laterally supported by adjacent masonry. The maximum corbel for each unit is the horizontal distance to be corbeled, divided by the number of courses from the bottom of the flue liner to the first corbeled course.

Lay the two last courses below the flue liner as headers. Cut them so they totally support the flue liner. Make sure they don't obstruct the flue liner opening.

Both flue area and chimney height affect proper draft. Figure 15-4 gives recommended flue areas. Figure 15-12 shows how a properly-constructed smoke shelf and chimney act to control downdrafts.

Chimney Construction

A chimney's main purpose is to create a draft. Draft is caused by the difference in weight between the heated air in the chimney and the relatively cooler air outside. As the heat increases, air expands and becomes lighter. Suction draws air into the fireplace and promotes combustion.

A chimney must extend 3 feet above flat roofs. It must extend at least 2 feet above the roof ridge or any raised part of the roof within 10 feet of the chimney as shown in Figure 15-13.

Make the flue as vertical as possible with no internal obstructions. Chimney flues work best when lined with a clay flue lining. Most codes require liners. Fireclay flue lining is made of a special mixture of clays that have been thoroughly burned to withstand excessive changes in temperature.

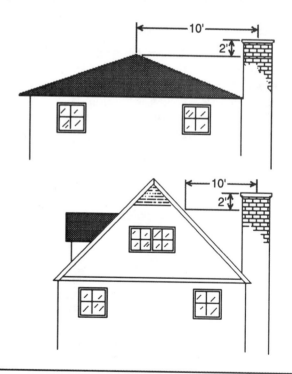

Figure 15-13
Chimney height specifications

Don't use the same flue for both a fireplace and a furnace. If more than one heating unit is connected to the same flue, the draft for each unit is reduced in half.

The size of the flue lining depends on the draft needed. As a rule, a fireplace flue lining should be $^1/_{10}$ to $^1/_{12}$ the area of the fireplace opening. For example, a fireplace opening 42 inches wide and 30 inches high has an area of 1,260 square inches. A 12-inch circular flue lining has an actual inside area of 113 square inches so it's satisfactory for the 42 x 30-inch fireplace opening.

A 13 x 13-inch flue lining (outside measurement) has a gross inside area of 127 square inches. But the effective inside area would be only 100 square inches. That's not enough. A square or oblong flue isn't effective over its entire cross-sectional area, because the column of smoke doesn't fill the corners. Gases and smoke rise with a circular swirling motion. A round flue is the most efficient because it offers less resistance to the rising column of smoke.

To prevent weathering caused by rain and changing temperatures, cap the top of the chimney with stone or concrete. Figure 15-14 shows a typical cap for a one-flue chimney. The flue lining extends above the top of the concrete cap by 2 to 4 inches. Surround the flue lining with mortar about 2 inches thick. Slope this mortar from the sides of the flue lining to the edges of the concrete.

Estimating Materials and Manhours

Figure 15-15 shows different sizes of chimneys and the number of bricks required per foot of height for each size. This table assumes a $^1/_2$-inch mortar joint. For example, assume your chimney will have two 8 x 8 and one 8 x 12 flues, and it's 22 feet high. That's the size shown on line "J" in Figure 15-15. It needs 70 bricks per foot of height, so you need 1,540 bricks (22 x 70 = 1540).

Standard-size bricks for the fireplace hearth are estimated at 6.5 bricks per square foot when laid on edge. Use 4 bricks per square foot when you lay the bricks flat. Estimate standard-size brick for the fireplace face at 6.5 bricks per square foot. Estimate fire brick (laid as stretchers) for the average-size fireplace (36 inches wide by 30 inches high) at 80 bricks.

It normally takes 5 or 6 bags of mortar to lay 1,000 bricks, and you need 3 cubic feet of sand for each bag of mortar. Allowing for waste, you need

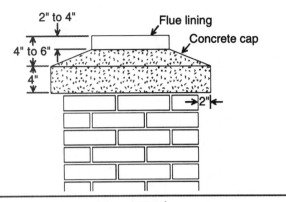

Figure 15-14
Chimney cap

about 1 cubic yard (approximately 2,250 pounds) of sand for 10 sacks of mortar.

Fireplace and chimney construction is exacting work that should be trusted only to a skilled mason. Often the mason contracts to furnish the labor, scaffolding, and tools. He will determine his cost based on the number and type of bricks, the style of fireplace and chimney, the height of the chimney, and any special work or conditions. You may furnish only the materials. The approximate manhours required are:

Per 1,000 brick	Mason	Laborer
Common brick chimneys	16	16
Common brick fireplaces	20	20
Brick veneer fireplaces	24	24
Washing (cleaning) per 100 SF	1	1

Estimate manhours for installing fireplace mantels as follows:

Work element	Unit	Manhours per unit
Prefab milled decorative unit 42" inches high, 6' feet wide	Each	3.2
Bracket-mounted hardwood beam, 10" wide, 3" thick		
6' long	Each	1.7
8' long	Each	2.0
Rough sawn oak or pine beam		
4" x 8"	LF	0.25
4" x 10"	LF	0.27
4" x 12"	LF	0.31

Time includes layout, cutting, drilling and placing shields where required, repairs and cleanup.

Sizes of chimneys and flues with their brick bonds

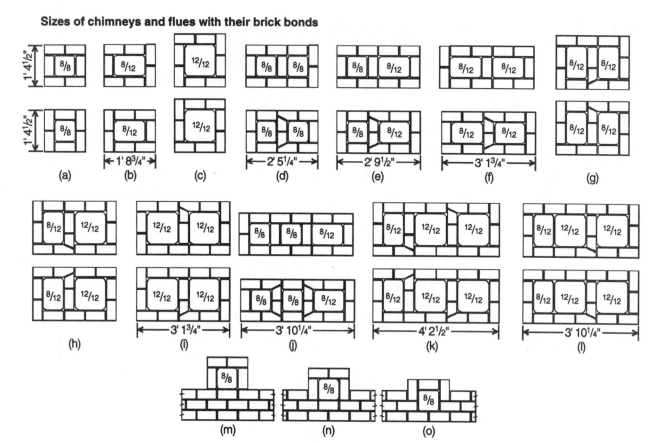

Number of brick required in chimneys per foot in height		
Size and number of flues	Number of brick	Cubic feet of mortar
(a) 1 - 8" x 8" flue	27	0.5
(b) 1 - 8" x 12" flue	31	0.5
(c) 1 - 12" x 12" flue	35	0.6
(d) 2 - 8" x 8" flue	46	0.8
(e) 1 - 8" x 8" and 1 - 8" x 12" flue	51	0.9
(f) 2 - 8" x 12" flue	55	1.1
(g) 2 - 8" x 12" flue	53	0.9
(h) 1 - 8" x 12" and 12" x 12" flue	58	1.0
(i) 2 - 12" x 12" flue	62	1.1
(j) 2 - 8" x 8" and 1 - 8" x 12" flue	70	1.2
(k) 1 - 8" x 12" and 2 - 12" x 12" flue	83	1.4
(l) 1 - 8" x 12" and 2 - 12" x 12" flue	70	1.2
(m) 1 - 8" x 8" extending 12" from face of wall	18	0.4
(n) 1 - 8" x 8" extending 8" from face of wall	9	0.3
(o) 1 - 8" x 8" extending 4" from face of wall	0	0.0

Figure 15-15
Chimney sizes and brick requirements

16

Electrical Work in Residential Additions

You won't get many add-on or conversion jobs that you can complete without doing some electrical work — usually adding circuits. But there are some things you should know before you consider doing the work yourself. The first is that you must comply with the existing codes. The second is that you must know what you're doing. Many residential fires are caused by faulty wiring which may be due to poor workmanship. Even if you hire an electrician to do the work, you still should know what the job entails and how it should be done. Here are some tips:

♦ Never work on hot wiring. Always disconnect the electricity before beginning work. Remove the fuse or trip the breaker in the main panel.

♦ Don't tighten the wire clamps on box connectors too tight. It can cause a short in the circuit. A snug fit is all that's necessary.

♦ Wrap wire nut connections with electrical tape. Wire nuts can crack and split open if you tighten them too much. Electrical tape insulates the wires if the wire nut cracks.

Most homes built today have a 150-amp or 200-amp main panel. Many older homes have 60-amp or 100-amp service which, in most cases, can't meet today's needs. A 200-amp panel is sufficient for electrical heating.

Volts, Amperes and Watts

Electricians use the terms volts, amps and watts when they talk about their work.

Voltage is like the pressure in a garden hose. An amp is the flow rate. Using the garden hose comparison, amps would be the gallons per minute. The watt is the unit which measures current usage. Let's continue

Wire size (copper)	Amps*	Watts**
No. 14	15	1800
No. 12	20	2400
No. 10	30	3600
No. 8	40	4800
No. 6	50	8400
No. 4	70	9600

*Use same size fuse or circuit breaker
**When using 120 volts

Figure 16-1
Wire capacity

Wire Size and Capacity

Figure 16-1 shows the wire sizes used in most residential electrical systems. The smaller the wire size number, the larger the diameter of the wire and the greater its capacity. Many electricians use nothing smaller than No. 12 for 15-amp circuits. They use smaller wire sizes, like No. 18 and No. 16, for low-voltage systems such as door bells, thermostats, or intercoms.

Heavy appliances such as water heaters, electric dryers, ranges, and deep-well pumps operate on 240-volt circuits. Use wire sizes No. 6, 8, and 10 for 240-volt appliance hookups. The amps rating of an appliance determines the wire size it needs. Use Figure 16-1 as a general guide.

Cable Identification Markings

Romex is a trade name for a nonmetallic (NM) sheathed cable. BX or Greenfield are trade names for flexible armored cable. Plastic-sheathed cable is a NM cable. It comes in an indoor type for indoor use, and underground type for outdoor use. Electrical cable is identified by special markings. On a cable marked 10-2 G NM:

♦ *10* is the size of the wire

♦ *2* is the number of conductor wires in the cable

♦ *G* says it has a ground wire (usually bare)

♦ *NM* says it has a nonmetallic sheath

A cable marked 10-3 G NM is No. 10 wire size with three conductor wires, ground wire, and a nonmetallic sheath.

the water hose analogy and suppose there's a small hole in the hose allowing water to leak out. This leak lowers the water pressure and rate of flow. Likewise, a current drain (wattage) in an electrical circuit affects the voltage (pressure) and amperage (rate of flow) of the electrical current. Here's how it works:

♦ 1 amp at 1 volt pressure = 1 watt

♦ 1 watt used for 1 hour = 1 watt-hour

♦ 1,000 watt-hours = 1 kilowatt

♦ volts x amps = watts

If you know the amperage and voltage for an electrical item, and want to find its wattage, multiply its voltage (in volts) by its amperage (in amps). For example, if your table saw is rated at 4.75 amps and you want to know its wattage, multiply its voltage by its amperage, or 120 volts x 4.75 amps, which equals 570 watts.

Wattage divided by voltage equals amperage. For example, an electric range uses 8,000 to 16,000 watts. But what's its amperage? Divide its wattage by its voltage (an electric range needs a 240-volt current):

8,000 watts ÷ 240 volts = 33.33 amps
16,000 watts ÷ 240 volts = 66.66 amps

So the range pulls 33.33 amps at 8,000 watts, and 66.66 amps at 16,000 watts.

Wire Color Coding

One of the most important things to remember about wiring is its color code. Without color coding we couldn't wire for electricity because we couldn't tell a hot wire from a neutral wire. Color coding helps you make sure you wire an electrical system safely. Here's the standard color code:

♦ Black wire is hot.

♦ Red wire is hot.

♦ White wire is neutral.

♦ Bare wire is grounding wire.

A 10-2 G NM has a black wire (hot), a white wire (neutral), and a ground wire (bare). A 10-3 G NM has a black wire (hot), a red wire (hot), a white wire (neutral), and a ground wire (bare). You can use the 10-2 cable for a 120-volt circuit, and the 10-3 cable for a 240-volt circuit.

Never connect a black wire to a white wire. Never connect a red wire to a white wire. Always connect a black wire to a dark or copper-colored terminal on fuse boxes, switches, and receptacles. Always connect a black wire to another black wire in lights and fixtures.

Ground a white wire, also called the continuous wire, at the main panel ground bar. Connect a white wire to a light or silver-colored terminal on all receptacles, and to the white wire on lights and fixtures.

There's an exception to the black-to-white wire rule. If the electric source (power lead) enters a light fixture and the switch is at the end of the run, you can connect a white wire to a black lead to form a switch leg or loop. In a switch loop, always paint a white wire insulation black at both ends.

A grounding (or ground) wire is normally bare. Connect it to a green grounding hex screw or to a metal box. A ground wire carries an electrical short to the ground. It protects people from shock, and electrical equipment from damage if there's lightning.

Ground-Fault Circuit Interrupters (GFCI)

A GFCI is a safety device that monitors the flow of electricity through a hot wire and a neutral wire. Normally, the same amount of electricity flows through both wires.

Here's how it works. Suppose you touch a hot wire, creating a temporary electrical path to the ground. Some of the electricity passes through your body and into the ground. When less current returns through a white wire (because a portion of it is passing through you), it results in an imbalance of electricity flowing through the hot and neutral leads. This is called a ground fault. The GFCI detects the imbalance

and cuts off the current within about 25/1000 of a second. This can prevent an electrocution.

There are three types of GFCIs. One type plugs into a grounded receptacle. Any appliance plugged into a GFCI has ground fault protection. The second type replaces a regular receptacle. The third type replaces a circuit breaker, giving ground fault protection to the complete circuit.

Guidelines for Residential Wiring

Here are seven basic guidelines to follow when you plan residential wiring:

1. Provide at least two 20-amp grounded circuits for a kitchen and laundry room, independent of lighting fixtures.

2. Allow one outlet for each 12 feet of wall space. You can put eight receptacles on a convenience circuit, unless otherwise specified by your local code.

3. Put receptacles 12 inches up from the floor.

4. Put switches 48 inches up from the floor, on the swing side (door knob side) of doors.

5. Put receptacles 8 inches above countertops and 48 inches apart. It's not a good idea to place receptacles over sinks or cooktops.

6. Provide a separate 15-amp circuit for a refrigerator.

7. Don't put receptacles or switches near bathtubs or showers. Someone standing in the tub or shower shouldn't be able to touch an electrical source.

Expanding an Electrical System

One of your most common jobs will be expanding an electrical system to accommodate an addition or conversion you've made to a house. Adding new circuits, outlets, switches and light fixtures is relatively easy when you're framing an addition or conversion. When the finish wall and ceiling are already installed, it's more complicated and difficult to expand the electrical service.

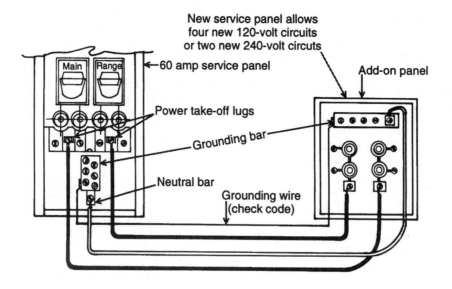

New service panel allows
four new 120-volt circuits
or two new 240-volt circuts

60 amp service panel

Add-on panel

Power take-off lugs

Grounding bar

Neutral bar

Grounding wire
(check code)

Figure 16-2
Add new circuits with an add-on panel

New Circuits

The main service panel is the household power distribution system. New circuits must begin at the service panel. Most fuse-type panels in older homes have two power take-off lugs located between the two left and the two right plug fuses. You can add more circuits by installing an add-on fuse panel or circuit breaker panel to the power take-off lugs as shown in Figure 16-2. If the panel doesn't have take-off lugs or any other hookup you can expand from, your best bet may be to replace the panel with one that has circuit breakers and a larger capacity.

Use No. 6 or larger wire to connect the panels as shown in Figure 16-2. Secure two black wires to the power take-off lugs. Attach a white wire to the neutral bar. Attach the ground wire to the grounding bar or strip. Be sure to check your local code regulations about doing this.

This hookup provides 120 volts between the black and white wires, or a 240-volt circuit between the two black wires at the add-on panel. In most of these main fuse panels, the power take-off lugs are fused at 60 amps in the main disconnect. Any take-off from the lugs must be to a fused or breaker-type box.

The Switch Leg or Loop Connection

Figure 16-3 shows a switch loop. You'll use a switch loop when the power lead enters a light fixture and the switch is at the end of the run. The two-wire cable power lead (with ground) runs from the power source to the ceiling box. The black (hot) wire loops from the ceiling box, through the switch and back to the light fixture.

The only time you would connect a black wire to a white wire is in a switch loop. The white wire is always neutral except when you use it in a loop. Then it becomes hot. Paint the white wire black at the switch and at the ceiling box. Whenever you're working on wiring and you see a white wire painted black, it's a hot wire. That's the theory, anyway. But in fact, not all electricians take the time to paint a wire. They assume that anyone who replaces a switch or goes into a ceiling box will know what they're doing and be able to tell if a white wire is hot or not. So don't assume that just because a white wire isn't painted black it's not hot.

Receptacles

Whatever the size of the remodeling work you're doing, you're sure to need lots of receptacles. You'll

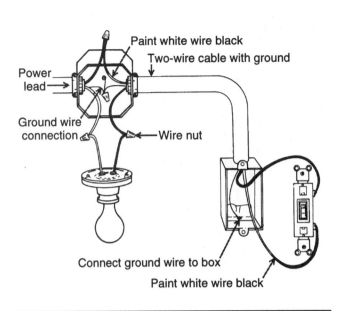

Figure 16-3
Switch loop

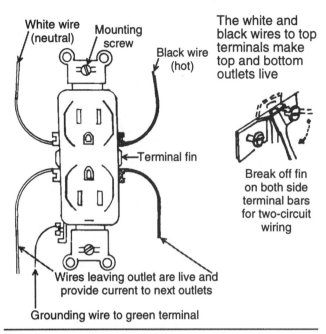

Figure 16-4
Duplex receptacle with single-circuit wiring

use 15-amp, 125-volt duplex outlets with grounding hex screws in most residential wiring. The outlets have two 6/32 threaded screws you use to fasten them to a wall box.

Normally, you can have eight receptacles on one general purpose circuit. These circuits supply power to all the lights and outlets in a home except for the kitchen, dining area, and laundry or utility rooms. Always check your code for restrictions on kitchen and appliance circuits. Mechanical equipment may also have special requirements.

Use only ground receptacles when you're adding outlets. Put wall outlets 12 inches from the floor and no more than 12 feet apart. Over counter space, put outlets no more than 4 feet apart and at least 8 inches above the countertop. Don't install outlets above a sink or stovetop surface.

The Split-Circuit Outlets

The Leviton receptacle, No. 264B, has push-in terminals and side-wired terminals with a break-off fin for two-circuit wiring. Break off the terminal fin at the dark terminals by prying downward with a screwdriv-

er. This interrupts the connection between the side terminals, letting you wire the duplex outlet to two separate circuits. You can have the top outlet on one circuit, and the bottom outlet to another. See Figure 16-4.

Figure 16-5 shows how to wire a split-circuit outlet. Notice that there's a switch loop and that the white wire is painted black, both at the switch and the outlet. The single-pole switch controls the top half of the outlet. The bottom half is always hot.

Adding a Switch and Light Fixture to an Existing Outlet

To add a switch and light fixture to an existing outlet:

1. Cut an opening for a wall box at the new switch location.

2. Put the switch 48 inches up from the floor on the swing side of the door.

3. Fish or snake a two-wire cable, with a ground from the outlet box, to the new switch box.

4. Extend the cable about 8 inches out of the box so there's enough cable to make the connections.

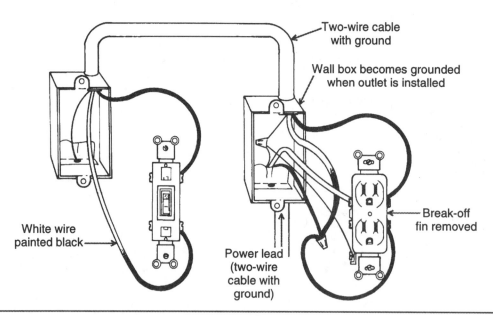

Figure 16-5
Wiring a split-circuit outlet

5. From the attic, drill a ³/₄-inch hole in the top plate and run a cable down to the switch location. See Figure 16-6.

6. Pull the other end of the cable to the light fixture location in the ceiling or wall.

7. Connect the wiring as shown in Figure 16-7.

Adding a Receptacle to an Existing Outlet

The duplex outlet is the one most commonly used in residential wiring. In a finish wall installation, you can use an existing outlet in an adjacent room to provide electricity to an add-on outlet. You can install the new outlet back-to-back with the old, or space them a stud apart.

First, cut an opening in the finish wall for the new outlet box. If possible, put the new outlet on the inside of the stud facing the existing outlet so you don't have to drill a hole in the stud for the cable. See Figure 16-8. Fish the cable from the existing outlet to the add-on. Figure 16-9 shows how to make the wiring connections.

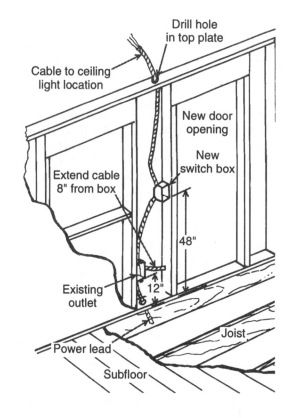

Figure 16-6
Adding a switch and light from an existing outlet

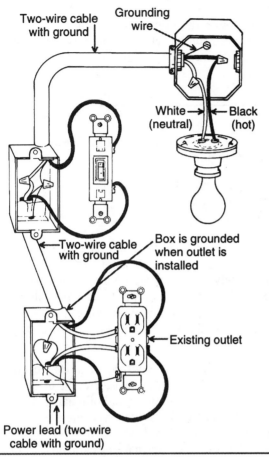

Figure 16-7
Wiring the switch and light to an existing outlet

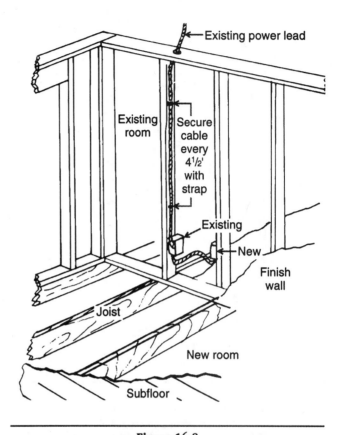

Figure 16-8
Adding a receptacle from an existing outlet in adjacent room

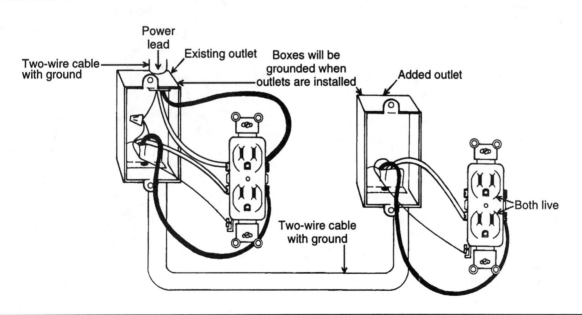

Figure 16-9
Wiring a new receptacle to an existing outlet

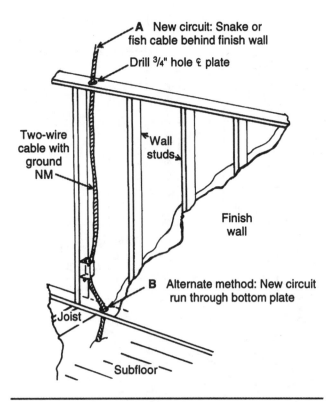

Figure 16-10
Adding a receptacle by running a new cable
through top or bottom plate

Adding a Receptacle on a New Circuit

Sometimes you'll have to add a receptacle to a new circuit instead of using an existing outlet. To do this, run the cable from a junction box or main panel through the top plate, as shown in A in Figure 16-10. Or, alternately through the bottom plate as shown in Figure 16-10 B. Drill a ³/₄-inch hole in the center of the plate between studs and fish the wire into the add-on box.

New Fixtures

In add-on and conversion work, all sorts of possibilities creep up where you can save time and money by simply looking around and finding the most efficient way to do something. Sometimes this'll be a shortcut you can take to simplify an otherwise drawn-out or complicated task. For example, you can take current from an existing ceiling box or light fixture and add new wiring for a receptacle or fixture. Run the wiring direct or through a switch. Figure 16-11 shows

how to make the connections. Figure 16-12 shows how you can run current from an existing fixture to an add-on fixture and have them controlled by a common switch.

New Switches

Three common types of residential switches shown in Figure 16-13 are:

- Single-pole switch
- Three-way switch
- Four-way switch

A single-pole switch controls a receptacle or light from one convenient location. Usually you put it immediately inside a room on the swing side of a door. The switch has two brass-colored terminals (screws), and on and off positions marked on the lever. Figure 16-12 shows the wiring connection for a single-pole switch.

Use a three-way switch, in pairs, to control a receptacle or light from two different locations. Use this type of switch at either end of a hall or the top and bottom of stairs. The switch has three terminals: one black or copper-colored, and two brass or silver-colored. The lever has no markings for on and off positions.

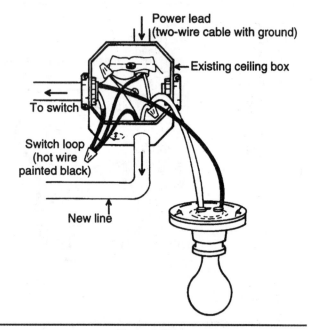

Figure 16-11
Taking off new wiring from existing ceiling box

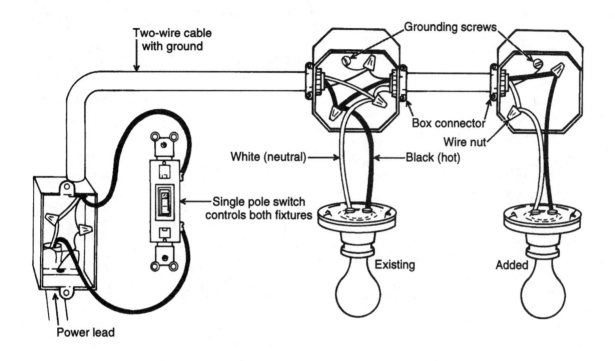

Two-wire cable with ground

Grounding screws

Box connector

Wire nut

White (neutral)

Black (hot)

Single pole switch controls both fixtures

Existing

Added

Power lead

Figure 16-12
Adding a light fixture to an existing fixture

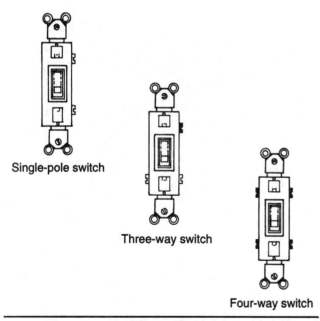

Single-pole switch

Three-way switch

Four-way switch

Figure 16-13
Three types of switches

Connecting three-way switches can be confusing if you don't have a diagram to follow. Figure 16-14 A shows how to connect switches which control a single light fixture with the power first going through the switches. When wiring three-way switches, connect the black wire to the dark-colored terminal. It's the common terminal for the hot line.

Figure 16-14 B shows how to install two lights at the end of three-way switches with the power lead first going through the switches. Both switches in Figure 16-14 are connected the same way.

Figure 16-15 A shows how to make the wiring connections for three-way switches located at the end of the circuit. Here the power lead enters the light fixture first. Figure 16-15 B shows a three-way switch at the end of the circuit controlling two lights, when the power lead first enters the light fixtures.

Figure 16-16 shows a light fixture installed between three-way switches with the power lead first entering the fixture.

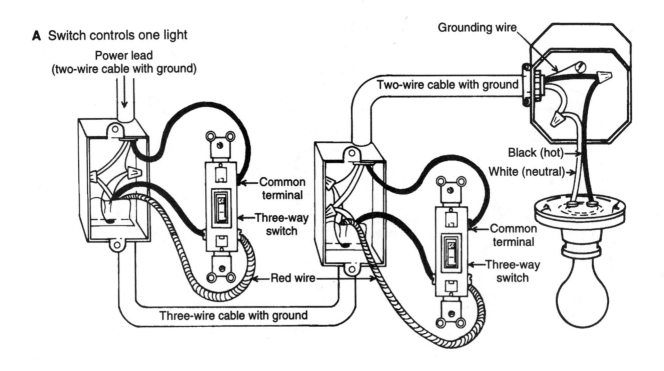

A Switch controls one light

Power lead
(two-wire cable with ground)

Grounding wire

Two-wire cable with ground

Common terminal

Three-way switch

Black (hot)

White (neutral)

Common terminal

Three-way switch

Red wire

Three-wire cable with ground

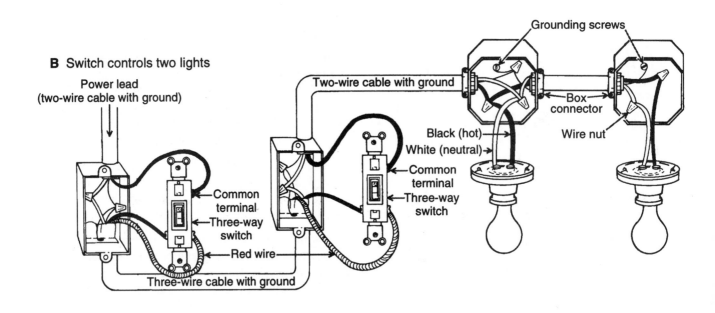

B Switch controls two lights

Power lead
(two-wire cable with ground)

Grounding screws

Two-wire cable with ground

Box connector

Black (hot)

White (neutral)

Wire nut

Common terminal

Three-way switch

Common terminal

Three-way switch

Red wire

Three-wire cable with ground

Figure 16-14
Three-way switches controlling lights — current first entering switches

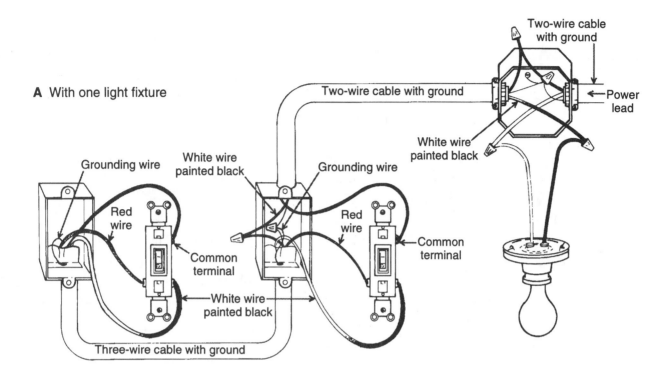

A With one light fixture

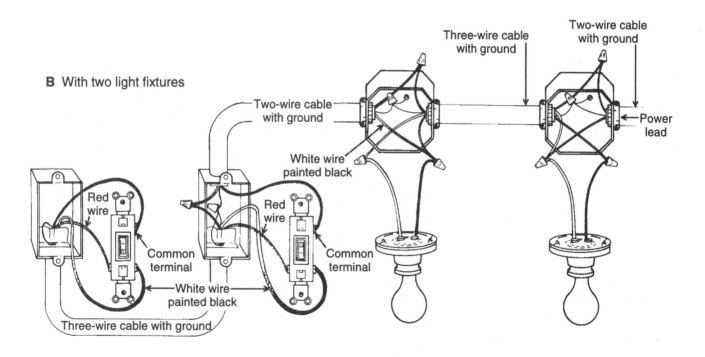

B With two light fixtures

Figure 16-15
Installing three-way switches at the end of the circuit

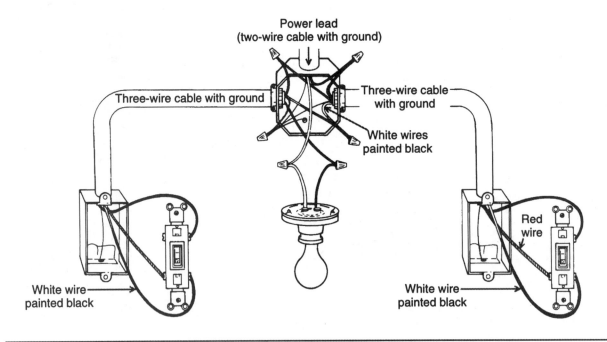

Figure 16-16
Fixture installed between three-way switches — current first enters light fixture

A four-way switch works with three-way switches to control receptacles or lights from three or more locations. The switch has four brass-colored terminals. The lever has no on/off markings. Make connections for each of the four-way switches you install, using the diagram in Figure 16-17.

Other Switch Connections

There are several ways to make connections with a single-pole switch. Figure 16-18 shows how to wire a switch to control two lights where the power lead enters the fixtures before it goes to the switch. The connection is similar to the one shown in Figure 16-15 B, except that it has only one switch.

Figure 16-19 A shows how to wire a single-pole switch to a light and outlet where the current comes into the switch first. The outlet is always hot in this type of connection.

Figure 16-19 B shows how to wire a single-pole switch, outlet, and light with the current first entering the light fixture. The outlet is always hot. Figure 16-20 shows a switch-controlled outlet where the current enters the outlet wall box before the switch.

Wiring with Plastic Boxes

When using plastic wall boxes, secure the NM cable to the framing within 8 inches of the box. If this isn't practical, use a box with built-in cable clamps. You can't ground a plastic box, so you have to wire them a little differently than metal boxes. Figure 16-21 shows how to wire an outlet at the end of a circuit run. The ground wire is attached to the grounding screw of the outlet.

When the outlet is within the run of a circuit — in the middle, for example — join the ground wires with a jumper, as shown in Figure 16-22.

Switches, as we have seen, do not have grounding terminals. If the switch is located within the circuit, as in Figure 16-23, tie the ground wires together.

Manhours for Electrical Wiring

Figure 16-24 gives a breakdown of estimated manhour figures for installing electrical wiring in new and finished construction.

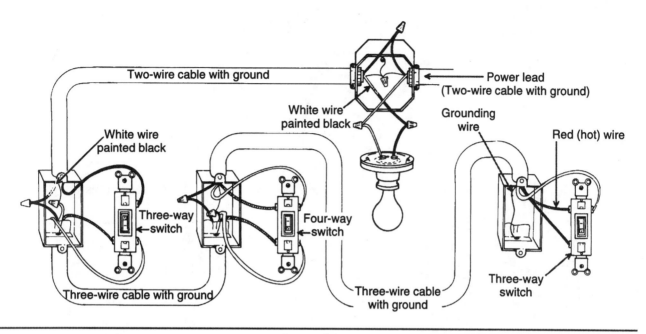

Figure 16-17
Connections using four-way switch — current first enters light fixture

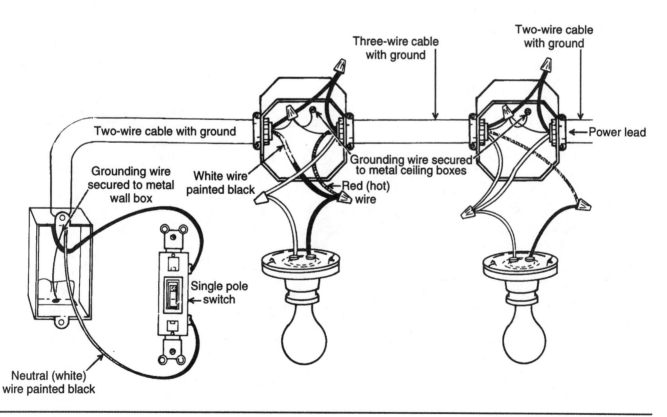

Figure 16-18
Connections with power lead first entering light fixture

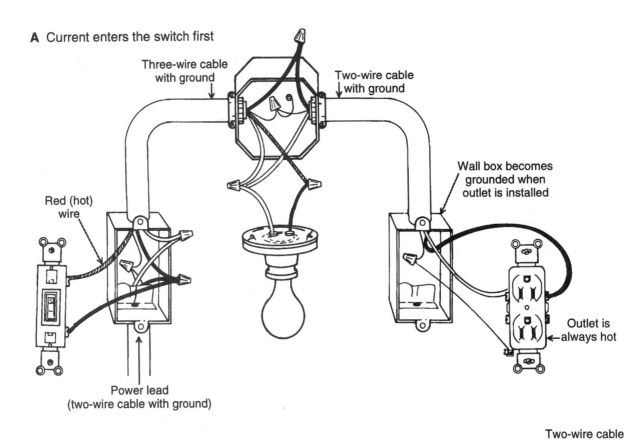

A Current enters the switch first

Three-wire cable
with ground

Two-wire cable
with ground

Wall box becomes
grounded when
outlet is installed

Red (hot)
wire

Outlet is
always hot

Power lead
(two-wire cable with ground)

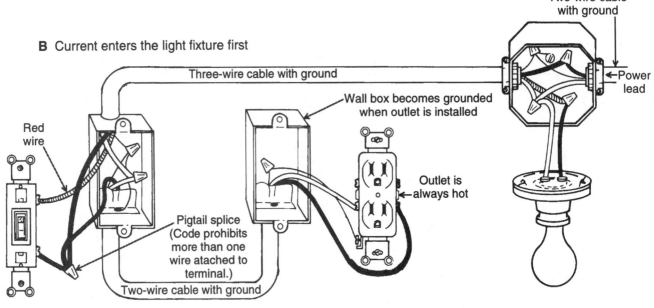

Two-wire cable
with ground

B Current enters the light fixture first

Three-wire cable with ground

Wall box becomes grounded
when outlet is installed

Power
lead

Red
wire

Outlet is
always hot

Pigtail splice
(Code prohibits
more than one
wire atached to
terminal.)

Two-wire cable with ground

Figure 16-19
Wiring a single-pole switch to a light and outlet

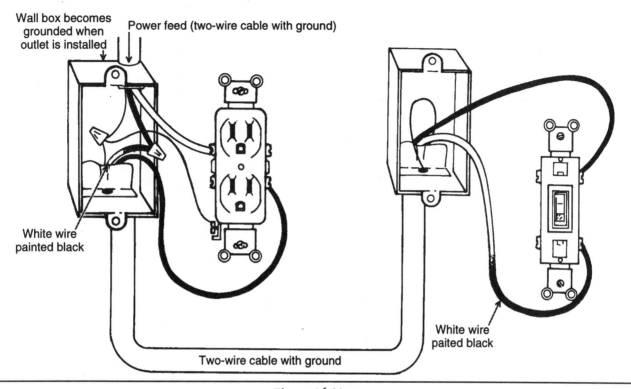

Wall box becomes grounded when outlet is installed

Power feed (two-wire cable with ground)

White wire painted black

White wire paited black

Two-wire cable with ground

Figure 16-20
Switch-controlled outlet with current entering the outlet before the switch

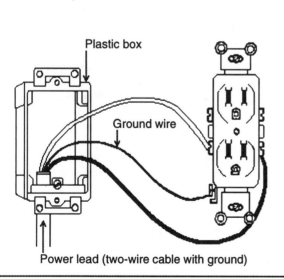

Plastic box

Ground wire

Power lead (two-wire cable with ground)

Figure 16-21
Wiring diagram — end of circuit outlet

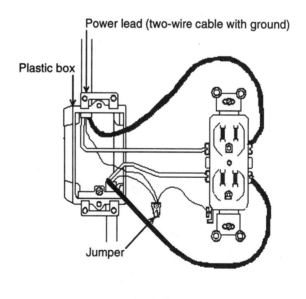

Power lead (two-wire cable with ground)

Plastic box

Jumper

Figure 16-22
Wiring diagram — within run of circuit

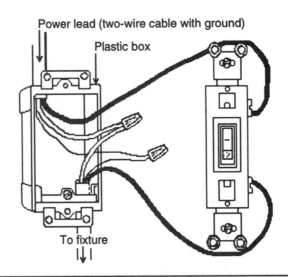

Figure 16-23
Wiring diagram — switch within circuit

Work element	Unit	Manhours	
		Finish construction	New construction
Add 60-amp panel from power take-off lug	1	8.0	5.0
Run electrical circuit (nonmetallic sheathed cable) with attic and crawl space access	50 LF	2.5	1.5
Install duplex wall outlet and cable in wall from existing outlet	each	2.5	1.0
Intall 4" octagon ceiling box and cable in ceiling from junction box (attic access)	each	2.0	1.0
Install wall box, switch and cable in wall from existing ceiling box (attic access)	each	3.0	1.5
Install flush mounted ceiling light fixture	each	1.0	0.7
Install wall-mounted light fixture	each	0.7	0.7
Three-way switch hook-up	pair	1.0	0.5
Four-way switch hook-up with pair of three-way switches	set	1.5	0.7

Figure 16-24
Manhours for electrical wiring

17

Finishing With Paint and Wallpaper

Paint, on both the interior or exterior of a home, is usually the least expensive way to finish and protect a house. And when you add a room to a house, the homeowner will often want the entire house repainted. This can be an added bonus for your profit margin.

How to Use Color and Texture

Most of your clients will have their own ideas about what paint colors they prefer. But if you're asked for suggestions, here are some guidelines you can use. Light from the south and west is warm and bright so rooms facing these directions will need cool colors such as green, blue, violet, and gray. Northern light is cold, and eastern light is harsh. Rooms facing either of these directions will look their best if you use warm colors — red, orange, brown, and yellow.

Walls are usually the largest area you'll paint so the color you use on them will dominate the color scheme. Carpeting, draperies, and upholstery should complement or blend with each other and the walls.

If you don't have an eye for color and texture, don't feel bad about it. A lot of remodelers don't, myself included. What you can do, however, is consult others who do. Paint stores, building material suppliers, and appliance manufacturers have people who will gladly advise you.

It's also a good idea to give some thought to paint texture. For example, use a high-quality latex, flat finish paint for a formal setting. Latex dries fast, has little odor, and you can clean it up with water. An eggshell finish works well in any setting. It is especially suitable for deep accent color and for high traffic areas. A high-gloss finish gives what's called the wet look. Use this in a contemporary room where a homeowner wants a pronounced effect. Gloss enamel finish washes well, which makes it a practical finish for trim, cabinets, doors, and play rooms. You can also use semi-gloss or gloss latex paint in kitchens and bathrooms to make the surfaces washable.

Textured exterior paints are available in three finishes: sand, rough, and stucco. A textured finish is ideal for a Mediterranean or Early American look.

Color and the House Site

The house and its setting should blend. This doesn't mean that a house on wooded property has to be green. There are many subtle tones in wooded areas. The beiges, browns, grays, and golds of bark, rock formations, and undergrowth offer many color selection possibilities.

A green house will appear greener when surrounded by shrubs and grass. The contrast between color and surroundings should be just enough to retain house definition and color.

Lighter shades give an impression of height, while darker shades minimize size. For a two- or three-level house, you might suggest painting the top level darker than the bottom so it doesn't look too tall for its width. If you use several colors, keep the colors in the same color family.

Creating Space and Mood with Color

A small room will look larger if its walls, ceiling, and woodwork are all the same color. A pale, bright color works best. The feeling of spaciousness is created by eliminating breaks in the flow of color at corners and ceiling lines. You can create a feeling of more space and continuity between rooms by using similar colors. This also applies to smaller houses. The total living space will appear larger if all rooms are done in coordinated colors.

You can make a square room more interesting by painting one wall a dramatic, contrasting color — usually the wall directly opposite the entrance to the room. Choose a color based on the dominant color in the furnishings — carpet, draperies, or upholstery. Square up a long, narrow room by painting the two end walls a deeper color. A room that's too large will seem better proportioned and more inviting if you paint it in darker shades. Lower a ceiling by painting it a color slightly darker than the adjacent walls.

Colors create moods. For example, a game room in a basement done in gay, cheerful colors will promote a happy outlook for activities in the room. Here's what the experts say about the moods created by some colors:

- Yellows and lime — bright and sunny
- Gold and bronze — rich and friendly
- Olive tones — somber and quiet
- Greens — cheerful and open
- Gray greens, aquas, and jades — calm and serene
- Pinks and reds — lively and aggressive
- Purples and violet blues — sophisticated and daring
- Blues and turquoises — refreshing and tranquil
- Oranges and peaches — active and inviting
- Spice tones — advancing and bold
- Camels, beiges, and taupes — subtle and elegant
- Earth tones — warm and cozy
- Grays, charcoals, and neutrals — cool and receding

Paint Properties

Most paints are based on a binder which is either dissolved in a solvent or emulsified in water. There are several solutions of such binders in a solvent:

- Clear finishes
- Varnishes (if they dry by oxidation)
- Lacquers (if they dry by evaporation)
- Paints (if opaque pigments of colors are dispersed in the binder)

It's the binders used in a paint that determine the way the paint performs. Figure 17-1 lists the important properties of the most common paint binders. There are a few more combinations that aren't listed in the table:

- Oil-alkyd — properties similar to oil and alkyd paints
- Cleoresinous — similar to alkyds but with less color retention
- Phenolic-alkyd — similar to phenolic and alkyd paints

	Alkyd	Cement	Epoxy	Latex	Oil	Phenolic	Rubber	Moistrue curing urethane	Vinyl
Ready for use	Yes	No	No³	Yes	Yes	Yes	Yes	Yes	Yes
Brushability	A	A	A	+	+	A	A	A	−
Odor	+¹	+	−	+	A	A	A	−	−
Cure normal temp.	A	A	A	+	−	A	+	+	+
Cure low temp.	A	A	−	−	−	A	+	+	+
Film build/coat	A	+	+	A	+	A	A	+	−
Safety	A	+	−	+	A	A	A	−	−
Use on wood	A	−	A	A	A	A	−	A	−
Use on fresh conc.	−	+	+	+	−	−	+	A	+
Use on metal	+	−	+	−	+	+	A	A	+
Corrosive service	A	−	+	−	−	A	A	A	+
Gloss - choice	+	−	+	−	A	+	+	A	A
Gloss - retention	+	X	−	X	−	+	A	A	+
Color - initial	+	A	A	+	A	−	+	+	+
Color - retention	+	−	A	+	A	−	A	−	+
Hardness	A	+	+	A	−	+	+	+	A
Adhesion	A	−	+	A	+	A	A	+	−
Flexibility	A	−	+	+	+	A	A	+	+
Resistance to:									
Abrasion	A	A	+	A	−	+	A	+	+
Water	A	A	A	A	A	+	+	+	+
Acid	A	−	A	A	−	+	+	+	+
Alkali	A	+	+	A	−	A	+	+	+
Strong solvent	−	+	+	A	−	A	−	+	A
Heat	A	A	A	A	A	A	+²	A	−
Moisture permeability	Moderate	Very High	Low	High	Moderate	Low	Low	Low	Low

A = Average
X = Not applicable
+ = Among the best for this property
− = Among the poorest for this property

¹ Odorless type
² Special types
³ Two component type

Figure 17-1
Comparison of paint binders' principal properties

♦ Oil-modified urethane — similar to phenolic and alkyd paints

♦ Vinyl-alkyd — similar to vinyl and alkyd paints

The pigment concentration of paint determines whether it has a high gloss, a semi-gloss, or a lusterless (flat) finish. There are special pigments in primers, such as zinc chromate, to make them corrosion-resistant. Metallic pigment is added to varnishes to make metallic coatings such as aluminum paints.

Figure 17-2 is a quick guide for selecting exterior paints.

Painting Tips for Exterior Painting

Clean off dust and dirt with a sturdy cloth or stiff brush. If there's a nail sticking out, drive it below the surface of the wood with a nail set. Then spot prime the area. When it's dry, fill the hole with putty. Seal any knots or pitch spots with an appropriate knot sealer to avoid brown spots coming to the surface of the paint.

Look for scaling, flaking paint. Where old paint is damaged, scrape down to a sound surface with a broad

	Aluminum	Cement base paint	Exterior clear finish	House paint	Metal roof paint	Porch-and-deck paint	Primer or undercoater	Rubber base paint	Spar varnish	Transparent sealer	Trim-and-trellis paint	Wood stain	Metal primer
Wood													
Natural finish	-	-	P	-	-	-	-	-	-	P	-	P	-
Porch floor	-	-	-	-	-	P	-	-	-	-	-	-	-
Shingle roof	-	-	-	-	-	-	-	-	-	-	-	-	-
Shutters and trim	-	-	-	P+	-	-	P	-	-	-	P+	-	-
Siding	P	-	-	P+	-	-	P	-	-	-	-	-	-
Windows	P	-	-	P+	-	-	P	-	-	-	P+	-	-
Masonry													
Asbestos cement	-	-	-	P+	-	-	-	P	-	P	-	-	-
Brick	P	P	-	P+	-	-	-	P	-	P	-	-	-
Cement & Cinder block	P	P	-	P+	-	-	-	P	-	P	-	-	-
Cement porch floor	-	-	-	-	-	P	-	P	-	-	-	-	-
Stucco	P	P	-	P+	-	-	-	P	-	P	-	-	-
Metal													
Copper	-	-	-	-	-	-	-	-	P	-	-	-	-
Galvanized	P+	-	-	P+	-	-	-	P	P	-	P+	-	P
Iron	P+	-	-	P+	-	-	-	-	-	-	P+	-	P
Roofing	-	-	-	-	P+	-	-	-	-	-	-	-	P
Siding	P+	-	-	P+	-	-	-	-	-	-	P+	-	P
Windows, aluminium	P	-	-	P+	-	-	-	-	-	-	P+	-	P
Windows, steel	P+	-	-	P+	-	-	-	-	-	-	P+	-	P

"P" indicates preferred coating for this surface "P+" indicates that a primer or sealer may be necessary before the finishing coat or coats (unless the surface has been previously finished).

Figure 17-2
Exterior paint selection chart

knife and wire brush. Smooth all rough areas with sandpaper. Remove rust and peeling paint by scraping or wire brushing. If there's no problem with water supply, you can wash protected areas — under the eaves, for example — with water. A strong stream from a garden hose does a good job. Apply primer when the surface is dry. If the old paint on a house is seriously deteriorated, pressure-wash it off. When the surface is thoroughly dry, apply a primer coat, and then paint.

To prevent drips and spatters from spoiling areas you've already painted, work from the top down. Paint the gutters and eaves first if they're the same color as the siding.

Work from side to side. It doesn't matter whether you work from right to left, or left to right, but try to minimize lapping. Paint across as far as you can comfortably reach (instead of painting from top to bottom) before you move the ladder.

When using a roller, pour a small amount of paint into the well of the roller tray. Work paint into the roller by rolling it in the paint in the tray. Be sure the entire roller surface is covered. Remove excess paint by rolling the roller over the ribbed portion of the tray. Apply paint in light even strokes, rolling first in one direction, then covering the same area again in the other direction.

When using a brush, coat under the edges of clapboard. Feather the ends of your brush strokes to blend one painted area to another. Don't bear down too hard on the brush.

All new wood surfaces must be dry, free of grease, mildew, mortar, and asphalt spatters. It helps to rough the surface with a stiff brush to remove loose fibers and splinters. Use a sealer to seal knots and sappy spots. Sand rough surfaces until they're smooth. Putty nail holes and cracks. Caulk window and door trim joints after you prime the surfaces. Before you stain any new wood, be sure the surface is dry and free of foreign matter.

You almost always need a primer coat on wood that's never been painted. Apply two finish coats over the primer for adequate coverage.

Finally, paint the trim and shutters, if there are any. If you can remove the shutters, take them off and paint them separately. Replace them when you complete the rest of the job.

Painting Interior Walls and Ceilings

Make sure the joint compound is thoroughly dry and that all the sanding dust is removed from drywall before you start painting. Repair damaged or defective joints with joint compound. Coat steel corner beading with sealer before applying water-thinned coatings. One coat of sealer and one finish coat is usually enough on drywall. Add a second coat if the finish is blotchy or uneven.

Before repainting plaster or drywall, remove any peeling or scaling paint. Sand these areas to feather the edges. Fill and sand cracks, holes, and blemishes so they're flush. Then spot-prime them to control residual bleeding. Wash greasy walls and ceilings with a strong detergent solution. Sand glossy areas until they're dull. Use primer to seal any ceiling with water stains. Use low-chalking paint on masonry to avoid streaks and stains.

When applying paint, start where the ceiling meets a wall in a corner of a room. Cut in a strip about 4 inches wide along both the ceiling and the wall beneath it. Then, with a roller, paint the rest of the ceiling, starting near the corner. Blend the new paint into the ceiling line you cut in. Paint across the width rather than the length of the ceiling — and don't stop until the ceiling is completely covered.

Next, cut in along the baseboard and around the door and window trim. After you've finished cutting in the rest of the room, paint one wall at a time, starting at an upper corner. Using the roller and slow, even strokes to minimize spattering, coat the wall. Paint the remaining walls the same way.

Painting Windows and Doors

Double-Hung Windows

When painting double-hung windows, first remove the sash lock. Lower the upper part of the sash and raise the bottom sash out of the way. Coat the window sash, then the rails. Don't paint the sash tracks. That would make the window stick. Return the upper sash to a near-closed position, lower the bottom section and paint it the same way. To complete the window, coat the check rails, frame, and sill. The best tool for this work is a 2- or $2\frac{1}{2}$-inch angular sash brush. You can also use it for flat trim work. Leave upper and lower sash slightly open until the paint has dried completely. When it's dry, use a razor blade to remove any paint smears or spatters from the glass.

Painting the Trim and Doors

For interior wood surfaces, you can paint, stain, or leave them with a natural finish. Use a fill material to keep the wood grain from rising. If you're painting or staining the trim, apply three coats of paint or stain (including primer coat). Lightly sand with the grain between coats.

Before you begin painting a door, remove all the door hardware. Open the door and place a block of wood on the floor between the door and its casing to brace it open. If the door is paneled, paint the panels first. Then paint the horizontal sections and finally, the vertical sections.

Begin at the top of flush doors and continue down until the door is completely covered. Keep the brush fully loaded and work rapidly, always brushing into

Work element	Unit	Manhours per unit
Brush painting, per coat		
Wood flat work	1000 SF	8.5
Doors and windows, area of opening	1000 SF	9.0
Trim	1000 SF	8.0
Plaster, sand finish	1000 SF	7.0
Plaster, smooth finish	1000 SF	6.0
Wallboard	1000 SF	5.5
Metal	1000 SF	8.5
Masonry	1000 SF	7.0
Varnish flat work	1000 SF	8.5
Enamel flat work	1000 SF	6.5
Enamel trim	1000 SF	8.0
Roller painting, per coat		
Wood flat work	1000 SF	6.0
Doors	1000 SF	8.5
Plaster, sand finish	1000 SF	2.5
Plaster, smooth finish	1000 SF	3.0
Wallboard	1000 SF	3.0
Metal	1000 SF	5.5
Masonry	1000 SF	3.0
Spray painting, per coat		
Wood flat work	1000 SF	2.0
Doors	1000 SF	3.0
Plaster, wallboard	1000 SF	2.5
Metal	1000 SF	3.5

The painting of interior surfaces includes minimum surface preparation, mixing paint materials, and application of paint to surface.

Figure 17-3
Labor for interior painting

the wet areas. Coat the door edges. Use a rag to stop paint that might run onto the other side of the door.

Apply two coats of paint or sealer to all exterior wood doors and wood windows. Paint the top and bottom edges of doors.

A good painter only uses trim brushes for the closest work. For other work, turn a large brush sideways and paint a neat trim line. Using the edge of a sash brush, carefully coat the edge of the window trim nearest the wall. Then paint the face of the trim. Coat door trim the same way. Extend the color over the door casing to include the door stop.

Usually you finish painting a room by painting the baseboards and molding. To protect the floor covering as you paint the baseboards, use a metal trim guard or rigid piece of cardboard. Wipe the paint from the trim

guard before you move it to the next location. If any excess paint ran between the trim guard and the molding, run a dry brush over the baseboard a few times to remove it. Use a rag dampened with an appropriate solvent — either water or mineral spirits — to immediately remove any paint that falls on the floor covering.

Estimating Manhours and Materials for Interior and Exterior Painting

Figures 17-3 and 17-4 give typical manhour figures for interior and exterior painting under normal conditions. Use Figure 17-5 as a guide for typical manhour figures for painting millwork. This is just a basic guide, since painting wood trim is subject to many variables. Location, height, surface conditions,

Work element	Unit	Manhours per unit
Brush paint, per coat		
Wood siding	1000 SF	7.5
Wood doors and windows, area of opening	1000 SF	9.5
Trim	1000 SF	8.5
Steel sash, area of opening	1000 SF	5.0
Flat metal	1000 SF	7.0
Metal roofing and siding	1000 SF	7.5
Masonry	1000 SF	7.5
Roller painting, per coat		
Masonry	1000 SF	5.5
Flat metal	1000 SF	4.5
Doors	1000 SF	7.0
Spray painting, per coat		
Wood siding	1000 SF	4.0
Doors	1000 SF	5.0
Masonry	1000 SF	6.0
Flat metal	1000 SF	5.0
Metal roofing and siding	1000 SF	6.0
Clean and spray waterproofing on masonry	1000 SF	10.0

Surface preparation for exterior painting includes removing dust with brush or cloth, removing oil and grease, masking and taping adjacent surfaces, and removing masking and taping. Sometimes it is necessary to lightly sand between coats or size and fill porous materials before painting, all of which is surface preparation.

Figure 17-4
Labor for exterior painting

Work element	Unit	Manhours per unit
Exterior wood trim, 3 coats	100 LF	1.7
Interior wood trim, 3 coats	100 LF	1.7
Kitchen cabinets, 3 coats	100 SF	2.7
Wood casework, 3 coats	100 SF	2.7
Metal casework, 2 coats	100 SF	1.7
Wardrobes, 3 coats	100 SF	2.7
Bookcases, 3 coats	100 SF	2.7

Time includes move on and off site, setup, surface preparation, masking and taping, light sanding between coats, remove masking and tape, cleanup and touchup as required. These figures will apply on most jobs.

Figure 17-5
Labor painting millwork

the amount of masking and covering, and other factors all affect how much time a job takes.

Figure 17-6 shows how to figure the paint for an add-on or an entire house.

Hanging Wallpaper

Wallpaper is a popular wall covering, often used in room additions and in attic conversion rooms, which has almost unlimited decorative possibilities. Always install wallpaper on a smooth wall. First drive any nails in the wall flush with the wall surface.

Installation procedures vary with the type of paper. Most manufacturers provide hanging instructions with their wallpapers.

To calculate the amount of paint needed, you must first determine the number of square feet of surface to be painted. The following steps provide a simple formula for determining square footage:

1. Figure the general area to be painted.
A simple formula for an entire house would be:
- A. (Length of house + width of house) x 2 = total distance around house.
- B. Distance around house x height of house = total sidewall area.
- C. (½ gable height x width of gable base) x 2 = total gable area.
- D. Total sidewall area + total gable area = total surface to be painted.

Note: You don't need to subtract window and door areas from the total surface figure if each opening is less than 100 SF.

Example:
- A. (50' + 42') x 2 = 184'
- B. 184' x 14' = 2,576 SF

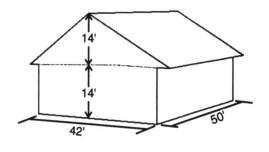

- C. ½ (14') x 42' x 2 = 588 SF
- D. 2,576 SF + 588 SF = 3,164 SF

2. Figure special areas:
These simple formulas will help you estimate paint requirements for the following special areas. Add the figures you get for each area together for the total square footage.

Balustrades
Measure the front area and multiply by 4.

Stairs
Count the risers and multiply by 8.

Lattice Work
Measure the front area and multiply by 2.

Porches
Multiply the length by the width.

Cornices
Measure the front area and multiply by 2.

Eaves
Measure the areas and multiply by 2.

Gutters & Downspouts
Measure the front area and multiply by 2.

Eaves with Rafters
Measure the area and multiply by 3.

3. Total surface figures to determine gallons of paint required.
To do this, divide the total surface area by the spreading rate (coverage rate) of a gallon of the paint of your choice. Spreading rates are usually included on the direction panel. Figure primer and finish coat needs separately.

Figure 17-6
How to calculate area and paint needed

Making a Business Plan

The hammer, saw, square, and pickup are common tools of the construction industry. You need them to get the work done. But running a successful business takes a lot more than a hammer, a saw, an old pickup truck and a contractor's license. The key tool you need to run your business is *management*. Every job must be planned and organized if your company (even if there's only you and one or two employees) is going to run smoothly and efficiently. That's the goal of management — and the reason for planning.

If you bought this book and stayed with me this far, it's probably because you have more than a passing interest in doing room additions and conversion work. But no matter what motivates you to start your own business, your bottom line is to earn money. That doesn't mean that now and then you won't lose your expected profit on a job. I don't know of a builder, including myself, who hasn't lost at one time or another.

What's the most important thing you can do to protect yourself against loss? Here's my answer to that crucial question: *documentation*. Make a written record of everything — inspections, estimates of materials and manhours, and the actual materials used and manhours spent on the project. Of course, a good written contract or agreement between you and your clients is essential.

But what about experience, you might say. Isn't that important, too? Of course, experience and know-how in the building trades is helpful. A skilled carpenter can look at a stud wall and know if it's properly constructed. He can take a set of plans and build the sturdy, professional project. A plumber or electrician can spot poor workmanship or improperly installed wiring or pipes a block away. If you have skills in the building trades, you're ahead of the game if you start your own business.

But there are people who run successful building companies without being skilled in any of the trades. They hire the necessary skills. And they know what constitutes professional performance when it comes to remodeling or building a home.

Most of us go into business for ourselves after we gain experience on somebody else's payroll. Or we start out by doing a few repairs or construction jobs on our own homes. Many of us prefer to stay small, keeping personally involved in all phases of the construction process. We get the jobs, sign the contracts, and drive the nails. We take our hourly pay, and hopefully, earn a decent profit from the business.

So if experience isn't the second most important factor in making your new company a success, what is? Well, it goes along with number one, documentation: a written business plan that defines your goals and how you plan to go about achieving them.

From a builder's standpoint, count on this: the only thing that happens without a plan is an accident. A good business plan can be your pathway to profit. To help you make a business plan, you'll need to answer some questions like these:

♦ What business am I in?

♦ What do I sell?

♦ Where is my market?

♦ Who will buy?

♦ Who is my competition?

♦ What's my sales strategy?

♦ How much money do I need to operate my firm?

♦ How will I get the work done?

♦ What management controls do I need?

♦ How will I carry them out?

♦ When should I revise my plan?

♦ Where can I go for help?

No one can answer these questions for you. As the owner-manager, you have to answer them yourself, before you draw up your business plan. If you do it right, your plan will follow a logical progression, from the starting point to reaching your goal.

When it's complete, your business plan will be your roadmap. It will guide your daily business activities. When you know where you want to go, it's easier to plan what you have to do to get there. Your business plan can also tell anyone who needs to know — key employees, suppliers and bankers — about your goals and your operations.

It'll also point out some of the strengths you can draw on and some of the personal weaknesses that may be a handicap. Knowing the things you do well and the things you need help with will make you a better, more successful contractor. For example, suppose you don't know much about law or accounting. Then you realize you have to get professional help when legal and accounting issues come up.

Creating Your Business Plan

All you need to create a plan like this is common sense and a little help. You provide the common sense and I'll be your helper. Get yourself a pencil and I'll take you through the process. But there's no way around it: Making the plan will take time and energy and patience.

As you complete your business plan, you'll fill in the forms in this chapter. If you don't want to write in the book, copy the pages and write on the copies. Collect the copies in a loose-leaf binder. That's because no business plan should be written in stone. You'll want to review these pages now and then to update the plan to fit changing conditions. And this you can depend on: conditions *will* change.

If you need more information on business planning, the Small Business Administration sells many guides and aids at modest prices. There's an SBA office in most larger cities. Check in the government listings at the front of your local phone directory. The SBA is supported by taxpayers' money (your money) so don't be shy about asking them for help.

Now roll up your sleeves and let's get to work. We'll begin at the beginning, with the most basic question of all.

What Business Are You In?

Are you a contractor? How much work do you subcontract? Do you limit your business to add-ons? Do you exclude attic conversions? Do you have someone else do your design work? Your planning depends on your definition of the kind of business you want to run.

I know a builder who started out strictly as a remodeler, confining his activities to small jobs. He refused to do bathroom work because he detested

What business am I in? _____

_____

_____

_____

_____

_____

Why did I answer that way? _____

_____

_____

_____

_____

_____

Figure 18-1
Business plan worksheet

working in small places, particularly when he had to deal with water pipes and drains. "I couldn't seal a leaking pipe even if there wasn't any water running through it," he claimed.

His wife talked him into remodeling the bathroom in their home. He enlarged the room, completely reworked the water and drain lines, and installed new fixtures. It turned out to be a showplace. He was so thrilled with his abilities he decided to specialize. His business plan took a big turn. Now his company has a reputation for quality kitchen and bathroom remodeling.

On Figure 18-1, fill in what business you're really in. Then use the rest of the space to give your reasons for that answer.

Try not to make the kind of business you want to do too limited. Unless you can come up with enough ideas to keep yourself and your crew working 12 months a year, maybe you're not ready for construc-

tion contracting. Obviously, the more employees you have, the more jobs you need. The other side of the coin is that a small builder — you and one or two employees — can stay busy with fewer jobs. That's one reason many builders prefer to stay small. They're satisfied to earn the equivalent of hourly wages and a limited profit.

Where Is Your Market?

Describe your market area in terms of customer profile (age, school needs, income, and so on) and geography. For example, if you're hoping to do a lot of additions and conversions, you need two main groups of customers. First, homeowners with growing families who have outgrown their present space. Second, owners who want to increase their monthly incomes by renting out part of their home. So concentrate on areas with older homes where families are growing.

My product	Types of customers	Location of customers
_____	_____	_____
_____	_____	_____
_____	_____	_____
_____	_____	_____
_____	_____	_____

What about my operation will make them want to buy?

_____

_____

_____

_____

_____

Figure 18-2
Customer profile worksheet

The significance of a customer profile is that it'll help you target your advertising to reach the right customers. In Figure 18-2, describe your market in terms of customer profile and geography.

What are the possibilities in your area? Are your opportunities purely local, or do they extend over a large surrounding area? How will the seasons affect your work?

Has the market for additions and conversions been limited in your territory for any reason in the past? Are there people who can use your service who don't know about it yet? Are there undeveloped markets where opportunities can be created for your class of work?

Now that you've described what you want in terms of customers and their location, what is it about your operation that will make these people want to buy your service? For instance, do you offer quality work, competitive prices, guaranteed completion dates, unique design, or other services that set you

apart? Use the bottom half of Figure 18-2 to describe your operation's selling points.

You've determined what it is you're marketing, who's going to need it, and why they'll want to buy it. Now you have to decide on the best way to tell your prospective customers about your product.

Planning Effective Sales and Advertising

Successful selling requires knowledge and training. If you feel that selling isn't your strong point, it probably isn't. Some builders find that hiring a specialist in sales promotion produces better sales results for each dollar spent than designing and carrying out their own sales campaigns.

What should your advertising tell about your company? Use the top of Figure 18-3 to answer. What

What should my advertising tell prospective customers?

_____

_____

_____

_____

_____

_____

_____

Form of advertising	Size of audience	Frequency of use		Cost of a single ad		Estimated cost
_____	_____	_____	x	_____	=	_____
_____	_____	_____	x	_____	=	_____
_____	_____	_____	x	_____	=	_____
_____	_____	_____	x	_____	=	_____
_____	_____	_____	x	_____	=	_____
		Total		_____	$	_____

Who are my major competitors?

_____

_____

_____

_____

How will I compete against them?

_____

_____

_____

_____

Figure 18-3
Advertising worksheet

form should your advertising take? Ask the local media (newspapers, radio and television stations, and advertising agencies) for information about their services and the results they offer for your money. Use the middle portion of Figure 18-3 to help you determine what advertising you need to sell your construction service.

How you spend advertising money is your decision, but don't fall for a high-pressure sales pitch by a media salesperson who may not know much about advertising copy. It takes experience in the advertising field to be competent enough to give advice in this area. You'll want to get as much help as possible for your money.

There's a definite advantage in selecting one or two points about your service and emphasizing them regularly in your advertising. What do you want prospective clients to think about when they hear your company's name? What features of your service are most important? Perhaps it's your ability to handle a contract from beginning to end: preparing the plans, arranging financing, and completing the job on time. Maybe your wife is an interior decorator who can contribute to the design and furnishing of the project. Use these or any other "bonus points" to identify advantages to potential clients.

Your advertising should:

♦ Make the public familiar with your name and the service you offer

♦ Make personal sales efforts more productive and create goodwill

♦ Keep you in touch with clients and prospective clients

♦ Bring in inquiries, so you can build a prospect list of potential customers

Here's a cliché you've heard over and over: *It pays to advertise*. But how do you figure out how much it pays — and try to ensure it's worth the money you spend? First, don't spread your advertising dollars over too wide an area. A small one-time ad in the local newspaper coupled with a 10-second spot on the radio isn't going to bring in a rush of queries.

Select the form of advertising that best suits your community, your advertising budget and your type of business. Try to visualize your prospects. What type of advertising will reach them most economically? Here are some of the possibilities:

1. Yellow Pages (always a good bet)

2. Newspapers

3. Local radio and TV stations

4. Billboards and posters

5. Direct mail letters

6. Advertising novelties (calendars, cards, pencils or rulers)

7. Bus stop benches

It's probably safe to say that most add-on and conversion builders do the bulk of their advertising through the Yellow Pages, newspapers, local TV and radio, and personal contacts. The medium I'm partial to is the Yellow Pages. Being listed in the Yellow Pages suggests to people that you're an established professional and not a fly-by-night operator in town for a quick steal.

Making a Prospect List

Every contact generated by your advertising is a prospect, even if there's no chance of an immediate sale. Keep a record of every contact you make to build up as large and complete a mailing list of prospects as possible. Keep a list of your past customers. They're your references and potential clients again in the future, when they have other work to be done.

Beating the Competition

What is your competition? How strongly entrenched is it? Does the competition offer what you have to sell: experience, training, ability to design and carry out that design in a smooth and professional manner? How does the quality of their service compare? Consider all these questions. They'll suggest areas where you can effectively advertise.

Competition is good for business — especially when it works against your competitor and in your favor. Competition in the construction industry often results in low profit margins. But if you're just starting or are a relatively small firm, this can be an advantage. A smaller firm can often compete with bigger outfits because its overhead is lower. For example, your office may be in your home, saving that expense. You can often work right out of your pickup, saving the expense of a field office. Larger outfits can't do that.

Competition is largely price competition, although a good reputation for quality and efficiency can lift you above some of the price fights. But because the construction industry is highly competitive, there's a high failure rate for poor planners and poor performers, particularly in the areas of estimating and bidding.

Now it's time to assess your competition. Answer the following questions on Figure 18-3:

♦ Who will be your major competitors?

♦ How will you compete against them?

Planning the Work

The market for the construction industry is unique in many ways. As a contractor, your market will be dependent on such variables as the state of the economy, local employment stability, seasonality of the work, labor relations, good subcontractors, and interest rates — things you have absolutely no control over. You'll also find that you're unavoidably dependent on others, such as customers or financing institutions for payment, and other contractors for performance of their work.

When your marketing efforts are successful, you've earned a job to do, at the right time and the right price. Now, how do you plan the work so that the job gets done on time? The plan you make should help you in two specific ways: First, it should help you maintain your production schedule. Second, it should allow you the flexibility to meet changing conditions, such as bad weather.

In planning the work, keep two things in mind:

1. Timing the starts

2. Timing the various steps in the construction process

If you have enough help and dependable supervisory personnel, you can take on as many projects as you can control. A work schedule should show, at a glance, the various operations in sequence, and whether the work is progressing on schedule. It should assign both a working day designation and a calendar day designation to each project. You can buy commercial scheduling boards designed for this purpose.

Figure 18-4 is a partial work schedule to show how you could set up one. Note that there's a column that you can fill in with a solid mark or an X to indicate either partial or completed work. A complete X

Estimated Job Completion Date: Dec 20, 1996

Activity	Working day		Calendar day	Completed
	Start	Finish		
1. Reinforce floor joist	1	4	11 / 7	☒
2. Build knee walls	5	6	11 / 9	☒
3. Install subfloor	6	7	11 / 12	☒
4. Frame walls	8	8	11 / 13	☒
5. Double collars	8	8	11 / 13	☒
6. Add gable windows	9	10	11 / 15	◨
7. Build dormer	11	13	11 / 20	◪
8. Build stairs	14	17	11 / 25	☐

Figure 18-4
Typical work schedule

on a particular calendar day means that you're on schedule. A partial X, like the one in item 6, add gable windows, means the work is three-quarters complete. An open square indicates a delay. You can see right away the trouble spots that may cause delays.

Save your work schedules. They'll form your basis for future estimates. Work schedules for completed similar jobs will give you information on:

♦ The steps of production

♦ What materials you'll need and when you'll need them

♦ How long the job will take

♦ Any peculiarities that may affect the completion of the job

When you consider all these things, you'll be more likely to submit an accurate bid. You'll also know how many workers you have available for new jobs that overlap current jobs. And finally, these records may help you decide the organizational structure that will work best for your firm.

Organization

Organization is the key to efficient operation, even if you're still doing everything yourself. As your company grows and expands, you won't be able to do it all yourself. You'll have to delegate work, responsibility, and authority. Your organization chart should show clearly who is responsible for the major activities of your business.

While your company is small, it's up to you to do almost everything. In this case the organization chart might look something like Section A in Figure 18-5. As the company grows, you'll probably add some specialists to take some of the load off of you. Your organization will change, and your chart will look more like Section B. If you decide to take on partners instead of employees to share the load, you'll need a chart that shows the division of responsibilities among the partners. Look at Section C.

Draw up an organization chart for your company as it exists now, and update it every time you make significant changes. Post it in a prominent place, so you and your employees always know who's responsible for what.

Bonding, Personnel and Equipment Planning

Some people say that a bond is the trademark of a professional builder. Getting bonds is a necessity of life for many contractors — especially those who handle big jobs. A bond is liability insurance. Bonding companies provide bonds for a certain percentage of the contract price. There are three main types of bonds:

♦ Bid bonds which assure that the bidder is prepared to perform the work according to the terms of the contract if successful in the bid

♦ Performance bonds which assure completion of the job according to plans and specifications

♦ Payment bonds which assure those dealing with the bonded contractor that they'll be paid

Bonding plays an important role in competition between larger construction companies. Bonding companies won't issue a bond unless a contractor can show both experience and the organizational and financial capacity to complete a project. Inexperienced contractors with too few assets to meet bonding requirements can't bid. Not being able to get a bond keeps many small builders from bidding on the more profitable jobs. This can be a real stumbling block for a new construction firm.

While the question of bonding may never come up with your customers, it helps to know about it anyway just in case. Many homeowners don't require that the contractor they hire be bonded. The good reputation or references of the builder are usually sufficient. Many builders who do additions and conversions use their credit with their suppliers and subs in lieu of loans since the turnaround time on these projects is short and payment can be made within a reasonable time. If you do get a bond, you may find that the banks you're trying to borrow from are more willing to deal with you.

The Small Business Administration has a surety bond program designed to help small and emerging contractors who have been denied bonds. The SBA is authorized to guarantee up to 90 percent of losses incurred under bid, payment, or performance bonds on contracts up to 1.25 million dollars. Apply for this assistance at any SBA district office.

Answer the questions on bonding in Figure 18-6.

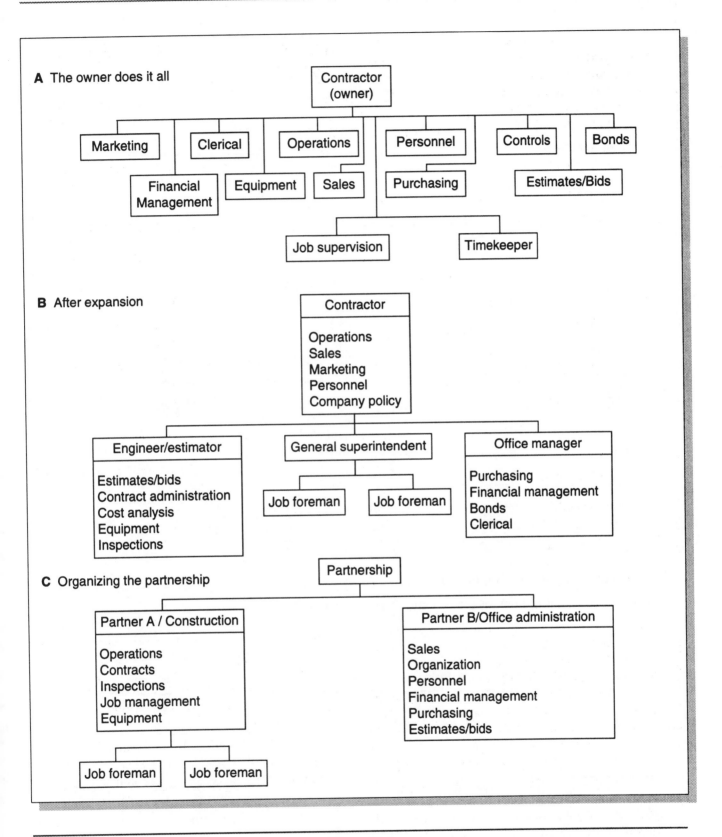

Figure 18-5
Typical organizational charts

Bonding

Will I need bonding   often _____ occasionally _____ seldom _____

Where will I get the bond? _____

What will the terms be? _____

Personnel

Will I carry a permanent crew or hire workers as needed? _____

Will I use union or nonunion labor? _____

How many workers will I need? _____

What is the hourly rate I will pay? _____

What will fringe benefits cost? _____

Will I supervise the work myself or hire a foreman? _____

If I hire a forman, what will his salary be? _____

Will I need clerical help? _____ What will it cost? _____

Equipment

Equipment	Rent	Buy	My cost
_____	_____	_____	$ _____
_____	_____	_____	$ _____
_____	_____	_____	$ _____

Will I need an office or use my home? _____

If I will need an office, what will the rent and other expenses be? _____

_____

_____

Figure 18-6
Bonding, personnel, and equipment requirements

Personnel and Equipment Requirements

Will you carry a permanent crew or hire workers as needed? Will you use union or nonunion labor? How many workers will you need? What will they cost in wages and fringe benefits? What about a fore- man? Will you need clerical help? Will you need special equipment? Will your crew provide their own hand tools? How many trucks will you need? Will you rent or buy special equipment? What about office space? Think these questions through, and answer on Figure 18-6.

Financial Planning

An important part of every business plan is cash planning. Will you have the money you need when you need it? As you do your business plan, remember that it's easy to leave out some important cost items. Anything you leave out of the picture will be an extra cash drain. Too many of these and your business will be headed down the drain.

The financial part of a job has to be planned as carefully as the actual construction. Your contract price must cover the direct and indirect construction costs, a share of overhead, and if you've planned well, a decent profit. You can get an accountant to help you set up an accounting system that meets your needs, but you have to do most of the financial planning yourself. You establish goals and set your own limits.

The first consideration in your financial planning is where the dollars will come from. In dollars, how much business (sales) will you be able to do in the next 12 months? Fill in the top line of Figure 18-7, the cash forecast worksheet, with the amount of cash you expect to take in for each of the months in the next year. Be as realistic as possible. Don't forget to anticipate weather conditions in your area.

Overhead

The cost of every job is more than just what you pay for materials and labor. You carry an overhead that includes several kinds of taxes, insurance, and miscellaneous expenses. When estimating a job, don't forget to include the overhead costs in your estimate.

The federal government collects Social Security taxes (FICA) and Medicare taxes from an employer each calendar quarter. It also imposes an unemployment insurance tax (FUTA) based on payroll. Most states also have an unemployment insurance tax on employers that's based on an employer's total payroll for each calendar quarter and history of unemployment claims. The actual tax percentage varies from state to state.

States generally require employers to carry workers' compensation insurance to cover their employees for job-related injuries. The cost of the insurance is a percentage of payroll based on the type of work each employee performs. The cost may vary from one reporting period to the next, depending on the history of injuries.

You should also carry liability insurance to protect yourself in case of an accident. The higher the liability limits, the higher your cost for the policy.

Other important overhead expenses include:

♦ Supervision

♦ Payroll and reports

♦ Interest on borrowed money

♦ Licenses

♦ Office expenses

♦ Car and truck expenses

♦ Advertising

♦ Legal and accounting fees

♦ Sales commissions

After you project 12 months of income, use Figure 18-8, the expenses worksheet, to help you figure your annual expenses. Find out the typical operating ratios for your kind of contracting from the trade association that covers your specialty in the construction industry. They'll be more accurate than the sample ratios on the form.

Matching Your Money and Your Expenses

How hard you work is just one factor — it doesn't guarantee you success. Always take your cash flow into consideration when you estimate and bid on a job. After you've planned for your month-to-month expenses, you need to figure out if there will be enough money coming in to meet these expenses and keep you going if there's down time between jobs.

The cash forecast is a management tool that can eliminate a lot of anxiety during lean months. Use the estimated cash worksheet, or ask your accountant to use it, to estimate the cash that will flow through your business during the next 12 months. You may find periods when you'll be short of cash. For example, you need materials and supplies to start a new job, even though it will be a month or two before your first payment. What do you do in the interim if you haven't established a credit line with your supplier?

Your bank may be able to help with a short-term loan. Any banker you approach will want to know whether your company's financial condition is weak or strong. The bank officer will ask to see a balance

	Jan	Feb.	Mar.	Apr.	May	Jun.	Jul.	Aug.	Sept.	Oct.	Nov.	Dec.
Expected available cash												
Cash balance												
Expected receipts:												
Job A												
Job B												
Job C												
Bank loans												
Total expected cash												
Expected cash requirements												
Job A												
Job B												
Job C												
Equipment payments												
Taxes												
Insurance and bonds												
Overhead												
Loan repayments												
Total cash required												
Cash balance												
Total loans due to bank												

Figure 18-7
Cash forecast worksheet

Expenses Worksheet	Percent of Your Sales	Your Annual Sales ($)	Your Jan. Sales	Your Feb. Sales	Your Mar. Sales	Your Apr. Sales	Your May Sales	Your June Sales	Your July Sales	Your Aug. Sales	Your Sept. Sales	Your Oct. Sales	Your Nov. Sales	Your Dec. Sales
Sales	*100.00%													
Cost of sales	44.45													
Gross profit	55.55													
Controllable expenses														
Outside labor	1.15													
Operating supplies	2.34													
Gross wages	22.78													
Repairs and maintenance	.59													
Advertising	1.12													
Car and delivery	2.04													
Bad debts	.03													
Administrative and legal	.48													
Miscellaneous expenses	1.03													
Total controllable expenses	31.56													
Fixed expenses														
Rent	1.00													
Utilities	1.41													
Insurance	1.16													
Taxes and licenses	.85													
	.10													
Depreciation	1.65													
Total fixed expenses	6.18													
Total expenses	37.74													
Net profit (before income tax)	17.81													

*These percentages are taken from Barometer of Small Business, Accounting Corporation of America. These figures are presented only as a sample and refer to specialty contractors with an annual gross volume between $50,000 and $200,000. The percentages vary from one business to another.

Figure 18-8

Expenses worksheet

Current Balance Sheet
for *(name of your firm)* as of _(date)_

	Assets
Current assets	$_____
Cash	$_____
Receivables	$_____
Inventories of supplies & tools	$_____
Total current assets	$_____
Fixed assets	$_____
Other assets	$_____
Total assets	$_____

	Liabilities
Current liabilities	$_____
Notes payable	$_____
Accounts payable	$_____
Miscellaneous current liabilities	$_____
Total current liabilities	$_____
Equipment contracts	$_____
Owner's equity	$_____
Total liabilities	$_____

Figure 18-9
Balance sheet

sheet. Figure 18-9 is a blank balance sheet. Even if you don't need to borrow, use it. Or have your accountant use it to draw a picture of your firm's financial condition.

To make your plan work, you'll need feedback at various stages. During the planning stage, you'll be estimating costs and bidding. Use your job cost analysis to make sure a job is going to make a profit. And then make sure estimated costs and actual costs are similar. This requires good supervision and a work schedule, competent tradesmen, and your personal follow-up. If you can't be on the job and supervise your crew, you'd better have a competent person in charge. Otherwise, it's a losing game you're playing.

As a business manager, you need to plan, direct, and control every job. That always includes financial planning. The management controls you establish should supply you with the information you need to keep your operation healthy.

How Workable Is Your Plan?

Did you follow along and plan this far? If so, step back and take a critical look at what you've done. Is it realistic? Can you do enough business to make a living at contracting before giving up your current job?

If your plan isn't workable, the time to revise it is now, not after you've committed time and money. If you feel that some revisions are needed before you start implementing your plan, make them. Go back to the cash flow and adjust the figures. Better yet, show your plan to someone who hasn't had a hand in making it. You may need fresh ideas. Your banker, contact man at the SBA, or any experienced contractor will be able to point out strengths and weaknesses in the plan.

If you have any strong doubts about your business or your ability to run it, it might be better to delay going into business until you feel as comfortable with the tools of management as you are with the tools of your trade.

Putting Your Plan into Action

The first action step is to get enough capital to get started. Do you already have the money? Will you borrow it from friends, relatives, or a bank? Where and when will you hire your employees?

Where and how will you get whatever licenses you need to be a contractor? The regulations for businesses vary from state to state. Contact the various levels of government for the ones which apply to you. Don't forget the IRS.

Your best bet is to go to your local SBA office. They can give you specific information for all levels of government. Local chambers of commerce can also often help you in this area.

Make a list of the things that you must do to get your business off the drawing board and into action. Date each item so it gets done on time.

Updating Your Plan

Expect things to change. The difference between successful and unsuccessful planning is often only the ability to keep alert and watch for changes. Watch for changes in your industry, market, and customers. Stay on top of changing conditions and adjust your plan accordingly. Once a month or so, go over your plan to see if you have to change it.

To stay current with the market, new building products, and trends, I recommend you subscribe to *Builder,* the magazine of the National Association of Builders. Write to:

Builder
P.O. Box 2029
Marion, OH 43306-2029

Another publication I recommend, aimed directly at remodelers, is *Remodeling*. Write to:

Remodeling
P.O. Box 5184
Pittsfield, MA 01203-5184

Building Your Management Ability

Most small business failures are due to poor management. If you need help to improve your management ability, you can get it from the Small Business Administration. The SBA can even help you start your business. It gives prospective, new, and established people in the small business community financial assistance.

Is yours a small business? The SBA defines a small business as one which is independently owned and operated, and not dominant in its field. To be eligible for SBA loans and other assistance, a business must meet a maximum size standard. Any construction company with fewer than 500 employees is likely to qualify as a small business.

Estimating

Knowing how to do a job means knowing how to estimate any new project for materials and manhours. As a practice session, you might want to draw plans for each kind of job you plan to do, work up a design, take off the materials item by item and estimate manhours by trade. Use any appropriate size floor plan for each project.

Management Tips

It would be a disservice to the reader to not include a few tips on management I've found that work over 25 years in the building business. There's no magic involved in acquiring management ability — just ordinary skills developed by everyday experience and, of course, effort. Here are some of the characteristics that I've seen in successful builders.

Integrity

Remodeling is such a lucrative business, it will come as no surprise that it attracts some low-lifes. There are more than enough crooks and incompetents around to give us all a bad name. But, if you do quality work, on time, and keep your commitments, your reputation will stand on its own and you'll get your share of the work.

In this day and age, integrity seems to be a lost word. The builder who appreciates what it means is the builder who will be in business ten years or more down the road.

In add-on and conversion remodeling (and all other types of remodeling), the homeowners' only real protection is their confidence in the integrity of the remodeler. That makes it especially important for you to be open and aboveboard in all your transactions. This doesn't mean you have to tell everyone all about your business. But you do want to treat your customers with frankness and fairness. Remember that a list of satisfied clients is about the best advertisement you can have. A reputation for square dealing is one of your most valuable business assets.

There's also another facet to integrity. It's just as important to treat your employees fairly as your customers. Insist on professionalism. Assign workers to tasks they're trained to do. Provide fair and just reward for work done, unbiased settlement of all disputes between employees, and prompt and friendly adjustment of mistakes in time and wages.

Discipline is the trademark of a successful business. You want workers to arrive to work on time, confine breaks and lunch periods to the specified times, and dress appropriately. Provide (and enforce) a dress code, work code, and behavior code. Make sure your employees know what you expect of them. Provide incentives to meet your expectations.

Creativity

You can also create confidence and goodwill by offering good suggestions to your clients. Point out any potential problems you spot. Offer suggestions for improvements. As a specialist in the field, you owe your client the full benefit of your knowledge and experience to ensure the project is well-designed and well-built.

Perseverance

Perseverance is profit. Every successful remodeler needs the ability to see ahead and come up with ways to cut costs and circumvent obstacles. You also must have the initiative to overcome problems, and to start and complete a project. Perseverance keeps it all going. If you're not persistent, find another line of work.

How to Build a Strong Company

Strong companies don't just spring up. You have to pull and tug at the thing — constantly. When you start your business, you'll be thinking and planning two or three months ahead. Later, as your company grows, you may be planning ahead for a year or more. The size and success of your company in the future depend on how well you:

♦ Adjust to technical and economic changes

♦ Build a management team

♦ Plan and achieve short-term goals

♦ Build for long-term growth

Pick and Train a Foreman

Have you ever tried to run a one-person building firm? If so, you know how easy it is to become discouraged about the heavy workload and the variety of skills needed to get the job done. You might have wondered if it was worth the effort.

What can you do to ease the burden? Consider putting your lead carpenter on salary while you teach him to take over as foreman or superintendent.

What do you look for in a potential foreman? First, choose a good craftsman who knows the technical details of add-ons and conversions. Second, you want a self-starter. Pick someone who shows initiative — who finds a way to get the work done without bringing you all the details and complaints. Third, look for the ability to become a manager. Remember, this person will be responsible for important aspects of your business. Anyone who can't manage their own time won't be able to manage the crews. Rate your candidate on these points. Could he or she, with training, run the company in your absence?

It's also important to choose candidates who can get along with people. Can they supervise workers without stirring up a conflict? Can they negotiate with subcontractors? Are they considerate and patient with demanding clients who don't understand a builder's problems?

Don't pick your twin. What you need is someone who complements your personality and skills. Try to select someone whose strong points balance your weak points. For instance, if you're good at paperwork, pick someone who's a good field supervisor.

Now you have to train the person. Start by delegating work. During the learning process, it will take a lot of coaching and checking. As soon as your foreman has shown the ability to handle tasks well, step back. Provide the authority, material, equipment, and labor needed to do the job, and let go of the reins. A properly trained foreman will know when to ask for help.

Keeping Records

Good records are the foundation for building a profitable business. Don't know anything about bookkeeping? Get a public bookkeeping service to set up your books. They'll install whatever system you need and train you to keep the necessary daily records. Then the accountant will spend only one or two days a month bringing your books up to date. Make sure your accountant sets up a system that will track your cash flow, so you can anticipate a problem before it becomes a crisis.

Your accountant will tell you that you should have a record of every dime earned, where it came from, and where it went. State and federal tax laws require that you keep good records, and good sense demands it. You must maintain a record of all money passing in and out of your business or you'll never be able to grow into a profitable company. You also have to know what materials and labor cost before you can set fair prices for your services.

The key to record keeping is to spend the minimum time needed to keep records that are just adequate for your needs. Start with the records you need to make up annual profit and loss statements and balance sheets. You'll need these to file tax returns. You'll also need these statements when you want to borrow money. No bank or S&L is going to lend you money without seeing your business records.

You may be able to get by with a single combined journal or cash book. Your accountant can advise you about simplified record-keeping systems.

How to Act on Your Records

If you don't use your records, what good are they? Study and understand what the numbers in your books mean. Compare this month's results with last month's results, and the results from this month a year ago. What do you see? If the trend is positive, understand why so you can do more of what you've been doing. If it's negative, figure out why while you still have time to make changes. When the reports show unexpected gains, try to devise some way to make the improvements a permanent part of your operation.

Your balance sheets and profit and loss statements are a good guide to making decisions about your business — if you know how to interpret them. A balance sheet tells how your business stands at a given moment. To see how your business is doing, take your month-end balance sheets for 12 consecutive months. Arrange the figures in 12 vertical columns across a page so you can compare asset and liability account totals for each month in the year. You'll begin to see trends in the figures. Then compare the month of November for this year and last year. See how things

are changing. Compare July for both years. What do you see? That's important information for anyone running a business.

Your profit and loss statement sums up your operations over a period of time. Comparing profit and loss statements will show changes in expense categories and the profit margin. Did you cut prices to meet competition? Then look for a lower gross profit, unless you cut construction costs proportionately. Did sales go up? If so, what about expenses? Did they remain proportionate? Was more money spent on office help? How about fixed overhead? Where did the money come from? By comparing operating income and cost account items from one period to another, you'll find the answers.

Summary

At the beginning of the book, I said that to be able to build room additions and convert attics and basements, you have to know how to build a house. By now you should realize that's true in two areas: doing the work and managing the business. Understanding and using the management techniques covered here will help you control your business, instead of being controlled by it. Skilled workers and the finest materials don't guarantee a success. You have to manage these resources to keep them working for you.

Know where your business stands in comparison with others in the same field. Search for ways to improve your profits. Is your expense ratio too high? Find out why and take steps to bring it into line. If your balance sheet shows unusually high labor costs, correct the problem or suffer loss of profits.

Organizing, planning, and careful record keeping are absolutely essential if you want to keep your company thriving. Successful management is a continuing process, and you should treat it as though your business depended on it — because it does.

Index

Other Practical References

Building Contractor's Exam Preparation Guide

Passing today's contractor's exams can be a major task. This book shows you how to study, how questions are likely to be worded, and the kinds of choices usually given for answers. Includes sample questions from actual state, county, and city examinations, plus a sample exam to practice on. This book isn't a substitute for the study material that your testing board recommends, but it will help prepare you for the types of questions — and their correct answers — that are likely to appear on the actual exam. Knowing how to answer these questions, as well as what to expect from the exam, can greatly increase your chances of passing. **320 pages, 8½ x 11, $35.00**

Professional Kitchen Design

Remodeling kitchens requires a "special" touch — one that blends artistic flair with function to create a kitchen with charm and personality as well as one that is easy to work in. Here you'll find how to make the best use of the space available in any kitchen design job, as well as tips and lessons on how to design one-wall, two-wall, L-shaped, U-shaped, peninsula and island kitchens. Also includes what you need to know to run a profitable kitchen design business. **176 pages, 8½ x 11, $24.50**

Renovating & Restyling Vintage Homes

Any builder can turn a run-down old house into a showcase of perfection — if the customer has unlimited funds to spend. Unfortunately, most customers are on a tight budget. They usually want more improvements than they can afford — and they expect you to deliver. This book shows how to add economical improvements that can increase the property value by two, five or even ten times the cost of the remodel. Sound impossible? Here you'll find the secrets of a builder who has been putting these techniques to work on Victorian and Craftsman-style houses for twenty years. You'll see what to repair, what to replace and what to leave, so you can remodel or restyle older homes for the least amount of money and the greatest increase in value. **416 pages, 8½ x 11, $33.50**

Manual of Professional Remodeling

The practical manual of professional remodeling that shows how to evaluate a job so you avoid 30-minute jobs that take all day, what to fix and what to leave alone, and what to watch for in dealing with subcontractors. Includes how to calculate space requirements; repair structural defects; remodel kitchens, baths, walls, ceilings, doors, windows, floors and roofs; install fireplaces and chimneys (including built-ins), skylights, and exterior siding. Includes blank forms, checklists, sample contracts, and proposals you can copy and use. **400 pages, 8½ x 11, $23.75**

Wood-Frame House Construction

Step-by-step construction details, from the layout of the outer walls, excavation and formwork, to finish carpentry and painting. Contains all new, clear illustrations and explanations updated for construction in the '90s. Everything you need to know about framing, roofing, siding, interior finishings, floor covering and stairs — your complete book of wood-frame homebuilding. **320 pages, 8½ x 11, $25.50. Revised edition**

National Renovation & Insurance Repair Estimator

Current prices in dollars and cents for hard-to-find items needed on most insurance, repair, remodeling, and renovation jobs. All price items include labor, material, and equipment breakouts, plus special charts that tell you exactly how these costs are calculated. Includes an electronic version of the book on computer disk with a stand-alone *Windows* estimating program FREE on a 3½" high density (1.44 Mb) disk. **560 pages, 8½ x 11, $39.50. Revised annually**

Contractor's Guide to the Building Code Revised

This completely revised edition explains in plain English exactly what the Uniform Building Code requires. Based on the newly-expanded 1994 code, it explains many of the changes made. Also covers the Uniform Mechanical Code and the Uniform Plumbing Code. Shows how to design and construct residential and light commercial buildings that'll pass inspection the first time. Suggests how to work with an inspector to minimize construction costs, what common building shortcuts are likely to be cited, and where exceptions are granted. **384 pages, 8½ x 11, $39.00**

Estimating & Bidding for Builders & Remodelers w/ CD-ROM

If your computer has a CD-ROM drive, the CD Estimator disk enclosed in this book could change forever the way you estimate construction. You get over 2,500 pages from six current cost databases published by Craftsman, plus an estimating program you can master in minutes, plus a 70-minute interactive video on how to use this program, plus an award-winning book. This package is your best bargain for estimating and bidding construction costs. **272 pages, 8½ x 11, $69.50**

Construction Forms & Contracts

125 forms you can copy and use — or load into your computer (from the FREE disk enclosed). Then you can customize the forms to fit your company, fill them out, and print. Loads into Word for *Windows*, Lotus 1-2-3, WordPerfect, or Excel programs. You'll find forms covering accounting, estimating, fieldwork, contracts, and general office. Each form comes with complete instructions on when to use it and how to fill it out. These forms were designed, tested and used by contractors, and will help keep your business organized, profitable and out of legal, accounting and collection troubles. Includes a 3½" high-density disk for your PC. For Macintosh disks, add $15. **432 pages, 8½ x 11, $39.75**

Basic Engineering for Builders

If you've ever been stumped by an engineering problem on the job, yet wanted to avoid the expense of hiring a qualified engineer, you should have this book. Here you'll find engineering principles explained in non-technical language and practical methods for applying them on the job. With the help of this book you'll be able to understand engineering functions in the plans and how to meet the requirements, how to get permits issued without the help of an engineer, and anticipate requirements for concrete, steel, wood and masonry. See why you sometimes have to hire an engineer and what you can undertake yourself: surveying, concrete, lumber loads and stresses, steel, masonry, plumbing, and HVAC systems. This book is designed to help the builder save money by understanding engineering principles that you can incorporate into the jobs you bid. **400 pages, 8½ x 11, $34.00**

National Repair & Remodeling Estimator

The complete pricing guide for dwelling reconstruction costs. Reliable, specific data you can apply on every repair and remodeling job. Up-to-date material costs and labor figures based on thousands of jobs across the country. Provides recommended crew sizes; average production rates; exact material, equipment, and labor costs; a total unit cost and a total price including overhead and profit. Separate listings for high- and low-volume builders, so prices shown are specific for any size business. Estimating tips specific to repair and remodeling work to make your bids complete, realistic, and profitable. Includes an electronic version of the book on computer disk with a stand-alone *Windows* estimating program FREE on a 3½" high-density (1.44 Mb) disk. **416 pages, 11 x 8½, $38.50. Revised annually**

Drafting House Plans

Here you'll find step-by-step instructions for drawing a complete set of home plans for a one-story house, an addition to an existing house, or a remodeling project. This book shows how to visualize spatial relationships, use architectural scales and symbols, sketch preliminary drawings, develop detailed floor plans and exterior elevations, and prepare a final plot plan. It even includes code-approved joist and rafter spans and how to make sure that drawings meet code requirements. **192 pages, 8½ x 11, $27.50**

Profits in Buying & Renovating Homes

Step-by-step instructions for selecting, repairing, improving, and selling highly profitable "fixer-uppers." Shows which price ranges offer the highest profit-to-investment ratios, which neighborhoods offer the best return, practical directions for repairs, and tips on dealing with buyers, sellers, and real estate agents. Shows you how to determine your profit before you buy, what "bargains" to avoid, and how to make simple, profitable, inexpensive upgrades. **304 pages, 8½ x 11, $19.75**

Residential Wiring to the 1996 NEC

Shows how to install rough and finish wiring in new construction, alterations, and additions. Complete instructions on troubleshooting and repairs. Every subject is referenced to the most recent National Electrical Code, and there's 22 pages of the most-needed NEC tables to help make your wiring pass inspection — the first time. **352 pages, 5½ x 8½, $24.50**

National Construction Estimator

Current building costs for residential, commercial, and industrial construction. Estimated prices for every common building material. Manhours, recommended crew, and labor cost for installation. Includes an electronic version of the book on computer disk with a stand-alone *Windows* estimating program FREE on a 3½" high-density (1.44 Mb) disk. **528 pages, 8½ x 11, $37.50. Revised annually**

Roof Framing

Shows how to frame any type of roof in common use today, even if you've never framed a roof before. Includes using a pocket calculator to figure any common, hip, valley, or jack rafter length in seconds. Over 400 illustrations cover every measurement and every cut on each type of roof: gable, hip, Dutch, Tudor, gambrel, shed, gazebo, and more. **480 pages, 5½ x 8½, $22.00**

Construction Estimating Reference Data

Provides the 300 most useful manhour tables for practically every item of construction. Labor requirements are listed for sitework, concrete work, masonry, steel, carpentry, thermal and moisture protection, door and windows, finishes, mechanical and electrical. Each section details the work being estimated and gives appropriate crew size and equipment needed. Includes an electronic version of the book on computer disk with a stand-alone *Windows* estimating program FREE on a 3½" high-density (1.44 Mb) disk. **432 pages, 11 x 8½, $39.50**

Craftsman Book Company
6058 Corte del Cedro, P.O. Box 6500
Carlsbad, CA 92018

☎ **24 hour order line**
1-800-829-8123
Fax (619) 438-0398

In A Hurry?
We accept phone orders charged to your
Visa, MasterCard, Discover or
American Express

💻 **Order online**
http://www.craftsman-book.com

Name _____
Company _____
Address _____
City/State/Zip _____

Total enclosed_____ (In California add 7.25% tax)
We pay shipping when your check covers your order in full.
If you prefer, use your ❑Visa ❑MasterCard ❑Discover or ❑American Express
Card#_____ Expiration date_____ Initials_____

Tax Deductible: Treasury regulations make these references tax deductible
when used in your work. Save the cancelled check or charge card statement as your receipt.

10 Day Money Back Guarantee

❑34.00 Basic Engineering for Builders
❑35.00 Building Contractor's Exam Preparation Guide
❑39.50 Construction Estimating Reference Data with FREE stand-alone *Windows* estimating program on a 3½" HD disk.
❑39.75 Construction Forms & Contracts with a 3½" HD disk. Add $15.00 if you need ❑Macintosh disks.
❑39.00 Contractor's Guide to Building Code Revised
❑27.50 Drafting House Plans
❑69.50 Estimating & Bidding for Builders & Remodelers w/ CD-ROM
❑23.75 Manual of Professional Remodeling
❑37.50 National Construction Estimator with FREE stand-alone *Windows* estimating program on a 3½" HD disk
❑39.50 National Renovation & Insurance Repair Estimator with FREE stand-alone *Windows* estimating program on a 3½" HD disk.
❑38.50 National Repair & Remodeling Estimator with FREE stand-alone *Windows* estimating program on a 3½" HD disk.
❑24.50 Professional Kitchen Design
❑19.75 Profits in Buying & Renovating Homes
❑33.50 Renovating & Restyling Vintage Homes
❑24.50 Residential Wiring to the 1996 NEC
❑22.00 Roof Framing
❑25.50 Wood-Frame House Construction
❑27.25 Builder's Guide to Room Additions
❑FREE Full Color Catalog

Craftsman Book Company
6058 Corte del Cedro, P.O. Box 6500
Carlsbad, CA 92018

☎ **24 hour order line**
1-800-829-8123
Fax (619) 438-0398

In A Hurry?
We accept phone orders charged to your
Visa, MasterCard, Discover or
American Express

💻 **Order online**
http://www.craftsman-book.com

Name _____
Company _____
Address _____
City/State/Zip _____

Total enclosed_____ (In California add 7.25% tax)
We pay shipping when your check covers your order in full.
If you prefer, use your ❑Visa ❑MasterCard ❑Discover or ❑American Express
Card#_____ Expiration date_____ Initials_____

Tax Deductible: Treasury regulations make these references tax deductible
when used in your work. Save the cancelled check or charge card statement as your receipt.

10 Day Money Back Guarantee

❑34.00 Basic Engineering for Builders
❑35.00 Building Contractor's Exam Preparation Guide
❑39.50 Construction Estimating Reference Data with FREE stand-alone *Windows* estimating program on a 3½" HD disk.
❑39.75 Construction Forms & Contracts with a 3½" HD disk. Add $15.00 if you need ❑Macintosh disks.
❑39.00 Contractor's Guide to Building Code Revised
❑27.50 Drafting House Plans
❑69.50 Estimating & Bidding for Builders & Remodelers w/ CD-ROM
❑23.75 Manual of Professional Remodeling
❑37.50 National Construction Estimator with FREE stand-alone *Windows* estimating program on a 3½" HD disk
❑39.50 National Renovation & Insurance Repair Estimator with FREE stand-alone *Windows* estimating program on a 3½" HD disk.
❑38.50 National Repair & Remodeling Estimator with FREE stand-alone *Windows* estimating program on a 3½" HD disk.
❑24.50 Professional Kitchen Design
❑19.75 Profits in Buying & Renovating Homes
❑33.50 Renovating & Restyling Vintage Homes
❑24.50 Residential Wiring to the 1996 NEC
❑22.00 Roof Framing
❑25.50 Wood-Frame House Construction
❑27.25 Builder's Guide to Room Additions
❑FREE Full Color Catalog

Mail This Card Today For a Free Full Color Catalog

Over 100 books, videos, and audios at your fingertips with information that can save you time and money. Here you'll find information on carpentry, contracting, estimating, remodeling, electrical work, and plumbing.

All items come with an unconditional 10-day money-back guarantee. If they don't save you money, mail them back for a full refund.

Name _____

Company _____

Address _____

City/State/Zip _____

Craftsman Book Company / 6058 Corte del Cedro / P.O. Box 6500 / Carlsbad, CA 92018

|||||

NO POSTAGE
NECESSARY
IF MAILED
IN THE
UNITED STATES

BUSINESS REPLY MAIL
FIRST CLASS MAIL PERMIT NO. 271 CARLSBAD CA

POSTAGE WILL BE PAID BY ADDRESSEE

Craftsman Book Company
6058 Corte del Cedro
P.O. Box 6500
Carlsbad CA 92018-9974

|||||

NO POSTAGE
NECESSARY
IF MAILED
IN THE
UNITED STATES

BUSINESS REPLY MAIL
FIRST CLASS MAIL PERMIT NO. 271 CARLSBAD CA

POSTAGE WILL BE PAID BY ADDRESSEE

Craftsman Book Company
6058 Corte del Cedro
P.O. Box 6500
Carlsbad CA 92018-9974

|||||

NO POSTAGE
NECESSARY
IF MAILED
IN THE
UNITED STATES

BUSINESS REPLY MAIL
FIRST CLASS MAIL PERMIT NO. 271 CARLSBAD CA

POSTAGE WILL BE PAID BY ADDRESSEE

Craftsman Book Company
6058 Corte del Cedro
P.O. Box 6500
Carlsbad CA 92018-9974